The Globalization of Managerial Innovation in Health Care

In 1983, the first patient classification system to be used on a national basis, the Diagnosis Related Groups (DRGs), was adopted as part of the Prospective Payment System in the United States. This system caught the attention of health policy makers in other countries, and a number of them began to implement similar approaches. What motivated them to adopt these systems? What similarities and differences were there among their experiences in implementing these systems? What can we learn about introducing change into national health systems by comparing their experiences?

The Globalization of Managerial Innovation in Health Care answers these and other questions by examining patient classification systems in fifteen different countries throughout the world. The result is a remarkable collection of case studies of how change can be introduced effectively into national health systems as well as a careful synthesis of what can be learned from them.

John R. Kimberly is the Henry Bower Professor of Entrepreneurial Studies and Professor of Management, Health Care Systems, and Sociology at The Wharton School, University of Pennsylvania. He is also Executive Director of the Wharton/INSEAD Alliance.

Gérard de Pouvourville is Professor and Chair of Health Economics and Management at the ESSEC Business School and Research Director of the National Centre for Scientific Research, Paris.

Thomas D'Aunno is the Novartis Chaired Professor of Healthcare Management and Professor of Organisational Behaviour at INSEAD.

The Globalization of Managerial Innovation in Health Care

Edited by

John R. Kimberly

Gérard de Pouvourville and Thomas D'Aunno

CAMBRIDGE
UNIVERSITY PRESS

CAMBRIDGE
UNIVERSITY PRESS

University Printing House, Cambridge CB2 8BS, United Kingdom

One Liberty Plaza, 20th Floor, New York, NY 10006, USA

477 Williamstown Road, Port Melbourne, VIC 3207, Australia

314-321, 3rd Floor, Plot 3, Splendor Forum, Jasola District Centre, New Delhi - 110025, India

79 Anson Road, #06-04/06, Singapore 079906

Cambridge University Press is part of the University of Cambridge.

It furthers the University's mission by disseminating knowledge in the pursuit of
education, learning and research at the highest international levels of excellence.

www.cambridge.org
Information on this title: www.cambridge.org/9780521711982

© Cambridge University Press 2008

First published 2008
First paperback edition 2020

A catalogue record for this publication is available from the British Library

Library of Congress Cataloging in Publication data
The globalization of managerial innovation in health care / [edited by] John R. Kimberly,
Gérard de Pouvourville, Thomas D'Aunno.
p. cm.
Includes bibliographical references and index.
ISBN 978-0-521-88500-3 (hardback) – ISBN 978-0-521-71198-2 (pbk.)
1. Diagnosis-related groups–Cross-cultural studies. I. Kimberly, John R. (John Robert), 1942–
II. Pouvourville, Gérard de. III. D'Aunno, Thomas A. IV. Title.
[DNLM: 1. Diagnosis-Related Groups–economics. 2. Organizational Innovation.
3. World Health. WX 157.8 G562 2008]
RA971.32.G56 2008
362.1–dc22   2008024024

ISBN 978-0-521-88500-3 Hardback
ISBN 978-0-521-71198-2 Paperback

Contents

List of figures   *page* vii
List of tables   ix
List of contributors   xi
Acknowledgements   xiv

Introduction   1

1   Origins of DRGs in the United States: A technical,
    political and cultural story   4
    Jon Chilingerian

2   Casemix in the United Kingdom: From development to plans   34
    Steve Sutch

3   Casemix implementation in Portugal   51
    Céu Mateus

4   From naïve hope to realistic conviction: DRGs in Sweden   73
    Rikard Lindqvist

5   Casemix in Denmark   92
    Annette Søberg Roed and Hanne Sjuneson

6   DRGs in France   116
    Xavière Michelot and Jean Marie Rodrigues

7   Introduction and use of DRGs in Belgium   144
    Marie Christine Closon, Francis H. Roger France, and Julian Perelman

8   DRGs in Germany: Introduction of a comprehensive,
     prospective DRG payment system by 2009   153
     Günter Neubauer and Florian Pfister

9   Casemix in Switzerland   176
     Hervé Guillain

10   The first decade of casemix in Italy   189
     Paolo Tedeschi

11   Casemix development and implementation in Australia   231
     Stephen J. Duckett

12   Diagnosis procedure combination: The Japanese
     approach to casemix   254
     Shinya Matsuda

13   Casemix in Singapore   272
     Chien Earn Lee and Eng Kok Lim

14   Experiences with the application of the DRG principle in Hungary 284
     Júlia Nagy, Csaba Dózsa, and Imre Boncz

15   Casemix systems – past, present, and future: The
     Canadian experience   320
     Sandra Mitchell and André Lalonde

16   Conclusions: The global diffusion of casemix   346
     Thomas D'Aunno, John R. Kimberly, and Gérard de Pouvourville

     Index   373

Figures

1.1 Three loosely coupled systems in the health policy environment *page* 7
1.2 Decision tree for major diagnostic category 11: disease and disorders of the kidney and urinary tract 11
1.3 Distribution of patients by length of stay: New Jersey 1979 12
1.4 Trends in Medicare length of stay and all hospital length of stay 1992–2003 18
1.5 Medicare acute inpatient margins under DRGs 1996–2003 19
1.6 DRG storyline 23
2.1 UK: Total expenditure on health, 1987/8 to 2004/5 35
3.1 Key institutions and relationships in the Portuguese health care system 52
3.2 Equivalent discharges, ALOS, and CMI: cumulative variations between 1997 and 2004 64
3.3 Number of readmissions in surgical DRG, 1997–2004 65
3.4 Percentage of normal deliveries and C-sections in the total number of deliveries, 1997–2004 66
3.5 Percentage of C-sections by region in 1997 and 2004 66
4.1 The Swedish health care model 74
4.2 Trends in MLOS, discharges, and health care expenditures in Sweden 1987–99 75
4.3 Health care costs per inhabitant, 2002, PPP-adjusted, US dollars 75
4.4 Potential years of life lost below age 70 per 100,000 inhabitants 76
4.5 Different driving forces moving to a prospective payment system 78
4.6 Financial risk for reimbursement systems 79
4.7 The new reimbursement system in several counties in Sweden 89
5.1 The development of activity-based financing in the Danish health care sector 101
5.2 Annual growth in activity in the hospital sector (percent) 108
5.3 Total waiting times for seventeen selected treatments, July 2002–July 2006 (weeks) 109

5.4   Annual growth in hospital productivity (percent)   109
5.5   Financing reform, January 1, 2007   111
6.1   The French health care system: organization and financing   119
6.2   Activity-based financing and other kinds of financing (lump sum)   130
8.1   System of hospital care provision in Germany   156
8.2   Length of stay, number of patients, and hospital days
       from 1993–2003   158
8.3   The alternative: differentiated base rates per provision level   164
8.4   The decided convergence phase 2005–9   165
8.5   Development of CMI from 2001 to 2005   168
8.6   Winners and losers in the hospital restructuring process
       1993–2003   169
8.7   The winners: the four biggest hospital chains 1992–2003
       (1992 = 100)   169
8.8   Integrated care: cost saving versus cost shifting   171
8.9   Complex lump-sum payments   171
9.1   Differences in reimbursement before and after recoding   184
12.1   Structure of social medical insurance scheme   255
12.2   Structure of DPC   260
12.3   An example of DPC-based payment for hospital   262
12.4   An example of DPC-based benchmarking   267
12.5   DPC and SWOT analysis   270
13.1   Casemix implementation: key drivers   279
13.2   IT infrastructure   280
14.1   Flow of financing in the Hungarian health care system   286
14.2   Closing the gap between base rates of different hospital groups   301
14.3   Monthly changes in the casemix index (CMI) in different
       years with different DRG versions   313
14.4   The activity (cumulative relative weight / 10,000 persons,
       by regions, September 2005)   316

Tables

1.1	US DRGs with highest volume FY2003	*page* 6
2.1	History of UK casemix groups	36
3.1	Key figures for Portugal	53
3.2	Sources of data for the calculation of Portuguese prices by DRG	54
3.3	Percentage of funding based in DRG	58
3.4	Cases treated, ALOS and casemix index (CMI) in the period 1997–2004	63
3.5	Final budget, equivalent discharges, CMI, ALOS, cost per equivalent discharge, and cost per equivalent discharge adjusted by CMI – statistical significance of the differences in the period before and after funding through DRG	68
3.6	Average number of diagnosis and procedure codes per record, 1998–2003	69
5.1	Key health care figures for Denmark, 2003	93
5.2	The political and administrative level, assignment and expenditure 2003	94
8.1	General demographic and health data (2004 if not otherwise stated)	157
8.2	Modules of the current DRG-reimbursement system	159
8.3	German system of reimbursement from 1995–2004	159
8.4	Indicators of hospital efficiency in the year 2003 (*2002)	161
8.5	The four phases of introducing DRGs in Germany from 2000–2009	162
8.6	Development of the German DRG system	166
8.7	Variation of base rates in 2004	167
8.8	Overview of the different effects of DRGs in Germany	174
10.1	Healthcare funding channels adopted by five Italian regions in 2000	193
10.2	Main features of DRG tariffs adopted by Italian regions (2004)	198
10.3	Overview of twenty-five MDCs and number of DRGs included (1994)	203
10.4	Current articulation of Italian hospital services referred to casemix system and tariffs	205
10.5	Financial flows leading to funding based on casemix systems	208

10.6   Changes in Italian hospital provision (1994–2003), public
       and private   213
10.7   Cost distribution in a sample of 42 public and 16 private
       Italian hospitals (2000)   215
10.8   Comparison in DRG ranking by frequency (ordinary
       admissions, 1994 to 2001)   216
10.9   Hospital discharges and days of hospitalization (2001–3)   220
11.1   Selected comparative statistics, public hospitals, NSW and
       Victoria, 1989–1990–2002–2003   239
12.1   Total medical expenditure in Japan, 1965–2003   256
12.2   An example of DPC definition table (stomach, malignancy 060020)   259
12.3   Major diagnosis category of DPC   259
12.4   An example of DPC definition table for reimbursement   262
12.5   Changes in resource consumption after the introduction of
       DPC between 2002 and 2003 (an example for "DPC
       0600203x01000x (Malignancy, Stomach, Total gasterectomy,
       No additional procedure, No CC)": 82 hospitals)   265
14.1   Characteristics of the official versions issued to date   297
14.2   Cost content of the Hungarian HBCS: average cost
       distribution of 1,000 HBCS cost-weights   299
14.3   Main characteristics of acute care in Hungary   313
15.1   Age categories based on cost and length of stay data   338
16.1   Variation in patient classification system adoption   348

Contributors

Imre Boncz Department of Health Policy, National Health Insurance Fund Administration, Budapest, Hungary, and Institute of Diagnostics and Management, University of Pécs, Hungary

Jon Chilingerian Professor of Organizational Behavior and Management of Health Care, Heller School for Social Policy and Management, Brandeis University, Boston, USA

Marie Christine Closon Health Services Research, School of Public Health, Université Catholique de Louvain, Belgium

Thomas D'Aunno Novartis Chaired Professor of Healthcare Management and Professor of Organisational Behaviour, INSEAD, Fontainebleau, France

Gérard de Pouvourville Chair in Health Economics and Management, ESSEC, Cergy-Pontoise, France

Csaba Dózsa Ministry of Health, Budapest, Hungary

Stephen J. Duckett Executive Director, Reform and Development Division, Queensland Health, Brisbane, Australia

Francis H. Roger France Health Services Research, School of Public Health, Université Catholique de Louvain, Belgium

Hervé Guillain Office of Finance, CHUV, Lausanne, Switzerland

John R. Kimberly Henry Bower Professor, The Wharton School, University of Pennsylvania, USA

André Lalonde Director, Corporate Planning and Quality Management, Canadian Institute for Health Information, Toronto, Canada

Chien Earn Lee Senior Director, Healthcare Performance Group, Ministry of Health, Singapore

Eng Kok Lim Assistant Director, Service Management, Healthcare Finance Division, Ministry of Health, Singapore

Rikard Lindqvist Centre for Patient Classification Systems, Stockholm, Sweden

Céu Mateus National School of Public Health, Lisbon, Portugal

Shinya Matsuda Department of Preventive Medicine and Community Health, University of Occupational and Environmental Health, Yahatanishi, Kitakyushu, Japan

Xavière Michelot Project Manager, Operational Performance, Capio Development AB, Stockholm, Sweden

Sandra Mitchell Manager, Grouper Redevelopment Project, Canadian Institute for Health Information, Toronto, Canada

Júlia Nagy Department of Curative and Preventive Services, National Health Insurance Fund Administration, Budapest, Hungary

Günter Neubauer University of the German Army, Munich, Germany

Julian Perelman Health Services Research, School of Public Health, Université Catholique de Louvain, Belgium

Florian Pfister Dipl.-Volkswirt, Institute for Health Economics, Munich, Germany

Jean Marie Rodrigues SSPIM, CHU Saint Etienne, France

Annette Søberg Roed Executive Adviser, Health Economics (DRG), National Board of Health, Copenhagen, Denmark

Hanne Sjuneson Head of Section, National Board of Health, Health Economics (DRG), Copenhagen, Denmark

Steve Sutch Sutch Consulting International Limited, UK

Paolo Tedeschi Center for Research on Health and Social Care Management, Bocconi University, Milan, and Management and Health Laboratory of Scuola Superiore Sant' Anna, Pisa, Italy

Acknowledgements

This book is a joint venture in every sense of those words. The authors of the individual chapters, Jon Chilingerian in the US, Marie Christine Closon, Francis Roger France and Julian Perelman in Belgium, Stephen Duckett in Australia, Hervé Guillain in Switzerland, Dr Chien Earn Lee and Eng Kok Lim in Singapore, Rikard Lindqvist in Sweden, Céu Mateus in Portugal, Shinya Matsuda in Japan, Dr Júlia Nagy, Csaba Dózsa, and Dr Imre Boncz in Hungary, Annette Søberg Roed, Hanne Sjuneson, and Poul Hansen in Denmark, Xavière Michelot and Jean Marie Rodrigues in France, Sandra Mitchell and André Lalonde in Canada, Günter Neubauer in Germany, Steve Sutch in the UK, and Paolo Tedeschi in Italy all responded fully and enthusiastically to the challenge that was put to them.

Finally, we are grateful to the Wharton/INSEAD Alliance and its Center for Global Research and Education for providing financial and logistical support for the two authors' meetings held at INSEAD and to Ana-Cristina De Sa and Laureen Sorreda for their help in organizing the authors' meetings and co-ordinating the work on the various chapters.

Introduction

On April 1, 1983, the first patient classification system (PSC) to be used for paying hospitals for the services they provided was adopted by the US Congress. For the first time, a payer – in this case Medicare – had a way of comparing the outputs of one hospital with those of another and a basis for paying hospitals in a standardized fashion for the "products" they produced.

This system, known as Diagnosis-Related Groups, (DRGs) was developed by a team of researchers at Yale University under the direction of Robert Fetter and John Thompson and sparked a revolution in the health care sector in the United States. At a moment in time when there was increasing concern in Congress and elsewhere about the rapid rise of costs in health care, hospitals could no longer justify higher costs simply by asserting their patients were sicker than anyone else's. By classifying patients according to the resource consumption patterns that were typically associated with particular diagnoses, the DRG case-based system promised to introduce both transparency and operational efficiency into a production process that had previously been largely opaque.

The US, however, was not the only country struggling with increasing costs in health care in the 1980s. A number of other countries, particularly in Western Europe, were experiencing similar increases and were in the hunt for solutions. When Congress adopted the Prospective Payment System with DRGs as the underlying patient classification system, other countries took notice, and soon a number of them began experimenting with various kinds of PCSs, most of which were modelled, directly or indirectly, on the DRG system. France, the UK, Portugal, and Belgium, among others, were "fast followers" and began to explore the possible use of PCSs in their own health systems.

In 1993, John Kimberly and Gérard de Pouvourville published a book titled *The Migration of Managerial Innovation: Diagnosis-Related Groups and Health Care Administration in Western Europe.* The book detailed the experiences of nine different countries in Western Europe with DRGs through 1991, including that of Germany, a country that at the time had decided not to go down that path. Viewing the spread of DRGs through the lens of innovation diffusion, the authors concluded that in addition to its potential to help control costs, a principal reason for the adoption of DRGs was the system's flexibility, flexibility that allowed it to be adapted to fit a variety of national priorities and policy contexts.

By 2005, fourteen years later, a number of other countries in other parts of the world had begun to use patient classification systems. What had their experiences been? How similar to or different from the original nine were they? What had happened in some of those original nine countries in the meanwhile? And what might be learned about introducing change into national health systems by comparing their experiences? To try to answer these questions, Kimberly and Pouvourville enlisted the help of Tom D'Aunno at INSEAD, and the three of us resolved to identify knowledgeable individuals in a number of countries who could write chapters for their country around a common set of themes. We turned to Jean Marie Rodrigues of France and Céu Mateus from Portugal, both of whom have been centrally involved in an organization called Patient Classification Systems International (PCS-I), for suggestions. After much discussion, we identified individuals in France, Belgium, the UK, Sweden, Switzerland, Portugal, Denmark, and Germany, eight of the nine countries in the original book, and in Hungary, Italy, Australia, Singapore, Japan, and Canada, new additions, to write chapters. We have also included a chapter on the US, feeling that it would be useful for the DRG story to be told as context for the rest of the accounts in the book.

An authors' meeting was held at INSEAD in December of 2004 to orient each chapter author to the principal themes in the book and to permit some sharing of experiences. We asked each author to provide a brief overview of the health system in their country to provide the context into which patient classification systems were being introduced and then to address a common set of questions: when was PCS introduced, what motivated its introduction, who were the key actors in its introduction, how did the implementation process unfold, and, finally, what has the impact been and what debates and controversies have emerged around its introduction and implementation?

First drafts were produced in 2005, and a second authors' meeting was held, again at INSEAD, in December of 2005 to discuss, review and identify strengths and weaknesses in each chapter that had been written up to that point. Final drafts and updates were produced in 2006, as was the concluding overview chapter.

Audience

The result is a book that provides rich descriptions of the fate of PCSs in each of the fifteen countries represented as well as an analysis of the commonalities and differences among them. As such, the book is intended to appeal to three principal audiences: *health policy makers and managers* concerned with designing and implementing new initiatives that will have broad impact and will engage many different sets of actors in complex and often highly contentious ways; *students*, both undergraduate and graduate, taking courses in health administration, comparative health systems, and/or the management of change; and *researchers* working on problems of innovation and change in general or, more specifically, on international and comparative health policy and management.

In an era when health reform is high on the political agendas of most countries around the globe, the book provides an overview of how health care is organized and financed in fifteen of these countries and how patient classification systems are being used in these efforts. In so doing, it illustrates a range of alternative solutions, and is thus likely to be of interest to those concerned with the problem of health reform in general as well. The story of health reform, of course, continues to unfold, and Patient Classification Systems and their continued evolution are only one piece of a much larger puzzle.

1 Origins of DRGs in the United States: A technical, political and cultural story

Jon Chilingerian

Introduction

In 1983, DRGs became the price-setting system for the Medicare program in the United States. Why did the United States choose DRGs?[1] The idea of setting 518 diagnostic payment rates for 4,800 hospitals seemed unimaginably complicated, too technical and an exercise in formula-driven cost control to some observers – an ambitious endeavor unlikely to succeed.[2] Nevertheless, since its inception, the DRG system has been called the single most significant post-war innovation in medical financing in the history of the United States (Mayes 2006), and may be the most influential health care management research project ever developed. As the chapters in this volume attest, worldwide adoption of DRGs followed in the wake of this American experiment.

Other competing patient classification systems could have been selected (Pettingill and Vertrees 1982). The range of policy options included flat rates per discharge, capitation, expenditure caps, negotiated rates, and competitive bidding (Smith 1992). Although researchers continue to experiment with alternative patient classification systems, a critical mass has formed around DRGs as the *dominant design* for measuring a hospital's casemix. A dominant policy design not only obtains legitimacy from the relevant community, future innovations must adhere to its basic features (Utterback 1996). A dominant design does not have to outperform other innovations; it merely has to balance the stakeholder interests.

Though the control of rising health costs is a major policy issue, American hospitals had come to expect "pass-throughs, bail-outs, and hold-harmless clauses" from the political system (Smith 1992, p 44). The implementation of DRGs, however, challenged this assumption and created a financial incentive for hospitals to manage Medicare patients more efficiently or lose money, contradicting the fundamental interests of hospital providers and professional monopolies. After Medicare shifted from retrospective reimbursement to prospective payment under DRGs, nine years later in 1992, Congress passed an equivalent prospective payment system for physicians. In 1997, outpatient services, skilled nursing care, long-term care, home health, and rehabilitation services also went to prospective payment. Hence, the implementation of DRGs stimulated a massive transformation of payment and financing for health care in the United States.

Transformational innovations like DRGs don't just happen; the inertia that characterizes health care organizations makes them remarkably resistant to policy changes. In fact, DRGs were never designed to be a payment mechanism; they were designed for managing hospitals. Support for DRGs did not come because the approach offered a perfect technical policy solution. This novel patient classification system was selected because it became closely aligned with the social–cultural system and the political system. To understand why the United States adopted a DRG-based payment system, the events, actors, and incidents within the historical context must be understood.

The remainder of this chapter is organized into five sections. The first section discusses the basic ideas behind DRGs. The second introduces a framework for understanding the policy environment in the United States. The third is a brief history of the introduction of DRGs in terms of the technical, political, and social–cultural systems. The fourth examines some of the impacts and controversies around DRGs. The final section summarizes and discusses the lessons learned.

ABCs of DRGs

In the United States, DRGs are a patient classification technique that defines and measures a hospital's casemix (ProPAC 1985).[3] Designed to segment clinically similar groups of patients by their hospital resource requirements, DRGs pay a flat amount per diagnosis. Each year the United States federal government uses DRGs to set 518[4] diagnostic payment rates for 4,800 short-term acute hospitals treating Medicare eligible patients.

Classification of patients depends on several partitioning variables such as: principal discharge diagnosis, a patient's age, and up to eight

Table 1.1 US DRGs with highest volume FY2003

DRG	DRG Name	Discharges %	No. (000)
127	Heart failure and shock	6%	693
89	Simple pneumonia and pleurisy > 17 w/cc	4	519
29	Major joint and limb reattachment	4	427
88	Chronic obstructive pulmonary disease	3	397
182	Esophagitis, gastroenteritis, and misc. digest. > 17	2	292
296	Nutritional metabolic disorder > 17 w/cc	2	261
174	GI hemorrhage w/cc	2	259
143	Chest pain	2	246
14	Intracranial hemorrhage / cerebral infarction	2	242
320	Kidney and urinary	2	211

Source: Federal Register, May 19, 2004, p 28195–28818

co-morbidities and complications. DRGs have a decision-tree structure, where each patient is categorized into one of twenty-five major diagnostic categories, and then into either a surgical or medical treatment strategy. Each DRG represents a class of patients with similar clinical work processes and medical service bundles. The most common DRGs are shown in Table 1.1. Ten DRGs account for nearly 30 percent of acute hospital admissions.

The number of DRGs has remained manageable, evolving from 468 when federal DRGs began in 1984 to 518 in 2005. However, as diseases and treatments change, so must DRGs. Each year they are reviewed and sometimes amended, or new DRGs are created. For example, there were no ICD–9 codes for HIV infections until 1986. MDC 25 was created for three new DRGs: HIV with major operating room procedure, HIV with major related condition, HIV without other related conditions. The Centers for Medicare and Medicaid Services (CMS) is the US federal agency that has been granted the power to establish new DRGs when a group of patients require more costly procedures. For example, DRG 482 was developed for tracheostomy and patients who require ninety-six hours or more of mechanical ventilation were put into DRG 541 or 542.

Each DRG is assigned a relative weight (RW) that represents national average costs (i.e. the expected resource consumption for a *typical* patient at an *average* hospital). So a DRG with a RW of 1 is expected to consume half the resources as a RW of 2. Each year, every hospital's diagnoses are aggregated and summarized into an overall RW. Pettengill and Vertrees

(1982) found that the casemix index range went from a low of .51 to a high of 1.83. Hospitals with higher RW receive more money.

Recalibration means a DRG's weight is increased or decreased. Each year the 518^5 different DRG weights are reanalyzed and recalibrated. For example, in 1985 a fracture of the femur (DRG 235) had a casemix index (i.e. relative weight) of 1.08; in 2005 the index was reduced to .7512.[6] To set prices with DRGs, Medicare calculates a national average unit price for every unit of service of care received during a hospital stay. In general, a hospital's DRG payment is: *Payment per discharge = (DRG relative weight × Standardized Base Payment)*. Medicare creates base payment rates that include operating (i.e. room and ancillary services) and capital costs (i.e. interest and depreciation). Adjustments are made for market conditions, medical education, care for low-income populations, casemix complexity, and new technology (see appendix).

The American health policy environment

Figure 1.1 displays a general framework for understanding the American policy environment. The health policy environment is composed of a shifting constellation of organizations – political institutions, associations, government agencies, research groups, NGOs, and so on. These organizations can be grouped into three loosely coupled systems, which influence behavior and must be managed: a technical medical care system, a

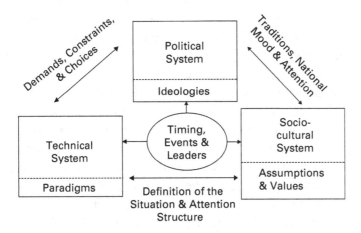

Figure 1.1   Three loosely coupled systems in the health policy environment

sociocultural system, and a political system (see Parsons, 1960; Tichy 1981; Tichy 1983; Tichy 1990; Chilingerian 2004).

The *technical system* is an invisible college of practitioners, delivery organizations, research scientists, planning staff, research and evaluation bureaus, consultants, and of course, academic professors working on ideas. Although personal and organizational values often influence how they frame problems, focus attention, and formulate paradigms, whenever new problems emerge the political system negotiates the demands, constraints, and choices for a problem (Pfeffer and Salancik 1978), and the socio-cultural system helps to interpret the situation (Kingdon 1984). The technical system goes right to work obtaining research funding, conducting research, writing reports, publishing and circulating papers, attending hearings, offering testimony, and testing new ideas (Kingdon 1984). Although technical policy proposals that are politically unappealing have little chance of surviving, timing the release of a technical solution can make a difference in its reception.

The *sociocultural system* reduces the likelihood that an idea's merit alone will cause it to rise to the top of the agenda, because solutions are closely embedded in personal relationships, attention structures, and networks (Granovetter 1985). The sociocultural system creates a context for under-standing, building commitment and offering justification for the superiority of a technical solution (Parsons 1960). Brickman (1987) has argued that decisions are important because we infer values from decisions; conse-quently, policy must fit with the cultural values of the mainstream (Kingdon 1984).

In the United States, health policy does not rest with a few powerful individuals; there is a *political system* that allocates power, influence, and attention to a political agenda, and resolves uncertainties about decision rights, relationships that affect resource allocation, internal status and career paths, and conflicts affecting the technical and sociocultural systems (Bacharach and Lawler 1982). Power is shared between the federal govern-ment and the fifty state governments. States experiment locally with health policy innovations, and if perceived as successful, new ideas may be adopted at the national level. This shared power is fragmented among a constellation of law-making politicians, executive branch bureaucrats, as well as providers and professional organizations. The fragmentation of power and influence was built into the foundation of American government with the phrase "checks and balances." Morone (1994) describes how this plays out:

Proposals must run an awesome political gauntlet: first, the Office of the President; then, the competing, overlapping committees in each branch of Congress (five separate committees have major jurisdiction over health care bills); after that, the Washington bureaucracy; and, finally, the multiple layers of American federalism – all divided by function and bedeviled by an extensive (much called upon) judiciary. It is not a policy-making apparatus designed for swift or concerted action. On the contrary, American government is designed to be maladroit at securing broad, coordinated policy changes – like national health care reform. (Morone 1994, p 154)

The health policy environment can be thought of as a weather system occasionally subject to severe conditions such as mini-tornados. Small events and incidences, and leadership inside the political system give rise to coalitions of powerful, influential people. Dominant coalitions determine how decisions are made.

Novel or complex problems and uncertainties can cause each of the systems to overload. Events in the situation (i.e., emergent leaders, chance meetings, values at stake, availability of information, struggle for control, etc.) will determine whether the political and/or cultural systems resolve the uncertainty. "Great ideas" are powerful, but their truth value is not enough to gain acceptance. Research has found that policy decisions represent a solution acceptable to the coalition (March and Simon 1958). So adoption and implementation require executive and political leaders who organize attention and advocate effectively, and build commitment to new ideas (Yergin and Stanislaw 1999). American policy leaders must convince bureaucrats, congress people, journalists, interest groups, and, indirectly, public opinion that an innovation makes sense. From time to time, leaders mobilize a *dominant coalition* around a great idea that fits with the *dominant ideology* of specialists, and the *dominant cultural values* of the mainstream. Under these conditions, an innovative idea can become a dominant paradigm. Urgency, timing and the depth of leadership matter more than well-designed solutions, competence, and commitment.

Why DRGs were selected: A brief history

Throughout the 1970s the United States experienced unbridled rising hospital costs. The technical experts argued that without a valid and reliable measure for hospital casemix, a fair prospective payment system would be difficult if not impossible. What virtually no one knew was that a small research group at Yale University had begun to develop a workable casemix measure. However, even the Yale researchers did not understand what they would eventually design, because of the way they had originally framed the problem. They asked – *In order for the hospital to manage and control cost-per-case, how can a hospital product be defined and measured?*

Research & Development at Yale University: "We have this new thing"

DRGs were the brainchild of two Yale professors: Bob Fetter, and John Thompson. Richard Averill, who later became director of health-related research at Yale, was a graduate student working with both Fetter and Thompson. Averill remembers that when they started to talk about these problems, Bob Fetter would ask "But John, what is the product?" John Thompson, whose background was in nursing, would say, "We treat patients." Then Bob Fetter would argue that to design a control process, you would have to be able to differentiate among a hospital's acute products.

While being developed at Yale, this method of describing the hospital's products was not called Diagnostic Related Groups (DRGs). In fact, when Thompson would encourage people to consider using DRGs he merely said "You have to do this new thing." This new thing that could describe and measure the entire range of patients treated in an acute hospital, from newborns and children to adults.

DRGs began as a "pure-research endeavor." In 1967, a group of local physicians asked for help with utilization review (Fetter 1991).[7] Could industrial engineering techniques be adapted to hospitals? Subsequent research in the early 1970s looked at why maternity and newborn care and costs varied among accredited, not-for-profit Connecticut hospitals. To address those questions, the Yale team worked iteratively among the conceptual, empirical, and policy domains. Fetter (1991) recalled in 1969 bringing together a panel of physicians to describe clinical work processes. As in the case of manufacturing, tens of thousands of "unique" hospital patient types existed. For example, there were thirty-nine ways to describe a cataract care process. Researchers were searching for an underlying structure focused on similarities to "identify the ordinary, the usual, the routine, and applying the techniques of statistical process control, to filter out the aberrant cases in order to understand the causes of aberrations" (Fetter 1991, p 6).

Previous work found significant correlations between length of stay (LOS), total charges and casemix complexity (see Lave and Leinhardt 1976;

Luke 1979). The research assumed that the amount of hospital resources consumed per customer was a function of the LOS. In retrospect, choosing LOS as a single, proxy measure of the underlying structure of hospital output was a stroke of genius. LOS was far less volatile than actual costs; it was clinically relevant, available, standardized, and a reliable measure of output.

With physician involvement, 10,000 hospital diagnostic (ICD–9–CM) codes[8] were segmented into twenty-three mutually exclusive and exhaustive categories called Major Diagnostic Categories (MDC). The MDCs were based on major organ systems inferred from the diagnosis, such as diseases and disorders of the eye; diseases and disorders of the circulatory system; diseases and disorders of the kidney and urinary tract, and the like. Diseases and disorders that did not belong to an organ (i.e. systemic infections) went into special or residual MDC categories.

The Yale team found three variables strongly associated with resource consumption: (1) surgical procedures, (2) the presence of complications or co-morbidity[9] (CC), and (3) the patient's age (seventeen years or less, eighteen to sixty-nine, or greater than seventy). Initial DRG segmentation was based on diagnosis (using ICD–9 code) and the presence or absence of an operating room procedure. Further partitioning was based on age and CC.[10] Homogeneous groups, as the Yale team defined it, meant that the unexplained sum of the squared differences in LOS would be minimized (Fetter *et al.* 1980).[11]

Figure 1.2 displays the decision-tree structure for MDC 11, diseases and disorders of the kidney and urinary tract. In this example, a surgical

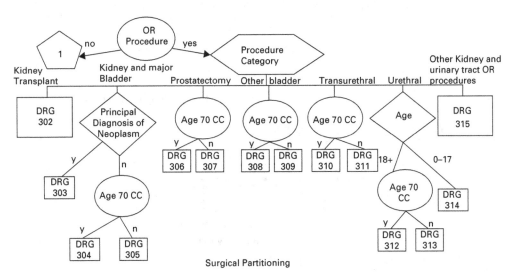

Figure 1.2   Decision tree for major diagnostic category 11: disease and disorders of the kidney and urinary tract

partition is grouped by a stand-alone procedure such as a kidney transplant (DRG 302) and procedures such as prostatectomy, which is refined by age and co-morbidity or complications (DRG 306 and DRG 307). If there is no operating room procedure, the medical partitioning includes diagnoses such as renal failure, neoplasm (age seventy CC), neoplasm (less than age seventy), kidney stones, and the like. After the first set of DRGs were developed, the 10,000 diagnoses were clustered into 383 cases.[12] Recalling that DRGs were guided by central tendency theory and clinical judgment, each of the 383 had patients with similar patterns of utilization, while maintaining clinical coherence. Consequently, not every patient could be assigned to a DRG – extreme LOS values were statistical outliers requiring a cutoff or trim ($< 5\%$), and some were inliers (Grimaldi and Micheletti 1983).

Two conclusions can be reached about DRGs. First, they are a crude, gigantic set of averages forcing standardization of care without an adjustment for severity within a diagnosis. Though lengths of stay (LOS) for some DRGs were normally distributed, many DRGs had strange LOS distributions. For example, Figure 1.3 shows the distribution of LOS for heart failure and/or shock in New Jersey in 1979 (adapted from Grimaldi and Micheletti 1983). The mean LOS of 12.8 days is misleading, since more than 30 percent of the patients stayed in the hospital less than five days or more than seventeen days.

Second, DRGs shifted the paradigm and changed the mind set of health policy and management. Prior to DRGs, hospitals were characterized as multiservice firms offering tens of thousands of activities. All of the possible

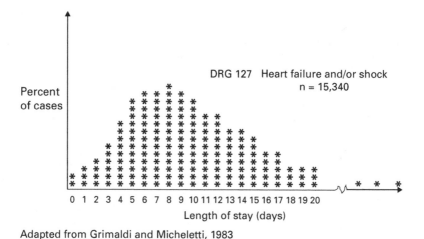

Adapted from Grimaldi and Micheletti, 1983

Figure 1.3   Distribution of patients by length of stay: New Jersey 1979

combinations of diagnoses, age categories, procedures, complications and co-morbidities could result in 400,000 groups.[13] With the "discovery" of a few hundred DRGs, the complexity of the hospital appeared manageable. In theory, every hospital could develop an information system capable of measuring the multiple service outputs of the hospital, and relating each diagnosis to the use of clinical resources. DRGs brought the medical records department out of the bowels of the hospital and into the hearts and minds of the hospital managers. A hospital's production function and medical strategy could be better understood. With better planning and control, hospital managers could become cost-conscious and more efficient. And Fetter finally had an answer to the fundamental health policy and management question – What is the product of the hospital? The answer, although imperfect, was DRGs.

New Jersey tries to do the DRG "thing"[14]

In 1980, New Jersey (NJ) became the first state to adopt DRGs. The principal reason was Dr. Joanne Finley, a physician with degrees in economics and public health and her association with (and respect for) Yale Professor John Thompson. In 1973, NJ's health department had been cited for weak cost control and negligence because they had become a political prisoner of the hospital industry. In 1974, Finley, New Haven's city public health officer and adjunct professor at Yale,[15] became NJ's Health Commissioner (Smithey and Fetter 1982; Hsiao *et al.* 1986; Mayes 2006). She was a mover and a shaker. Under pressure from lawsuits to reform NJ, she recalled Thompson's vague words before she left: "you got to do this new thing."

After some preliminary meetings, Finley requested a proposal from Thompson and the Yale DRG team. In 1976 a proposal was submitted to the Social Security Administration (SSA) to design and implement an all-payer DRG system in NJ. Politically, Dr. Finley would have a fight on her hands with the hospital association and Blue Cross. However, Finley developed a proposal that accommodated the primary interests of the key stakeholders:

Urban hospitals desired financial assistance for providing care to their disproportionately poor patients; commercial insurers wanted relief from increased cost shifting imposed on them by all hospitals; state legislators desired an increased measure of cost control to address Medicaid's cost escalation; and the federal government wanted states to experiment with different forms of hospital reimbursement in order to develop a national model of reform for Medicare. (Mayes 2006, p 17)

Finley negotiated directly with the NJ Hospital Association and the NJ Blue Cross for DRG-based payment. On the hospital side, Jack Owen, the head of the NJ Hospital Association, publicly criticized DRGs but privately advised Joanne Finley on how to mobilize the hospitals' dissatisfaction and create an alliance with a small number of early adopter "volunteer" hospitals. Owen understood the clash of interests between suburban and urban teaching hospitals, and personally convinced twenty-six hospital managers to give up some of their interests, arguing that DRGs could yield net benefits.[16]

In 1980, twenty-six NJ hospitals volunteered to receive the first DRG payments.[17] In 1981 another forty hospitals were paid by DRGs, and in 1982 the final thirty hospitals came under DRG reform. DRGs achieved a measure of success between 1980 and 1986 (Rosko and Broyles 1986; Rosko and Broyles 1987). NJ hospital revenues were below the national averages, and though hospitals with surpluses did not reduce their costs, hospitals with deficits achieved significant cost reductions (Hsaio *et al.* 1986). Lower costs per case were achieved because LOS decreased more than 10 percent (Weiner *et al.* 1987). DRGs appeared to control hospital costs without affecting their financial health (Rosko 1989).

By 1982, the Reagan administration needed an acceptable solution to what had become a healthcare cost crisis. More importantly, Richard Schweiker, Reagan's Secretary of Health and Human Services, became convinced that DRGs were the new thing "he had been looking for" (Smith 1992, p 38).

The political system's response to urgency and social pressure

Long before NJ's introduction of DRGs, the seeds of change had been sown. In 1965, after five decades of discussion and debate about national social insurance, the Medicare and Medicaid programs were enacted. Medicare was a compulsory social insurance program for people over sixty-five, plus a government-subsidized program to pay physicians; both programs covered about half of the health expenditures for older Americans. With the passage of Medicaid, there was expanded assistance to the fifty states to care for the poor (covering about 30 percent of the poor).

Medicare, which included a cost-plus 2 percent reimbursement system, gave hospitals and physicians *carte blanche*. To accommodate hospital interests, the politicians had created legislation promising to reimburse all hospital costs, rather than set prospective rates for illnesses. Hospitals were paid on an accelerated basis for asset depreciation. So in 1967, after the first full year of operation, the hospital average daily service charge increased 22 percent. The Medicare forecast of $1.3 billion was off by $3.3 billion. By 1969, the media characterized the health care situation as on "the brink of chaos" and the president of the United States declared a "massive crisis" in health care (Morone 1994). When politicians articulated the view that Medicare and health care were out of control, the public agreed (Smith 1992). In 1971, 75 percent of the respondents to a national survey agreed that there was a health care crisis (Alford 1975; Starr 1980). Medicare's annual rate of increase was more than 20 percent each year. Between 1966 and 1976, growth in hospital costs skyrocketed 345 percent, against a Consumer Price Index increase of 89 percent (Mayes 2006). In ten years, public spending on health lurched from $11 billion to $78 billion (Enthoven 1980).

In 1980 President Ronald Reagan was elected on a political platform to "get government off the backs of the people" – implementing trickle-down economics, deregulation, and more market-based competition. Despite the rhetoric, hospitals costs soared in 1980, 1981, and 1982, up 13, 16 and 15 percent respectively (Brown 1991). National health care spending had skyrocketed from $35.9 billion in 1965 to $355.4 billion by 1983. Politicians finally stopped threatening hospitals to behave or be controlled. In 1982, Congress enacted the Tax Equity and Fiscal Responsibility Act (TEFRA) and asked President Reagan to deliver prospective prices with casemix.[18]

The federal government also tried various policies and regulatory solutions, such as professional reviews, capital budgets, planning, and even voluntary efforts. With the exception of wage controls every attempt to contain hospital costs failed. During President Carter's administration (1976–80) a behind-the-scenes group of senior health policy analysts from the Bureau of Health Insurance wanted to help reform Medicare. To explore policies aimed at controlling cost-per-case, they assigned Julian Pettengill, a young economist who had experience with earlier attempts to control routine hospital costs[19] (Pettengill 2002). In 1979 Pettengill was part of a team investigating the value of DRGs, because he assumed cost-per-case limits required a casemix index. He and his colleague James Vertrees conducted the largest DRG pilot study, 1.93 million discharges in 5,957 hospitals (Pettengill and Vertrees 1982). They wrote an internal report recommending DRGS as a "valid and generally accurate representation of the expected costliness of an individual hospital's casemix" (Pettengill and Vertrees 1982, p 124).

Small events and incidences

When President Reagan was elected, he appointed Richard Schweiker[20] Secretary of the Department of Health and Human Services, and the Pettengill report went on a shelf (Mayes 2006). Schweiker had seen health costs rise for twenty years and hospitals fail to manage costs. His vision was to contain hospital costs with a prospective payment system, and he established a high-level committee to investigate alternatives (Smith 1992).[21] By the fall of 1981 the committee narrowed the choices to either: (1) setting flat rates per discharge based on each hospital's historic costs, adjusted for inflation; or (2) employing DRGs for individual patient discharges. Just as the committee was about to recommend flat rates, Schweiker gave the order, "Develop the DRG approach!"

Why were DRGs selected by the leader of the federal agency? Three months earlier, when the American Hospital Association convened in Washington, Schweiker met Jack Owen,[22] former president of the New Jersey Hospital Association and an advocate of DRGs (Smith 1992). During this impromptu meeting, Owen talked about the "New Jersey experiment" and persuaded Schweiker that DRGs could be used to set individual hospital prices. From a technical standpoint, learning about the existence of DRGs made this meeting fortuitous; from a political standpoint, having the largest American hospital association support DRGs was momentous (Smith 1992). Shortly thereafter, Schweiker discovered the work at Yale and Pettengill's research. Schweiker sent a senior group to NJ. In December 1982, reassured that DRGs were working in NJ, and that the Yale team would be available to lend their academic credibility, a report went to Congress proposing DRG-based payments. Congress passed a DRG amendment on March 23, 1983. DRGs were used to pay for Medicare services beginning on October 1, 1983.[23]

After 1983, American states interested in improving their payment system would have to consider DRGs as a reference point (Mayes 2006). Between

1983 and 1994, DRGs diffused to every region of the United States; almost half of the United States adopted various aspects of the DRG system for their own use (Jacobson 1994). By 1991, twenty states were using DRG-based payment systems (Jacobson 1994). However by 1997, the United States government reported that eighteen different patient classification systems were in use. Today, the federal government and some states such as New York and Maryland are developing severity-adjusted DRG categories.

Impacts and controversies

The 2005 MedPAC[24] report to Congress began with the following analysis regarding hospital and ambulatory services:

The evidence on payment adequacy for hospital is mixed. Beneficiaries' access to care, volume of services, and access to capital are positive, and results on quality are mixed. However, unusually large cost increases recently have led to a downward trend in Medicare margins. (p 41)

Several reasons are given for lower margins. First, medical costs increased faster than "market basket" inflation. Between 2002 and 2003 malpractice costs rose from 26 percent per adjusted discharge to 34 percent. Administration and general expenses, which account for 15 percent of hospital costs, rose by 7.5 percent per adjusted discharge (MedPAC, 2005).

In the years following the implementation of DRGs, academics hypothesized that financial pressure from DRGs would lead to quality shading, hospital closures, and targeting profitable, or transferring out less profitable patients. In the early years, no evidence of quality reductions was found (Carroll and Erwin 1987; Des Harnais *et al.* 1988; Feinglass and Holloway 1991; MedPAC 2004). Pressure from DRGs between 1998 and 2003 did not negatively affect in-hospital mortality or mortality thirty days after discharge – both have decreased across all DRGs (MedPAC 2004). Other studies found no reductions in the utilization of intensive care units (Sloan, Morrisey and Valvona 1988). Moreover, significant quality improvements were achieved in congestive heart failure and coronary artery by-pass graft (MedPAC 2005, p 23.)

Between 1990 and 1999 340 more hospitals closed than opened; however, these hospitals were very small and had very low admission and occupancy rates. Finally, there has been little or no evidence that patients in

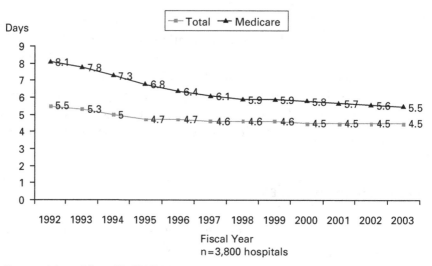

Source: Adapted from MedPAC 2004

Figure 1.4   Trends in Medicare length of stay and all hospital length of stay 1992–2003

"unprofitable DRGs" were transferred to city and county (public) hospitals (Newhouse 1989).

The most significant change in behavior after the advent of PPS was the reduction in days of acute patient care. For example, ProPAC found that average LOS dropped 9 percent in 1983, the first year DRGs were introduced. Between 1983 and 1988 the change in average LOS totaled 9.2 percent (Hodgkin and McGuire 1994). MedPAC's report to Congress in March 2002 revealed a 32.3 percent LOS reduction from 1989 to 1999 for all US hospitals.

Over the next several years, the magnitude of the change under DRGS was significantly greater. Figure 1.4 reveals that overall LOS for all hospital admissions fell 18 percent from 5.5 days to 4.5 days, while LOS for patients under DRGs fell 32 percent, from 8.1 days in 1992 to 4.5 days in 2003. If LOS declined, did admissions increase? Prior to DRGs, admissions had been increasing. Contrary to the NJ experience, admissions dropped 11 percent between 1983 and 1991 (Hodgkin and McGuire 1994).

Early studies found that DRGs were associated with reduced expenditures (Zwanziger and Melnick 1988). In the later years, costs-per-adjusted admission[25] were flat from 1993 to 1996, declined in 1997 and 1998, and rose between 1999 and 2002 (MedPAC 2004). Between 2001 and 2002 costs-per-adjusted admission increased 5.4 percent from $6,980 to $7,355 (MedPAC 2004).

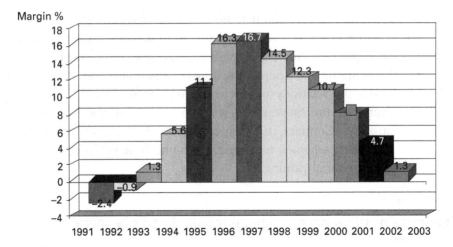

* Margin = revenue minus cost, divided by revenue.
Source: Adapted from MedPAC Report to Congress, 2003

Figure 1.5   Medicare acute inpatient margins under DRGs 1996–2003

A few years after the introduction of DRGs, the annual rate of increase from Medicare revenues was below the rate of hospital inflation. Without controversy, from 1986 to 1992, acute hospital margins owing to Medicare declined. Acute inpatient margins under DRGs are displayed above. Figure 1.5 shows that margins increased between 1992 and 1997, from a small negative margin to a high of 16.7 percent. The Balanced Budget Act saw margins falling, and in 2003 they were only 1.3 percent.

Do DRGs creep?

Under a DRG system, casemix matters. Small changes in the coding of diagnostic and other information can influence casemix and can have a large payment effect (Steinwald and Dummit 1989). For example, in 1990 it was established that each 1 percent increase resulted in an additional $400 million in revenue for hospitals and expenditures for Medicare (Carter, Newhouse and Relles 1991).

In 1981, the term "DRG creep" was coined to describe a potentially unethical or pathological managerial behavior – coding and record keeping designed to elevate casemix weights and payments (Simborg 1981). In fact the national casemix index did increase. After the first year of DRGs the national average casemix weight went from 1.05 to 1.13

(Steinwald and Dummit 1989). Subsequent studies found that most of the increase in casemix reflected a mix of more complex cases (two-thirds was true change) and the remainder was due to more accurate narrative descriptions and coding (see Carter, Newhouse and Relles 1991). Before DRGs the relatively unimportant medical records department was often found in the basement of the hospital, underfunded, ignored and in atrophy. Contrary to highly publicized cases of fraudulent revenue enhancing schemes, most research found little evidence of DRG upcoding or managerial gaming.

Influence of DRGs on managerial mindsets and behavior

Studies of managerial behavior inside New Jersey hospitals found that DRGs were not used for internal control. New Jersey hospital managers found DRGs too complex to use for daily, weekly or monthly management, since it required very precise information and cost accounting data. In addition, managers did not necessarily target the "unprofitable" DRGs, nor did they manage intensive care costs, reduce more expensive clinical staff, or manage LOS for surgical DRGs differently than the medical DRGs. LOS for outlier DRGs decreased in matching proportions, which hurt the hospitals financially (Weiner *et al.* 1987). Decreasing LOS across the board while increasing new admissions was easier for managers (Weiner *et al.* 1987).

In theory, hospital management controls work best at the level of the individual physician (Fetter and Freeman 1991; Chilingerian and Sherman 2004). DRGs offered management control tools that could uncover inefficient or low-performing physicians. NJ hospital executives did not use DRGs to manage practice patterns (Hsaio *et al.* 1986). Why? Exposing the less efficient or the top twenty money-losing physicians created unexpected political problems, because the list often included:

the senior surgeons in the hospital, who have had the most genuinely severe cases referred by their colleagues ... the chief of psychiatry ... the hospital oncologists, who are employing appropriately new expensive chemotherapy regimens ... None of this physician behavior could be challenged by hospital administrators. (Hsaio *et al.* 1986, p 41)

Using DRGs to manage clinical processes and behavior became the exception, not the rule.[26] For hospital managers, the importance of DRGs is not prospective payment. It is all about the annual increase – the tighter the DRG rate, the bigger the political battles.

Garden state flowers for Algernon[27]

The worst case scenario for DRGs came true when New Jerrey ran into serious problems. Between 1986 and 1991, the positive effects of DRGs slipped away, and the three letters "DRG" became a political liability. By 1990, $1.5 billion of unsettled claims had accumulated and the State of NJ paid $1 billion in settlements in 1991–2. The newly elected New Jersey Governor Florio set up a task force attacking DRGs. In 1992 DRGs and rate setting in NJ were repealed. The political and cultural forces that had found DRGs acceptable had shifted and they now found them a disaster. As swiftly as they were introduced DRGs were DEAD! Left with a bad taste, NJ never considered going back to an all-payer DRG system. Yet, without DRGs NJ hospitals achieved even greater distinction – they became the most expensive in the United States, charging 415 percent above their costs (Forum Institute for Public Policy 2004).

Lessons and conclusions

DRGs were not only a breakthrough for payment and finance policy in the United States (Smith 1992; Kimberly and Pouvourville 1993; Mayes 2006); they may be the most far-reaching and influential health services research projects of the twentieth century. Some have gone so far as to attribute DRGs to a series of changes leading to the Managed Care revolution in the United States (Mayes 2004).

Three conditions made the timing right for DRGs (Brown 1991). There was both a national sense of dissatisfaction with hospitals' ability to contain their costs and non-partisan perceptions of urgency/crisis. New leaders had been appointed in the political system, government agency, and the hospital association, who identified the need for a prospective payment system with a casemix index. These leaders forged a dominant coalition that declared casemix classification by DRGs not only available, but an appealing alternative – reproducible by key technical people in government, and "politically acceptable." Nevertheless, what truly shaped DRGs and changed history was a set of conditions and explanatory variables that aligned the technical system with the sociocultural and political systems. DRGs were embedded in interpersonal networks, national political agendas, and leadership attention structures. Each of these conditions and variables will be discussed.

Small incidents and events that tell the DRG story

Many small events, elements and social incidences fused by social relationships shaped the selection of DRGs. The Yale research team had won several research grants, and as a result had become household names to certain staff members in the federal Health Care Finance Agency (HCFA) Office of Research. When Dr. Joanne Finley became New Jersey Health Commissioner, she maintained contact with John Thompson at Yale. She knew she could trust Thompson and Fetter to help her implement DRGs.

Jack Owen, former head of the New Jersey Hospital Association, became the newly appointed Washington representative of the American Hospital Association and Richard Schweiker, a former Senator frustrated by rising health costs, became Secretary of Health and Human Services. They met. Owen advocated for DRGs. The interaction motivated Schweiker to learn about DRGs and educate his staff. He discovered Pettengill's internal DRG database and Pettengill's DRG report. Schweiker became a DRG champion and vowed to implement DRGs immediately.

Schweiker and Finley's confidence in the solution depended on their personal relationships, social networks, and trust relations (Granovetter 1985). These non-academic political leaders communicated inferences about casemix and hospital behavior, rather than the evidence, and absorbed a great deal of uncertainty when dealing with other stakeholders (March and Simon 1958). Schweiker used his position to order his staff to recommend DRGs for national policy (Smith 1992).

Finally, Yale had a strong name brand image. Though Fetter, Thompson, Averill and others were not well known to the political stakeholders, Congress, or Secretary Richard Schweiker, a *Yale* research team was credible and brought brand value. Prior experience with Yale and the Office of Research reduced the remaining uncertainty – Yale would provide whatever technical assistance was needed to implement DRGs.

Figure 1.6 contextualizes the DRG story. Decades of scientific development and a series of small incidents or events (i.e. chance meetings, appointments of key people, networks) and strong persistent goal-directed leadership led to the selection of DRGs.

Triggering Events

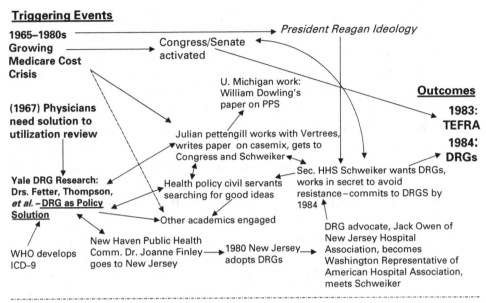

Figure 1.6   DRG storyline

Underlying conditions: Perceived Social Security and Medicare crisis, no better policy alternatives available; strong executive support for DRGs, PPS fit with contemporary Reagan ideology (capitalism/social Darwinism); broad-based coalition between executive and legislative branch and hospitals; budget revolution.

Urgency and time pressure. The circumstances that initially directed the attention of key people such as Dr. Joanne Finley or Richard Schweiker to DRGs was a hospital cost "crisis" that required immediate attention. Finley and Schweiker translated the pressure of the external crisis internally by setting challenging goals using special project implement-ation teams with deadlines. March and Simon (1958) have observed that the occasions for innovation are more likely if resources are allocated to independent planning units (away from daily tasks) and deadlines are set by hierarchical authority.

Timing and perception of an acceptable technical design. DRGs had only been tested in NJ on a limited basis. Had the federal government waited, the NJ problems would have surfaced. Nevertheless, in 1983 people believed that DRGs were working in NJ and could be successful on a national scale.

Importance of technical experts, leadership and attention structure. DRGs were very complex. Only a few[28] technical experts (i.e. Fetter, Thompson, and the Yale research team, staff like Julian Pettengill, NJ project team) and political leaders (i.e. Dr. Joanne Finley, Jack Owens, Richard Schweicker) had first-hand knowledge and direct access to the real evidence on DRGs. In both the New Jersey and the HCFA cases, the technical experts and thought leaders summarized knowledge and inferences about hospital behaviors, persuading key people that DRGs would work.

Organizations need an implicit or explicit strategy for dealing with a problem-filled world. A leader's attention structure is a pattern of personal involvement with the task environment (and in particular the technical, political, and social systems) (Chilingerian 1987). Schweiker and Finley were actively involved in the definition of the situation and the decision to adopt DRGs. They invested time and focused their attention on DRGs and offered their credibility that it would work.

Availabilty and reproducibility. Complex innovations like DRGs are more likely to be accepted if the data is available and authoritative decision makers or staff can visibly reproduce the methods and results. In March 1981, research completed by HCFA staff members, Julian Pettengill and James Vertrees, with a sample of Medicare patients from 5,576 hospitals, substantiated that DRGs were a valid and reliable measure of the expected costs of a hospital's casemix (Pettengill and Vertrees 1982). After Schweiker discovered this research it became highly influential (Smith 1992).

DRG as nearly dominant design. DRGs were and remain an *acceptable, not a perfect,* solution to casemix. The first external scientific assessment of DRGs using a national database found that DRGs' relative weights explained *only 30 percent of the variation in cost-per-case.* If, however, hospital size, wage index, teaching, and urban location were added, as much as 72 percent of the variation could be explained (Pettengill and Vertrees 1982). Subsequent studies found that DRGs explained only 17 percent of the variation in cost-per-case in Michigan hospitals, as little as 3 percent of the variation in psychiatric DRGs, and 25 percent of neonatal diagnosis.

DRGs capture the complexity, but none of the severity within a DRG. Horn *et al.* reported that adding a severity of illness index explained 61 percent of the variability in cost-per-case versus 28 percent without a severity factor (1985). Other studies have found that the incremental effect of severity of illness was small in comparison with the addition of the DRG casemix index (Rosko and Chilingerian 1999). Although DRG weights were designed to equalize accounting profits, studies found inequitable payments and substantial variation in accounting profitability among

DRGs (Newhouse 1989). Super-speciality hospitals performing cardiac, orthopedic, or cataract surgery have flourished because some DRGs are very profitable, while others, such as oncology, pediatrics, geriatrics, etc. are unprofitable. More work is needed to create a fair payment system.

The future of DRGs: Exceptions and anomalies

From 1969 to today, DRGs have continually been revised to adapt to diagnostic codes, changing physician behavior and new technology add-on payments. As evidence surfaces, rate appeals are filed to CMS.[29] The US government is up against the entire drug, bio-medical technology industry and professional associations. In 2002, for example, the FDA approved *InFuse*, a bone stimulation product[30] developed by Medtronic for use with spinal fusions (DRG 487 and 498). CMS rejected Medtronic's request for an add-on payment, because the threshold cost requirements of $41,923 for DRG 497 and $58,040 for DRG 498 were not met. By 2003 new data on physician practices and hospital costs revealed that the total costs across both DRGs was $62,752, exceeding the threshold. Since the average orthopedic surgeon was using two doses of InFuse at a cost of $17,800, CMS agreed and approved a DRG add-on payment of $8,900 – 50% of the average cost (HealthPoint Capital 2003).

Although DRGs were designed to create homogeneous groups, a growing body of research has found heterogeneity. Academic researchers found that high-risk patients had large LOS deviations from published Medicare averages. Differences among patients within a DRG explain over 80 percent of total variation in net-price-per-patient admission (Lynk 2001). The growth in anomalies has led to the development of DRG special interest groups. The National Association of Children's Hospitals and Related Institutions, for example, argued for an expansion from seven DRGs to forty-seven, by including clinical findings and other clinical variables such as discharge status and birth weight. As the exceptions, anomalies and interests accumulate, DRGs may be attacked politically and eventually could collapse.

In response to these problems, CMS has promised to implement severity adjustments. A new system called "All Patient Refined" (APR) DRGs is being developed to include the base DRG, severity within DRG (i.e. extent of physiologic decompensation or organ loss experienced) and risk of mortality or likelihood of dying. Each DRG will have four severity of illness categories: 1 = minor, 2 = moderate, 3 = major and 4 = extreme. Once a patient is given an APR-DRG such as DRG 127, heart failure and shock, a severity of illnesss subclass is assigned based on secondary diagnosis, presence of non-surgical procedure, and the interaction effects of other diagnoses, age, and APR-DRG. Neonatal patients will have their own severity subclass.

Seldom has academic policy research produced results as dramatic as DRGs. The DRG paradigm conceptualizes and defines the products of the hospital, with a clear methodology for measuring those products. DRGs are not only anchored in the technical programs of acute care, and deeply embedded in the culture of hospital management, but they are also utilized by hospital decision makers to allocate resources to care programs. Despite the small-scale failure of DRGs in NJ and some critical external assessment DRGs have survived changes in leadership, political parties, and challenges from more powerful ideas. DRGs have become institutionalized.

The United States government uses DRGs as a tool for balancing and controlling the national health care budget. In fact, the politicians and policy makers alike have been willing to adjust hospital reimbursement rates to serve larger goals such as reducing the budget deficit.

By restraining the annual increase in diagnosis-related groups (DRG) payment rates below the market basket rate of medical inflation, the difference between what Medicare actually paid and what it would have paid if increases matched the market basket was counted as budget savings. (Lee *et al.* 2003, p 483)

When the President of the United States wants to reduce the budget, his staff can use the DRG system as the mechanism to achieve budgetary savings.

Most policy and management experts believe (anomalies notwithstanding) that the DRGs continue to be the *right* way to measure hospital casemix. Although DRGs have not been used extensively to manage physician and hospital performance, the potential is still there. Clearly, it has been used as a tool to reduce macro lengths of stay, to bring clinical information and medical records into hospital boardrooms. And as one expert reflecting on the American system said:

looking back on DRGs, it was a good move. I didn't see how the hospitals were going to get their doctors to cooperate in getting the patients out [of hospitals], but they did. (Alan Enthoven 2002)

TECHNICAL APPENDIX

Example of a US DRG Payment: Heart Failure and Shock (2005) Hypothetical patient admitted to a suburban hospital X in USA

DRG 127:	Heart failure and shock
Mean length of stay	5.2 days
Local wage index:	.8292[31]
Hospital X's operating cost to charge ratio:	.432
Hospital X's capital cost to charge ratio:	.060
Hospital X's SSI ratio:	.1044
Hospital X's Medicaid ratio:	.3322
Disproportionate share factor (SSI + Medicaid)	.4366
Operating Federal Payment (OFP):	4,071.98[32]
Casemix index:	1.0390
Weighted Federal Payment (OFP × casemix index)	4,230.79
Operating indirect medical education:	0[33]
Capital indirect medical education:	0
Total cost outlier reimbursement	0[34]
New technology payment:	0[35]
Total operating payment = Weighted federal payment + IME payment + DSH payment	
Weighted Federal Payment =	$4,230.79
IME payment = IME factor × weighted federal payment =	0.00
DSH payment = DSH factor × weighted federal payment =	507.69
Total operating payment:	**$4,738.48**
Capital federal payment	$392.09
Capital IME payment	$0.00
Capital DSH payment	$0.00
Total capital payment	$392.09
Hospital-specific add on (SCH or MDH)	$326.82
Cost outlier payment (operating + capital)	$0.00
New technology payment (Value code 77)	$0.00
Total reimbursement amount	**$5,457.39**

NOTES

1. The agency responsible was Health Care Financing Administration in Health and Human Services.
2. One might argue that a simpler approach based on gross revenue adjusted by DRG could have worked as well.

3. *Casemix* lacks a precise definition and could include illness severity, major organ failure, mortality, diagnostic uncertainty, obstacles to treatment such as obesity, age, health status, or socio-economic factors.

4. The original research aggregated 10,000 illnesses into 383 diagnostic categories.

5. In March 2003 there were approximately 527 DRG categories, however nineteen were declared obsolete.

6. In 1985 Medicare's payment for DRG 235 was $6,323.08. In 2005 the payment dropped to $3,945.71.

7. Medicare patients had to be reviewed after every thirty days in the hospital.

8. The work at Yale used ICDA8 until 1982. By 1979, all US hospitals began using ICD–9–CM.

9. If a complication and/or co-morbidity (CCs) increased the LOS one day for 75 percent of the patients, they were assigned a separate DRG. There are approximately 200 DRGs with CCs present.

10. The list of CCs is the same for most DRGs (Averill 1991).

11. Total sum of the squared difference (TSSQ) for the number of patients discharged over a time period was calculated: $TSSQ = \Sigma (Yi - Y)^2$, where Yi = length of stay for the ith patient and Y is the average stay for all patients. The Yale team developed a computer algorithm, AUTOGRP that minimized unexplained variance between observations by segmenting patients based on diagnosis, surgery, age, co-morbidity or complications, etc. The rule was to find a variable that minimized the total within group sum-of-squared difference (TWGSSQ). So, hypothetically, if the TWGSSQ patients older than seventy were 412 and the TWGSSQ for patients with co-morbidity were 819, then age would become the partitioning variable.

12. When examined closely, the clusters were somewhat imperfect. For example, DRG 304 (see Exhibit 2) included procedures such as: bilateral nephrectomy, ureteral meatotomy, radical dissection of iliac nodes, renal diagnostic procedure, aorta-renal bypass, renal biopsy, and implantation of a mechanical kidney (Fetter *et al.* 1980).

13. Development was supported by research grants from Social Security in 1974 and 1975 to investigate cost containment and later from Health Care Financing Administration. A more important event was in 1979. The World Health Organization released ICD–9–CM. Yale was given a grant by HCFA to update DRG based on ICD–9.

14. This section draws heavily on personal interviews with Joanne Finley, Sandy Weiner, and the papers by Smithey and Fetter (1982), Weiner and Sapolsky (1995), and Mayes (2006).

15. While at Yale, she had attended DRG symposiums, and knew Thompson and Fetter.

16. According to Smith (1992) and Mayes (2006) Jack Owen played a key role in selling DRGs to Secretary of Health and Human Services, Richard Schweicker.

17. Just before DRGs were used for hospital billing and payment in 1980, the New Jersey Hospital Association filed a lawsuit on behalf of twenty-five hospitals (Smithey and Fetter 1982). The lawsuit did not disrupt implementation.

18. Two other facts led to DRGs. First, Medicare nearly bankrupted the Social Security Trust fund. Second, the Reagan Administration Economic Recovery Act had cut federal taxes, which led to budget deficits. By the spring of 1982, the Congress and some of the leading Republican Senators saw the critical importance of controlling Medicare spending.

19. He had been a principal author of section 223 of the Social Security Amendment of 1971.

20. Schweiker had spent ten years in the Senate and ten years in Congress, a total of twenty years in Washington. He had been ranking minority member of the Health Subcommittee on the Finance Committee. He knew health care and he understood politics.

21. This section draws heavily on Smith (1992), who writes in great detail about the politics of DRGs.

22. Jack Owen was a newly appointed Washington representative of the American Hospital Association.

23. Carolyn Davis, Head of HCFA reports that in October 1982 she told her staff that by October 1983 "Make no mistake. We are going to get DRGs done" (Davis 1995).

24. MedPAC was established as an independent Federal Commission to offer Congress payment recommendations for Medicare Program, which includes: acute hospitals, physicians, skilled nursing homes, home health, etc.

25. This is defined as admissions (inpatient + outpatient revenues) / inpatient revenues.

26. One noteworthy exception in the USA is Intermountain Health Care in Utah.

27. Charlie's pet mouse, Algernon, undergoes a special brain surgery and Algernon becomes a genius. Charlie also undergoes that surgery and he becomes an intellectual. However, Algernon's intelligence begins to fade and decline and Algernon dies. What will happen to Charlie?

28. Many other key people were involved with DRGs such as Stuart Altman, Bruce Vladeck, Carolyn Davis, to name a few. Due to the page limits of this introductory chapter, these important people could not be included.

29. CMS analysts change DRGs to accommodate new technology. To adapt DRGs to new technology approved by the FDA requires at least one year of experience. If physician practice behavior uses higher dosages that the DRG has assumed, it could take another two to three years to change the DRGs. The CMS rule is to increase the payment by 50 percent of the average cost for the procedure.

30. Bone stimulation for spine fusion procedures reduces the uncertainty for patients whose histories are associated with poor healing (i.e. obese patients, smokers, patients with chronic problems, etc.)

31. If wage index is greater than 1, labor-related share is 71.1 percent, and non-labor is 28.9 percent. If the wage index is less than or equal to 1, the labor-related share is 62 percent, and non-labor is 38 percent.

32. The operating federal payment (labor + non-labor) = $4,554.26. Since the local wage rate is less than 1, the labor portion is 71.1 percent or $2823.64; the non-labor is $1,730.62. The labor portion $2,823.64 multiplied by the local wage rate of .8292 to get the labor portion of $2,341.36 plus $1,730.62 for a total weighted federal payment of $4,230.70.

33. This hospital is not a teaching hospital. If it were the formula would be: $((1+ \text{Intern to Bed Ratio})^{.405} - 1 \times 1.42)$, where 1.42 is the multiplier for the period 10/1/04–9/30/05.

34. The total cost outlier = operating + capital payments. The operating cost outliers = (standard operating costs – operating threshold)* .8 marginal cost factor. The capital cost outlier = (standard capital costs – capital threshold)* .8 marginal cost factor.

35. Hospitals are paid (the lower of) either 50 percent of the cost of the service, or 50 percent of the covered costs that exceed the DRG payment. If InFuse was used, a hospital would get an additional $1,995.00, 50 percent of $3,910.

REFERENCES

Alford, Robert (1975). *Health Care Politics: Ideological and Interest Group Barriers to Reform.* Chicago: University of Chicago Press.

Altman, Stuart (2005). Transcripts of an oral history interview with the informant conducted by Jon Chilingerian on 1 November 2005.

Altman, Stuart and Cohen, Alan (1993). The Need for a Global Budget. *Health Affairs* 12 (Supplement): 194–203.

Averill, Richard F. (1991). Development. In Robert Fetter (ed.) *DRGs: Their Design and Development.* Ann Arbor, Michigan: Health Administration Press.

Averill, Richard F. and Kalison, Michael L. (1991). Structure of a DRG-based Prospective Payment System." In Robert Fetter (ed.), *DRGs: Their Design and Development.* Ann Arbor, MI: Health Administration Press.

Bacharach, S. and Lawler, E. (1982). *Power and Politics in Organizations.* San Francisco, CA: Jossey-Bass.

Brickman, Paul (1987). *Commitment, Conflict and Caring.* Englewood Cliffs, NJ: Prentice Hall.

Brown, Lawrence D. (1991). Knowledge and Power: Health Services Research as a Political Resource. In Eli Ginzberg (ed.) *Health Services Research: Key to Health Policy.* Cambridge, MA: Harvard University Press.

Brown, John Seely and Duguid, Paul (2000). *The Social Life of Information.* Cambridge, MA: Harvard Business Press.

Carroll, Norma V. and Erwin, W. Gary (1987). Patient Shifting as a Response to Medicare Prospective Payment. *Medical Care* 25: 1161–67.

Carter, Grace M., Jacobson, P.D., Kominsky, G.F. and Perry, M.J. (1994). Use of Diagnosis-Related Groups by Non-Medicare Payers. *Health Care Financing Review* Winter 16(2): 127–58.

Carter, Grace M., Newhouse, Joseph P. and Relles, Daniel A. (1990). How Much Change in the Case Mix Index is DRG Creep? Report 3826 to HCFA. Rand/UCLA/Harvard Center for Health Care Financing Policy Research.

Chilingerian, J. A. and Glavin, M. P. V. (1994). Temporary Firms in Community Hospitals: Elements of a Managerial Theory of Clinical Efficiency. *Medical Research and Review* Fall 51(3): 289–334.

Chilingerian, J. A. and Sherman, H. D. (1987) For-Profit vs. Non-Profit Hospitals: The Effect of the Profit Motive on the Management of Operations. *Financial Accountability & Management* 3(3): 283–306.

Chilingerian, Jon (1987). *The Strategy of Executive Influence: An Analysis of the Attention Structure of the Hospital Chief Executive.* Unpublished Doctoral Dissertation, Cambridge, MA: MIT.

Chilingerian, Jon A. and Sherman, H. David (2004). DEA Applications in Health Care. In William W. Cooper, Lawrence M. Seiford and Jow Zhu (eds.) *Handbook on DEA.* Ann Arbor, MI: Kluwer.

Cost of Living Council (1974, January 24) Control of Hospitals' Costs under the Economic Stabilization Program. *Federal Register* 2694.

Davis, Carolyn (1995). Transcripts of an oral history interview with the informant conducted by Edward Berkowitz on November 8, 1995.

Davis, Karen (2003). Transcripts of an oral history interview with the informant conducted by Rick Mayes on August 1, 2003.

Des Harnais, Susan, Chesney, James and Fleming, Steven (1988). Trends in Regional Variations in Hospital Utilization and Quality during the First Two Years of the Prospective Payment System. *Inquiry* 25: 373–82.

Enthoven, Alan (1980). *Health Plan: The Only Practical Solution to the Soaring Cost of Medical Care.* Reading, MA: Addison-Wesley.

Enthoven, Alan (2002). Transcripts of an oral history interview with the informant conducted by Rick Mayes in 2002.

Feinglass, Joe and Holloway, James J. (1991). The Initial Impact of the Medicare Prospective Payment System on US Health Care: A Review of the Literature. *Medical Care Review* 48: 91–115.

Fetter, Robert B. (1991). Background. In Robert Fetter (ed.) *DRGs: Their Design and Development.* Ann Arbor, MI: Health Administration Press.

Fetter, Robert B., Brand, David A. and Gamache, Dianne (1991). *DRGs: Their Design and Development.* Ann Arbor, MI: Health Administration Press.

Fetter, Robert B., Shon, Youngsoo, Freeman, Jean, Averill, Richard F. and Thompson, John D. (1980). Case Mix Definition by Diagnosis-Related Groups. *Medical Care* Vol. 8, No. 2: 1–53.

Finley, Joanne (2006). Transcripts of an oral history interview with the informant conducted by Jon Chilingerian on March 1, 2006.

Forrester, Jay W. (1968). *Principles of Systems.* Cambridge, MA: Wright-Allen Press.

Forums Institute for Public Policy (2004). An Overview of Charity Care in New Jersey: Past, Present and Future. Report to the Robert Wood Johnson Foundation: 1–13.

Granovetter, Mark (1985). Economic Action and Social Structure: The Problem of Embeddedness. *American Journal of Sociology* 91: 481–510.

Grimaldi, Paul L. and Micheletti, Julie (1983). *Diagnostic Related Groups: A Practitioners' Guide.* Chicago, IL: Pluribus Press.

HealthPointCapital (2003) In a testament to second chances, InFUSE gets CMS approval for $8,900. Research Daily, retrieved February 20, 2006 from www.healthpointcapital.com/research/2003/08/04.

Hodgkin, Dominic and McGuire, Thomas G. (1994). Payment Levels and Hospital Response to Prospective Payment. *Journal of Health Affairs* 13: 1–29.

Horn, S. D., Bulkley, G., Sharkey, P. D., Chambers, A. F., Horn, R. A. and Schramm, C. J. (1985). Inter-Hospital Differences in Patient Severity: Problems for Prospective Payment Based on Diagnosis Related Groups (DRGs). *New England Journal of Medicine* 313: 20–4.

Hsiao, William C., Sapolsky, Harvey M., Dunn, Daniel L. and Weiner, Sanford L. (1986). Lessons of the New Jersey DRG Payment System. *Health Affairs* 6: 32–45.

Kimberly, John R. and de Pouvourville, Gérard (1993). *The Migration of Managerial Innovation.* San Francisco: Jossey Bass.

Kingdon, John (1984). *Agendas, Alternatives, Public Policies.* Boston, MA: Little Brown and Company.

Lave, Judith and Leinhardt, Samuel (1976). The Cost and Length of a Hospital Stay. *Inquiry* 13: 327–43.

Lee, Jason S., Berenson, Robert A., Mayes, Rick and Gauthier, Anne K. (2003). Medicare Payment Policy: Does Cost Shifting Matter? *Health Affairs* W3 480–8.

Luke, Royce (1979). Dimensions in Hospital Case Measurement. *Inquiry* 16: 38–49.

Lynk, William J. (2001). One DRG, One Price? The Effect of Patient Condition on Price Variation within DRG and Across Hospitals. *International Journal of Health Care Finance and Economics* Vol. 1, No. 2: 111–37.

March, James and Simon, Herbert (1958). *Organizations.* New York: Wiley.

Marmor, Theodore (1973). *The Politics of Medicare.* New York: Aldine Publishing Company.

Mayes, Rick (2004). Causal Chains and Cost Shifting: How Medicare's Rescue Inadvertently Triggered the Managed Care Revolution. *The Journal of Policy History* Vol. 16, No. 2: 144–74.

Mayes, Rick. (2006). The Origins, Development, and Passage of Medicare's Revolutionary Prospective Payment System. *Journal of the History of Medicine and Allied Sciences*, Vol. 62, No. 1: 25–55.

Medicare Payment Advisory Commission MedPAC (2004). "Medicare Payment Policy" Report to Congress. March 2004.

Medicare Payment Advisory Commission MedPAC (2005). "Medicare Payment Policy" Report to Congress. March 2005.

Morone, James A. (1994). The Bureaucracy Empowered. In James A. Morone and Bary Belkin (eds.) *The Politics of Health Care Reform.* Durham, NC: Duke University Press.

Newhouse, Joseph (1989). Do Unprofitable Patients Face Access Problems? *Health Care Financing Review* 11: 33–42.

Office of Technology Assessment (1985). First Report on the Prospective Payment Commission (ProPAC). March 25, 1985. Pursuant to Section 1886(e)(G)(i) of the Social Security Act. Washington, DC.

Olsen, Johan P. (1976). Choice in an Organized Anarchy. In James March and Johan P. Olsen, *Ambiguity and Choice in Organizations.* Norway: Bergen Universitetsforlaget: 82–139.

Parsons, Talcott (1960). *Structure and Process in Modern Societies.* Glencoe, IL: Free Press.

Pettengill, Julian (2002). Transcripts of an oral history interview with the informant conducted by Rick Mayes on October 29, 2002.

Pettengill, Julian and Vertrees, James. (1982). Reliability and Validity in Hospital Case Mix Measurement. *Health Care Financing Administration, Office of Research and Demonstrations* Vol. 4, No. 2: 101–28.

Pfeffer, Jeffrey, and Salancik, Gerald R. (1978). *The External Control of Organizations. A Resource Dependence Perspective.* New York: Harper and Row.

Prospective Payment Assessment Commission (1985). *Report and Recommendations to the Secretary of US Department of Health and Human Services.* Washington, DC: PPAC.

Prospective Payment Assessment Commission (1986). *Adjustments to the Medicare Prospective Payment System. Report to Congress.* November 1985. Washington, DC: PPAC, 1–88.

Rogers, Everett M. (1995). *Diffusions of Innovations.* New York: The Free Press.

Rosko, Michael (1989). A Comparison of Hospital Performance under the Partial-Payer Medicare PPS and State All-Payer Rate Setting Systems. *Inquiry* 26: 48–61.

Rosko, Michael and Broyles, Robert W. (1986). The Impact of the New Jersey All-Payer DRG System. *Inquiry* 23: 67–75.

(1987). Short-Term Responses of Hospitals to the DRG Prospective Pricing Mechanism in New Jersey. *Medical Care*, Vol. 25, No. 2: 88–99.

Rosko, Michael and Chilingerian, Jon (1999). Estimating Hospital Inefficiency: Does Case Mix Matter?" *Journal of Medical Systems* Vol. 23, No. 1: 57–71.

Schein, Edgar H. (1977). *Organizational Culture and Leadership*, 2nd edition. San Francisco, CA: Jossey-Bass.

Simborg, Donald W. (1981). "DRG Creep: A New Hospital-Acquired Disease," *New England Medical Journal* Vol. 304: 1602–4.

Smith, David G. (1992). *Paying for Medicare: The Politics of Reform.* New York: Aldine de Gruyter.

Smithey, Richard W. and Fetter, Robert B. (1982). Rate Setting in New Jersey. In Robert B. Fetter, John D. Thompson and John R. Kimberly (eds.) *Cases in Health Policy and Management.* Homewood, IL: Richard D. Irwin, Inc.

Starr, Paul (1982). *The Social Transformation of American Medicine.* New York: Basic Books.

Steinwald, Bruce A. and Dummit, Laura A. (1989). Hospital Case Mix Change: Sicker Patients or DRG Creep?" *Health Affairs* 8: 35–47.

Tichy, Noel M. (1981). Networks in Organizations. In P. C. Nystrom & W. Starbuck (eds.) *Handbook of Organizational Design.* New York: Oxford University Press.

(1983). *Managing Strategic Change.* New York: Wiley.

Tichy, Noel M. and Devanna, Mary-Anne (1990). *The Transformational Leader.* New York: John Wiley and Sons.

Utterback, James M. (1996). *Mastering the Dynamics of Innovation.* Boston, MA: Harvard Business School Press.

Weiner, Sanford L., Maxwell, James H., Sapolsky, Harvey M. and Hsiao, William C. (1987). Economic Incentives and Organizational Realities: Managing Hospitals under DRGs. *Milbank Quarterly* Vol. 65, No. 4: 463–87.

Weiner, Sanford L. and Sapolsky, Harvey M. (1995). Life Cycles of Health Care Reform: Rate Setting in New Jersey 1980–1995. Unpublished report. Cambridge, MA: MIT.

Yergin, Daniel and Stanislaw, Joseph. (1999). *The Commanding Heights: The Battle between Government and the Marketplace that is Remaking the Modern World.* New York: Simon & Shuster.

Zwanziger, Jack and Melnick, Glen, (1988). The Effects of Hospital Competition and the Medicare PPS Program on Hospital Cost Behavior in California. *Journal of Health Economics* 7: 301–20.

2 Casemix in the United Kingdom: From development to plans

Steve Sutch

Introduction to the UK healthcare system

UK healthcare is dominated by the National Health Service (NHS). This was established in 1948 and financed by general taxation. The OECD reported[1] that in 2002 the UK spent 7.7 per cent of its GDP of which public expenditure accounted for 83.4 per cent of the total. The spending had increased from the 1993 figure of 6.9 per cent of GDP.

Under the UK government's NHS Plan,[2] record levels of increased funding for the NHS were planned to rise over the period 2003/4 to 2007/8 by an average of 7.4 per cent a year in real terms. By 2004/5 total spend[3] on the NHS totalled £82.5 billion (7.01% of GDP), up from £66.2 billion in 2002–3 (6.26% of GDP). Figure 2.1 shows the increase in government health expenditure and the percentage of GDP from 1987/8 to 2004/5.

The public healthcare sector in the UK is divided into four principal National Health Services (NHS) for England, Scotland, Northern Ireland and Wales. Each of these services, whilst following the founding principle of the NHS to provide healthcare free at the point of service to all, has differences in policy dictated by the four different legislative and political assemblies for each of the member countries. These differences include free prescription charges in Wales, free elderly personal nursing care in Scotland, and differences in the strategic structures of hospitals and commissioning organisations.

At the beginning of the 1990s the Conservatives, who were in power between 1979 and 1997, reformed the healthcare sector in England. At the time it was relatively centralised. The reform meant that a number of areas that had been under the central authorities were decentralised to regional health authorities with local responsibility. At the same time reforms were introduced to create an internal market, most noticeably the General

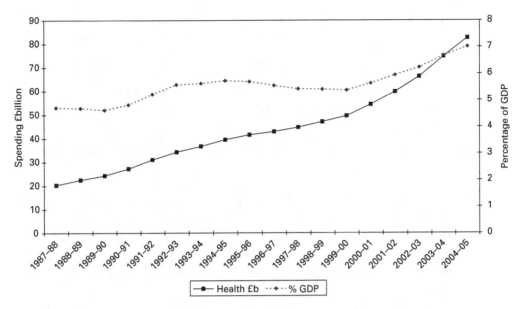

Figure 2.1   UK: Total expenditure on health, 1987/8 to 2004/5

Practitioner fund-holding system. Through the changes the government stressed the role of contractual relations between the demand side and the supply side in the healthcare sector, the 'purchaser/provider split'. Trust Hospital organisations were created that were distinct from the Health Authorities, the latter of which now had responsibilities to purchase healthcare services from the former for their residential population.

The Labour government that came into power in May 1997 stated that these contractual relations had required unnecessary resources. Although certain elements from the previous system were to be maintained, the new government wanted to enhance increased internal co-operation within the healthcare sector. One way that this was to be achieved was by making co-operation mandatory. Contracts between purchasers and providers introduced by the previous government were changed to commissioning agreements. It was expected that the duration of these agreements was to be three years, rather than one year for the previous contracts.

In the original purchaser/provider organisations created by the Conservative government there had been approximately 3,800 organisations. The new system, with more integrated care, was to move responsibility for the purchase of healthcare services to 500 new commissioner organisations, the Primary Care Groups, which later became Primary Care Trusts. The purpose of this limitation of the number of purchaser organisations was to

Table 2.1 History of UK casemix groups

Year	Version	Policy Purpose
1987	USA Diagnosis Related Group v5	Resource management initiative
1991	Healthcare Resource Groups v1	'English DRGs'
1994	Healthcare Resource Groups v2	Costing for contracting
1997	Healthcare Resource Groups v3	1998 reference costs
2003	Healthcare Resource Groups v3.5	Payment by results

reduce administrative costs. The new primary care groups were each intended to cover a population of about 100,000. In each group there was a requirement to have general practitioners (about fifty) and community nurses. Each group was responsible for a budget which was meant to cover the cost of the majority of hospital treatments as well as treatment and care in the primary sector.

The most important task for the old Health Authorities (now being reduced in number from 100 to 30) was to provide guidance and to monitor and regulate healthcare at the local level. The authorities were required to establish overall healthcare plans, collect healthcare statistics and monitor providers. The new Strategic Health Authorities (SHAs) were to have seats on hospital boards and be able to influence hospital investments and certain appointments. Furthermore the SHAs were to continue to be responsible for the purchase of some highly specialised hospital services.

A brief history of the introduction of casemix in the UK

The early research into casemix in the UK began from about 1981,[4,5] and by the late 1980s work on a refined version of US DRGs was being proposed and developed, leading to the creation of the National Casemix Office (NCMO) and the creation of the English casemix groups or Healthcare Resource Groups (HRG) by 1991 (Table 2.1). The NCMO was led by Dr Hugh Sanderson, a public health physician, with the work being commissioned by the English Health Department. The usage of the groupings over the next ten years was primarily in the area of informing contracts and commissioning, but by 1999 the NCMO had been absorbed and taken over by the NHS Information Authority (NHSIA), responsible for the development of informatics in England. There were significant advances in the areas of benchmarking information, with performance data based on HRGs being made available across the NHS by both private companies and the NHSIA, which allowed the free use within the NHS of detailed activity and performance data from all NHS organisations.[6] Latterly this work has increasingly been provided by private companies, after the progressive development within the NHS. The work to revise the HRGs continued, after the closure of the NHS Information Authority in 2005, within the newly created NHS Health and Social Care Information Centre, which was responsible for the provision of health information and statistics. The changes in the organisations responsible for the development of casemix groups in England, from a dedicated office to inclusion within a wider information technology organisation, and latterly a health information/statistics organisation, reflected the constant reorganisation within the NHS over the same period of hospital and purchaser organisations. This also reflected the changes in policy over the usage of the HRGs and other casemix tools.

The development of Healthcare Resource Groups

The first version of HRGs produced in 1991[7] was created following the work of six pilot sites in the Resource Management Initiative in England. These sites used the US DRGs fourth revision[8] which was also reviewed for its applicability to the English National Health Service (NHS). The conclusions of this work during the 1980s were that England should develop and own a casemix classification and that an ideal classification should be clinically acceptable.[9] More specifically, the need to redesign the US DRGs for the UK was based on perceived differences in clinical practice in the US and UK[10] (Sanderson 1998) and that any modification would need structural changes to reflect UK clinical practice. In order to achieve any clinical acceptance, there would need to be clinical modification and control over the development of a classification.

The use of this version of HRGs was not prescribed,[11] but it was suggested that they could be used for the purposes of aggregating activity and analysing length of stay, and used as a planning tool. It was anticipated that in the future it would become possible to analyse resource use, and this version was subsequently used to provide information for hospital contracting from 1992 to 1994, but it was not used as part of national policy for costing.

The second version of HRGs was published in 1994.[12] This version of the HRGs again relied on clinical input and included an independent assessment of the groups by the appropriate Royal Colleges. Efforts were made to improve the statistical performance of the grouper and this resulted in the deletion of groups with fewer than 200 cases per annum (unless specific clinical arguments were made for their retention, such as for transplants) and the review of any groups that did not contribute to the predictive power of the overall classification system using the Reduction in Variance (RIV) statistic. The analyses were supported by the use of Classification and Regression Trees or CART,[13] with length of stay being used as the dependent variable.

Due to the tendency for elderly patients to be retained in hospital for longer and for these patients to be coded with fewer secondary diagnoses, a number of HRGs were created that used age splits in combination with complication and co-morbidity splits.

The chapter system was changed to reflect the body system of the primary operation or primary diagnosis (for non-surgical patients) rather than the specialty of the consultant providing the care. A number of problems had arisen with the use of specialty in the first version, with the same diagnosis and procedure codes appearing in more than one group. The alignment of the chapters to the body system recognised that cross-specialty work needed to be resolved within the system.

A procedure hierarchy was introduced ranking the surgical procedures on a scale of 0 to 4. This was used to identify non-operating room procedures (Rank = 0) and an ordering of the surgical procedures in a patient record was used to determine the one that should drive the final HRG assignment, rather than the implicit use of the primary (or first listed) procedure as in version 1 of HRGs. The surgical HRGs continued to use the resource level of procedures (for example h06 Foot Procedure, Category A), but also used the type of surgery (e.g. h02 Primary Hip and other Major Joint Replacements).

The second version of HRGs was introduced as the basis for costing inpatient activity in English hospitals from 1994 and early pilot costing exercises from 1992 had also informed the HRG design. The third version of HRGs was initially published in 1997,[14] with three successive revisions (versions 3.1, 3.2 and 3.5). In general, version 3 differed from previous versions in the limited inclusion of minor operative procedures, the expansion of the procedure hierarchy categories and the introduction of complex elderly groups.

Concurrently with the HRG groups, Health Benefit Groups (HBGs)[15,16] were also developed. HBGs are patient groups that present homogeneous healthcare needs and who, under the presumption of a similar level of healthcare intervention, may be expected to reach more or less similar results. The HBGs were designed primarily to be used by planners of healthcare services to assess healthcare needs in a given population.

The first HBGs were developed for certain cancers, heart disease, head injury, venereal diseases in women and heart attack, and later developed within areas such as diabetes and painful hip disorders. The development stopped, with the primary focus of commissioner-based groupings being concentrated on the simpler classification for programme budgeting, based on the primary diagnoses of the patient treated.

The development of an outpatient grouper that makes use of the supplementing classifications was begun in 1998. Whilst the classifications were published and the reporting of costs was mandated, the outpatient minimum dataset was seen by many trusts as a huge administrative burden and this led to a simplification of the classification of outpatient activity largely back to the specialty of the consultant providing care, although this classification was expanded to include more clinic types and to include clinics led by other healthcare professionals. In addition, work was also undertaken to create groupings for Accident and Emergency departments, community care, mental health, radiotherapy and chemotherapy.

The development of the fourth revision of HRGs began in 2004, and was primarily designed to support hospital payment, described in the next section. This requirement led to increased work to integrate the casemix groupings developed for acute hospital, outpatient and other settings, and reflected the move within the NHS to more integrated, patient-focused care.

The current situation

The NHS Plan[17] committed the government to a radical change in the organisation and delivery of healthcare. Essentially the UK system was to be changed from a state-dominated, centrally controlled monopoly provider of health services, to one where there will be a plurality of providers and real patient-based choice on where and how they are to be treated.

The Wanless[18] Report on the funding of the English NHS, concluded that it should remain predominately a tax-based socialised system. Wanless did, however, recommend that the English system needed substantial investment if it were to match the standards and quality of comparable European systems. The government's response to Wanless was to commit itself to record levels of increased funding for the NHS. Over the period 2003/4 to 2007/8 it was to increase funding by an average of 7.4 per cent a year in real terms. To maximise the benefits from this investment and to underpin the delivery of the NHS reforms, the government also concluded that it needed to change the way that funds flowed through the NHS. Cumulatively, this gave an additional £34 billion increase (43% in real terms). It will take UK spending to near or just above European averages.

The government concluded that it required a system of 'payment by results'[19] to provide the necessary levers to drive through the system reforms and changes. It will do this by introducing a prospective tariff-based system of reimbursement for providers of services to NHS patients. Payments by results will be based upon casemix-adjusted payment principles. This is replicating the best elements of prospective systems that already operate widely in the world. It will be built on the English Healthcare Resource Groups (HRGs). The key timelines are: for 2003/4, tariff applied to fifteen HRGs; for 2004/5, tariff applied to 48 HRGs. A step change occurs in 2005/6 when a tariff-based system will be applied to most NHS activity. In essence, all activity that can be classified into HRG/SCT measures will be included.

The objective of the reforms is to produce a fair, transparent and rules-based system for paying providers. Currently there is no rationale in funding for providers, where budgets are still based on historic levels. Currently, funding varies for trusts providing similar services and this needs to be addressed together with supporting patient choice and plurality. The reforms also aim to provide incentives to increase capacity and reward efficiency, allowing trusts to retain surpluses to invest in services and to put pressure on high-cost providers to reduce costs and avoid deficits.

The Admitted Patient Care (Inpatients and Daycases) HRGs were revised through a rigorous analytical and clinical review process. This work is now continuing into other settings such as outpatient and community HRGs and projects are now investigating the use of ever-increasing data returns on hospital, community and family doctor-led services. Other care management approaches are being considered for inclusion in casemix design, such as the process of care approach and components of care to aid both the design of casemix classifications and the understanding of efficiency and effectiveness.

In order to maximise the benefits from this investment and to underpin the delivery of the NHS reforms, the government also concluded that it needed to change the way that funds flowed through the NHS. Whilst the system of financing and allocating the local commissioning agents (the Primary Care Trusts) was unchanged, the way that commissioning and payments to providers is organised is being revolutionised.

Reimbursement system – 'payment by results'

In its progress report on Delivering the NHS Plan,[20] the government concluded that it required a system of 'payment by results'[21] to provide the necessary levers to drive through the system reforms and changes. The new system was required to:

- pay providers (NHS and independent sectors) fairly and transparently for services delivered;
- reward efficiency for services delivered;
- support greater patients' choice;
- enable commissioners to concentrate on quality and quantity rather than price.

It was to do this by introducing a prospective tariff-based system of reimbursement for providers of services to NHS patients. This tariff was a fully inclusive payment covering associated fixed costs, medical salaries and all direct costs. The payment by results system uses a standard tariff to commission services and is intended to remunerate providers fairly and transparently. It was also intended to support patient choice by a true 'money follows patient' process and to require cost and volume-based commissioning.

It replaced a system that, with degrees of sophistication that were variable across the country, was essentially a block grant system of local funding. Whilst Primary Care Trusts are financed on a nationally applied weighted responsible (geographical) population basis, they then commissioned on the basis of local providers, prices and costs. There was often incomplete knowledge of the volumes and severities of the services they would pay for, and relative efficiency was extremely variable, so patient access differed across the country. The system was intended to provide a standard for the payment of services, as there was little transparency in the relative costs or totality of commissioning packages. Perverse incentives are inherent in this system, one being that under block agreements it was possible for providers to both under- and over-achieve volumes with no penalty or reward.

Payments by results were therefore to be based on a standard price tariff (which allows for unavoidable regional cost variations). It was also to be based upon casemix-adjusted payment principles. In this, it was expected to replicate the best elements of prospective systems that already operate widely in the world. It was to be built on the English Healthcare Resource Groups (HRGs) and other Service Classification Tools (SCTs) where HRG/DRG measures are not developed or do not fit.

'Payment by results' was initially introduced in a limited way, with the tariff applied to just fifteen HRGs in 2003/4, then applied to forty-eight in the following year. Alongside this, the commissioners were expected to develop casemix-adjusted contracts, of a cost and volume nature, for the main surgical (2003/4) and other (2004/5) acute specialties. A step change was expected in 2005/6 when a tariff-based system was to be applied to most NHS activity, but issues arose over emergency activity following the large numbers of same-day admissions[22] as a direct result of the government's four-hour waiting target for emergency room attendances. To meet this target, many hospitals began to admit the patients expected to wait more than four hours into inpatient beds to avoid being included in the target statistic, despite many of these subsequently being discharged the same day. This large increase in same-day admissions and the potential for hospitals to receive full HRG-based inpatient payment led to a delay to the full extension of Payment by Results in 2005/6. The object of the reforms, however, remained the same – all activity that could be classified into HRG/SCT measures would be included, and so would cover acute inpatients, out-patients, Accident and Emergency services and adult critical care.

In terms of NHS spend it was intended to encompass over 60 per cent of the total budget from 1 April 2005, leading to one of the most extensive coverages of any prospective payment system. It is clearly a very ambitious and pressurised development plan. However, there are many issues that have not yet been fully resolved, such as the change in activity currency to the full hospital stay (referred to as a 'spell') from the use of the episode of care under each consultant ('consultant episode'), and the full consideration of the costs of research and development, specialised (technology) reim-bursement, teaching, and the 'unbundling' from HRGs and packages of care.

The HRG revision process

The casemix grouping programme in England had been responsible for producing a set of casemix classifications (the Healthcare Resource Groups – HRGs) for admitted patient care, A&E, chemotherapy, community, critical care, outpatient, mental health, palliative care, pathology, radiology and radiotherapy. The initial planned use of the admitted patient care HRG prompted a rapid revision of (the then) current version 3.1, which was first introduced into the NHS in 1997 for costing. The revision process was firstly set out to update (the then) current set of groups to ensure they were fit for use during 2004/5 and to further develop their design to fit the wider purpose of commissioning across all healthcare sectors beyond 2005.

The revision of HRGv3.1 began in September 2002 to support the introduction of HRG-based tariffs from 2003/4. The project team within the NHS Information Authority began the process of re-establishing the nineteen clinical working groups that supported the HRG design. The working groups' membership was made up of nominated physicians and surgeons from the respective medical associations and Royal Colleges in the UK, with project, analytical and coding support. The NHSIA analytical team produced reports to support the work of the clinical working groups in three phases. The initial reports showed the current activity (2001/2 hospital episode statistics consisting of over 11 million patient records) within the respective HRGs for each chapter; the analysis reports followed the initial meetings of the working groups; the additional analysis reports finalised the recommendations of the working groups. A set of initial design rules was specified to act as a guide which included reduction in variance tests, covariance, minimum cost and volume criteria for new groups and variance differences resulting from splits and mergers.

The final output of the clinical and analytical design process was a set of recommended changes to the HRGs, which revised the original 572 HRGs to 610 HRGs and a set of further recommendations and areas for investigation to be considered in the future design. The quality assurance of the new group definitions was finalised in April 2003, bringing to a close the design process in just over six months. The new group definitions were then taken forward to be incorporated into the software released to the NHS in October 2003. These HRGv3.5 groups were costed by hospitals in 2005, and used as the basis of reimbursement to English Hospitals from April 2006.

During the revision process there was recognition of the need to look at the generic design of the HRGs with respect to particular patient types that exist across the classification and the need to have a consistent approach across the chapters and clinical working groups to the consideration of these patient types. This led to the formation of four expert reference panels, which were expected to produce recommendations through specific studies to the design of HRGs. Each of these panels was responsible for overseeing HRG development from the perspective of specific patient groups covering children and paediatrics, chronic illness, specialised services and cancer.

The patient-centred approach which was adopted by the expert reference panels provided an opportunity to look at the care patients receive across organisations, care settings and sectors. However, the ideal design of the

groupings was to be assessed against alternative designs to assess the effectiveness of any design given the constraints of the cost of new data collection
or the practicalities of a useable system within the existing structures in the
health service.

A number of the studies were set up to take advantage of new clinical data
collection systems that existed at national or sub-national level such as the
Central Cardiac Audit Database, Delayed Discharge data, Single Assessment
Process data for long-stay patients and the Cancer Audit Databases.

The design of groupings in investigating the issue of setting, in particular,
was to concentrate on the interface areas of traditional care settings such as
primary care and outpatients, outpatients and same-day inpatients. It was
crucial that the reimbursement system was designed to provide the correct
incentives in these areas irrespective of the grouping system. The priority area
was where the same care is provided in the same environment, but the
classification of a patient event varies between and within organisations. This
was particularly evident in same-day diagnosis surgery, where practice varied
considerably between organisations in recording these events as outpatients
or day cases, where differences existed in the reimbursement rates. The
system should investigate whether it wishes to favour or provide incentives
towards activities being carried out in particular settings or, more specifically, particular sectors of care (e.g. providing incentives to GPs to carry out
minor surgery as opposed to a patient undergoing an outpatient attendance).

In considering unbundling and bundling, the care provided to a patient
can be viewed in two ways: longitudinally over time; or vertically over
inputs. The longitudinal or output approach will typically measure the
processes of care such as investigation, diagnosis, treatment and follow-up
care. The vertical or input approach will look at the individual services
provided by an organisation(s) such as pathology, imaging, theatre, and
drugs. Casemix classification has at its core the concept of defining outputs
and therefore traditionally favours the measurement of the former view of
care. However, the measurement of inputs (sometimes described as intermediate outputs or components) is important in aiding the design of
casemix classifications and the understanding and even tracking, of key
resource components and drivers.

There are a number of natural barriers to bundling and unbundling of care
around the organisations that may contribute to care at any given time.
Either the casemix classification and reimbursement will need to be designed
around traditional organisational barriers, or systems of co-payment will
need to be considered. Unbundling of services can lead to problems of

overproduction, poor recognition of duplication and a barrier to innovations in treatment. The process of care approach will require rules for the movement of patients between processes where they exist in a single provider, such as acute care to rehabilitation, and rehabilitation to intermediate care. This will require changes to the current administrative minimum datasets, based on rules set to avoid the perverse incentive to over-record that has been seen in the current system, which records consultant episodes during an admission spell in a single hospital organisation.

A number of specific pilot projects were set up to consider new areas of clinical work in the NHS not currently or adequately covered by HRGs and several areas were identified as rapid areas of change (e.g. the critical care groupings based on organs supported, palliative care, interventional radiology and plastic surgery based on combined working with other specialties). These initiatives are also producing requirements to record procedures and interventions that will feed into the development of a revised intervention classification system, which is replacing the current surgical classification OPCS. Initially, a new system, the National Intervention Classification (NIC) was to be developed, but this was abandoned in 2005 and replaced by a less ambitious revision of the surgical classification (OPCS). Whilst aiding the inclusion of new procedures, OPCS will continue to suffer the difficulties of a classification with out of date concepts of classification and a low level of investment dictated by the anticipated replacement by READ and latterly the SNOMED-CT coded nomenclatures.

The English Department of Health therefore set out plans for fundamental changes to the way that funds flow through the National Health Service in its project, Reforming NHS Financial Flows.

Introducing payment by results

The proposals included the creation of a nationally agreed set of prices, commissioning based on volumes adjusted for casemix using Healthcare Resource Groups, and a shortlist of those Healthcare Resource Groups which should be commissioned and monitored individually. The planned system was due to cover 60 per cent of the total budget from 1 April 2005. This is highly ambitious and, if successful, will lead to one of the most (if not the most) extensive prospective payment systems.

The objective of the reforms was to produce a fair, transparent and rules-based system for paying providers. There had been no standard rationale in funding for providers – budgets were still based on historic levels. This had led to different funding for trusts that were providing similar services and this needed to be addressed, together with supporting patient choice and plurality. The reforms also aimed to provide incentives to increase capacity and reward efficiency, allowing trusts to retain surpluses to invest in services and to put pressure on high-cost providers to reduce costs and avoid deficits.

The Admitted Patient Care (Inpatients and Daycases) HRGs have now been revised using a rigorous analytical and clinical review process. Further requirements to revise these groupings and others such as outpatient and community HRGs have been identified and projects are now in place to investigate the use of ever-increasing data returns on hospital, community and family doctor-led services.

The casemix classification and the reimbursement rules should be seen as separate but dependent parts of a reimbursement system. If these two processes were to be owned by separate organisations, the need to interact at appropriate stages in the respective design processes should be carefully considered. There is a need for effective and timely communication between the key partners in the design system (i.e. the Health Department, project managers, technical staff and clinical associations). Key design requirements need to be in place at the start of the process, with appropriate input from the key parties, to ensure both ownership and that the final results meet the requirements.

The ability to use a casemix classification is highly dependent on the level of practical and technical knowledge within a health system. Whilst HRGs have been used in a limited capacity, they had not been substantively revised for almost six years. This not only led to a loss of 'corporate knowledge', but also the loss of inter-organisational relationships. A regular and ongoing revision process ensures the maintenance and required knowledge to provide a robust system that can be effectively implemented as the basis of a reimbursement system.

The universal collection of cost data by all hospitals following the adoption of a new version of HRGs, which in turn produced a set of reference costs, added eighteen months to the implementation timetable. The creation of an annually updated patient-level costs model, supplied by a discrete number of hospitals, would provide a significant resource in both the design of the groups and in the systematic creation of cost weights or reference costs. Other casemix designs such as the process of care approach should be considered, but the cost of additional data should be weighed against the gains given in explaining cost against existing methods of data collection. Components of care should be collected where possible to aid both the design of casemix classifications and the understanding of efficiency and effectiveness.

The design of the reimbursement system and associated casemix classifications need to be transparent and reputable to maximise the ownership and ensure that changes can be made once issues and problems have been identified. This will also ensure that learning continues, avoids 'reinventing-the-wheel' and aids the perception of the process within the Health Service.

Whilst these reforms initially only applied to England, they have been considered by the rest of the UK. From 1994, the All Patients Diagnosis Related Groups (AP-DRG) system was used in Wales,[23,24] adapted from the original US version of the grouper to use UK coding standards, and was used predominantly to report reference costs from Welsh hospitals. However, this changed in 2001 when the transition to the English HRGs[25] (Activity and Costs in Welsh Hospitals) was made. In Scotland, costing has also been carried out using HRGs (Scottish Health Service Costs[26]) and the initial use of HRGs for commissioning services was being introduced in 2005 with the development of tariffs.[27]

Impact, debates, controversies

The implementation of casemix systems within the UK has been a slow and sometimes abortive process over the last two decades. The full use of the system has yet to be realised, as it is still in its initial implementation, with final implementation of the 'payment by results' system not expected until 2008. Hospitals, commissioning organisations and policy leaders are still able to influence the progress of the system and its final outcome.

Up until 2003, little attention had been paid to the funding system in the NHS whilst the increased spending was in place, but in 2006, there were early signs that hospitals needed to ensure they could maintain fiscal control and undertake fully accountable financial planning as the historic block funding began to be replaced by a system driven by activity-based funding, with alternative providers of healthcare such as independent treatment centres, general practitioners and other NHS and private hospitals. A number of hospitals announced funding shortfalls, with reports by the British Broadcasting Company in April 2006 noting that 25 per cent of NHS hospital trusts had failed to balance their books in 2004/5, resulting in a total deficit of £250 million.

Increased financial pressure has also been brought about due to the changes in the contracts between the NHS and general practitioners, and the NHS contracts for medical staff. Some work has argued that changes to contracts, whilst improving the transparency of payments, have led to an underestimated increase in cost to the NHS without necessarily producing changes to clinical practice.[28] The new system to pay general practitioners includes the Quality and Outcomes Framework (QOF), a points system related to disease areas and clinical targets.[29]

With the increased financial pressure, concerns over 'upcoding' by hospitals have been increasing and there is increased pressure on staff to maximise the HRG and therefore the resultant tariff paid to the hospital.[30] This issue also illustrates the concerns of commissioning organisations whose funding within England has not been fundamentally reformed despite the changes to hospital funding, whilst the other countries in the UK have undertaken reform of the funding mechanisms for health commissioners.[31] There is also increasing evidence that hospitals are narrowing the scope of their services, or reducing their casemix to become more efficient, leading to concerns that specialised and 'non-profitable' services will be reduced. This presents a challenge to the casemix system to become sophisticated, to represent the breadth of clinical services and for the funding system to recognise the need to maintain the full scope of clinical services.

The policy agenda in healthcare in the UK is dominated by many apparently competing initiatives such as: the National Service Frameworks, four-hour A&E waits, eighteen-week waits, NICE clinical guidelines, changes in the configuration of providers in the NHS to the increased use of independent/private sector organisations and new contracts for primary care doctors and hospital consultants. The challenge for policy is to see if these areas can be accommodated within a financing system that is fair and transparent as laid down by the policy leading from the NHS Plan. The UK system has an opportunity to create a common system with the correct drivers to facilitate integrated care and a reimbursement system that considers all areas of healthcare provision.

NOTES

1. OECD (2006), OECD Health Data 2005: Statistics and Indicators for 30 Countries. [Online]. Available at www.oecd.org/ [last accessed 19 April 2006].
2. Department of Health (2000), The NHS Plan: A Plan for Investment, A Plan for Reform. Available at www.dh.gov.uk/assetRoot/04/05/57/83/04055783.pdf [last accessed: 10 January 2006].

3. HM Treasury (2006), Treasury Report Total Expenditure on Services by Function, 1987–88 to 2004–05. Available at www.hm-treasury.gov.uk/economic_data_and_tools/ [last accessed: 19 April 2006].

4. Coles, J. M. (1993), England: Ten Years of Diffusion and Development. In Kimberly, J. R. and de Pouvourville, G. (eds.), *The Migration of Managerial Innovation: Diagnosis-Related Groups and Health Care Administration in Western Europe.* San Francisco, CA: Jossey-Bass, pp 17–59.

5. Sanderson, H., Anthony, P. and Mountney, L. (1998), Resource Groupings: History of Development and Current State. In Sanderson, H., Anthony, P. and Mountney, L. (eds.), *Casemix for All.* Abingdon, UK: Radcliffe Medical Press, pp 11–26.

6. Sutch, S., Spark, V., Benton, P., Farrell, G. and Light, M. (2001), The NHS Performance Analysis Toolkit. In Hofdijk, J., Roger France, F. H. and Pironet, D. (eds.), *Proceedings of the 17th PCSE / 3rd EFMI Working Conference.* Brugge, Belgium: Patient Classification Systems Europe, pp 226–33.

7. National Casemix Office (1991), *Healthcare Resource Groups Definitions Manual Version 1.0.* Winchester: National Casemix Office.

8. Health Systems International (1987), *Diagnosis Related Groups: Fourth Revision, Definitions Manual.* New Haven, CT: Health Systems International.

9. Newman, T. and Jenkins, L. (1991), *DRG Experience in England 1981–1991.* London: CASPE Research.

10. Sanderson, H. (1996), Localisation of DRGs in the UK. In *Conference Proceedings: The Eighth Casemix Conference: Casemix and Change – International Perspectives.* Sydney: Commonwealth Department of Human Services and Health, pp 283–7.

11. National Casemix Office (1991), *Healthcare Resource Groups Definitions Manual Version 1.0.* Winchester: National Casemix Office, p 18.

12. National Casemix Office (1994), *Healthcare Resource Groups Version 2 Definitions Manual.* Winchester: NHS Executive.

13. Brieman, L., Friedman, J. H., Olshen, R. A. and Stone, C. J. (1993), *Classification and Regression Trees.* New York: Chapman & Hall.

14. National Casemix Office (1997), The Version 3 Healthcare Resource Group Documentation Set. Winchester: NHS Executive.

15. Sanderson, H. (1997), Health Benefit Groups – One Year On in Patient Classification System/Europe (PCS/E): 13th International Working Conference, Florence, Italy, 1–3 October 1997: Proceedings Book, pp 159–60.

16. Walker, A., Jack, K., Twaddle, S. and Burns, H. (1998), Health Benefit Groups in NHS Decision-Making. In Sanderson, H., Anthony, P. and Mountney, L. (eds.), *Casemix for All.* Abingdon. UK: Radcliffe Medical Press, pp 111–24.

17. Department of Health (2000), The NHS Plan: A Plan for Investment, A Plan for Reform. Available at www.dh.gov.uk/assetRoot/04/05/57/83/04055783.pdf [last accessed: 10 January 2006].

18. Wanless, D. (2002), Securing Our Future Health: Taking a Long-Term View. London: HM Treasury.

19. Department of Health (2002), Reforming NHS Financial Flows: Introducing Payment by Results. Available at www.dh.gov.uk/assetRoot/04/01/87/04/04018704.pdf [last accessed: 10 January 2006].

20. Department of Health (2001), Delivering the NHS Plan. London: Department of Health.

21. Department of Health (2002) Reforming NHS Financial Flows: Introducing Payment by Results. London: Department of Health.

22. Rogers, R., Williams, S., Jarman, B. and Aylin, P. (2005), 'HRG Drift' and Payment by Results. *BMJ* 330: 563 (12 March).

23. Sutch, Steve (1996), The CaseMix Policy of England and Wales or Do You Speak English a Rydych Chi'n siarad Cymraeg. In Patient Classification System/Europe (PCS/E); 12th International Working Conference, the Australian CaseMix Week, Sydney, Australia, 16–21 September 1996: Proceedings Book, pp 119–26.

24. 3M Health Information Systems (1995), NHS Cymru Wales All Patient DRG, Version 12.0 Grouping with ICD–10 and OPCS4.2 Codes: Users Manual. Wallingford, Connecticut, 3M Health Information Systems.

25. Sutch, S.P. (1997), Grouping Issues in England and Wales – The Use of APDRGs in Wales with the Advent of HRGs Version 3 in Patient Classification System/Europe (PCS/E); 13th International Working Conference, Florence, Italy, 1–3 October 1997: Proceedings Book, pp 160–4.

26. ISD Scotland (2005), Scottish Health Service Costs. Available at www.isdscotland.org/isd/files/Costs_Exec_Summary_2005.pdf [April 2006].

27. ISD Scotland (2005), Scottish National Tariff Development. Available at www.isdscotland.org/ [April 2006].

28. Williams, S. and Buchan, J. (2006), *Assessing the New NHS Consultant Contract: A Something for Something Deal?* London: King's Fund.

29. Department of Health (2004), Quality and Outcomes Framework (QOF). [Online]. Available at www.dh.gov.uk/PolicyAndGuidance/OrganisationPolicy/PrimaryCare/PrimaryCareContracting/QOF/fs/en [last accessed: April 2006].

30. E-Health Insider (2005), 'Upcoding' a Hazard as PbR Pressure Grows. London: E-Health Media Ltd.

31. Townend, P. (2001), Targeting Poor Health: Professor Townsend's Report of the Welsh Assembly's National Steering Group on the Allocation of NHS Resources. Cardiff: The National Assembly for Wales.

3 Casemix implementation in Portugal

Céu Mateus

Céu Mateus

Introduction

Since 1979, the Portuguese health care system has been based on a National Health Service (NHS) structure, with public insurance, universal coverage, almost free access at the point of use, and general taxation financing. The state is committed to providing health protection for the whole population and equity objectives are prominent. This has been reinforced by successive legislation, which also attributed to the Portuguese health care system the objectives of promoting efficiency, quality, and accountability (Assembleia da República 1990). Nonetheless, it should be highlighted that, in reality, the Portuguese NHS has never conformed to the general characteristics of the Beveridge model, mainly because of an incomplete transition from a previously fragmented social insurance system. Occupation-based insurance schemes that existed in 1979 are yet to be integrated into the NHS, meaning additional coverage for the one provided by the NHS for around 20–25 percent of the population (OECD 1998). These occupation-based insurance schemes, which benefit from additional public funding and allow families to enjoy double coverage, contribute to inequalities in access. A large private sector co-exists with the NHS and its role was explicitly recognized in the 1990 NHS law that instituted a mixed health care system involving both the public and private sectors (Assembleia da República 1990). The private sector is mainly responsible for visits to specialists, elective surgery, ancillary tests and kidney dialysis.

Figure 3.1 depicts key institutions and financial/service relationships between the stakeholders in the Portuguese health care sector (Oliveira and Pinto 2005). The central government level still exerts the most influence, with a tradition of centralized management. Regional Health Authorities (RHAs) manage the provision of primary care and are responsible for state reimbursement of prescribed drugs to the Pharmacy Association. The

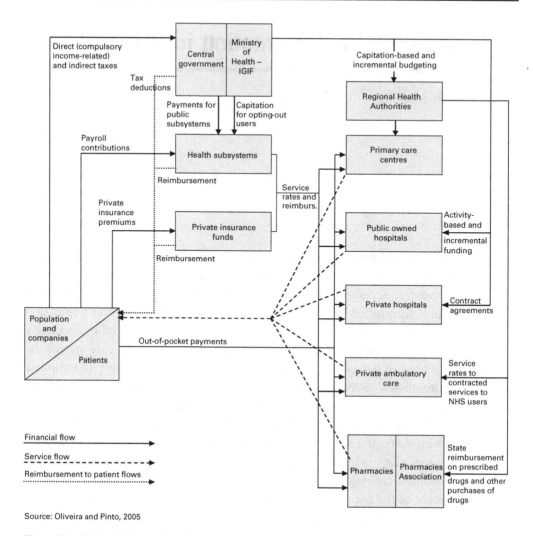

Source: Oliveira and Pinto, 2005

Figure 3.1   Key institutions and relationships in the Portuguese health care system

Institute for Financial Management and IT (IGIF) is an agency of the Ministry of Health whose main responsibility is the management of NHS financial resources for primary and hospital care. In addition, it also produces statistical information and regulates IT in both hospitals and health care centers. Patients are given an NHS general practitioner (GP) within their area of residence. Primary care GPs are expected to act as gatekeepers and refer patients to secondary care provided by medical specialists. Access to emergency services has been unrestricted, contributing to an imperfect gatekeeping system.

Table 3.1 Key figures for Portugal

Population (2004)[a]	10,043,763
% over 65	17
% over 80	4
Life expectancy (2002)[b]	
Male	73.8
Female	80.5
Resources (2003)	
N. acute care hospitals[c]	92
N. acute beds (1000)[a]	3.6
N. admissions (1000)[a]	117.4
N. outpatient visits per capita[a]	3.8
% GDP spent on health care[d]	9.6
% Public	6.7
% Private	2.9
NHS expenditures by sector[d]	
Hospitals	46.4
Primary care	50.3

Source:
[a] National Institute for Statistics (www.ine.pt)
[b] OECD Health Data 2004
[c] Centros de Saúde e Hospitais: Recursos e produção do SNS:
Ano de 2004. Direcção-Geral da Saúde, 2005. (www.dgs.pt)
[d] Serviço Nacional de Saúde – Contas Globais 2003. IGIF,
2005. (www.igif.min-saude.pt)

The Portuguese health care system is mainly financed by the state budget. Over the past two decades, expenditure has increased steadily. Among EU nations, Portugal is presently a high health care spender in terms of percentage of GDP spent (in comparison with other countries that have NHS-based systems) (OECD 2004). Private financing was responsible for 29 percent of total expenditures in 2002 (OECD 2004) mostly for "out-of-pocket" payments (visits to specialists, pharmaceuticals, dental care, physiotherapy, and so on).

A brief history of the introduction of casemix systems in Portugal

Back in 1984, the Portuguese Ministry of Health started a pilot project to study the feasibility of implementing DRGs as a measure of output of cases

Table 3.2 Sources of data for the calculation of Portuguese prices by DRG

Variable	Country	Source
Costs	Portugal	Analytical accounts (DGF – IGIF)
Relative weights	USA	Maryland cost weights
Inpatient discharges	Portugal	DRGs database (DDSFG – IGIF)
National base rate	Portugal	Ministry of Health

treated in hospitals. The starting point was a proposal presented by Yale University for technical assistance to support the development of a hospital DRG-based information system. As noted by Urbano *et al.* (1993), DRGs were seen as a hospital cost control project and were financially supported by the US Agency for International Development. Since the results of the pilot study were very favorable, a decision was made to extend the system to all public acute care hospitals. In 1987 more than 50 percent of NHS hospitals were included in the project and by 1990 that figure had risen to 90 percent (Bentes *et al.* 1993; Bentes *et al.* 1996). Within ten years all NHS hospitals were collecting patient data to feed the DRG information system.

The implementation process followed a top-down approach. The adoption of a patient classification system was envisaged by the MoH, and, taking advantage of the centralization of the Portuguese political system, hospitals had to comply with the decision. The double role of the MoH as both provider of and payer for care should not be forgotten. Dynamics toward implementation started in the MoH and were spread to NHS hospitals through the involvement of physicians and hospital managers in selected hospitals. A small team lead by João Urbano, an experienced hospital manager, worked closely with the Secretary of State for Health. One of the members of the team was Margarida Bentes, who, after Urbano's departure, led the Portuguese project and was the most influential person in implementing DRGs in Portugal.

Urbano *et al.* (1993) explain that "the first objective of the project was to create an integrated information system for hospital management based on a set of necessary and uniform data, which would allow all levels of management to measure and control their productivity, support their decision making, make plans and budgets, and establish equitable financing criteria. The second objective was to develop an information system that could efficiently collect, treat, analyze, and transmit information within hospitals, between hospitals and central departments, and among central departments." The main goal was to rationalize the allocation of resources to NHS hospitals by linking resources given for inpatient care to the production of treated inpatient cases. Campos (quoted by Bentes *et al.* 1993) considered the major problems of the Portuguese health sector to include the chronic under-financing of public hospitals, the accumulated deficits that have resulted from this under-financing, limited management power, delays in meeting expenditures, and an overall lack of confidence in the sector from both users and suppliers. It was thought that by implementing a DRG-based resource allocation model, its objectivity and rationality in setting budgets would help to solve or minimize some of these problems. Moreover, as stated by Dismuke and Sena (2001), the Portuguese MoH sought to encourage a more efficient utilization of resources in public hospitals to help productivity and curb the uncontrolled growth of public expenditure in the health care sector.

Portuguese team leaders carefully followed the DRG experiment in the US and established close contacts with other European countries, envisaging the implementation of patient classification systems. It was clear to the Portuguese team that no national resources were available for investment in a nationally developed system and the DRG system appeared to have been suitably tested and evaluated by others.

There were seminars and training sessions involving hospital managers and physicians, primarily to promote DRGs and their use as a hospital management tool. Urbano *et al.* (1993) highlight the key role played by hospital managers in the acceptance process once they had been persuaded that improvements in information systems and management tools could help them in their profession. However, it should be noted that later one of the main critiques of DRGs also came from hospital managers, especially after hospital funding was calculated based on DRGs.

The current situation

Taking into consideration the aims of the project presented above, an integrated information system was created; however, it is mainly used to define funding criteria. In my opinion, all the other aims of the project, which are feasible, are still to be fully achieved.

DRG use in Portugal concerning the payment for hospital activities is threefold:

- national tariffs for reimbursement of care are provided to the beneficiaries of occupation-based schemes, insurance companies (mainly for traffic accidents and occupational injuries) and other third-party payers;
- a prospective global budget for inpatient care can be calculated;
- payment for surgeries performed on patients received from waiting lists.

The full cost of hospital stays is supposed to be covered by the price of the DRG, and costs related to physician care are included in the national tariff. There are no specific adjustments for research and teaching activities, but these are supposed to be taken into account using the adjustments in place for a hospital's group.[1] Innovative drugs and devices not included in any DRG are treated on an *ad hoc* basis. It should be noted that, regarding cochlear implants and replacement of automatic cardiac defibrillators, the price of the medical device is added to the price of the DRG for hospital reimbursement. For intestine and spleen transplants, hospitals are reimbursed according to the costs of the procedure, and each inpatient day is paid according to a *per diem* rate; the same applies for chemotherapy drugs, endo-prosthesis, ocular prosthesis, external prosthesis and walking aids. Patients being permanently ventilated are excluded from the DRG system and their treatment costs are reimbursed according to the daily rate of the ICU.

The key components of the inpatient resource allocation model are the determination of DRG weights, hospital casemix indices, hospital adjustment rates, and the total number of discharges. Each DRG relative weight expresses a relationship between that DRG and any of the others in terms of resource consumption, and in relation to the average case in Portugal, which has a relative weight of 1. The greater the relative weight of a DRG, the more significant the consumption of resources associated with it. In Portugal, relative weights do not vary by hospital; a single value is computed for each DRG and is used nationwide. Determination of Portuguese relative cost weights suffers from the non-existence of cost-per-patient data in NHS hospitals. To surmount that problem, a top-down costing approach was adopted, and global inpatient costs of each hospital are allocated to each DRG based on Maryland cost weights and on lengths of hospital stay. The shortcoming of this methodology lies in the assumption of an identical profile of treatment in Portugal and in the State of Maryland in the USA. Since 1994, when necessary, panels of physicians (by major diagnosis category) have convened at IGIF with the aim of validating Portuguese cost weights.

Costs included in the model originate in the cost accounting of each hospital and are reported in terms of principal inpatient sections. Nevertheless, it should be noted that hospitals' cost accounting still presents different reporting criteria, which negatively impacts the DRG model. A working group was put in place in 1997 in order to improve the linkage between hospitals' cost accounting and the DRG cost model. For all hospitals, items to be included in each cost center were revised in order to assure greater comparability with costs included in the model.

For Portugal, the national base rate results from the quotient of the total of costs of each year divided by the total number of discharges for the same year, and it expresses the average cost for the average patient for that year. The passage from costs to prices, in the end, is simply the modification of the original base rate into the national base rate. The final decision regarding the value of the national base rate is made by the MoH, bearing in mind its impact on third-party payers and on the expenditure of the NHS, because that value is going to be used for funding purposes. The national casemix is set equal to one and, after changes in cost weights or base rates, the model is recalibrated.

Maryland cost weights are developed by the Maryland Cost Review Program and reflect the cost of a service relative to other services in each DRG. By assuming that Portuguese hospitals have the same pattern of service use as hospitals in Maryland, but at different levels, it is possible to determine the relative costs of each service that comprise total hospital costs by DRG. It would have been impossible to obtain Portuguese cost weights, as information regarding total resource use for an individual patient has never been routinely collected because individual patient billing has never existed.

The current model computes a hospital budget by multiplying the number of patients the hospital is expected to treat during budget year N by its casemix index, then by its blended base rate.

Hospital inpatient budget $H_i = CMI \times \sum equivalent\ discharges \times group\ base\ rate$

Adjustments to this formula are made to account for outlier and transfer cases and to ensure overall budget neutrality.

DRGs are not used to set the totality of inpatient funding; they have been introduced smoothly (Table 3.3). Inpatient care funding through DRG represents around 75 to 85 percent of a hospital's inpatient budget, with the remaining percentage billed to third-party payers.

When losses are limited to zero, that means that, in cases where the budget was lower than the one received in the previous year, it was decided

Table 3.3 Percentage of funding based in DRG

Year	DRG	Previous year's budget	Limit of losses
1997	10%	90%	Zero
1998	20%	80%	No limit
1999	30%	70%	No limit
2000	30%	70%	Zero
2001	40%	60%	Zero
2002	50%	50%	?

by the MoH to keep the same funding. It should also be kept in mind that the amount spent under the DRG funding system cannot exceed the national budget for inpatient care and, frequently, it is necessary to adjust the national base rate to conform to that constraint.

Since the inception of DRGs, feedback reports to hospitals are produced every year. This information facilitates an evaluation of hospital performance on a routine basis, enabling managers and physicians with knowledge about national practices and ability to monitor institutional deviations from observed standards. A set of national and hospital peer group indicators is generated for the purpose of feedback reports. Hospitals are classified in five peer groups, in an attempt to reflect differences in cost structures and casemix largely associated with differing roles played by those hospitals in delivering health care (Bentes 1992). As Bentes *et al.* (1997) put it, "the use of groups for statistical analyses ensures that only hospitals with similar cost and case-mix potentials are compared to each other, thus augmenting the significance of reference values generated within the groups."

Feedback reports contain casemix-adjusted performance and quality indicators and aim to provide hospitals with benchmark practice-based measures that can be used to assess performance, identify latent quality problems, and improve utilization review activities. Each hospital can always perform clinical reviews of individual cases in situations where major deviations from reference values are found. Hospital feedback reports are composed of three sets of information: performance measures, quality of care alerts, and data quality evaluation.

Performance measures include inpatient volume and average length of stay (ALOS) by DRG and casemix evolution. Hospital-expected overall ALOS is also included, which corresponds to the global length of stay that the hospital would have if the ALOS for each of its DRGs was the same as that observed for the DRG of the peer group or at the national level. Having the expected overall ALOS as a reference, a hospital can easily compare itself with other hospitals in its peer group and at the national level in the use of days to treat patients. Information regarding outlier patients is given as well. Outlier patients in each DRG are considered to be those whose lengths of stay are below (short-stay patients) or above (long-stay patients) the trim points of the DRG, as well as transferred cases. To complete this set, information concerning the evolution of the CMI of the hospital is presented.

The next set of information contains quality of care alerts attempting to call hospitals' attention to gaps between expected and actual outcomes in terms of patient health status for groups of similar patients. Nevertheless, when looking at these indicators, one should not forget that each hospital possesses its own reality, which may influence the meaning of results. Quality of care alerts reported to hospitals include information regarding the percentage of readmissions on surgical DRGs, mortality on selected DRGs, and information about complications related to surgical procedures, pregnancy, delivery and puerperium and decubitus ulcer as secondary diagnosis. Complications occurring during a hospital stay, because of their implications for patient well-being and recovery, are powerful outcome indicators. In spite of the fact that some complications cannot be avoided, it is known that the occurrence of a high number of certain diagnoses is associated with deficient quality of care in hospitals. Thus, a set of ICD–9–CM codes were identified for hospital feedback reporting and were grouped in the areas already mentioned. It should be noted that the existence of these diagnoses does not provide evidence about the quality of care in individual cases or even in small samples. However, when the incidence of these secondary diagnoses is analyzed for a large group of patients, it can be expected that deviations from reference values might indicate potential quality problems.

The last set of indicators concerns evaluation of data quality. The correct and complete filing of medical records and adequate administrative proceedings are also important in comparing each hospital's performance. The analysis of representative samples of hospital records enabled the identification of the main problems at the national level. Data is a cornerstone of the whole system, because it influences the quality of information available as well as its impact on funding levels. Data quality indicators have evolved since their inception in order to set higher standards for hospital registries.

Feedback reports can prove to be very helpful in targeting excellence or problem areas within the hospital, enabling hospital managers to better dialog with physicians.

Since the early 1990s, all acute NHS hospitals are included in the DRG's casemix system for inpatient care. There have never been any attempts to implement casemix systems for psychiatric care or rehabilitation. During the mid-1990s, two pilot studies were undertaken to test the feasibility of implementing Ambulatory Patient Groups (APG) to ambulatory care provided in hospitals (Valente *et al.* 1998). However, despite positive results from the second study, no action has been taken as yet.

In 1996 a process to adapt DRGs for the classification of ambulatory surgeries was initiated (Bentes *et al.* 1996; Mateus and Valente 2000). The rationale for this was rooted in the growing trend to shift care from in-patient to ambulatory settings and an ever-growing number of one-day surgeries being paid by DRG as either a short-stay outlier or an inlier admission, depending on the low trim point of the DRG assigned. From the viewpoint of the payer (the MoH itself), this was a clear distortion of the inpatient DRG system, considering that it was neither designed nor intended to classify ambulatory surgeries.

The first step was to define which procedures would be eligible. Based on a list of ICD–9–CM procedure codes developed by the Irish Department of Health, representing procedures which, in the opinion of Irish physicians, could be done on an outpatient basis, a similar one was developed for Portugal. A survey, where ambulatory surgery was defined as "a scheduled procedure, requiring operating room facilities, but no overnight stay," containing a list of potential ambulatory surgery procedures was sent to selected hospitals (fifty-six) to ascertain the national practice. In the survey, ICD–9–CM procedure codes were mapped to DRGs, because the goal was to have "ambulatory surgery DRGs." Usable responses were received from thirty-four hospitals (60% response rate). The answers were received from a number of physicians working in different specialities in each hospital and had to be made consistent within each hospital regarding procedures done by more than one speciality. When a procedure was selected by more than one speciality, it was assumed that it was a potential ambulatory procedure. As a result of the survey, a set of thirty-three DRGs were selected as eligible to classify ambulatory surgeries based on four criteria: physician responses, DRG content homogeneity, reported volume of zero-day stays for the most common selected procedure code above 30 percent, and, to preserve face validity, a low DRG trim point (less than or equal to two days). To ensure validity and acceptability of results, panels of physicians were assembled, and through consensus techniques a final list of thirty-eight "ambulatory surgery DRGs" was achieved (five other DRGs were included).

The last step was to compute a price for each ambulatory surgery DRG. According to the Portuguese DRG cost model, hospital costs were separated into those that could be assumed to vary with length of stay (e.g. physician, hotel) and those that were likely to be similar for each inpatient admission in the same DRG (e.g. laboratory, pharmacy). The price of each ambulatory surgery DRG was composed of the following components of the price of the corresponding inpatient DRG (100% of operating room; 100% of physician for one day; 100% of hotel and nursing for one day; 100% of administration for one day; 80% of the supplies; 25% of imaging and laboratory; 25% of drugs; 0% of intensive care unit and other ancillary).

The first prices were published in 1998 and used in budget setting the same year. Ambulatory surgery DRGs were first updated in 2001 and again in 2003, containing, at present, seventy-one ambulatory surgery DRGs. However, it is not clear whether the link to the initial methodology has been kept.

Since the pilot study, it was decided to adopt HCFA DRGs[2] without any adaptation to the Portuguese setting. Several versions of HCFA DRGs have been used and, at present, version sixteen is in place. Version updates do not occur on a regular basis and depend on the MoH. Other patient classification systems have been tested on Portuguese data, like AP-DRG[3] and APR-DRG. However grouping results with these groupers did not show enough improvement to justify the change. When compared with the HCFA DRGs, procedures and diagnosis are coded through ICD–9–CM for the year corresponding to the HCFA DRG version in use.

Patient demographic and clinical data and data related to each admission are routinely collected in all hospitals according to a uniform minimum basic data set (UMBDS). These data, which are primarily aimed at assigning the appropriate DRG to each discharge, are forwarded to IGIF (a central department at the Ministry of Health) where a national DRG database is kept, with an approximate total of 900,000 cases per year.

It was understood that high-quality data was a prerequisite to its use and would strengthen the utilization of DRGs. Therefore, the establishment of a hospital-wide framework for data evaluation was a major priority (Bentes *et al.* 1997). In Portugal, coding is done by physicians who are voluntarily trained as coders. The coding training program is run by IGIF and comprises three dimensions: (i) to train physicians in coding; (ii) to train physicians to audit coding; and (iii) to update physicians' coding knowledge.

Internal and external hospital coding audits have been carried out on a regular basis since 1995. Each hospital is required to have an internal auditor, who coordinates the data collection process and supervises the clinical coding completed by the group of in-hospital physician coders. An external auditing team, composed of specialized physicians and a senior manager from IGIF, has been appointed to promote, support and monitor audit activity at the hospitals, thus complementing the ongoing internal audits. Audits are supported by software, developed by a Portuguese physician, that identifies the main data errors and inconsistencies in samples of hospital records. That software returns information about the average number of codes per record, the percentage of invalid codes for diagnoses and procedures and administrative data, coding errors (opposite codes, for instance) and alerts to eventual coding problems or deficient information in the medical records (diagnosis and procedure duplication, unspecified principal diagnosis, questionable admission, unacceptable principal diagnosis, unspecified operating room procedure, operating room procedure unrelated to principal diagnosis, lack of external cause of injury or poisoning, record without procedures) and atypical length of stay. Analysis of representative samples of hospital records enabled the identification of the main problems at national level and action toward their resolution.

It is worth noting that, in some years, as part of the financing criteria, the quality of coding performed at a hospital has been linked to adjustments to the hospital's preliminary budget, in terms of premiums and penalties, thus creating an additional incentive for data quality improvement (Bentes *et al.* 1997).

Hospitals keep a local database of their DRG data and are expected to upload new records to the national database every month, as well as updates and corrections of older ones. Depending on the size and internal organizational structure, both centralized and decentralized abstraction and coding processes can be found among Portuguese hospitals. There is no interference from the MoH regarding the collection of data from hospitals, which has always been seen as fundamental to the development of the national database.

Once data is added to the hospital database, it becomes readily available for the physicians and hospital managers working there. After being included into the national database, the data is available within the department coordinating the project in Portugal. If requested by the MoH

Table 3.4 Cases treated, ALOS and casemix index (CMI) in the period 1997–2004

	1997	1998	1999	2000	2001	2002	2003	2004
Total discharges	831,216	838,847	864,243	926,792	933,692	940,342	963,781	954,206
Inliers	713,177	719,765	740,793	801,693	794,875	789,599	792,177	768,879
Short stays	71,223	73,135	75,497	76,050	79,768	83,354	89,142	89,611
Long stays	26,579	25,613	23,103	22,192	21,193	19,654	19,096	17,895
Ambulatory surgeries	20,237	20,334	24,850	26,857	37,856	47,735	63,366	77,821
ALOS	7.5	7.5	7.3	7.1	7.1	7.0	6.8	6.8
CMI	0.99	1.00	1.02	1.04	1.07	1.08	1.08	1.10

Source: National DRG Database – DDSFG/IGIF, 2005

or institutes within it, data can be made available; however, this should be seen as an exception.

It should also be noted that, before 2005, no information was published or made available to the public based on DRG data. Moreover, access to the data by researchers has become more and more difficult, preventing the development of a body of knowledge in the area. In 2005 IGIF published national DRG data for the years 2003 and 2004 (www.igif.min-saude.pt) and it is now possible to have an idea of the number of patients discharged, number of inpatient days and ALOS for each DRG. Information for the top twenty-five DRGs in terms of number of admissions, number of inpatient days and highest ALOS was also produced. Quality alerts were also made available. Despite this very positive step, there is still a long way to go.

Impact, debates and controversies

ALOS has been decreasing steadily in Portuguese hospitals, while the number of patients discharged shows the opposite trend (Table 3.4). This has been a constant since the introduction of DRGs and might point towards more efficiency in the treatment process. Moreover, occupancy rates have been constant at around 75 percent (Bentes *et al.* 2004). CMI increased 11 percent (Figure 3.2) between 1997 and 2004, which also shows that more complex patients are being treated in less time.

One important question is related to the impact of DRGs on hospital costs. In a work carried out in 2002, Mateus appraised the impact of DRGs

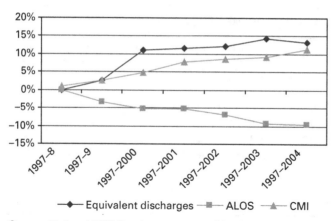

Source: National DRG Database, computed by the author

Figure 3.2   Equivalent discharges, ALOS, and CMI: cumulative variations between 1997 and 2004

on hospital funding in Portugal by analyzing key variables in two periods: before and after the introduction of DRGs. With the data available at the time, it was possible to conclude that the differences found in each period for the value of final budget, number of equivalent discharges, CMI and ALOS were statistically significant. Nonetheless, the differences found in cost per equivalent discharge and cost per equivalent discharge adjusted by CMI were not statistically different for the two periods under analysis.

Mateus (2002) attempted to measure the impact of DRGs in the redistribution of resources among groups of hospitals by comparing the budgets of each group before and after the introduction of a DRG-based funding model. It was concluded that the average budget increased for all the hospitals. Central and teaching hospitals saw their weight in the total budget diminish (from 20.3 to 18.5 percent). Specialized hospitals' weight declined as well, though not as severely (from 18.9 to 18 percent). District hospitals were the big winners (their share of the total budget rose from 54 to 57 percent). There was no change for county hospitals.

Quality of care is a complex issue. To capture its dimensions, several indicators should be used that are inextricably linked to perspective: MoH, hospital manager, physician or patient. DRGs are not suitable to measure quality of care, since they were not designed for that goal, but their data enable the identification of problem areas regarding quality of care. These data can be seen as a proxy for quality of care for readmissions, C-sections (in the total of deliveries), pressure ulcers, and many other areas. For instance, in Figure 3.3 one can observe the number of readmissions in surgical DRGs between 1997

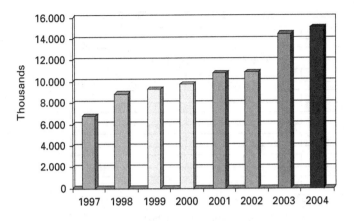

Source: National DRG Database – DDSFG/IGIF, 2005

Figure 3.3   Number of readmissions in surgical DRG, 1997–2004

and 2004. In the period under analysis, the number of readmissions increased by 121 percent; this might denote a practice of premature discharges in surgical patients, poor working conditions in the operating theater or lack of a policy to control infections. Nevertheless, this information should only be used to investigate further, since it does not necessarily mean that quality of care has been decreasing due to the DRG system.

It is surprising that such trends are not discussed further by those involved in the health care arena, especially in times where quality accreditation is becoming more and more important. It is acknowledged that DRGs can be used to target areas for utilization review; nevertheless, the Portuguese utilization review project has been at a standstill for more than a decade. As an example, it is worthwhile to look at the case of C-sections. Between 1997 and 2004, the number of deliveries diminished by two percent, yet the number of C-sections rose by 20 percent. In 2004, for 100 deliveries, 31 C-sections were performed (Figure 3.4). These figures point to a worrying trend in Portugal and further analysis should be carried out by the MoH to ascertain its causes.

Looking at the same indicator by region (Figure 3.5), the difference in the performance of the procedure becomes obvious; nearly ten percentage points separate the regions in which it is performed less often from the region where the rate is highest. Could this be due to physician choice, or to characteristics of the mothers? Is it related to the way provision of care is organized? Answering these questions should interest the Portuguese MoH,

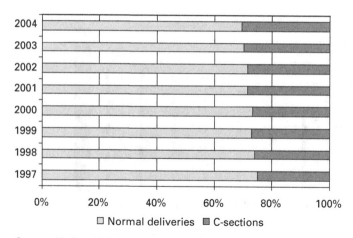

Source: National DRG Database, computed by the author

Figure 3.4   Percentage of normal deliveries and C-sections in the total number of deliveries, 1997–2004

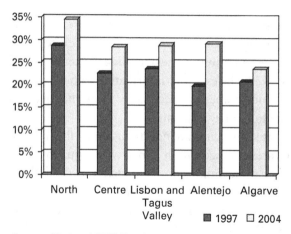

Source: National DRG Database, computed by the author

Figure 3.5   Percentage of C-sections by region in 1997 and 2004

as C-sections present a greater risk of infection to mothers than normal deliveries and should only be performed when deemed clinically necessary.

The reasons behind this trend are not clear. This sort of information is yet to be utilized by the MoH to either attempt to change physician behavior or to increase understanding of the costs of optional treatments in an era of limited resources and growing demands.

In 2001, Dismuke and Sena evaluated the influence of DRG-based payment on the technical efficiency and productivity of diagnostic technology in

Portuguese public hospitals. Analysis was performed for district and central hospitals to ascertain if payment methodology had an impact on productivity growth in terms of technology and technical efficiency change. Authors assessed three diagnostic technologies commonly used in Portuguese NHS hospitals – computerized axial tomography scanner (CAT), electrocardiogram (ECG), and echocardiogram (ECO) – using frontier analysis techniques. It was concluded that the technical efficiency of technologies increased both for central and district hospitals, with the exception of CAT. Furthermore, the authors found evidence that movements in productivity could be attributed to the DRG payment system for the technologies under evaluation.

Dismuke and Guimarães (2002), using Portuguese DRG data, estimated a count data model at the hospital level with inpatient mortality as a quality indicator. No evidence was found that the casemix-based payment system had pernicious effects on hospital quality, as measured by hospital mortality for the most frequent non-obstetric DRG (DRG14 – specific cerebrovascular disorders except transient ischemic attack) during the three-year time period under study (1992–4). Based on the results of the analysis, the authors concluded that hospitals with higher technology utilization and lower than predicted ALOS tend to have lower mortality rates.

In the past there has been some evidence of DRG creep and splitting stays to increase revenues. The first problem has been addressed through audits of data and patient records. To deal with split stays, controls on readmissions are done as follows: when a patient is readmitted into the same hospital in a period of seventy-two hours according to the discharge data, only the DRG of the first admission is eligible for reimbursement claims or funding. Exceptions to this rule apply when the second admission is not clinically related to the first one or if it represents a consolidation of treatment, such as in the area of oncology, and in those cases two DRGs are considered for reimbursement claims or funding.

The number of diagnoses and procedures per record can be considered to be low after twenty years of implementation of DRGs.

This snapshot of the evolution of coding shows that, in spite of the investments made in training physicians in coding, some doubt can be cast on its return. Figures presented for the number of diagnoses mean that, besides the primary diagnosis, there is not much more information being inserted into the system except the number. However, coding quality is not only related to quantity, but also to the content of the information transmitted, and looking at the top ten procedures recorded, one surmises that quantity is preferred over quality.

Table 3.5 Final budget, equivalent discharges, CMI, ALOS, cost per equivalent discharge, and cost per equivalent discharge adjusted by CMI – statistical significance of the differences in the period before and after funding through DRGs

Difference is statistically significant	Final budget	Equivalent discharges	CMI	ALOS	Cost per equivalent discharge	Cost per equivalent discharge adjusted by CMI
Yes	x	x	x	x		
No					x	x

Source: Mateus 2002.

There is agreement in considering the virtues of DRGs as a classification system for inpatient care, with the exception of some physicians. The situation is very different regarding the use of DRGs for hospital funding. Despite all the efforts made by the MoH to improve the funding model, voices against it are increasing. One of the goals of the current funding model was to allocate resources based on hospital production and national average costs, regardless of the costs incurred by each hospital. However, hospital managers still clamor for a reimbursement model of funding. Bearing this in mind, it is not difficult to understand persistent claims that the budget allocated to their institution is not enough to cover current costs. More recently, pharmaceutical companies have come to the conclusion that using a DRG-based system for funding prevents hospitals from adopting newer, and more expensive, pharmaceuticals and medical devices. From their point of view, this system does not facilitate the adoption of innovation, since the costs of new technologies are very high and DRG national tariffs do not cover them. Physicians also hold use of DRGs responsible for restraining a wider acceptance of new technologies. Nevertheless, it should be noted that, in fact, no hospital can produce its actual costs per patient treated. This turns the discussion into an exchange of opinions, without any data to support the claim that national tariffs are lower than the true cost of hospital treatment.

In a health care system like the Portuguese, the fate of DRGs is politically dependent on two dimensions: the continuation of the system itself and its uses. Changes in the MoH might mean a questioning of the importance of the system and its results and perhaps the option of no system at all. Moreover, more important in terms of continuity of use of DRGs in Portugal would be a change in the current model of hospital resource allocation. It seems doubtful that hospitals would still feed data into the

Table 3.6 Average number of diagnosis and procedure codes per record, 1998–2003

Year	Average number of diagnosis codes	Average number of procedures codes
1998	2.05	2.25
1999	2.18	2.61
2000	2.41	3.51
2001	2.58	3.92
2002	2.67	4.12
2003	2.72	4.28

Source: National DRG Database – DDSFG/IGIF, 2004

system if their funding or charges to third-party payers was set without the use of DRGs.

Gazing at the crystal ball

The potential of the information collected for classifying discharges according to DRGs is impressive. Nevertheless, in Portugal it has remained unused except in three major fields: hospital funding, hospital comparisons, and setting of national tariffs for inpatient and ambulatory surgery care. It should be noted that there is no other database with morbidity information and treatment profiles of the Portuguese population.

More recently, two other uses for DRG-produced information have been instituted: setting prices to reimburse operating teams (physicians and nurses) for surgeries performed on patients on the waiting list and contracting production goals with hospitals based on past trends. However, in the author's opinion the methodological shortcomings of these extended uses of DRG information should prevent their continuation.

The author believes it would create added value for Portuguese health policy makers to use DRG information for the following additional purposes: to profile morbidity characteristics of the Portuguese population at national and regional levels; to organize provision of care according to need; to target areas for utilization review and quality assurance; and to control the achievement of goals set in existing national health plans for different pathologies. Furthermore, data collected in patients' registries could be used, as pointed out by Noe *et al.* (2005), to support health economics research in fields such as: identifying practice patterns and evaluating variations based on setting; examining regional differences; conducting population subgroup analyses; determining characteristics of high- and low-cost patients; and so on.

The creation of a database with enormous information potential is, in my opinion, one of the major strengths of the implementation of a patient classification system. Nevertheless, its use cannot ever be dissociated from the interests of the different key players in the field.

Patient classification systems, namely DRGs, empower decision makers and hospital managers to better understand hospitals' production and resource consumption at both the macro and micro level. At the same time, a common language to communicate to physicians is created. These features can lead to more successful establishment and monitoring of objectives and targets for the services and for the NHS itself.

New adopters should bear in mind the investment required to implement a patient classification system: groupers' licenses or development; training of personnel (physicians, nurses, hospital managers, coders, and others); consultancy; equipment; and so on. However, the expected benefits should greatly exceed the costs.

The Portuguese program is still limited to a single department of the MoH both in terms of technical knowledge and data use. The non-existence of willingness to divulge data, results and information contributes to preventing research and development in this area, to bad utilization of the system, and to the image of DRG use as a "black box."

In Portugal, the ongoing debate centered on how the gap between hospital costs and national tariffs can compromise the continuity of the system, particularly in places where increasing pressures on cost containment are foreseeable in the near future. It would be a major achievement to develop national cost weights, and a sample of representative hospitals should be sought. Nevertheless, it should be stressed that, after twenty years, the DRG system is still the single "*prêt-à-porter*" tool to characterize and cost hospital production.

NOTES

1. For financing goals, hospitals are usually grouped based on casemix indices, average hospital base rate, total costs, teaching status, and so on.
2. For further information see *Diagnostic Related Groups, Definitions Manual Version*, 3M HIS
3. For further information see *All Patient Diagnosis Related Groups Definitions Manual*, 3M HIS

REFERENCES

Assembleia da República. Lei 48/90: Lei de Bases da Saúde. *Diário República* 1990; 195: 3452–59.

Bentes, M. (1992). DRG-based funding in Portugal: Two years after. Proceedings of the Third EURODRG Workshop, May, Madrid, Spain.

Bentes M., Dias C. M., Sakellarides C., and Bankauskaite, V. (2004). *Health Care Systems in Transition: Portugal.* Copenhagen: WHO Regional Office for Europe on behalf of the European Observatory on Health Systems and Policies.

Bentes, M., Mateus, C., Estevens, S., Valente, M. C. and Veertres, J. (1996). Towards a more comprehensive financing system for the Portuguese NHS hospitals. Proceedings of the 12th International PCS/E Working Conference, September 19–21, Sydney, Australia.

Bentes, M., Urbano, J., Carvalho, C. and Tranquada, S. (1993). Using DRGs to Fund Hospitals in Portugal: An Evaluation of the Experience. In *Diagnosis Related Groups in Europe: Uses and Perspectives*, M. Casas and M. Wiley (eds.), Berlin: Springer-Verlag.

Bentes, M., Valente, M. C., Mateus, C., and Estevens, S. (1997). Feedback and Audit: Ingredients for Quality improvement. Proceedings of the 13th PCS/E International Working Conference, October 1–3, Florence, Italy.

Casas, M. and Wiley, M. (1993). *Diagnosis Related Groups in Europe: Uses and Perspectives,* Berlin: Springer-Verlag.

Dismuke, C. E. and Guimarães, P. (2002) Has the Caveat of Case-mix Based Payment Influenced the Quality of Inpatient Hospital Care in Portugal? *Applied Economics,* 34 (10): 1301–7.

Dismuke, C. E. and Sena, V. (2001). Is there a Trade-off between Quality and Productivity? The Case of Diagnostic Technologies in Portugal. *Annals of Operations Research,* Vol. 107, Issue 1–4: 101–16.

Kimberly, J. R., de Pouvourville, G., *et al.* (1993). Portugal: National Commitment and the Implementation of DRGs. In *The Migration of Managerial Innovation: Diagnosis-Related Groups and Health Care Administration in Western Europe*, J. R. Kimberly and G. de Pouvourville (eds.), San Francisco: Jossey-Bass.

Mateus, C. (2002). *O impacto dos grupos de diagnósticos homogéneos no financiamento hospitalar em Portugal entre 1995 e 2001* (The Impact of DRGs in the Funding of Portuguese Hospitals between 1995 and 2001).

Mateus, C. and Valente, M. C. (2000). The impact of ambulatory surgery DRGs. Proceedings of the 16th PCS/E International Working Conference, September 27–30, Groningen, The Netherlands.

Noe, L., Larson, L., and Trotter, J. (2005). Utilizing Patient Registries to Support Health Economics Research: Integrating Observational data with Economic Analyses, Models, and other Applications. *ISPOR Connections,* Vol. 11, No. 5: October 15.

OECD (1998). *OECD Economic Surveys 1997–1998, Portugal.* Paris: OECD.

OECD (2004). *OECD Health Data 2004.* Paris: OECD

Oliveira, M. D. and Pinto C. G. (2005). Health Care Reform in Portugal: An Evaluation of the NHS Experience. *Health Economics,* 14, S1: S203–S220.

Urbano, J., Bentes, M. and Vertrees, J. C. (1993). Portugal: National Commitment and the Implementation of DRGs. In *The Migration of Managerial Innovation: Diagnosis-Related Groups and Health Care Administration in Western Europe*, J. R. Kimberly and G. de Pouvourville (eds.), San Francisco: Jossey-Bass.

Valente, M. C., Estevens, S., Costa, C. T., Barardo, A. and Bentes, M. (1998). Portugal: On the Route to APGs. Proceedings of the 14th PCS/E International Working Conference, October 1–3, Manchester, UK.

4 From naïve hope to realistic conviction: DRGs in Sweden

Rikard Lindqvist

Introduction

Sweden, with about nine million inhabitants, has a decentralized public health care system. Three political and administrative levels – central government, county councils and local municipalities – are involved in financing, providing and evaluating health care activities. The central government has only a legislative supervisory role, while county councils and municipalities are responsible both for financing and providing health services (Figure 4.1). The county councils are entitled to collect direct income tax revenues as their major financial source, but they are also politically accountable through their directly elected political assemblies. The vast majority of Swedish hospitals are public, owned and financed by the county councils. Primary care settings are also financed by the county councils but they are both publicly and privately owned.

Swedish hospitals have traditionally been financed via global budgeting. This is due to the fact that Sweden has a tradition of publicly owned hospitals and that cost control has been an important issue. Moreover, before the introduction of DRGs, there was no accepted system in use to describe performance. The counties had poor knowledge of hospital activity and productivity. There was a great need to find ways to measure productivity.

In Sweden, DRGs have been used as a prospective payment system, to describe performance and increase the transparency of hospital activities, as an analyzing tool and to measure productivity. The tradition of collecting data at individual patient level is strong in Sweden; the National Discharge Register has been in use since the 1960s and contains all individual inpatient records. All data can be linked to the individual patient using the individual identification number given to every citizen at birth. The register has

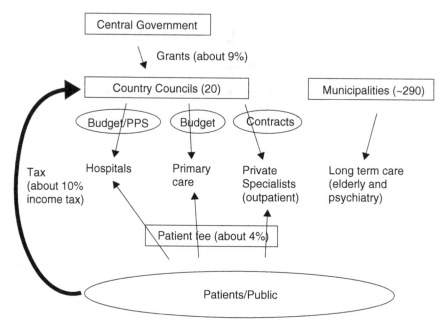

Figure 4.1   The Swedish health care model

traditionally been used for research purposes. Today the use of the register is increasing, to measure both productivity and various types of follow-up in health care.

During the early 1990s some county councils introduced quasi-market-oriented systems with prospective payment systems for hospital reimbursement. Others introduced DRGs later on and used them for other purposes.

Regardless of whether the counties introduced prospective payment systems, the county councils have been focusing on productivity in delivering health care services for the past fifteen years. A focus in the health care debate has been to maintain the same level of care, but with lower costs.

In 2002 Swedish health care expenditure per capita was a little above the Western European average but, unlike some other European countries, health care expenditure as a percentage of GDP has been relatively stable during the past ten years (around 9 percent). The overall MLOS in acute care is decreasing, but the number of discharges is relatively stable (Figure 4.2).

After having been much higher than in almost all other countries throughout the 1970s and 1980s, total health spending is now in line with other OECD countries (Figure 4.3).

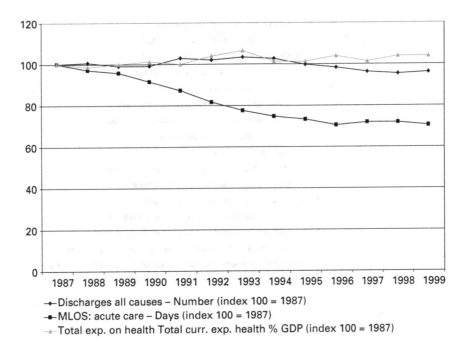

-◆-Discharges all causes – Number (index 100 = 1987)
-■-MLOS: acute care – Days (index 100 = 1987)
-▲-Total exp. on health Total curr. exp. health % GDP (index 100 = 1987)

Figure 4.2   Trends in MLOS, discharges, and health care expenditures in Sweden 1987–99
Source: OECD Health Data 2004

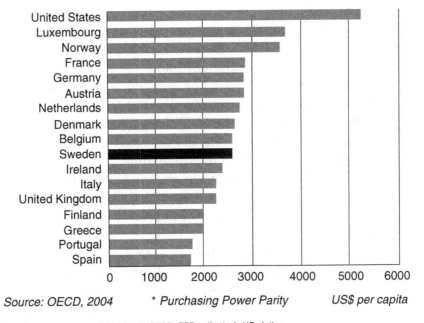

Source: OECD, 2004   * *Purchasing Power Parity*   *US$ per capita*

Figure 4.3   Health care costs per inhabitant, 2002, PPP-adjusted, US dollars

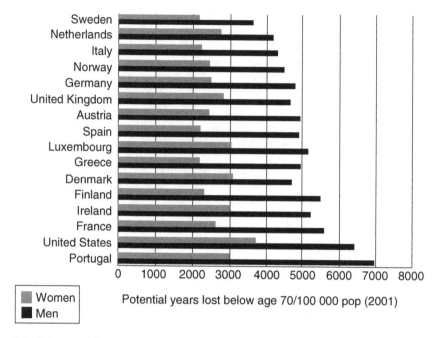

Figure 4.4   Potential years of life lost below age 70 per 100,000 inhabitants

Sweden's population is old but relatively healthy. Most indicators of health status have been well above average for several decades (see OECD Economic Surveys Sweden, June 2005).

Life expectancy is long, while medically avoidable deaths are relatively low for almost all disease groups (Figure 4.4).

The main problems in Swedish health care at present are access, productivity in primary care and care for the elderly, waiting times for elective surgery and the transition from hospital care to social care (especially for patients in mental health). Within the county there is also variability in costs, quality and medical practice – this needs to be leveled out. Another important field to improve is management systems in all sectors of health care.

The focus on productivity has changed toward a focus on efficiency, where productivity is one of several measurements. As the information systems in health care develop, the ability to compare results and quality has improved. Today, the focus is on the transparent comparisons of quality and efficiency between the counties.

DRGs in Sweden

The DRG system was introduced by the Swedish Institute for Health Services Development (Spri) in the mid-1980s with the main purpose of obtaining a tool for benchmarking and cost analyses. From the outset, the approach was quite academic and to a large extent oriented towards the physicians.

In 1991 DRGs came into use as a payment system for acute inpatient care in Stockholm county council, and two other large counties (Scania and Region of Västra Götaland) followed in the mid/late 1990s. The adoption and development of DRGs were the concern of the county councils. This background and a tradition of a high degree of local autonomy resulted in a situation where the central coordination on DRG issues in Sweden was relatively weak. This was particularly true when it came to financial questions; if or how DRGs are used for reimbursement was, and still is, a question for individual counties to deal with.

From a situation where the county councils did more or less all the development and adoption of DRGs in Sweden there was a change of direction in the late 1990s. County councils which had used DRGs for activity-based financing started to see a need for coordination, and began working together in informal networks. The discussion in these networks resulted in a formal request to the Ministry of Health and Social Affairs to constitute an organization for national coordination on DRG issues. The Centre for Patient Classification Systems (CPK) was established in 1999. This comprises the Federation of Swedish County Councils[1] (Landstingsförbundet) and the National Board of Health and Welfare (Socialstyrelsen) and has responsibility for developing and maintaining the Swedish version of NordDRG, the prevailing classification which was developed amongst Nordic countries. CPK does not have responsibility for reimbursement issues in the country; these issues are still the responsibility of the county councils and the regions.

The introduction of prospective payment systems based on DRGs

In the 1990s Swedish health care needed to save money and to move towards a more patient-oriented system. The motives for introducing prospective payment schemes have been first to increase productivity and

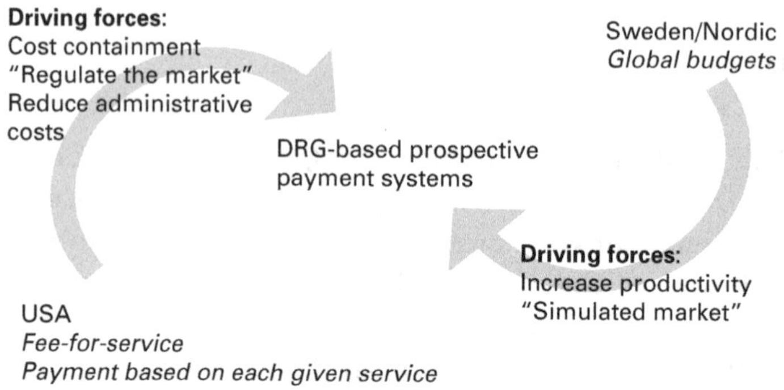

Figure 4.5   Different driving forces moving to a prospective payment system

thereby save, or make better use of, the money used for health care. Long waiting lists for elective surgery were another reason. A third important reason for introducing prospective payment systems was to introduce a "freedom of choice" for the patient, so as to allow her/him to select a hospital for treatment. The idea was that the patients were given freedom of choice. If reimbursement followed the patient, a degree of competition would be introduced among the hospitals in the counties. By providing good services and thereby attracting patients, the hospitals would gain higher revenues. There was also a need for better information and higher transparency in health care. The global budget did not encourage either productivity or patient-oriented care, therefore a move to an activity-based funding system was begun (see Figure 4.5).

In some counties the introduction of DRGs as a PPS (Prospective Payment System) was also introduced as a part of a provider–purchaser system with more clear responsibilities and shared financial risk (Figure 4.6).

However, some counties have not yet moved to a PPS system, both for political reasons (health care is not considered a market), and, most probably, because of the concern for cost control when strong incentives for productivity are introduced. These counties are quite small with few hospitals.

The introduction in Stockholm County Council – "Stockholmsmodellen"

The first county that introduced DRGs for reimbursement purposes was Stockholm County Council (which comprises about 1.5 million inhabitants) back in 1992. DRG as a tool for hospital financing was one of the

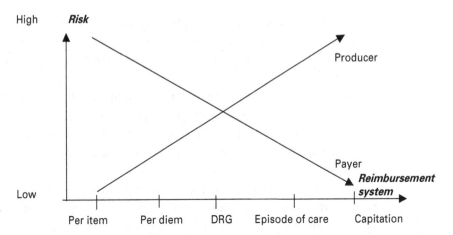

Figure 4.6   Financial risk for reimbursement systems

elements in what was called the "Stockholmsmodellen" (the Stockholm Model). The background of the model was a general opinion that the efficiency of the health care sector could be improved by regulated market mechanisms inspired, among others, by the reforms passed in Great Britain.

The concept of the Stockholm model included:

- *A purchaser/provider split.* Before the introduction of the reform, Greater Stockholm was divided into nine local health care districts with responsibility for providing health care, including the management of hospitals, for the residents in their geographic area. These local health districts were now changed to purchasing organizations with a small administrative staff and a political assembly. The districts received money from the central council and were responsible for paying for care provided to the residents. The districts were obliged to negotiate and come to agreements with the hospitals on prices and volumes of care. However, if no agreement was reached, a general pricing list was to be used based on actual cost for the specific care.
- *Economic allocation based on needs.* Before the introduction of the reform, the central council allocated resources to the hospitals, via the districts, by global budgets – basically, budgets based on the hospital's historical costs rather than the needs of the inhabitants. The change meant that money would be allocated to the districts using a socio-economic index based on the residents' socio-economic conditions. [1]
- *Hospital financing based on prospective payment.* From global budgets based in practice on a yearly adjustment, the change was quite dramatic – the model implied that all hospital services should be charged with a

fixed price both within the hospital (medical services etc.) and within districts. DRGs were chosen for reimbursement for somatic inpatient care, and for outpatient care, a "homemade" system called "KÖKS" was developed.

- *Freedom of choice for the patients.* Patients in Stockholm were traditionally treated in hospitals based on geographic catchment areas; after the introduction of the reform, the patients had the right to choose another hospital within the county, and the districts had to pay for the care.

In one way, the introduction was gradual; in the first year (1992) only four-and-a-half medical specialities were reimbursed by DRGs – general surgery, orthopaedics, gynaecology/obstetrics, urology and the cataract surgery in ophthalmology. The other hospital specialities followed in 1993.

In another way, the introduction was rapid. The planning and preparation phase was short, which meant that adaptations of the working practices, modification of computer systems as well as education and training were in many cases neglected to some extent. There was, however, a focus on involving department heads from all hospitals in regular meetings, where concerns and solutions were addressed.

The general opinion about the system among the political representatives was generally conservatively positive – all political parties from left to right approved of the introduction. Among the heads of the involved departments the discussion was full and frank, but the impression was that they accepted the change. Whether this acceptance was based on approval or in the absence of alternative solutions is difficult to assess, but one suggested explanation is that most of the heads of departments thought that the reimbursement by DRGs would generate more money for their departments.

As stated earlier, the introduction of DRGs was rapid and to some extent abrupt, from a situation with global budgets with yearly adjustments to a system where practically all resources to the hospitals were to be allocated by the prospective payment. There were some exceptions such as research and development, and education and training. But nevertheless the introduction has been described as a situation of "jumping into deep water and then learning to swim". As a consequence of this, many mistakes and misjudgments were made. For example, the outpatient registration/pricing system "KÖKS" was developed as a temporary solution designed to be used for one to two years and then to be replaced by something better. NordDRG has just replaced the system after more than ten years of use.

Initially, the risk-sharing between purchasers and providers was quite distorted: if the hospitals avoided agreements with the districts they could charge a price based on actual cost and work without volume restrictions. This naturally gave the hospitals almost all the control in the system. The large increase in production volumes following the introduction generated substantial deficits in district budgets during the early years. The deficits, combined with a general decrease in tax revenues due to the recession in the mid-1990s, led to a reaction in a totally opposite direction. The prices in 1998 were fixed at the level of the price of the hospital with the lowest cost, and fixed volumes were set for the hospitals. This just transferred the deficits back to the hospitals. A conservative conclusion is that during the 1990s, Stockholm Council County never got risk-sharing to work.

Other counties introduce prospective payment systems

In the mid-1990s, the regions of Västra Götaland and Scania (the second and third largest regions in Sweden) introduced prospective payment systems based on DRGs. Many of the concepts introduced in these regions were basically the same as in Stockholm, but there were some differences. The most substantial of these was the approach to the introduction. Both Västra Götaland and Scania used longer planning and preparation periods, and spent more time on educating staff and adapting computer systems. As in Stockholm the introduction was aiming at covering all hospitals and specialities but the level of reimbursement was more modest – starting with a mixed model with 10 to 50 percent of the hospital revenues based on DRGs and the rest on global budgets. The lower rate of prospective reimbursement had a more conservative impact, but gave much more scope for handling areas more difficult to reimburse through prospective payments, such as new drugs and innovative techniques.

The regions of Västra Götaland and Scania have claimed that when they introduced their systems, they developed a totally different and implicitly better model than Stockholm County Council. This is hard to recognize, when looking at the solutions. However, a more careful implementation, and (most likely) the ability to learn from Stockholm's mistakes, have been of great advantage for them.

Quality of care

In addition to DRGs there is a need for data on quality and results in health care services. In order to measure efficiency, quality data are essential. In Sweden there are at present about sixty quality registers of various size and depth. Some of the registers have been collecting data for more than twenty years and are vital tools in quality improvement work. The registers are mainly developed by clinically active professionals, and are focused on specified medical areas such as, for example, Riks-Stroke, the Swedish national quality register on stroke care [2], Swedish National Cataract Register [3] and Swedish National Total Hip Arthroplasty Register. [4]

Sweden also has national health data registers in which many performance indicators are available; for example, registers have been used for analysis of differences in case fatality within 28 days after acute myocardial infarction. [5] A lot of effort is now being made, both at national and local level, to find valid and accepted quality indicators to follow-up health care performance, in addition to productivity measurements. Some counties are already using models for performance indicators follow-up. During 2006, Sweden implemented national performance indicators to measure performance at county level on a yearly basis.

The current situation

Today, the counties in Sweden can be divided into two groups with regard to usage of DRGs. The first group uses DRGs for reimbursement to hospitals and covers a large extent of the care (both inpatient and to some extent outpatient). The five counties/regions are Stockholm County Council (since 1992) and the regions of Scania, Västra Götaland, Halland and Östergötland (since the mid/late 1990s). The County of Uppsala implemented NordDRG as a payment system for all hospitals in 2007. These six counties represent more then half of Swedish health care calculated on health care expenditures. Mental health care is not yet included in the counties' PPS, but some are planning to include this in coming years. In 2006, three counties also included the new outpatient groups in the NordDRG system in their PPS.

The second group of counties uses DRGs as a component in a reimbursement system for a smaller part of health care, for example for "cross-county border patients" or for one single hospital in the county.

All in all, more than 50 percent of all admissions in Swedish acute somatic inpatient care are reimbursed by NordDRG.

Long-term care and primary care are not covered by NordDRG. Global budget and/or capitation are used for these areas. Some counties are also paying primary care per visit. The income from patient fees is very low in Swedish health care – about 3–4 percent of the revenues.

As stated earlier – the counties decide themselves if and how they want to use the DRGs in their reimbursement systems, and what supplementary rules should be applied (e.g. reimbursement of outliers, cost ceilings, patient fees, etc.). All counties, with prospective payments systems based on DRGs, finance research and teaching separately and use some form of outliers' reimbursement either based on actual cost or bed days. Some counties use additional payments for very expensive drugs and services, but the trend is towards using cost outliers and/or a mixed model where expensive services are financed by block grants. Traditionally in Sweden, physicians who work in hospitals are employed on a fixed salary, therefore their costs are included in the reimbursement to the hospitals.

All counties working with PPS have some kind of mixed model in which a part of the hospital financing is with a global budget, another part is based on DRGs, and, in some cases, a third part is dependent on achieved goals such as, for example, quality improvement in specific areas. The level or percentage of coverage by DRGs based on reimbursement varies between counties, but also between different hospitals within the counties.

The counties are also responsible for the monitoring of fraud and other misuses of the system. The control over the supply of health care is also in the hands of the county councils. The most usual way to stop inappropriate activities has been to shorten supply.

Today only the common Nordic version of DRGs, NordDRG, is in use in Sweden. Other systems such as HCFA-DRG and AP-DRG have been used by some counties, but have now been abandoned in favour of NordDRG. The Nordic grouper was originally developed from HCFA-DRG (in 1995) and from this original clone, the system has been developed into a free-standing version of DRGs. The system is jointly developed by the Nordic countries and Estonia.

The first reason why a Nordic version of DRGs was developed was that there was a need to adjust the grouper to Nordic conditions (i.e. classification of diagnoses according to ICD–10 and classification of procedures according to NCSP (NOMESCO classification of surgical procedures, the common Nordic Surgical classification). The second and more important reason was the need to develop a DRG system that was fully transparent and in which the Nordic countries had a realistic possibility of influencing the development of the system.

NordDRG is currently in use nationwide in hospitals in Norway and in the majority of the regional health care administrations in Finland and Sweden. The system has also been introduced in Iceland and Estonia. Denmark has developed and uses a modified DRG system (DkDRG) originally based on NordDRG. In Denmark, DRG is used to finance all hospital activities, both in- and outpatients.

In Sweden, CPK (The Centre for Patient Classification Systems) is responsible for the Swedish version of the grouper, both for maintenance and development. The actual updating of the set of rules determining the DRGs (the logic of the system) is carried out by the Nordic centre.

CPK has done considerable development work within the NordDRG system during recent years. The system now includes a new grouping logic for mental health inpatient care and from 2006, all outpatient care (except primary care) is included in the system. All in all, the Swedish version of the NordDRG system 2007 comprises about 1,000 groups.

In Sweden there are two versions of NordDRG 2007. The full version can handle both inpatient care (including mental health care) and all outpatient care except for primary care. The classic version is for inpatient care only.

Before making a major change to NordDRG, the quality of the data where problems were reported should be checked. Obvious errors of primary coding and costs data should be excluded. The material has to be large enough for statistical analysis, and possible systemic bias has to be ruled out.

The development process of the NordDRG system includes all Nordic countries. All the changes in NordDRG are analyzed and discussed in the NordDRG expert group. The expert group suggests changes to the NordDRG steering group who make the final decision about changes to the system.

Changes in DRGs may be initiated by problems with either cost heterogeneity or clinical relevance, according to the basic idea of all DRG systems: patient cases are to be assigned to clinically relevant groups with the least possible variance in cost.

Main criteria for changes in NordDRG

- The change has relevance for the whole system and is supposed to be functional even in the future.
- The change is motivated either by a need for better clinical relevance, or by a need for better cost homogeneity, or both.
- If the change is motivated by the need for better cost homogeneity, it may not threaten clinical relevance.
- If the change is motivated by the need for better clinical relevance, it may not lead to reduced cost homogeneity.
- The change may not lead to an uncontrolled increase in the number of groups.

For all types of changes (splitting DRG, merging DRG, partial or total reassignment) specific statistical criteria must be evaluated with cost-per-case data from at least one of the Nordic countries. Changes can sometimes be made, even if not all criteria are met, but in those cases a clear rationale has to be put forward.

The CPK produces national cost weights for NordDRG (in- and outpatients) on a yearly basis. It is not mandatory to use the national weight-sets; local weights are also used in the counties. Most counties do use the national weights and it is an objective that in the future all counties will use the same weights. National cost weights are based on the national case-costing ("bottom-up" costing approach) database [6] which comprises 50 percent (in 2006) of all inpatients in Sweden. The work of collecting case-costing data for outpatient care has just started; four hospitals delivered case-costing data for outpatients for 2004.

Impact of prospective payment systems based on DRGs

First of all, the differences in adaptation of DRGs and PPS in the counties make it difficult to draw conclusive statements as to the benefits and drawbacks of the system.

Secondly, it is very hard to sort out the effects of the adoption of PPS from other changes in health care.

However, the common perception is that the prospective payment system increases hospitals' productivity. [7, 8] The system also gives better information for analysis and improvement and better quality in coding of diagnoses and procedures. [9] The use of DRGs has also helped to bridge the gap between the medical and economic/administrative sides of health care.

One of the largest problems of using PPS, at least from a Swedish perspective, has been the mechanisms of cost control. In the case of Stockholm County, productivity rose quite dramatically during the years following the introduction, but the increased production also led to higher total expenditures. To secure cost control, budget ceilings were introduced – which led to a reduction in the increased rate of productivity. Finding the balancing point between the urge to increase productivity and the need to control costs, given limited resources, has been the largest problem when introducing PPS.

There has also been a discussion about whether the increased productivity is merely an effect of "running faster", not from working more rationally. [10]

The reduction in length of stay over the last decade can be attributed to a number of factors, but it is probably also due to the use of DRGs. [11] Counties and hospitals that use DRGs tend to have shorter length of stay than others. Whether the present length of stay is too short or not is a question people will disagree about. Basically a shorter length of stay is preferable, but concerns have been raised that elderly people are sent back to their homes too early.

Compared with the 1990s, there is more knowledge, as well as more realistic expectations, concerning the use of NordDRG; this enables us to see the good and bad in the system, which has led to more acceptance of it. The enlargement of PPS to embrace both outpatient care and psychiatry is also important, especially in the light of the trend to move treatment to an outpatient setting.

To conclude, the most obvious benefits of the system are a rise in productivity, more transparency in the activity and performance of hospitals, the creation of a common "language" between professionals and administrators, a financing system that focuses on hospitals' activities instead of the organization as a "blackbox," a better description of performance, and a tool for benchmarking.

Lessons learned

DRGs are not a "miracle cure"

The most important experience of working with DRGs and PPS is that the introduction of prospective payment systems doesn't solve all the problems facing health care. When PPS was introduced in some counties back in the early 1990s, PPS was thought of as a "miracle cure." Those few who were opposed to the transformation, saw the change as the end of the Swedish health care model as they knew it. [12] Both of these expectations were proved wrong. Other political decisions and changes, economic conditions and the general public's expectations have had more impact on health care than the introduction of prospective payment systems.

A casemix reimbursement system improves productivity

It's basically quite simple – when a founding system based on recorded activity is introduced, activity increases or, to be more explicit, recorded activity increases. The first problem is to determine if the increase is an effect of better/changed recording or an actual increase in volume. The experience in Sweden, especially in the outpatient care setting (where there was no tradition of good recording) is that the initial increase seen after the introduction of PPS was to a large extent due to changes in recording. However, the number of inpatient admissions also increased, and this effect is better documented since the medical recording of admissions was of good quality in Sweden.

The next question is whether the desired growth in productivity should be generated by increased volume with capped expenditures, or stable volume with decreasing unitary costs. Regardless of which way one goes, the incentive structure has to be well thought-out, clear and understandable.

The productivity incentive has to be balanced by mechanisms for cost containment

As mentioned earlier, the balance between strong incentives for an increase in production and containment of total expenditures has to be recognized. In a situation where, as in Sweden, most health care is financed by tax, the resources are basically limited. When changing from a system with a high level of expenditure control, as in the Swedish traditional budget system, to a system with more focus on production, the effects can be faster and more extreme than imagined. This can, as in the case of Stockholm County Council during the 1990s, lead to drastic and ill-considered actions that result in negative effects and a general distrust of the system.

Good information systems and good data are crucial

When shifting to a system where clinical data are the basis for reimbursement, the importance of data and information systems increases. In Sweden the tradition of collecting clinical data and the use of the personal identi-fication number has been useful, but a new information system for follow-up and analysis had to be developed. This development was regrettably slow when it came to tools for analyzing production at hospital and department level. This was quite ironic, considering that the responsibility for a hospital's economy was to a large extent moved to the department heads.

The data quality has also to be considered. In spite of a long tradition of data collection, the quality of data was poorly analyzed. This needed work to improve the quality of basic clinical data.

The focus has to change from the technical aspects to the incentive structure

It is striking how every newcomer in the DRG family tends to focus on the technical aspects of the systems. The preparation phase and first years of use are often characterized by endless discussions of technical details. These discussions are to some extent essential, but there is a great risk of losing the focus on what the system should achieve, which problems are to be solved and which goals are to be reached. The solution, a prospective payment by DRG, is secondary to the goal of getting more and better health care at a constant or lower cost.

Reflect before developing a national grouper

It is hard to have a general opinion about whether or not it is worth the effort to develop our own version of a DRG grouper. Our experience is that there are many benefits to having our own system, such as transparency and influence on the development of the system. But it is also hard work to establish a grouper, and this continues with the maintenance and devel-opment of the system. The Nordic collaboration has been crucial for a small country, with an obscure national language, such as Sweden.

The future of DRGs in Sweden

If the trend in the 1990s was mainly to implement PPS in Sweden, in the 2000s, the picture of the reimbursement systems is somewhat different. Today it is recognized that there are many ways to reimburse hospitals, as is the fact that all these methods have good and bad impacts on the health care system.

| Payment by results / achieved goals |
| Prospective payment systems
Retrospective payment |
| Global budget / Capitation |
| Other grants (R&D, education, etc.) |

Figure 4.7   The new reimbursement system in several counties in Sweden

Today's trend is therefore to use a combination of several methods, for example (see Figure 4.7):

- global budget / capitation;
- retrospective payment;
- prospective payment;
- payment by results / achieved goals.

The intention is to find the right combination of reimbursement methods to balance the good and the bad from each method.

Another trend in Sweden is "going back to the basic data quality." More efforts are being directed towards correct registration and regular revisions of coding. One key question concerns the access to, and quality of, data. Working with prospective payment systems based on DRG means working with core health care data, and the performance of the systems is heavily dependent on the quality of the basic data. To implement the systems we need access to individual patient data, both to reimburse and to assess performance in a more accurate way.

Technical appendix

NordDRG

The NordDRG groupers are owned and developed by the national health care authorities in the Nordic countries (Denmark, Finland, Sweden, Norway and Iceland). The collaboration also includes Estonia as a partner.

The groupers are updated on a yearly basis and six versions are produced, one "common" Nordic version and one (or two) versions for each country in the consortium. The Danish version of NordDRG is not used in Denmark for reimbursement – the Danes are using their own grouper called DkDRG originally based on the NordDRG framework.

The common version of NordDRG covers all inpatient care including psychiatric care and day surgery. From 2006, the Swedish version of NordDRG also includes groups for ambulatory care. The system has a total of 929 groups of which 527 are inpatient care, 170 are day surgery and 170 ambulatory care.

Coding systems used in Sweden

The Nordic countries have a long tradition of collaborating on classification systems – manifested in the Nordic Centre for Classifications in Health Care (WHO collaborating centre). The Nordic countries are collaborating on the basic classifications but are also forced to obtain national versions of the classifications on account of the national languages.

For coding diagnosis the Nordic countries are using a national version of ICD–10 and for surgery procedures the common Nordic classification of surgery is used (NCSP). In Sweden a new national system for non-surgical procedures was introduced in 2006 (KVÅ).

Cost weight

Cost weights in Sweden are based on cost-per-case data collected from the hospitals which have systems for cost-per-case calculation. National guidelines have been developed for cost-per-case calculations and the database, collected on a yearly basis, now consists of about 50 percent of all admissions in Swedish health care. National weights are calculated and published on a yearly basis.

The full NordDRG grouping logic is available online in English at: http://www.nordclass.uu.se/

NOTES

1. Since 1 January 2005 the name has been changed to Swedish Association of Local Authorities and Regions

REFERENCES

[1] Diderichsen, F., Varde, E., Whitehead, M. (1997). Resource Allocation to Health Authorities: The Quest for an Equitable Formula in Britain and Sweden. *BMJ* 315 (7112): 875–8.

[2] Asplund, K., Hulter Asberg, K., Norrving, B., Stegmayr, B., Terént, A., Wester, P. O. (2003). Riks-stroke – A Swedish National Quality Register for Stroke Care. *Cerebrovasc Dis* 15 Suppl. 1: 5–7.

[3] Håkansson, I., Lundström, M., Stenevi, U., Ehinger, B. (2001). Data Reliability and Structure in the Swedish National Cataract Register. *Acta Ophthalmol Scand* 79(5): 518–23.

[4] Söderman, P. (2000). On the Validity of the Results from the Swedish National Total Hip Arthroplasty Register. *Acta Orthop Scand Suppl* 71(296): 1–33.

[5] Köster, M., Andersson, J., Carling, K., Rosén, M. (2003) [Mortality after Myocardial Infarction Has Decreased in Nearly all Swedish Counties during the 1990s. Greatest Improvement Seen in those Counties with the Worst Initial Results]. *Lakartidningen* 100(37): 2838–44.

[6] Heurgren, M., Nilsson, H., Erlö, C., Sjöli, P. (2003) [What Does the Individual Patient Cost? CPP – the Cost Per Patient Method – Is the Answer]. *Lakartidningen* 100(42): 3312–5.

[7] Quaye, R. K. (2001). Internal Market Systems in Sweden: Seven Years after the Stockholm Model. *Eur J Public Health* 11(4): 380–5.

[8] Charpentier, C., Samuelson, L. A. (1999) [*Impact of a Health Care Reform – A Study of the Stockholm Model*] *Effekter av en sjukvårdsreform – En analys av Stockholmsmodellen.* Stockholm: Nerenius & Santérus Förlag AB.

[9] Serdén, L., Lindqvist, R., Rosén, M. (2003). Have DRG-based Prospective Payment Systems Influenced the Number of Secondary Diagnoses in Health Care Administrative Data? *Health Policy* 65(2): 101–7.

[10] Forsberg, E. (2001). *Do Financial Incentives Make a Difference?* Uppsala: Acta Universitatis Upsaliensis.

[11] Lindqvist, R., Möller, T. R., Stenbeck, M., Diderichsen, F. (2002). Do Changes in Surgical Procedures for Breast Cancer have Consequences for Hospital Mean Length of Stay? A Study of Women Operated on for Breast Cancer in Sweden, 1980–95. *International Journal of Technology Assessment in Health Care* 18(3): 566–75.

[12] Diderichsen, F. (1993). Market Reforms in Swedish Health Care: A Threat to or Salvation for the Universalistic Welfare State? *International Journal of Health Services* 23 (1): 185–8.

5 Casemix in Denmark

Annette Søberg Roed and Hanne Sjuneson

1. The Danish health care system

The Danish health care system is characterized by free and equal access to health care services. This principle has the same high priority regardless of the party in office. Free and equal access to health care services and universal coverage go hand in hand with a strong determination to control costs. Within the last fifteen years, the freedom to select the hospital of one's choice has also become a very important part of the health care system.

The health care system in Denmark is mainly publicly financed through taxes,[1] and is decentralized, with three administrative levels: state, county and municipality.[2] The state's task in health care provision is, first and foremost, to initiate, coordinate, advise, and legislate. The counties are responsible for providing health care services within the limits set by the state.[3] The municipalities are responsible for district nursing, public health care, school health care, and child dental treatment.

The provision of health care services by municipalities and counties is negotiated every year in the national budget negotiation. The budget negotiation takes place between the government on the one hand, and the Danish regions[4] (counties) and Local Government Denmark[5] (LGDK) on the other. Agreements are typically in the form of recommendations for local and country tax rates and agreements on injecting capital into specific health care areas or projects, such as cancer treatment or waiting times. Introduction of activity-based financing has also been agreed on in budget negotiations. Although the agreement is not legally binding, in practice there are few examples of significant tax increases beyond the agreed level, and the state government can, in principle, sanction county and municipality behavior by withholding block grants and extraordinary grants.

Table 5.1 Key health care figures for Denmark, 2003

Population			5,385,507
% of population over 67			12
% of population over 80			4
Life expectancy			
Male (2004)			75.2
Female (2004)			79.9
% of GDP spent on health care			7.0
	1999	**2001**	**2003**
Activity			
Number of acute-care hospitals	69	60	57
Number of acute-care beds (measured in 1,000)	18.8	18.2	17.5
Number of discharges (measured in 1,000)	1,023	1,037	1,083
Number of bed-days (measured in 1,000)	5,763	5,630	5,375
Average length of stay (days)	5.6	5.4	5.0
Number of outpatient visits (measured in 1,000)	4,388	4,663	5,314
Types of services	(in million DKK)		
Hospitals (public)	53,106	55,511	58,389
Primary sector	12,587	14,187	16,120

Source: Indenrigs- og Sundhedsministeriet (2005), pp. 2, 14, 25, 53 and www.statistikbanken. dk, October 31, 2005.

The counties are responsible both for primary sector and hospital sector care. The primary sector deals with general health problems and its services are available to all. This sector can be divided into two parts. One chiefly deals with treatment and care, which includes general practitioners (GPs),[6] practicing specialists, practicing dentists, physiotherapists, etc. (the practicing sector) and district nursing; the other is predominantly preventive, and deals with preventive health schemes, health care and child dental care.

When seeking medical treatment, the population first comes into contact with primary health care. General practitioners act as "gatekeepers" with regard to hospital and specialist treatment. The hospital sector deals with medical conditions that require more specialized treatment, equipment, and intensive care.

In 2003, the total costs of the Danish health sector were 98 billion DKK, which accounted for 7 percent of GDP. Of the total health costs, public expenditures accounted for 82 percent, and private expenditures for 18 percent. The total public expenditures in the health care sector are distributed, with 1.6 percent, 88.5 percent and 9.8 percent, respectively, for state, counties and municipalities (Table 5.2).

Table 5.2 The political and administrative level, assignment and expenditure 2003

Level	Assignment	2003 (in million DKK)
State	Legislation	1.294
Parliament	Coordinate	
Minister of Interior and Health	Surveillance	
National Board of Health		
Counties	Hospitals	70.444
13 counties	Primary health care	
Copenhagen	Hospital prevention	
Corporation		
Municipalities	Nursing homes and district nursing	7.837
271 municipalities	Child dental treatment	
Public expenditure		**79.575**

Source: Indenrigs- og Sundhedsministeriet (2005), p. 2

Both counties and municipalities collect local taxes. The tax revenue is equalized between counties and municipalities based on objective criteria. Approximately 80 percent of county-based health care is tax financed, whereas in the municipalities, 50 percent of health services are tax financed and 50 percent are state-grant financed. The taxes collected by the state are transferred to the counties through block grants according to objective criteria, which, among other things, includes demography.

Private hospital care is limited, providing only about 2 percent of all hospital service, whereas public hospitals provide around 98 percent. Also, the number of private hospital beds is only 0.1% of the total number of hospital beds. Even though the volume of the private hospital sector is very small, it has an important role in promoting competition within the hospital sector; patients' free choice between public and private hospitals puts pressure on public hospitals to provide timely and high-quality service.

2. The introduction of casemix systems

Denmark has a long tradition of registering all activity, in both the hospital sector and primary health care. The National Patient Registry contains data for inpatients from 1977 onward. Outpatient activity has been included in the register since 1995. All patients can be identified by social security numbers.

Technically, the conditions for introducing casemix systems have therefore been available at a very early stage. During the late 1980s and early 1990s, a few pilot studies using casemix methods were carried out. However, these studies led the Danish regions, among others, to conclude that it was not worthwhile to introduce a casemix system in Denmark.

The introduction of casemix systems in Denmark was later initiated and carried out by a small group of persons employed by the Ministry of Finance and the Ministry of Health. In 1994, a white book from the Commission on Hospital Economy was published. On the initiative of Deputy Permanent Secretary Jørgen Lotz from the Ministry of Finance, the report suggested that casemix methodology should be tested thoroughly on Danish hospital data (on somatic treatment). Deputy Permanent Secretary Karin Kristensen from the Ministry of Health had a major role in the introduction of a casemix system in Denmark. However, Head of Division Poul Erik Hansen from the Ministry of Health (renamed the National Board of Health in 2002) is the person who has had the greatest single influence on the introduction and use of DRGs in Denmark.

Hansen has a degree in economics, and prior to his employment in the Ministry of Health, he worked for Statistics Denmark and at the Danish School of Public Administration. For a longer period, he has also been an associate professor at the University of Copenhagen. Hansen took part in the initial work on DRGs, together with Kristensen, and has carried through the development of a Danish casemix system and a Danish cost database. Within the process of introducing DRGs in Denmark, Hansen has primarily had the role of innovator. He has a strong ability to identify the potential of the system and to predict the initiatives needed to develop it.

The successful introduction of DRGs in Denmark was due to a combination of political will, personal relations, and hard work. Political will was the primary condition. The political will has, among other things, expressed itself through the decision to use DRGs for distributing a special government fund. However, delivery of county data to the Danish cost database has never been politically mandated. The DRG system was developed strictly on a voluntary basis. Also, counties are not obliged to use the DRG system in their local activity-based financing models. The calculation of reliable DRG rates is therefore dependent on voluntary participation by all Danish counties and hospitals. For this reason, both personal relations and hard work were other important conditions for the successful introduction of DRGs in Denmark. The use of DRGs can only be successful if counties feel that they benefit from participating in the development of the system. Hansen has managed to find the balance between these conditions, and has, on this basis, been successful in developing the Danish DRG system.

Productivity

Following the Commission on Hospital Economy's 1994 white book, the Ministry of Health set up a committee, led by Kristensen, to test the casemix methodology by conducting a productivity analysis based on casemix. The Danish counties were not very enthusiastic about participating in this test. However, it was agreed that an initial analysis would be performed in the county of Northern Jutland. The committee found that, among casemix systems, DRG systems were the most promising. The first productivity analysis was therefore based on the DRG system used in the Nordic countries (NordDRG). A productivity analysis of Northern Jutland hospitals, based on DRGs, was published in August 1995. When presented in North Jutland by Kristensen and Hansen, the productivity report was quite well received by politicians, administrative staff, and clinicians. This was due partly to the fact that the DRG project was backed up by the local management, and partly because all relevant parties' administrators, clinicians, etc. participated in the project.

After the first pilot study in North Jutland, a productivity analysis was carried out on all Danish hospitals, resulting in a report published by the Casemix Commission in November 1996. In Denmark, this was the first public productivity analysis at hospital level based on DRGs. Despite the fact that the first report by the commission was well received, and that counties, clinical and administrative staff had participated in the commission, the second report was not well received. The benchmark led to considerable debate and criticism of the casemix methods. The administrative staff stated that the analysis was not valid because it used cost weights from Norway. On the other hand, the clinical staff stated that the Nordic grouping (NordDRG) did not reflect Danish clinical practice. After the publication of the benchmark, casemix methodology was established as an option for measuring hospital output in the Danish hospital environment. However, due to the criticism of the casemix method, very few analyses on productivity were made publicly available before 2005.

NordDRG ⇒ DkDRG

As a result of the debate on the validity of the Nordic DRG system for Danish data, the Ministry of Health undertook two initiatives. First, the ministry asked the DSI (Danish Institute for Health Services Research) to examine the possibilities for calculating Danish cost weights. These initial Danish cost weights were based on cost studies at three Danish hospitals.

In 1997, the Ministry of Health conducted two pilot projects on clinical validation and concluded that it was necessary to make modifications to NordDRG. Therefore, it was recommended that the clinical validation of DRG groups should cover all clinical specialties (Status for udvikling af DRG-metoden 2000–2001: kap. 5). From 1998 to 2001, the Ministry of Health carried out a clinical validation of NordDRG in cooperation with physicians from the scientific specialty societies. In the clinical validation, three demands were made on the new Danish DRG groups. First, DRG groups should be clinically meaningful. Second, DRG groups should be resource-homogeneous, meaning that the cost of treating patients within a DRG group should be approximately the same. Third, there should not be too many groups, to keep the system as simple as possible. The new system, called DkDRG, was implemented from January 1, 2002.

Since 2002, a new clinical validation has taken place every year between the National Board of Health and the scientific specialty societies (Takstvejledning 2005: 44). A casemix system for ambulatory care, called the Danish outpatient grouping system (DAGS), was also implemented in 2002. The DAGS groups have been developed to reflect treatment costs, hence clinical practice is only taken into consideration in a secondary sense. The American Ambulatory Patient Group-system (APG) inspired DAGS (hospital funding and casemix).

The first cost studies were made by DSI at three hospitals in 2000, and in 2004, the Danish cost database was extended to all public hospitals, and to both stationary and ambulatory patients.

DRG as a means of payment

Until 1993, Danish patients only had the right to receive hospital treatment at the particular hospital in their home county to which their family doctor referred them.[7] In 1993, however, a new law gave somatic patients the right to use a referral from their family doctor to receive basic-level treatment at any public hospital they chose. The new law was a reaction to pressure by the public and the media. For instance, some patients had been unable to receive treatment at a hospital close to their relatives if this meant that treatment had to be delivered outside the home county.

Specialized hospital departments were, in the beginning, exempt from the new law, but since 2003 they too have been included. With the new law, a flow of cross-county free-choice patients began. In the first years, the inter-county payments[8] of these patients took place without any interference from the central government or Parliament.

In 1995, the Ministry of Health set up a Hospital Commission that was to examine the organization of Danish hospitals and, among other things, evaluate whether a change in structure or a better use of resources could reduce waiting times. The creation of the Hospital Commission was due to a political agreement between the social democratic government and the conservative party. In the report from the commission, which was published in January 1997, it was recommended that the payment for cross-county free-choice patients should be based on diagnosis-related rate per treatment instead of rates per bed-day. It was also recommend that the rate for highly specialized treatment should be calculated for total treatments and not on a fee-per-service basis.

In December 1996, the Copenhagen Hospital Corporation submitted an application to the Ministry of Health to examine the differences in the rates used for highly specialized treatments. Following this application and the recommendations by the Hospital Commission, the Ministry of Health constituted a Patient Charge Commission. Kristensen and Hansen, respectively, chaired the commission and the two related working groups.

In January 1998, the Patient Charge Commission published a report on the payment structure for Danish patients. The report showed a confused payment structure: inside the same specialty, some hospitals charged patient bed-day prices that were ten times higher than bed-day prices at other hospitals with comparable functions. On top of these payment differences, the hospitals charged different amounts for special services, making the overall patient payment structure quite confused. As a consequence, the report by the Patient Charge Commission suggested that a casemix payment system should be used for cross-county free-choice patients. This recommendation was realized in the parliamentary compromise in the national budget of 1999, where it was decided that casemix would constitute the new payment structure for cross-county free-choice patients by the year 2000. This decision was reinforced in the 2000 economic agreement between the Danish regions and the state government.

The DRG system established in 2000 was based on the Danish cost-weights from the DSI cost study while the grouping was still based on the NordDRG.

The Danish counties were at this point still in opposition to the use of a DRG system. The introduction of DRGs as a means of payment was therefore exclusively a government decision. To comply with a wish from the counties, it was agreed in the 2000 budget negotiation that the payment for cross-county patients should be settled with a 100 percent DRG rate (as opposed to a rate below 100 percent).

Currently, payment for cross-county patients is still 100 percent of the DRG rate, even though marginal patients can, in most cases, be treated at a lower cost.[9] Financing at 100 percent of the DRG rate gives the counties incentives to try to attract patients from other counties and, at the same time, provide a sufficiently high service that their own patients do not choose hospitals in other counties. Choice of hospital, together with DRG financing, has therefore introduced new incentives in the provision of health care services. It is difficult for counties to agree on lowering the rate for cross-county patients because, in every case, there will be both a winner and a loser, depending on who treats the most patients from outside the county.

Hospital choice has also influenced the counties' ability to control total expenditure. The home county pays for the hospital treatment of its own residents, regardless of whether the patient utilizes cross-county hospital choice. Increased waiting times can therefore no longer be used to control costs. At the same time, the total budget restraint, which is negotiated annually between the national government and the regions, is quite tight.

The 2000 economic agreement for the counties also introduced the so-called 90/10 model. In this new budget structure, 10 percent of counties' hospital funding was to be dependent on activity measures such as DRG. Due to problems some counties experienced in upgrading their IT qualifications to casemix funding, counties were given the option to use activity-based measures other than casemix in the 90/10 model. However, a number of counties and the Copenhagen Hospital Corporation decided to implement the 90/10 model on a casemix basis. One county even chose to base its hospital contracts on an 80/20 basis.

In March 2002, the 90/10 model was evaluated in a report[10] by the Ministry of Interior and Health. The evaluation showed that the use of activity-based funding in 2000 and 2001 for patients treated at hospitals in their home county was modest, with only 1.3 percent of the counties' hospital costs activity-based. If the costs of cross-county free-choice patients, together with the costs of highly specialized hospital treatments, were included, then the share of activity-based financing increased to 15 percent in both 2000 and 2001. Many counties chose to target their 90/10 model at delimited areas and on a marginal funding principle (Evaluering 2005: 40). This explains the relatively limited share of activity-based financing for the counties' own patients.

3. The situation in 2006

In Denmark, casemix was originally introduced as a tool for hospital productivity analysis. The DRG system was first used for financing purposes for cross-county free-choice patients and (in some counties) for implementation of the 90/10 model. Until the introduction of the 90/10 model, hospitals were managed through framework management / block grants combined with contract management, in which the hospital and department received a grant in each budget period that could not be exceeded. Within the given appropriation, the hospital should deliver the politically agreed activity. By introducing the intra-country payment system and the 90/10 model, block grants were combined with activity-based financing. An evaluation of the 90/10 model showed that it did not create the necessary incentives to increase efficiency and minimize waiting lists.

Waiting time for hospital treatment has been a very important political issue during the 1990s. A number of different initiatives have been introduced to bring down waiting times. Among other things, health care sector grants were increased and experiments with waiting time guarantees for different groups of patients were carried out. None of the initiatives had the desired effect.

The November 2001 election led to a change of government. The new government introduced two new initiatives in 2002: an activity-based government pool and extended hospital choice. The purpose of these initiatives was to increase efficiency and minimize waiting lists by creating a direct connection between activity and financing. To further strengthen this connection, it was agreed in budget negotiations between the state government and the regions that, from 2004, a minimum of 20 percent of hospital financing should be activity based. Figure 5.1 illustrates the development of activity-based financing over the last two decades.

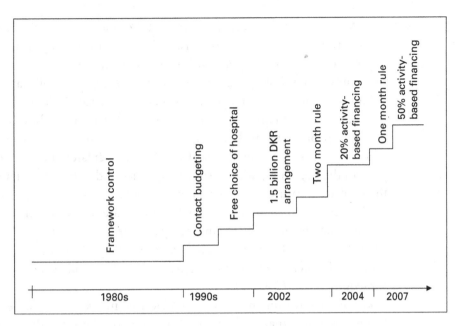

Figure 5.1   The development of activity-based financing in the Danish health care sector

Hospital choice and the activity-based pool

Since January 1, 1993, citizens in need of hospital care have been able to choose freely among all public hospitals that offer basic treatment. From July 1, 2002, patients have had the opportunity to choose among private hospitals or clinics in Denmark (this is conditional on the private hospital having an agreement with the Danish regions for offering treatment) or abroad if the waiting time for treatment at a public hospital exceeds two months.

Extended hospital choice has increased the pressure on public hospitals and counties. If the counties do not treat patients themselves within two months, they risk having to pay a higher price for treatment at a private hospital or a hospital outside the county. The rates for treatment at private hospitals are negotiated annually between the hospitals and the Danish regions. The starting point for these negotiations is the DRG rates. In 2006, the private hospitals and Danish regions were not able to agree on rates, so they were determined by the Minister of Health.

Patient awareness of hospital choice has increased since the introduction of extended free-choice hospitals. Within the first three years after its introduction, 62,000 patients had used extended free choice.

As noted above, in 2002 the government put aside 1.5 billion DKK for an activity-based pool,[11] with the purpose of strengthening county and county hospital incentives to decrease waiting time, increase responsiveness and competition among public hospitals, and at the same time, give a larger role to private providers. The activity-based pool amounts to 1–2 percent of total public hospital costs. The funds in the pool are allocated to the counties when they produce more hospital services than their baseline production.[12] The baseline production is calculated on the basis of activity in the previous year, including a productivity demand of 1.5 percent for each county. The National Board of Health calculates the baseline every year. In the beginning of the year, the counties' individual drawing rights to the pool are measured utilizing a demographic key. Money is paid from the pool when a real increase in activity above baseline is documented. As a ground rule, the departments that carry out the extra activity are considered when the hospital's share of the activity-based pool is distributed. More funds for financing activity above baseline have been put aside in each of the subsequent years (2003–6).

When the government pool was introduced in 2002, it was agreed by the Danish regions that county level production beyond the predefined baseline should be rewarded with 100 percent of the DRG/DAGS value. This implies that a county would receive 100 percent of the DRG value when county production exceeded its predefined baseline level. In 2003, the share of the DRG/DAGS value was reduced to 80 percent. Since 2004, the share of the DRG/DAGS value that is reimbursed has been reduced to 70 percent.

There was an immediate and very significant effect on activity after the introduction of the government pool. Among other reasons, this was probably due to the fact that the initial reimbursement rate was somewhat higher than the cost of marginal production. The current reimbursement rate is seen as an estimate of the marginal DRG rate. The government pool finances marginal production costs, so the reimbursement rate need not cover all fixed costs etc.

It is important to note that the government pool was and continues to be a fixed sum of money, meaning that control of total costs is not compromised from a government point of view. If counties are not able to control production within the limits set by the government pool, the counties assume all economic risk. Also due to limits set in the annual budget negotiations between the government and Danish regions, the counties are not free to raise taxes to cover deficits.

The introduction of the government pool contributed to changing the counties' attitude toward the DRG system. This was partly due to the fact that the government pool gave the hospitals a real possibility to increase activity with a (more than) sufficient coverage of the costs. The government pool introduced new money into the system. However, the calculation of the baseline production is a persistent source of discussion between the counties, on the one hand, and the Ministry of Health and National Board of Health, on the other.

The initial acceptance of the DRG system was also largely due to the fact that the government pool was introduced at the same time as the first version of the Danish DRG system. As mentioned above, both clinical and administrative staff from the counties participated in the development of this system, which was based on a Danish cost database and adapted to Danish clinical practice.

Information systems

To provide the counties with information on the activity-based pool, the National Board of Health has developed an Internet-based information system called "eSundhed" (eHealth). eSundhed contains data on county activity and productivity, and builds mainly on DRG-grouped data from the National Patient Registry.[13] All Danish hospitals register activities and report to the National Board of Health online each night. By the very next day, the hospitals have a calculated production value (production and DRG-production value) returned to them through eSundhed.

Once a month the counties receive an overview that shows activity compared to baseline in relation to the activity-based pool. The time lag of these estimates of earnings from the government pool is approximately three months. The hospital activity calculations are controlled for large increases in the registered value per contract (creep). eSundhed helps hospitals control their budgets by supplying updated, real-time information regarding relevant activities, resources and financial data.

Access to eSundhed is restricted to county and hospital staff who use eSundhed data for their daily work. Administration of eSundhed access is decentralized and is managed by the counties.

In order to support hospital choice, a list of waiting times has been published on the Internet by the National Board of Health since 2002. The information on waiting times is supplemented by information on the number of operations, average length of stay, quality indicators, etc. The publicly available information on the Internet enables patients to compare different hospitals' achievements, and is also expected to increase technical efficiency.

Activity-based financing

In the economic agreement between the government and Danish regions for 2004, it was agreed that the deployment of activity-based financing should be gradually increased. Since 2004, each county has been required to settle a minimum of 20 percent of hospital grants based on actual activity. The share of activity-based financing is measured as the relation between the value of activity-based financing and total DRG production value (total revenue). The increased use of activity-based financing was initiated by the government for the purpose of increasing activity and productivity by creating an economic incentive for efficient service provision. The main concern by the government and the Ministry of Finance in particular was that the increased use of activity-based financing would make it difficult for counties to control total costs.

It is at the discretion of the counties to settle payments with the hospitals and to decide on the specific models used. It is also the responsibility of the counties to set tariffs by which hospitals are paid. All counties have chosen to use the Danish casemix system (DkDRG) as a point of reference in setting tariffs.

According to the economic agreement, the counties' models for activity-based financing should take the following objectives into consideration: (1) high level of activity and short waiting times, (2) high degree of control of public spending, (3) high productivity, and (4) high quality patient treatment.

Activity-based financing must be supplemented by a number of other instruments, such as monitoring quality of care, monitoring health services referrals, etc.

The models of activity-based financing should comply with the following principles:
- Somatic treatment areas should be covered.
- The tariffs should be determined starting from a valuation of the underlying structures of expense and from the priorities of the activity etc.
- The payment should, at a minimum, cover expenses that are directly related to patient treatment (e.g. medicine).
- The models should be transparent, robust, and fair, for example, through visible consequences for the hospitals if the productivity or activity deviates from the defined requirements.
- Payments for treatment of patients outside their county of residence are settled between the counties in such a way that payments for hospitals are independent of patient's residence.
- Activity-based financing must be supported by enhanced managerial discretion at hospital, department, and department level.
- The hospital management should, to an appropriate extent, fund the performing department by activity, in order to strengthen the incentive for effective provision of service.

As a by-product of the increased transparency regarding hospital productivity, emphasis should be placed on a more systematic dissemination of best practice in terms of efficient service provision across counties.

As mentioned earlier, each county is free to form its own model of activity-based financing within the guidelines described by the economic agreement between the government and Danish regions.

The different parameters that can be adjusted are mainly:
- Activity-based financing can start from the first patient or only above a certain level of activity.
- Different tariffs can be applied for different levels of activity.
- Differentiated tariffs can be applied, meaning that certain fields of action, determined by speciality or DRG-group, etc. are given higher priority (higher tariffs) than others.
- There can be a maximum payment, meaning that activity above a certain ceiling is financed by the hospital itself.
- The counties can control for large increases in the registered value per contact (DRG-creep) with the hospitals before payment of the activity-based funds.

The last point avoids hospital receipt of activity-based funds based on a registered increase in production value that is not reflected in actual production. Typically, the value per admission (measured per hospital or per county) is not allowed to increase more than 1.5 percent annually.

In implementing a minimum of 20 percent activity-based financing, the fifteen Danish counties chose more or less fifteen different combinations of the possibilities listed above. In 2004, six counties chose a model where hospitals were paid by results only above a certain level of basic production, while nine counties chose a model where hospitals were paid a certain tariff starting from the first patient treated. With the purpose of controlling expenditure, nine counties chose to define a maximum level of payment (ceiling), meaning that the hospitals assume all economic risk. Also, to control expenditure, seven counties chose different tariffs for different levels of activity (e.g. lower tariffs for higher levels of production). Only five counties chose to use differentiated tariffs to give certain areas of treatment a higher priority than others.

The introduction of activity-based financing by the government on a national scale is an example of the increasing degree of interference by the government in the operation of the hospitals. Until the first half of the 1990s, counties were more or less free to run the hospitals within the limits of the block grants. The increasing number of demands by the government has decreased this degree of freedom. The Minister of Health and the government are held responsible for the running of the health care sector, the reduction of waiting times, the quality of care, etc., even though hospital management is decentralized. As previously mentioned, persistent problems with waiting times have been a very important political issue during the 1990s, causing severe criticism of the changing Ministers of Health. Seen in this light, it may not be surprising that the number of initiatives taken by the government is increasing.

The Danish National Board of Health has calculated the extent of activity-based financing in the counties in 2004. The level varied from approximately 20 to 70 percent of total public hospital activity. This implies that the activity-based financing models chosen by the counties have very different impacts on the level of activity-based financing, and that the crucial parameter is whether activity-based financing starts from the first patient or at a certain level of activity.

According to the economic agreement between the government and Danish regions for 2005 and 2006, the counties are to continue settling a minimum of 20 percent of hospital revenues based on actual activity. A number of counties introduced minor changes in their activity-based financing models in 2005. A larger number of counties chose a model where hospitals are paid a certain tariff starting from the first patient treated. The number of counties defining a maximum level of payment also increased. The share of activity-based financing in the counties in 2005 has been estimated to vary from 21 to 68 percent.

In February 2005, the government announced its intention to increase the minimum share of hospital budgets that should be allocated on a casemix basis to 50 percent within the next few years. The Ministry of the Interior and Health published a report in spring 2006 with suggestions on how to form new models of activity-based financing. One of the important recommendations in the report was an increased focus on fixed versus variable costs. The fixed costs should be settled through block grants, while the variable or marginal costs should be settled through the activity-based financing model. When the fixed costs are separated from variable costs, differences between hospitals with high and low productivity will become clearer.

Summary of DRG system use by 2006:
- Settling payment for basic treatment between counties.
- Distribution of a government pool for increased activity.
- Activity-based financing within counties.
- Productivity analysis.
- Purposes of planning, working and controlling in the counties.

Activity-based financing outside the DkDRGs

DkDRG does not cover psychiatric care. Instead, treatment of psychiatric patients outside the patient's home county is rewarded with a fixed rate per bed-day. The government pool for increased activity, as well as the minimum of 20 percent activity-based financing at the county level, does not account for psychiatric patients. As of 2007, psychiatric patients are expected to be included in DkDRG.

GPs and specialists outside the hospitals are also not covered by the DRG system. GPs and specialists outside hospitals are 100 percent activity based, and the rates used are negotiated between the Danish regions and the doctors' association.

The DRG rates cover all hospital activity, including highly specialized treatments at university hospitals. When distributing the government pool for increased activity DRG rates are also used for measuring highly specialized treatments. However, the tariffs used to settle payments between counties for highly specialized treatments are calculated by the university hospitals themselves. These rates are cost based and include public servant pensions, payment of interest, and depreciation.

The home county is obliged to pay for treatment when patients choose to use extended hospital choice to receive private hospital treatment. As noted above, the rates used are negotiated between the Danish regions and the private hospitals. The basis for these negotiations is the DkDRG rates, but the final price may differ.

4. Impact, debates, controversies

As part of the economic agreement for the year 2004 between the government and the Danish regions, the level of activity-based financing was re-evaluated in 2005. The Copenhagen Hospital Corporation, the Danish regions, the National Board of Health, the Ministry of Finance, and the Ministry of Interior and Health published the evaluation in May 2005.[14] It showed that the effects on activity, waiting times, and productivity had been positive. Furthermore, expenditure did not explode, as many had feared.

The governmental activity-based pool, which was introduced in 2002, seems to have had a great effect on activity, though it is still difficult to measure the effect of the 20 percent activity-based financing of hospitals that was implemented in 2004.

Measured in value of production by DRG points, activity increased by 17.7 percent in the period 2000–2004. The largest growth in activity, 7.6 percent, took place in 2001–2, the first year after the introduction of the governmental activity-based pool.

Measured in number of treated patients and number of operations, the picture is the same. The number of treated patients and the number of operations increased by 7.6 percent and 15.9 percent respectively, in the period 2000–2004. Again, the largest growth took place from 2001–2, where the number of treated patients and the number of operations increased 3.4 percent and 11.6 percent, respectively (see Figure 5.2).

Waiting times have fallen since the introduction of activity-based financing and the introduction of extended hospital choice. The waiting time for seventeen selected treatments has fallen from approximately twenty-six days in July 2002, to eighteen days in July 2006 (see Figure 5.3).

Hospital sector productivity has risen between 1.2 and 0.8 percent annually from 2000–2003 (see Figure 5.4).

According to the evaluation, there is still 'room for improvement.' The counties' models of activity-based financing only comply to some extent with the principles in the economic agreement. Also, counties lack sufficient knowledge of the underlying cost structures to set adequate

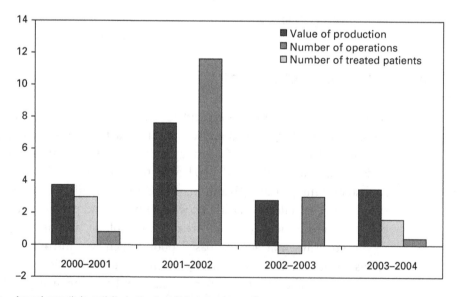

Figure 5.2   Annual growth in activity in the hospital sector (percent)

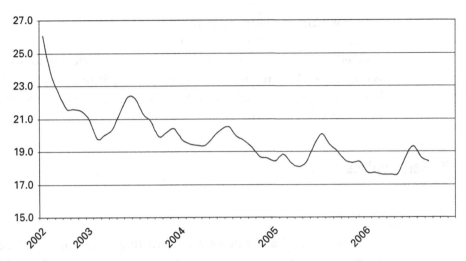

Source: The Danish Waiting Time Information System – Predicted waiting times for the uncomplicated patient

Figure 5.3   Total waiting times for seventeen selected treatments, July 2002–July 2006 (weeks)

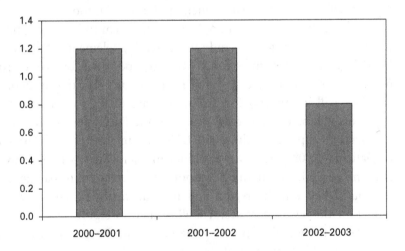

Figure 5.4   Annual growth in hospital productivity (percent)

marginal tariffs etc. On this basis, the evaluation of activity-based financing recommended:

- more efficient economic incentives;
- better knowledge of cost structures and marginal tariffs;
- identification of productive and efficient units;

- development of information systems;
- more competition between hospitals.

As noted above, a report by the Ministry of Health in spring 2006 recommended how the regions should build their models of activity-based financing when the share of activity-based financing is increased to a minimum of 50 percent.

5. Perspectives

The structural reform

The Danish political–administrative structure is currently undergoing its biggest reform for more than thirty years. By January 1, 2007, the 14 counties and the Copenhagen Hospital Corporation will have been reduced to 5 regions, and the 271 existing municipalities will have been reduced to 98 new municipalities. Many tasks will be transferred from the counties to the municipalities and the state, while the single most important task of the regions will be hospital management and administration.

Moreover, the regions will not be given the right to levy taxes, but will be financed by block grants and an increasing element of activity-based financing. The governmental activity-based pool will be raised from 1–2 percent to 5 percent of the overall hospital costs. Starting in 2007, municipalities will jointly pay for the health care of their own citizens. These payments will be calculated as a share of the DRG rates, with a maximum payment of approximately 4,000 DKK for inpatients and 270 DKK for outpatients (2003 prices). In addition, municipalities will also pay a fixed amount per inhabitant of the region. The size of this payment will be negotiated between the region and its municipalities. The new financing model for the health care sector is illustrated in Figure 5.5.

Some of the main purposes of the Danish health care reform are:
- a simple and efficient public sector;
- better service with unchanged tax levels;
- clear responsibility and elimination of grey areas;
- increased citizen involvement.

The co-payment is expected to increase municipalities' involvement in prevention, care and rehabilitation.

As the new regions will not have the right to levy taxes, the largest part of county financing will consist of a block grant from the state, based on

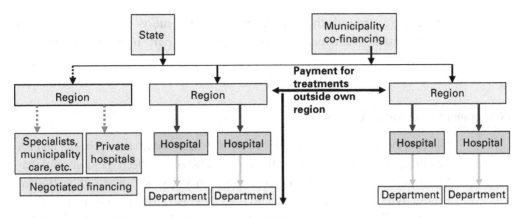

Figure 5.5   Financing reform, January 1, 2007

objective criteria. If regions wish to improve services in the future, they will need to improve productivity to make resources available for the new initiatives. When negotiations take place between a region and its municipalities on the municipalities' contribution per inhabitant, the region's productivity analysis results may also be of great importance.

To improve transparency in comparing and improving outcomes, the government published productivity analyses at country, region and county levels in 2005. From 2006, productivity analyses at the hospital level have been published; publication of department level analyses has also been attempted. The DRG system will be used for the calculation of the productivity indexes.

The Danish government, which was re-elected in February 2005, has declared that activity-based financing of hospitals should be increased from the existing 20 percent to 50 percent. This will further increase the use of the DRG system.

The structural reform changes the balance of power between the three administrative levels. Both the state and the municipalities are given a larger role, and both will wish to influence the new regions. The regions will be completely dependent on financing by the municipalities and the state. However, the regions will be large enough to be strong opponents to the government.

The current counties have been very much in opposition to the structural reform, partly because they will lose control over a number of tasks, and partly because of the new financing model. However, the on the whole, the municipalities have welcomed the reform. After the initial discussions, the atmosphere around the reform has become more positive, with both counties and municipalities taking an active part in preparing for the reform.

Development of the use of DRGs

DRGs are used to an increasing extent as a means of financing in the Danish health care sector. The introduction of DRGs has been gradual and has taken place over a period of more than ten years. The first publication of productivity analysis based on DRGs in 1996 gave rise to criticism, both of the methods used and, in particular, of the DRG system itself. In the intervening period, a significant effort has been made to improve the DRG system and to adjust it to Danish clinical practice. Both hospital administrative staff and clinicians have been involved in this process. As of today, there is wide acceptance of the system, among both clinicians and administrative staff at the county and hospital level. The general opinion is that there is no turning back. It was found that there is no better alternative than DRGs as a means of "measuring" economy in the health care sector, and that it would be unwise to return to a situation where there is little knowledge of cost structures.

As of 2006, the Danish DRG system covers all inpatient and outpatient hospital treatment. However, the DRG system is not (yet) used for settling payments between counties for highly specialized treatment. Within the last couple of years, significant efforts have been made to adjust the DRG system to describe highly specialized treatment more precisely. On this basis, decisions will be made within a relatively short period of time as to whether to begin using the DRG system for settling payment for highly specialized treatment between regions.

By summer 2006, a DRG system for treatment of psychiatric patients had been developed, using DRG rates based on ABC studies on a number of psychiatric hospitals. From January 1, 2007, municipalities co-pay for both somatic and psychiatric treatment of their own citizens. It is expected that the calculation of the co-payment for psychiatric treatment will be based on the psychiatric DRG rates.

As a result of the extended use of the DRG system, Danish hospitals and counties (regions) are increasingly dependent on the system. As a result, the demand for precision, both in grouping and in the calculation of DRG rates, has also increased. To accommodate this demand, the Danish cost database is being further developed and improved. Likewise, clinical validation is updated on an annual basis.

The development of the cost database aims at establishing a basis for the calculation of unit costs, marginal rates, and the contribution margin. The full benefits from activity-based financing can only be obtained if counties and hospitals have a detailed knowledge of the cost structures. In order to calculate unit costs, etc., it is necessary to identify the costs of production for each patient contact (e.g. costs for surgery, utensils, implants, blood tests, etc.). Therefore, great efforts are being made to collect the necessary data and compile it in a comparative way.

6. Technical appendix

The Danish DRG system covers inpatients (DRG) and outpatients (DAGS). Each year the National Board of Health calculates both DRG and DAGS rates. The DRG system for 2007 was the sixth version of DkDRG. There are three main steps in the calculation process:
1. Clinical validation.
2. Cost database.
3. Calculation.

Clinical validation has already been mentioned. Every few years, all DRG groups are validated. In the intervening years, there can be minor adjustments in the groups.

The cost-weights are calculated on the basis of the Danish cost database. This covers all public hospitals and both stationary and ambulatory patients. The cost database is based on on hospital cost information in cost centers, and registration of individual treatment. Part of the costs can be directly related to patients, some costs are distributed using point systems, and others are distributed as a fixed cost per bed-day or per ambulatory visit. The DRG rates for a particular year are based on the hospital's accounts two years earlier. The collection of data and the improvement of the Danish cost database is an ongoing process.

The average discharge costs are calculated for the discharged patient in each DRG group. The DRG rates include internally financed research, education, expensive drugs, etc. DRG rates do not include public servant pensions, payment of interest, and depreciation. The DAGS rates are exclusive of drugs costing more than approximately 700 DKK per day. Hospitals can charge the home county for the cost of these expensive drugs when treating a patient who resides outside the county. The DAGS rates are also exclusive of public servant pensions, payment of interest, and depreciation.

DRG groups with more than twenty observations are trimmed at the 99 and 1 percent fractals. Groups with fewer than twenty observations are trimmed at the 95 and 5 percent fractals. All DAGS groups are trimmed at the 90 and 10 percent fractals. During the trimming, extreme values are replaced with the value of the trim point.

The trim point defines the maximum number of bed-days covered by the DRG rates. Patients with a longer admission than the trim point are settled with a fixed rate per bed-day above the trim point. In 2006, the rate per bed-day was 1,608 DKK.

Hospital activity is registered in the National Patient Registry. Diagnoses and procedures are registered using ICD–10. It is the responsibility of the hospitals to register the activity.

NOTES

1. Citizens co-pay expenditures for medical and dental services.
2. Denmark has three political and administrative levels: state, counties and municipalities (national, regional and local levels).
3. In Denmark there are fourteen counties and the Copenhagen Hospital Corporation, which consists of the Municipality of Copenhagen and the Municipality of Frederiksberg. The Copenhagen Hospital Corporation is responsible for delivering hospital services to citizens in Copenhagen.
4. An interest organization for the fourteen counties.
5. An interest organization for the 268 municipalities.
6. Self-employed GPs, who operate wholly within the public health care system.
7. Naturally, emergency cases overruled this practice.
8. The home county pays for treatment of its own citizens.
9. Counties are, however, free to agree on another level of payment.
10. "Aktivitetsbestemt finansiering i Danmark – foreløbige erfaringer."
11. The activity-based pool covers all somatic activity except telephone consultations, sterilization, and alcohol treatment.
12. The counties can request for adjustments in the baseline production due to organizational changes.
13. The National Patient Registry has, since 1977, been the nationwide registration of all somatic hospital admissions. Since 1995, data on outpatients and emergency patients have been submitted. Data on contact with psychiatric hospital departments have been reported since 1995. All patients are classified according to hospital department

admitting the patient, diagnosis, surgical procedures, date of admission, date of discharge, and mode of admission. All patients are given a unique, lifetime identity number that is used for all contact with public services.

14. "Evaluering af takststyring på sygehusområdet."

REFERENCES

Danish Ministry of Health (1999). *Hospital Funding and Casemix.* www.sst.dk/upload/hospital_funding_ and_casemix_drg.pdf

H:S, Amtsrådsforeningen, Sundhedsstyrelsen, Finansministeriet & Indenrigs- og Sundhedsministeriet (2005). *Evaluering af takststyring på sygehusområdet.* Salogruppen A/S.

Indenrigs- og Sundhedsministeriet (2001). *Status for udvikling af DRG-metoden 2000–2001.* Schultz Grafisk.

(2002). *Aktivitetsbestemt finansiering i Danmark – foreløbige erfaringer.* GraPhia.

(2005). *Sundhedssektoren i tal – september 2005.* www.im.dk/publikationer/sundhedssektoren_i_tal/SIT_sept_05.pdf

Ministry of the Interior and Health (2002). *Health Care in Denmark.* 5th edn. www.im.dk/publikationer/healthcare_in_dk/index.htm

Sundhedsministeriet (1995). *Måling af sygehuses produktivitet. En DRG-analyse for Nordjyllands Amt.* Nyt Nordisk Forlag Arnold Busk.

(1996). *DRG-analyser for danske sygehuse, 1993.* Nyt Nordisk Forlag Arnold Busk.

(1997). *Udfordringer i sygehusvsenet. Betnkning fra Sygehuskommissionen.*

(1998) *Takststrukturen i sygehussektoren. Rapport fra Takstudvalget.* Nyt Nordisk Forlag Arnold Busk.

Sundhedsstyrelsen (2004). *Takstsystem 2005. Vejledning.* Schultz Grafisk.

6 DRGs in France

Xavière Michelot and Jean Marie Rodrigues

France, with its population of around 62 million, is one of the largest countries in the EU, first by geographic size and second, after Germany, by population. US DRGs were introduced into France as GHM (Groupes Homogène de Malades) as early as 1983, but they weren't used as a resource allocation tool until 1997, and had no major impact until 2004. This project, called PMSI (Programme de Médicalisation des Systèmes d'Information), has been shaped by the fragmented design of the French health care system and by the cultural framework embedding socio-economic reform in France.

A brief description of the French health care system

Ranked the number one health care system in the world by the World Health Organization in 2000, the French health care system provides a high level of service, but at what could be considered a very high price when compared to many other OECD countries.

Hospital care is characterized by the coexistence of public, private for-profit, and private not-for-profit hospitals, whose ownership, organization, management and financing differ widely.

Core indicators

The French population enjoys a good health care status and benefits and easy accessibility (despite geographic inequalities) to the entire health care system. However, the cost of this system, and therefore its tendency to increase deficits, has been a major issue in public debates for over three decades.

Satisfaction with the French health care system is traditionally high – much higher than in most other countries. However, the performance of the system in terms of quality of care has only been evaluated since the creation of a so-called hospital "accreditation" procedure in 2000, which is only now being extended to all physicians. There is no evidence of important flaws in terms of quality of care, but the 14,000 extra deaths that occurred during the August 2003 heatwave invites a critical appreciation of the WHO ranking.

Until the introduction of a referral system in 2004, patients benefited from a complete freedom to choose and use private and public health services. Physicians are free to settle wherever they want (which results in wide discrepancies in access to care, especially for general practitioners and some specialties such as ophthalmology, cardiology, gynecology and surgery). There are almost no waiting lists (with the noticeable exception of emergencies and heart or kidney transplants) and accessibility to the system remains generally very good. Since the development in the 1990s of a new information system based on a patient's individual electronic card (named Vitale), all French citizens and permanent residents are entitled to access public or private hospital care (inpatient or outpatient), with a contribution strictly limited to the amount of the out-of-pocket payment.

The French population enjoys a relatively high life expectancy (79 years), especially for women (82.7 years), compared to the average across OECD countries. Infant mortality is very low, having experienced a very strong decrease in the past few decades – 4.6 deaths per 1,000 live births. The obesity rate among adults, at about 10 percent, remains one of the lowest in the developed world, although it is rising, especially among children.

One of the real low points lies in the mortality rate for adults before sixty-five, which is one of the highest in Europe and results in a wide gender gap in life expectancy (7.5 years). The relatively high mortality rate among men is mostly due to violent deaths (fatal accidents, suicide, homicide) and alcohol and tobacco consumption. Geographical inequality in health status is important, with high-mortality clusters in the most deprived areas (e.g. a five-year difference in life expectancy between north and southwest regions).

Health expenditures

France ranks above the OECD average in terms of health care spending, both per capita (€2,580) and as a percentage of its GDP (9.5%) – about one percentage point higher than the average across OECD countries. Yet it remains well below the US expenditure level, both in absolute (per capita) and relative terms.

However, there is concern, as expenditures show steeper and steeper annual growth rates (2.2 percent during the 1990s, 3.7 percent in 2000 and 2001 and may reach 12.6 percent by 2020 if the trend continues) – all data in real terms. The share and growth of pharmaceutical expenses is particularly worrying: France ranks second after the US for drug expenses per inhabitant, with a 21 percent share of total health care expenses. What is more, drug expenditure experienced one of the steepest increases among OECD countries

This results in a structural deficit of the health care system, despite permanent adjustments and reforms. The deficit thus reached €10 billion in 2003, and has remained more or less at this level ever since.

Access to and financing of health care

Though health care services are delivered both by the public and private sectors, funding is essentially operated through public sources. The national and universal compulsory public health insurance system accounts for 75 percent of total funding with three major funds and several smaller ones. Complementary private insurance schemes (covering more than 80 percent of the population) account for 13 percent of funding. Out-of-pocket payments (mostly for eye and dental care) represent about 12 percent of the system's resources.

Public funding covers access to two different health care sub-systems: a national public health care system and a private contractual system. The national public health care system is publicly owned, organized and managed, and consists nearly exclusively of hospitals. The contractual private healthcare system consists of nearly all ambulatory care (e.g. independent physicians) as well as an increasing part of hospital care (about 40 percent of acute care hospital admissions occur in private for-profit hospitals). The role of the complementary private funds is to address the increasing financial burden supported by patients in both sub-systems (not just in the private sector as in most other countries).

Since the adoption of the Universal Health Coverage Law (Loi sur la Couverture Maladie Universelle or CMU) in 2000, people with low income have free access to the system, financed by taxes. People with a low income who are not entitled to health insurance benefits thus have access to free health care.

Figure 6.1 below shows the outline of the organization and financing of the French health care system.

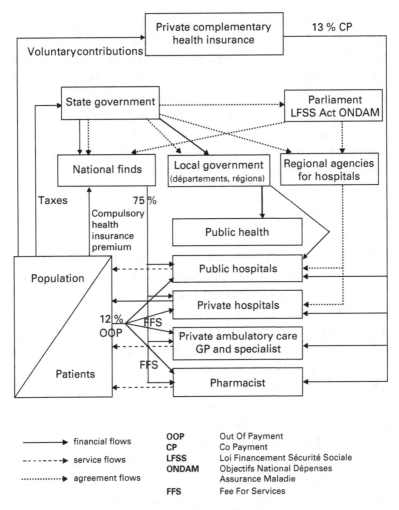

Figure 6.1   The French health care system: organization and financing

Beside the small share mentioned above and financed through general taxation (Couverture Maladie Universelle), the financing of health care is now mainly linked to taxes through a direct universal contribution proportional to income (58%) and indirect taxes on alcohol and tobacco (2%) and to employment, as the health care system is still financed through employees' and employers' fees (40%).

Funding of health care is rather complex, due, on the one hand, to the different processes for public and private for-profit hospitals, and to the respective role of the state and of health care insurers, on the other. Regarding public hospitals, twenty-two regional agencies (called ARH) are responsible for planning and allocating funds according to the limit set each year by the parliament; the health care insurance fund only acts as a payer. Regarding private for-profit hospitals and private health care professionals, the health insurance fund is in charge of regulating spending through a price–volume monitoring of tariffs, also according to the limit set each year by the parliament. This mix of a public and a private health care system funded in different ways by the same universal health care insurance fund controlled by the state corresponds neither to a fully integrated national health system nor to a purely contractual private one.

Organization of health care

The relationships between the state, health care insurance funds, local authorities (involved in health care investments), and care providers are governed by several agreements, called COM (Contrats d'Objectifs et de Moyens), which are negotiated every five years – the balance of power inclining, however, clearly in favor of the state. At the hospital level, if public hospitals are autonomous with respect to care organization and internal management, they must comply with a national and regional framework. This is also true, but to a lesser degree, for private for-profit hospitals (most of which are aggregated in corporate networks).

Regarding primary and secondary care, there are 1.7 million health care professionals in France, among whom 200,800 are physicians (i.e. about three doctors per 1,000 inhabitants) which is slightly above the OECD average. Fifty percent are specialists, 36 percent work in public hospitals or structures and are civil servants, and the rest work in private practice (both hospital and ambulatory settings) and are paid on a fee-for-service basis. The main concerns raised by the demographics of French health care professionals are the following: an uneven geographic distribution, raising issues of inequality of access to health care services, and a rising disproportion between general practitioners and specialists, resulting in too few GPs and too many specialists, combined with a disproportion among specialists, with some specialties, like obstetrics or anesthesia, having experienced decreased interest among medical students.

Regarding the hospital sector, there are 3,171 hospitals in France, accounting for 486,069 beds (i.e. 8.4 beds per 1,000 inhabitants) and about 4 acute care beds per 1,000 inhabitants). Hospitals are divided into two categories: public hospitals (1,032 hospitals and 65 percent of all beds) and private for-profit and not-for-profit hospitals (2,139 hospitals and 35 percent of all beds – 20 percent for-profit and 15 percent not-for-profit).

The public sector hence prevails in terms of number of beds, and has the greatest market share in medicine (77.7%) and obstetrics (67.3%), but more than 51.2 percent of surgical procedures and 60 percent of cancer treatments take place in the private sector.

Brief history of the introduction of casemix in France

In June 1982, the Ministry of Health's Direction for Hospitalization sent public and private hospitals an invitation to participate in a project to record patients' medical data. The objectives of the experiment were pinpointed as follows: "The project seeks to test the creation of a French hospital database in a selection of hospitals within their short-term care section. This database will facilitate the description of hospitals' output or medical activities through a range of typical patient cases and medical procedures in order to generate a new management style in hospitals." Participating institutions would commit themselves to providing a standardized discharge summary, or uniform hospital discharge dataset (known as Résumé de Sortie Standardisé, or RSS, and designed according to the EU MBDS, or Minimum Basic Dataset) for each hospitalized patient.

This invitation marked the first step in DRG introduction in France – a process that would nevertheless require more than fifteen years to be fully completed. The history of casemix development in France can be related to a specific period, a few DRG "champions," state-managed early experimentation, slow implementation, and finally, illustrates how a fragmented health care system is challenged by a centralized state.

The French PMSI (Programme de Médicalisation des Systèmes d'Information) has been implemented in all French hospitals since 1985. It is a program aimed at describing hospital output based on medical activity, via a medico-economic patient classification system called GHM (Homogeneous Patient Groups, or Groupes Homogènes de Malades). The GHM classification aims at classifying, using a limited set of descriptive variables (diagnosis, procedures, co-morbidities, age, length of stay, etc.) and a grouping algorithm, patients in groups which are homogeneous both in terms of cost and care.

Timing

The casemix issue was first raised in the late 1970s, along with a reform of the public hospital funding system meant to deal with peaking hospital expenses, due to a poorly regulated *per diem* payment system. The government decided in 1982 to implement a new cost-containing system based on a so-called "global budget" set for each individual public hospital. Following the advice of some academic experts, it was then planned to adjust resource allocation to hospitals by measuring their clinical activity. This was also meant to make possible the fair evolution of funding in relation to activity, and to create exhaustive hospital clinical databases for internal management, clinical, epidemiological, and economic research. It should be noted that nothing was done for private for-profit hospitals, whose expenses were increasing as well, and for similar reasons as in public hospitals.

Five steps can actually be identified to characterize this process:
- 1982–6: conceptualization and pilot testing of the model based on Fetter's work;
- 1986–91: development of the tools required for experimentation;
- 1989–91: generalization of the PMSI to all hospitals;
- 1991–6: medico-economic evaluation (experimentation led in the Languedoc-Roussillon region, Marrot report, national cost study);
- 1997–2003: adjustment of hospital budgets according to casemix following the 1996 Juppé reform;
- since 2004: implementation of the T2A, the new casemix-based financing system.

The Law of January 19, 1983, which instituted global budgeting for all public and private not-for-profit hospitals, can be considered as setting the framework for initial development of casemix, along with the Decree of January 19, 1983, whose article 8 determines the rules for calculating global budgets, and states that these must be modulated by the hospital's level of activity.

As with most DRG projects, PMSI was methodologically supported by the Yale University Health Services Management Group, led by Professor Robert Fetter. It was, in fact, a joint development program between the few French DRG promoters and the Yale University group, from the initial visit of a French delegation to Yale (March 1982) until 1989.

Like all DRG projects in Europe, PMSI's initial development followed the following four steps:
- assessment of the technical feasibility of assigning DRG numbers to uniform hospital discharge abstracts databases, which was achieved in France with the Grenoble-based DOSTAM system in 1983;
- evaluation of whether the utilization model defined by DRGs is adequate to fit the national hospital database (i.e. whether or not relationships

observed between length of stay (LOS) and different variables (diagnosis, procedure, age discharge status) provide an explanation of significant amounts of costs variability); this was assessed in France in 1984, with the approximately 300,000 discharge abstracts in the database from DOSTAM and later on from Caen and Marseille databases, and was finalized before the systematic recording of hospital discharges, starting with the national RSS in 1985;

- design and implementation of a cost-accounting and budgeting model, taking into account actual and expected patient activity levels through both DRG and national accounting and financial data framework; this was fully achieved in two hospitals (Vienne and Annemasse DOSTAM Rhône-Alpes region) in 1984;
- implementation and development of software and information systems, including training for data collection, processing (assigning patients to DRGs and computing cost by DRG) and analysis on an in-house microcomputer. It started in France in 1986 with the French grouper software based on HCFA DRGs Version 3 1985.

In 1985 the uniform hospital discharge dataset (known as Résumé de Sortie Standardisé, or RSS) was created. And the first Version (called "V0") of the GHM classification, the French patient classification system, was released.

In 1989, private for-profit hospitals required an experimentation of PMSI, first in about 40 hospitals, then in more than 150. Medical Information Departments (Département de l'Information Médicale, or DIM) were created within each hospital the same year.

In 1991, the recording of PMSI data and the setting up of a DIM were made mandatory by an Act of Parliament.

In 1992, the realization of a national per-case cost database from a voluntary sample of public and private not-for-profit hospitals was undertaken.

Then, in 1994–5, an experiment was undertaken in the Languedoc-Roussillon region with all public and private hospitals (representing forty-eight public and private not-for-profit and fifty-five private for-profit hospitals, totaling 500,000 stays per year) that demonstrated the feasibility of routine activity data collection and casemix-based financing for non-voluntarily participating hospitals. The experiment also revealed important budgetary disparities between public hospitals and between the public and private hospital sectors.

The generalization of the PMSI to all public and private not-for-profit hospitals occurred in 1994, while its generalization to all for-profit private hospitals was realized in 1996. That same year, as part of the Juppé reform, a system of budget adjustment based on casemix was introduced that was essentially in the hands of the regional agencies for hospitalization and was aimed at reducing budgetary inequalities among hospitals that had arisen within the global budget system.

In 1999, considering the limited impact of this mechanism and the persistence of inequalities across hospitals and regions, a law was passed stating the implementation of an experimentation of a truly casemix-based financing system, then called "tarification à la pathologie." A task force, called Mission d'Expérimentation de la Tarification à la Pathologie and headed by M. Jean Marrot, an Inspector of Social Affairs, was created in January 2000 in order to conduct the experiment, which resulted in a report in 2002. This set the main technical and political conditions to the implementation of casemix-based financing in France and proposed to follow up on this project, which was deemed to be feasible. It should be noted that this report, though it still serves as a reference, has never been officially published.

The final step was the Social Security Financial Bill of 2003, which commanded the implementation of casemix-based financing in all public and private hospitals between 2005 and 2012.

Drivers

Until the 1980s, French hospital budgets directly derived from activity through the payment of a *per diem* rate, the level of which was set at the beginning of each year and re-evaluated annually through a nationwide increase rate. This rate was also modulated, depending on the nature of the medical unit providing the service. This proved to be a good system for the development of hospital care, but also proved to be a poor one insofar as it soon became inflationary, as the *per diem* rates were based on historical costs. So, at the beginning of the 1980s, the decision was made to implement global budgeting to put a lid on overflowing hospital expenses, thereby inciting hospital managers to limit costs per unit. The development of a casemix tool was then undertaken as a potential means of modulating these global budgets.

Though, in fact, its aim as a financing tool existed from the beginning, the PMSI was originally presented as an epidemiological tool in order to gain acceptance from doctors and hospital managers. At the end of the 1980s, little by little the Ministry of Health started promoting a new discourse around PMSI: it emphasized the need to modernize both hospital internal management and the relationship between the state and the hospitals. The administration's core message then became that, while PMSI was a necessary element of hospital's new management tools, both on an internal/microeconomic/hospital level and from an external/macroeconomic/state level point of view, it would not yet be used as a pricing tool. However, due to the slow development of PMSI, casemix was unveiled as a financing tool only in the 1990s, when, following the "ordinances Juppé" of 1996 (named after the then Prime Minister in charge), casemix started being used to modulate global budgets at the inter-regional and intra-regional levels.

During the first ten years, the development of casemix in France was one tool unconnected with any health care reforms. The 1991 hospital reform Act introduced a regional planning process, and legalized the DRG system and clinical information department (DIM) for any type of hospital, but without any formal link between the two. The Ministry of Health's core message was that, while PMSI was a necessary element of hospitals' new management tools, both from an internal/microeconomic/hospital level and an external/macroeconomic/state level point of view, it would not yet be used as a pricing tool. Hospital Information Systems and DRG Technology investments were low, no managerial innovation was developed, and the exhaustive recording of hospital discharges and grouping with the French GHM was only reached in 1997–8.

After the 1996 health care reform, health care resource allocation among the twenty-two regions became a complex process, taking into account health care needs, inequity in hospital resource allocation based on a DRG casemix index, hospital spending per inhabitant, and geographic origin of the patient. Within each region, the regional agency for hospitalization (ARH for Agence Régionale de l'Hospitalisation) used several tools for planning and funding. They computed for each hospital and for the total region the precise casemix index (called ISA points). This computation was based on GHM national cost-weights, edited each year from a bottom-up cost analysis of a national sample of eighty hospitals, by the national casemix agency, the ATIH, and was finally set in 2000. There was an official policy to reduce the differences between the actual budget of each hospital (over- or under-funded) and their expected budget with the regional arithmetic mean of the ISA casemix index. Unfortunately, the reduction of the important differences between hospitals (1 to 3 at the beginning) followed a slow rate of around 5 percent each year, while, on the other hand, the second half of the system reform (private health care professionals, drugs, and health insurance) completely failed to contain costs by a contractual price–volume regulation.

After the 2002 re-election of the president and parliamentary majority, having passed the previous integrated reform, a new top-down contradictory health care reform was developed. Three separate Acts in 2003 and 2004 introduced market competition between the actors: increase in payment by the individual patients or by voluntary health insurance and individual reimbursement of each hospital stay based on GHM, to ensure competition between public and private hospitals without harmonization of the governance and funding rules. This new policy was supported by IT implementation plans: a new coding system for intervention procedures named CCAM, a web-based platform named Epmsi, and a communicating or shared unique electronic medical record named DMP. This shift from a UK-like national service to a US-like free market system was impressive in a such a short period of time (1996–2004) with the same political power.

Key players

PMSI was introduced by Jean de Kervasdoué, Director for Hospitalization at the French Ministry of Health. So initially, initiative was taken at the national political level when the global budget was introduced in the early 1980s, with a view to modulating the global budget according to hospital activity, as previously mentioned. This state-level impulse was given to the detriment of debate with hospitals and other stakeholders, and also to the detriment of on-site training and information programs. It was also given without the usual clear support from top civil servants. It should therefore not have succeeded.

The implementation of a casemix system in the early 1980s could not have arisen in France from an initiative at hospital level for several reasons. First of all, for technical reasons: French hospitals had never been legally compelled to routinely register data on medical services provided. Contrary to most developed countries' hospitals, they had no central department to manage and store medical files – central archives did exist, but only for storage purposes. What is more, they had no personnel trained to handle international coding systems, which also means there was no one to advocate for the use of such tools. Luckily, there were a few happy exceptions, due to random pioneers such as Valois in Grenoble, Thouin in Caen, Noirclerc in Marseille, and an emerging medical informatics community, with young MDs following the track opened by Gremy in Paris. Finally, there was a general lack of accounting systems to identify patient resource utilization in public hospitals and a lack of openness in the detailed billing of private for-profit hospitals. There were also political reasons: opposition of doctors to any initiative which could hinder their freedom as practitioners, especially in the context of the election of the first left-wing president in 1981 and distrust of hospital managers, who feared increased control from the central level with the development of casemix data collection.

Moreover, there was no real implication for the national health care insurance funds at this stage either, although the major one (the Caisse Nationale d'Assurance Maladie, or CNAM) was studying new utilization review methods when PMSI was launched.

Thus, PMSI's development was undertaken within the ministry, using a team composed of people who were not the traditional high-ranking civil servants, but who had original profiles with a more entrepreneurial spirit, supervised by a then left-wing government. These people came from academic and research fields and were open to the spirit and ideas of American universities.

The decision to implement casemix came along with a major political change (i.e. the election of a left-wing socialist president and parliamentary majority for the first time since World War II). The new under-secretary of state for hospitals (de Kervasdoué) and his clinical information adviser (Rodrigues) were aware of the research work done at Yale by Fetter and his colleagues to develop a new tool to measure clinical activity known as DRGs. They convinced senior ministers, and an impulse was given with the support of a few health economics researchers (de Pouvourville in Ecole Polytechnique and Moisdon in Ecole des Mines), medical informatics pioneers (Valois in Grenoble), and an emerging medical informatics community with young MDs following their founding leader, Gremy, in Paris. Indeed, the Director of Hospitalization assigned project development to a specifically created task force within the Directorate for Hospitalization (the administrative body in charge of French hospital management within the French Ministry of Health).

This impulse was given without a debate with hospitals and other stakeholders, who had different reasons to resist the initiative: doctors, hospital managers, and the national health care insurance funds. Later on, the development of the PMSI and its use as a financing tool was always achieved through the work of dedicated task forces within or outside the ministry, not by the ministry's services themselves.

On the other hand, these champions held their legitimacy from a specific political situation that changed in 1986. Almost eight years (1986–94) were needed for the system to gain acceptance, first by health care stakeholders (hospital managers and physicians, health insurance systems) and finally by government officials of the right-wing political majority in 1994 (Balladur government) and 1996 (Juppé government).

The system is currently maintained by the Technical Agency for Hospital Information (Agence Technique de l'Information Hospitalière, or ATIH), created by a decree in 2000. The main tasks assigned to the agency are:

- development and maintenance of the PMSI in the fields of medicine/ surgery/obstetrics, home hospitalization, rehabilitation, and psychiatric care;
- contribution, along with the National Healthcare Insurance Fund (CNAM), to the development and maintenance of the French classification of medical procedures (CCAM) and of the International Classification of Diseases (ICD);
- supply to all hospitals of the tools (software mainly) required to collect PMSI data;
- supply to the Regional Agencies for Hospitalization (ARH) of the tools required to control coding and data collection;
- production of the tools required for the implementation of the new casemix-based financing system (T2A) – especially cost-weights and tariff calculation;
- development of various tools to serve as a basis for health care organization planning, financial decision support, epidemiological studies, and hospital performance measurement.

Supervision of the agency is the responsibility of the Directorate for Hospitalization at the Ministry of Health, which also sets the agency's yearly objectives and is project manager on most of its projects. The agency has a budget of €5.1 million and is funded partially by the state, partially by the Healthcare Insurance Fund, and also collects €550,000 of its own resources. It employs forty-six people, mainly doctors, computer scientists, and statisticians.

Beside the ATIH, and within the Ministry of Health, the Mission Tarification à l'Activité, created in 2003, is in charge of the implementation of the new casemix-based financing system. It is headed by Mme. Martine Aoustin, a doctor who spent most of her career within the National Public Healthcare Insurance Fund.

Implementation

The choice was made in the 1980s to operate a transposition of the American classification system, including its grouper, as this was the only operational tool available at the time anyway. The initial GHM version in 1986 was a transposition of HCFA DRG 3 1985, but used the ICD–9 for diagnoses (not ICD–9 CM) and a new French coding system for procedures named CDAM (Medical Procedures Catalogue). Regarding collection of cost data, the initial choice was to use Fetter's cost modeling system, despite objections raised regarding accounting issues: this system relies on the principle of an overall cost calculation method.

Further on, the Ministry decided to develop a French version of the classification but the investment it required was initially underestimated, which resulted in the use of the old GHM/HCFA 1985 version until 1996, and in the need to transpose another US grouper (AP12) in 1997 – always using French coding systems (ICD–10 for diagnoses and CDAM/CCAM for procedures). New versions of the French classification and grouper have been realized and published. Currently, the tenth version of the GHM classification (V9), comprising 701 groups and published in 2004, and a thirteenth grouper are being used – and a V10 of the GHM classification should shortly be enforced.

The development of casemix in France can be considered as an archetypal example of how the French public authorities manage a complex, fragmented, and fuzzy health care system in the absence of public debate on health care organization and financing during election campaigns, given the role of expert committees and commissions, the number of different minister's special advisers, and the politically correct way of promoting each reform as the only possible way. In the case of casemix, these features can explain its early initial development, the long time taken to identify problems, and finally, its entitlement to completely change the health care system. This reminds one of the "Enlightened Despotism or Absolutism," defined as the following: "only a monarch can be enlightened and powerful enough to apply a socioeconomic modernization of a country when too many actors have divergent goals and values." [1],[2],[3].

Current development and uses of casemix in France

Contrasting with the early development of research on DRGs, the first real comprehensive data production year was 1996, and the first national utilization for funding was in 1998.

While casemix is now used in all acute care hospitals for their acute care activities, it is still under continuous improvement and under development

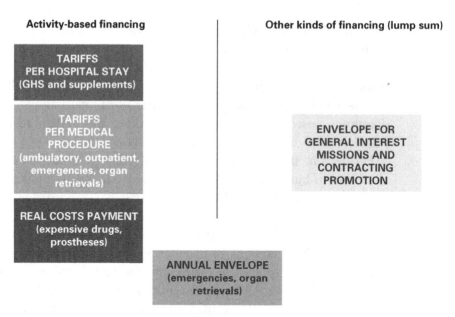

Figure 6.2   Activity-based financing and other kinds of financing (lump sum)

as well, most notably in the areas of psychiatry and rehabilitation, where experiments are currently being conducted. What is more, use of the casemix tool recently experienced a major change with the introduction of casemix-based payment.

Extensions of casemix

Casemix has reached its full development for hospital inpatient acute care in the areas of medicine, surgery and obstetrics: each and every hospital must comply with PMSI's rules and collects and transmits exhaustive activity data. New tools are under development by the ATIH in order to encompass rehabilitation and psychiatric care within the field of PMSI.

From a quantitative point of view, the completeness of data collection within the PMSI has been evaluated from 1996 on, and was achieved as early as 1998 in the public hospital sector; it reached 97 percent that same year and 98 percent in 1999 in the private sector.

From a qualitative point of view, before the PMSI was generalized, the rate of errors implying a change of GHM was relatively high (around 15 percent on average, but much higher in large hospitals with a decentralized data collection system, where it reached 25 to 30 percent) but its impact on valorization was limited, rarely above 5 percent. After the generalization of the PMSI, a distinction must be made between the public and private hospital sectors.

In the private sector, systematic controls by external inspectors (doctors from the public health care insurance funds) were operated between 1997 and 1999. The rate of errors implying a change of GHM had then diminished, and was lower than 5 percent in 1999. Since 1999, there are no more systematic controls, but only punctual controls freely initiated by the Regional Agencies for Hospitalization. As a result, the realization of external controls has been very variable, both in its extent and durability, depending on the region considered.

In the public sector, since 1995 a two-step validation procedure has existed, articulating a systematic internal control (operated by the Medical Information Department of each hospital) on a random sample of 100 cases per semester, and an external control (operated by doctors commanded by the Regional Agencies for Hospitalization) on a sample of 20 files randomly selected among the 100 re-coded by the Medical Information Department of each hospital. However, no assessment of these controls has been published to date.

Uses made of casemix

The main use made of casemix today in France is for financing hospitals, casemix-based financing having been introduced in 2004 and gradually replacing the former systems in use. The new financing system should be fully implemented in 2012.

Financing

It must be noted first and foremost that the implementation of casemix-based financing operates in a very special context. France is currently moving from an unsatisfactory system, where public and private hospitals were financed in two different fashions. French public and private not-for-profit hospitals were financed through a global budget system, while negotiated fee-for-service (FFS) tariffs constituted the main source of financing for French for-profit hospitals.

Public and private not-for-profit hospitals have so far depended on global budgets, which were mainly fixed on a historical basis, although these budgets have also depended, since 1997, on both specific hospital costs and an adjustment based on a regional casemix index giving the average cost per case.

In private for-profit hospitals, so far payment has mainly been based on a whole set of tariffs, including *per diem* prices (covering the cost of accommodation, nursing care, drugs, and minor devices) and lump sums covering the running costs associated with the use of technical equipment. Doctors working at these hospitals have been paid directly for their hospital activities on a separate FFS basis.

The trouble was that global budgeting had become very unfair over the years, with some public hospitals much better off than others, having become a black box in which the regulator had no insight. FFS financing of private for-profit hospitals had become very complex and unfair, as each hospital negotiated its own fees with the health care insurance fund, and, as a consequence, were hard to regulate. Different systems resulted in an unequal treatment of public and private hospitals, resulting in unexplainable but huge cost differences between public and private hospitals (estimated at about 30 percent).

As an answer to these issues, the Social Security Financial Bill for 2003 required the implementation of casemix-based financing in all public and private French hospitals between 2004 and 2012. This new financing system is called "tarification à l'activité", or T2A. A new task force called Mission Tarification à l'Activité was created to implement the new system.

The T2A system is a real prospective per-case payment system or PPS, the basic idea being to implement a prospective payment system that aims at financing hospitals according to their actual activity and, for the treatment of each given case, at a standard price.

Although the previous public hospital funding system did not entirely ignore the nature of hospital activities, the way these activities were taken into account differed significantly from the approach involved in the latest method. Formerly, payment was the means enabling hospitals to perform activities, whereas hospitals are now funded on the basis of their actual activities. The entire approach to hospital payment has therefore been reversed: it is no longer based on past expenditure, but on hospital activity. Moreover, hospitals will have to bill the health insurance funds to be refunded after patients' stays. This represents a significant conceptual change in management practices at the hospital level.

Indeed, when it began, the following objectives were assigned to the new payment system: to link financing to the actual level of hospital activity; to establish a common financing system for public and private hospitals; to create incentives for hospital managers and medical staff to analyze their casemix, medical practices, and cost structure; to promote the development of some activities (e.g. ambulatory surgery) and hinder the growth of others.

Also, the following principles had to be followed while setting up the new financing scheme:

- the extension of the new payment system was limited to the field of hospital activity in medicine, surgery and obstetrics (thus excluding psychiatry, rehab, etc.);
- implementation had to be gradual, with many transition adjustments;
- a global price–volume regulation was to be implemented (i.e. if global hospital activity grows in year n, the tariffs will be lowered in year n+1 to make sure the hospital budget is not exceeded);
- the scheme had to make provision for convergence of the tariff scales initially applied to the public and private sector separately;
- within each sector, the scheme also had to make provision for convergence of the tariffs and conditions between hospitals.

Indeed, tariffs cover the full cost of hospital stay for the public sector, but do not include doctor's fees in the private for-profit sector, resulting in different tariff scales for public and private hospitals. But other factors (tariff calculation methodology, and structural factors as well) that will be further detailed later on also impact both tariff scales differently.

In public hospitals, casemix-based financing started in 2004, representing 10 percent of the budget in 2004 and 25 percent in 2005. It reached 50 percent in 2007 and should reach 100 percent in 2012.

In private hospitals, casemix-based financing started on March 1, 2005, with 100 percent casemix-based financing, but only for the hospital part (fees for physicians are paid separately). The transition will be made progressive through the transition part of the adjustment index applied to the tariff (hospital part) scale of each hospital, which should equal one in 2012.

The French T2A system is a mixed system combining pure casemix-based payment and other types of financing, which are:

- tariffs per medical procedure: some activities benefit from a *per diem* (neonatology, home hospitalization, reanimation, intensive care, continuous monitoring) or a fee-for-service payment (dialysis, radiotherapy, outpatient activities like consultations, MRI, PETscans, hyperbaric chamber). Palliative care is one case where there is more than one GHS tariff for one GHM, the tariff being increased by 30 percent if the service has dedicated beds, and by 40 percent if there is a specific palliative care unit;
- lump sum payments for research, teaching, innovation, and other public interest duties;
- mixed systems: emergencies and organ retrievals and transplants benefit from a twofold financing, with a fixed and a variable per-patient share;

- real cost payment for expensive drugs and medical devices: some particularly expensive drugs and implants are excluded from the GHS tariff perimeter and are an additional reimbursement, based on hospitals' real costs, unit by unit, each time they are prescribed by a hospital, provided they fulfil certain criteria: a high cost per unit and a non-generalized use (because these two factors introduce an important cost heterogeneity within the cost of the DRG to which they are attached); and the inscription on a list published yearly (or more often depending on the arrival of new products on the market) by the French Ministry of Health.

Other possible uses of casemix

An important indirect consequence of casemix development in France has been the development of expertise in ICTs and clinical terminology of all stakeholders: hospitals, universities, health administration, and the press. The DIMs (Medical Information Departments) provide the resource pool in medical coding systems and information systems, which were lacking in the early 1980s. They play an increasing role within hospitals and are federated in regional and national colleges.

Casemix has not been recommended as a tool for internal management, because the total cost approach that was chosen implies that the tariff attached to a given DRG takes into account transversal costs (i.e. costs not directly attached to the unit where the patient is treated, but also those linked to support units and accessory activities gravitating around this category of patients, while hospitals are being managed on a unit basis (per medical specialty). In practice, however, this is used more and more for hospital internal management and strategic planning. Hospital managers are now taking casemix into account in day-to-day management, and most hospital finance directors are completely familiar with casemix-based accounting:

- to analyze their activity (studies of segments of activity defined by medical unit, length of stay, patient's age, type of diagnosis, type of care, etc.) and to appreciate the fit between the organization and its actual activity;
- to realize a prospective calculation of their budgets, estimate their marginal and overall costs, and the gap between costs and revenue for each type of activity;
- to realize benchmarks with other hospitals or with the national database on various criteria (cost, casemix, length of stay, etc.);

- to implement internal contracting, hospital-level strategic planning;
- to estimate a target level of activity and a target size to achieve, with a view to the negotiation with the Regional Agency on capacity planning.

Casemix is then used for planning at the regional level through the Regional Schemes for Sanitary Organization (Schémas Régionaux d'Orientation Sanitaire, or SROS) established by the Regional Agencies for Hospitalization as a planning tool.

Most universities have developed curricula in medical information (masters as well as doctoral) with an initial training for each different school of health care professionals.

The national hospital organizations (for university hospitals, public hospitals, cancer centers, private for-profit and private not-for-profit hospitals) have developed their own research teams on casemix, and sometimes their own national database.

Casemix is not yet used for quality assurance, except by looking regularly at some indicators. However, it should be noted that this type of use is currently under development (COMPAQH project).

Some epidemiological applications have also been developed using the Anonymous Unique Patient Identifier (e.g. in neonatology in Burgundy and for cancer in the Rhône-Alpes region).

Casemix is used for benchmarking, but the only comparisons that have been made public up to now were undertaken by the press, and these comparisons have been heavily criticized. Consequently, benchmarking based on casemix data cannot yet be regarded as institutionalized, but the data are public and can be accessed from the ATIH for benchmarking. The only limit is that all data must be anonymous, which explains, for instance, why no data are provided on death rates. [4]–[8]

Impact, debates, controversies and future prospects

While the introduction of casemix through the PMSI has been a slow process and has encountered many setbacks and much opposition, the use of casemix as a means to reform the hospital financing system has been progressively and surprisingly well-accepted by all stakeholders – it could even be argued that, in its basic principles, this reform is rather consensual.

However, debate over casemix and its uses has not yet ended. The extension of casemix to new areas of care poses many new questions, and the technical options taken to implement casemix-based financing generate passionate discussions. All these elements might serve as a basis for lessons to potential new adopters of casemix systems.

Regarding project management

Though an initiative at the national level with strong political support may be useful as a first step, important efforts and time must also be invested to convince the different stakeholders

This was demonstrated notably by the important promotion work performed by Mme. Aoustin, head of the team in charge of the implementation of the new system.

The French example shows that for successful implementation of a casemix system, an initiative at the national level with strong political support may be necessary, especially where doctors are traditionally resistant to any form of control, and where hospital managers fear an increase in state control. This may not be true when applied to a traditionally more decentralized country, or in a country where the relationship between stakeholders is more peaceful. However, from an institutional point of view, it is interesting to note that the development of casemix in France has been essentially driven by semi-autonomous bodies, whether they were dedicated task forces within the Ministry of Health, or took the form of an independent agency.

The French case shows that casemix can be successful even though it is not immediately used for financing

This may be France-specific, but it demonstrates that slow implementation is not necessarily a hurdle.

Regarding casemix itself

The French GHM classification does not effectively describe everything that happens within a hospital, hence the necessity of separate forms of financing for teaching, research, etc.

The principle of activity data collection within acute care hospitals can be regarded as irreversible at this stage: little more than twenty years after its first steps, the PMSI works and it works well – even if data collection remains an issue in some borderline areas when the field of what should be described is not precisely known (e.g. "frontier procedures" – those procedures at the limit between hospital and ambulatory care) or when the choice has been made to exclude certain areas that arguably should be included within the PMSI perimeter (e.g. ambulatory radiotherapy). This can be regarded as unavoidable, and no country has implemented a pure per-case hospital payment system as of yet; it generates many difficulties and results in a fairly complicated system.

If PMSI works well for acute care activities in the fields of medicine, surgery, and obstetrics, it can be regarded as a worrisome inconvenience to exclude whole areas of hospital care. At this stage, the French GHM classification does not take into account what happens outside of the hospital, be it upstream or downstream of hospital care, or in the mental health care field

Extension of the casemix methodology outside the acute care sector has started with the development of an Anonymous Unique Patient Identifier (AUPI) in 2002 to link hospital and ambulatory care procedures. This opens the opportunity for the collection of comprehensive information regarding each patient, as planned by the ambitious project of Shared Medical Records (named DMP). Regarding rehabilitation care (named SSR) and psychiatric care, the clinical information recording tests have not been conclusive, and the new classification tools are still under field testing. Regarding ambulatory care, the newly-developed coding system, CCAM, appears very promising, and has piqued foreign countries' interest as a universal tool to code for procedures.

What is more, beyond the global assessment that PMSI works well, it can be argued that the quality of coding is insufficiently evaluated/assessed at this stage.

The only evaluations that have been made as to the overall quality of coding are old or incomplete, and no continuous follow-up is performed. Evaluations estimate the rate of coding errors inducing classification in the wrong GHM as 5 percent in the private sector and 10–20 percent in the public sector. This may appear to be a "reasonable" rate, but could probably be improved. However, a comprehensive procedure for external control (i.e. control that is external to the hospital, operated under the responsibility of the Regional Agency for Hospitalization) was developed in 2004 to allow a systematic automated "on file" control and a selective "on the field" control. Sanctions incurred by faulty hospitals encompass payback of unjustified billing, as well as financial penalties (limited to 5 percent of the hospital's total yearly budget).

**Linked to the development of such interesting new tools as the CCAM,
another concern lies in France's ability to promote its tools abroad: in the past,
France has proved unable to properly market its classification system**

This has resulted, for instance, in the adoption by Germany of the
Australian classification a few years ago, while the French classification
would have been a sensible choice. The lack of international cooperation
regarding the development of classification systems, combined with the
traditional French tendency to stand on its own, probably means that,
regrettably, France will remain isolated for the foreseeable future.

Debates regarding casemix-based financing

Rarely has a health reform in France been supported as much and as broadly
as casemix-based hospital financing. Both public and private hospitals, all
medical organizations, and all public institutions involved have agreed with the
major principles of the reform. The first explanation for this general agreement
has much to do with the fact that no one was satisfied with the former system,
and everyone agreed that a change had to be made. Moreover, casemix-based
financing appears to be a fair system, which is a primordial advantage considering that the major flaw of the former system was its unfairness (as well as
its lack of transparency from the regulator's point of view). Besides, the need
for more transparency and better management of public hospitals had long
been recognized by most stakeholders. However, this initial consensus on the
reform has naturally receded as the actual implications of the new system were
better understood, and as technical details began to be discussed.

Both public and private hospitals complained about the level of the tariffs
for 2005, claiming that for the same level of activity, they would receive less
funding, while, on the contrary, and in order to smooth the transition toward
the new system, overall expenditures on hospital acute care were increased.
Stakeholders have also been complaining that the tariff calculation method
and the determinants for calculation of the various budgets and their allot-
ment to the hospitals were not clear and, more worrying when you're supposed to set up pluriannual strategic plans, not foreseeable enough.

**Most of the initial complaints and reactions concern issues linked
to the implementation process, in particular the delays in announcements
and the lack of transparency and communication.**

To take an example, the tariff scale applicable to private hospitals in 2005
was only announced in the first week of March 2005, leaving no room for

preparation by the concerned hospitals. Similarly, the list of drugs and medical devices to be reimbursed in addition to the GHS tariffs has been published quite late. The lack of clear information on several technical aspects regarding payment also generates confusion. It was difficult for most providers to have a clear view of what their budget situation would be by the end of 2005.

Also, the share of the total hospital budget devoted to casemix-based or other activity-based types of payment, and the share to be allocated on a budget basis to account for certain specific costs not directly related to care, are not precisely defined, which is another source of uncertainty.

A tariff calculation system based on average observed costs is not satisfactory in the long run: the current GHS tariff calculation system, even if it undergoes continuous improvement, cannot be regarded as the ultimate ideal methodology and will have to be cumulated with other methods, the first of which is the approach in terms of standard costs.

First of all, the system's transparency and predictability are deemed insufficient by the involved actors, who complain that they don't know how tariffs are being calculated, so they are not able to anticipate their evolution and take this into account in their strategy. Furthermore, they are incapable of adapting their behavior in a rational way, which could prevent fulfillment of the objectives pursued by national public health care authorities.

The system is characterized by the fact that it mixes tariff macroeconomic management (through global variation of tariffs in order to ensure that the national objective for hospital expenses is met – this mechanism is called price–volume regulation) and microeconomic management (through the targeted fluctuation of some tariffs in order to provide incentives or disincentives).

Finally, it can be said that the average cost does not constitute a sufficient grounding on which to build the GHM weighted cost scale: just as the average observed cost should not serve as a tariff, it is not necessarily valid as a means to weight tariffs. As a matter of fact, the average observed cost is not necessarily the right cost . . .

The calculation and allocation of the budget devoted to public interest duties promises to remain a source of important conflicts and rivalries.

Both the public and the private hospital sectors expressed their concern as to the share and global amount of this budget (supposed to cover the costs linked to teaching, research and other public interest duties not described as part of the hospitals' activity by the PMSI) relative to what is devoted to casemix-based financing. The allocation of this budget also constitutes an important and controversial issue. Private hospitals fear that the budget could be used as a mechanism to make up for the relative inefficiency of larger public hospitals, while public hospitals have expressed doubts about estimating these kinds of costs properly and accurately. However, the requirement for public hospitals to identify and assess the cost of the different public interest duties they support may prove an effective means of improving the transparency of public hospital budgets and management.

Concerning convergence of the GHS tariff scales of public and private hospitals, comparing and bringing closer two different tariff scales proves a difficult task.

It has already been said that the GHS tariffs are currently much higher in the public than in the private sector – partly because they include doctors' fees, but also for other reasons. According to the 2005 Financial Bill for Social Security, "For the years 2005 to 2012, ... the national DRG tariffs ... are calculated while taking into account the convergence process ... which must be over, except for the differences justified by differences in the nature of the costs covered by these tariffs, latest in 2012. The target tariffs convergence will have to be met by 50% by 2008." Thus, the objective of achieving the "right reference cost" being set, the assessment of cost production within hospitals (and, more specifically, on the quantification and qualification of cost differences within and between hospital sectors) has now become a priority.

Regarding convergence of the lists of drugs and medical devices reimbursed in addition to the GHS tariffs, political pressures are likely to be felt strongly.

The drugs gathered on this list represent today about 24.4 percent of the total amount of French hospital expenses (e.g. oncology treatments, blood-derived drugs, orphan drugs, EPO, most implantable devices, etc.). In 2004 the list for medical devices was originally composed of cardiovascular devices, but it now includes a great number of implantable medical devices, among which are most of the devices used in orthopedic surgery.

The choice of such a system is risky: though it guarantees access to the products that are on the list (mostly innovative products), it is also potentially inflationary and may generate distortions in medical practices (i.e. in the use of other products of the same category in the event that they are not on the list). Thus, this system implies the implementation of a specific regulation, which in France is twofold with:

- a macroeconomic price–volume regulation (not specific to drugs and medical devices) according to which, if the global hospital activity grows in year n, the DRG tariffs will be lowered in year n+1 to ensure that the global hospital budget is not exceeded;
- a microeconomic regulation, both medical (through contracts passed between each hospital and the regional agencies to guarantee that drugs and medical devices are prescribed according to national and international medical standards and recommendations) and financial (through a maximum unit price for each drug and medical device on the list, above which a hospital will not be reimbursed).

The contents of this list differ, depending on whether it applies to public and not-for-profit private hospitals (formerly financed through a global budget) or to for-profit hospitals (formerly financed on a fee-for-service basis). Under their former financing system, for-profit hospitals benefited from a full reimbursement, unit by unit, for all the medical devices they bought: the list which applies to them is thus longer and more detailed than the one used for public and not-for-profit private hospitals to smooth the transition to the new financing system.

The willingness of public hospitals to regain market share in surgery has led their unions to put pressure on the government to extend their list of medical devices reimbursed in addition to the GHS tariffs and make it as close as possible to the one used for private for-profit hospitals. There is concern that the system will be hard to maintain: even when all the conditions required to remove a category of devices from the list and reintegrate it so the GHS tariffs are met, hospitals (whether public or private) will exert pressure to prevent this from happening.

In conclusion, some lessons can be drawn from the French experience.

While the various stakeholders remain favorable to the new system in principle, there are many debates about the technical details of the new system's definition and implementation. However, the implementation of casemix-based financing can now be deemed an irreversible process: the new system is now operational and casemix being used in practice for financing in both public and private hospitals, it is unlikely that a political decision could be made which would completely stop the reform in its tracks.

Nevertheless, the balance between the part of revenue directly related to care and the other parts of the revenue and how they are defined is permanently on the agenda.

The French example demonstrates clearly that strong political support is a necessary, but not sufficient, condition for the success of an initiative at the national level. Significant investment in efforts and time to develop the support of key stakeholders is also required.

An interesting debate for others is the contradictory role of "winner" and "loser" hospitals when a new financing method is introduced (as in the 1996 reform, which showed inequity and inefficiency across regions and types of hospitals). [9][10] Some decisions in favor of reducing such differences were made, and the losers were some well-known university hospitals and over-funded regions, the most important one being Ile de France which includes Paris. The winners were under-funded regions and smaller hospitals, like those from Picardie and Poitou-Charentes. There were also opponents who considered that the changes were not fast enough. The joint efforts of the opposing actors were effective in the PPS reform of 2003.

Concerning public/private hospital sector convergence, an important French specificity lies in the fact that the T2A reform must be applied to two sectors formerly financed in different ways: interesting lessons will also be learned from this experience in the coming years. It is, however, a little early to say if convergence will be successful and what the major success/failure factors will be.

Finally, to be fair, it is necessary to stress that the French example is not showing important accompanying measures that have been or are underestimated (e.g. integrating the casemix implementation clearly within a health care reform, early investment in DRG and information technology, training programs and economic incentives for managerial and government innovation, and transparency in the entire annual funding decision process).

REFERENCES

[1] Gay, P. (1996). *The Enlightenment: An Interpretation.* New York: W.W. Norton Company.

[2] Gay, P. (1959). *Voltaire's Politics.* Princeton, NJ: Princeton University Press.

[3] Rodrigues, J. M., Trombert-Paviot, B., Martin, C., and Vercherin, P. (2002). Is the French enlightened despotism able to change a casemix adjusted budget allocation with a national hospital service into a US-type Prospective Payment System to create market competition? Budapest: Proceedings 20th PCS/E International Conference.

[4] Décret n 83.744 du 14 août 1983 relatif à la gestion et au financement des établissements d'hospitalisation publics et privés participant au service public hospitalier.

[5] Fetter, R. B., Shin, Y., Freeman, J. L., Averill, R. F., and Thompson, J. D. (1980). Casemix Definition by Diagnosis Related Groups. *Medical Care* 18 (Suppl 2):1–53.

[6] Loi n°91–748 du 31 juillet 1991 portant réforme hospitalière.

[7] 560 hôpitaux le palmarès 2000. *Le Figaro*. October 2000; n 17467, Dossier spécial, 48 pages.

[8] Ordonnances n 96–344 du 24 avril 1996 portant mesures relatives à la maîtrise médicalisée des dépenses de soins.

[9] Coca, E. (1998). *Hôpital Silence! Les inégalités entre hôpitaux*. Paris: Berger-Levrault.

[10] Quentin, C., Bouzelat, H., *et al.* (1998). How to Ensure Data Security of an Epidemiological Follow-up: Quality Assessment of an Anonymous Record Linkage Procedure. *International Journal of Medical Informatics* 49:117–22.

7 Introduction and use of DRGs in Belgium

Marie Christine Closon, Francis H. Roger France, and Julian Perelman

A brief history of casemix systems in Belgium

All Belgian citizens are today covered by the social security system (following the Bismarck model), which is mainly financed through employment-related social contributions and general taxation. The health care system is regulated by the state and managed by INAMI (the National Institute against Illness and Disability). In INAMI, mutualities and representatives of medical professionals negotiate medical services, such as procedures and drugs, included in the nomenclature. For each service, a national fee and percentage of reimbursement is determined. Fees cover full costs and are owed to the physician, who is paid by service for ambulatory care, outpatient and inpatient care.

The Ministry (Federal Public Service) of Public Health defines the price of a day's stay for each hospital, based upon its infrastructure, accommodation and nursing care (45 percent of hospital financing). This price is based on the advice of several committees, including members of the hospital administration, physicians, and financial partners.

Physicians' activities in hospitals are covered by the reimbursement of fees for services (41 percent of hospital financing) and drugs by fees (14 percent). Inside each hospital, physicians negotiate with the medical and financial managers to determine the portion of their fees retained for overhead costs (equipment, materials, infrastructure, worker s, etc.). This open hospital financing system (by day and by service), which operates without a predetermined budget, has generated a rapid increase in the number of days, medical services and procedures performed, resulting in an exponential growth in the overall cost.

In this context, it appeared necessary to control the rise of payments in the current day and fee for services system through the development of a more cost-efficient financing system.

To achieve this, a way to calibrate prospective hospital budgets had to be developed. In 1983, the Minister of Social Affairs and Public Health, Mr. J. L. Dehaene, assigned a quota of days for each hospital, and introduced a partial prospective budget for laboratory procedures based on a hospital's casemix, which was approximated by the surgical procedure data available from the fee-for-service based financing system.

The progressive implementation of DRGs in Belgium is thus the result of a combination of a context of growing hospital expenditures and a few very motivated individuals, as well as hospitals, university researchers and political decisions. Interest in implementing DRGs arose after Robert B. Fetter spent a sabbatical year at the Université Catholique de Louvain toward the end of the 1970s, from his model for a prospective payment program for Medicare claims in the United States. DRG can be implemented only if medical data are available, and availability of casemix data in Belgium has been a long, gradual process. In 1971, the Scientific Policy initiated an inter-university study on hospital data collection that resulted in the first medical record summary. This was proposed by F. H. Roger France, and was implemented first in Belgium and soon thereafter at the European level (1982). DRGs were initially tested at the Centre for Medical Informatics of the Université Catholique de Louvain in 1980. In 1985, the Ministry of Health financed a research study comparing university hospitals. The very detailed information system contains resources used, available by patient, including payment for services and drugs, and is linkable to the medical record summary for each stay and a minimum financial data set. This research showed a high variability of the length of stay (LOS) and resources used according to DRG across hospitals, and the usefulness of the medical and financial summaries for internal management, health care services financing, evaluating quality of care, and tracking epidemiological trends. The study was extended on a voluntary basis to forty hospitals. At this point, it was a question of research and development, which explained the enthusiasm of hospitals to participate. They felt themselves to be an integral part of the process of working out a new system of financing. The development approach was based on a bottom-up voluntary demonstration of convincing results, rather than a top-down imposition of ready-made solutions. This prompted the Minister of Health, Mr. Ph. Busquin, to legally enact in 1990 mandatory registration of a minimum basic data set using ICD–9–CM codes in all acute care hospitals. These data had to be sent to the Ministry of Public Health. The translation of the ICD–9–CM code into French and Flemish allowed the groups to be applied in Belgium immediately, both for operations and diagnoses.

How DRGs are used in Belgium

In 1995, All Patient Diagnosis Related Groups (APDRGs) of 3M were chosen as the grouping method to establish comparisons for financial purposes. This version was selected due to its ready accessibility at an affordable price and its ability to enable international comparisons. The new financing system was applied first to financing LOS only. Each acute care hospital in Belgium received, for each admission, a prospective number of justified days corresponding to the national average LOS by pathology (APDRGs) and age (plus or minus 75 years and geriatric profile). Hospitals were progressively held responsible for any excess of days, whereas a number of days below the prospective amount generated profits. Meanwhile, a reward or penalty was also applied based upon whether a hospital's percentage of one day surgeries for thirty-two surgical APDRGs was above or below the national average. However, the progressive extension of the new payment system to other sources of hospital financing (medical and drugs fees) was a much more difficult issue.

Belgium potentially has an extraordinary hospital information system, as for each patient medical data and detailed standardized resource utilization data (all medical services, drugs, etc.) are available at the hospital level. However, medical data are processed by the Ministry of Public Health, while billing data are sent to the mutuality for reimbursement. Information was considered a source of power and each party was afraid to lose it by merging the data. The question of privacy was also important. As a result of these difficulties, it would take a long time to define the conditions for data bank merging and access. The availability of such a database could extend the DRG payment system from LOS to all physician fees for services.

However, there is a further difficulty linked to the type of physician payment in Belgium. In most countries where a DRG or casemix system was applied to hospital financing, the system moved from an historical budget to a budget linked to casemix. In such a move, the real activities of the physicians appear to be considered more carefully. In Belgium, physicians are now paid for each individual service they provide, independent of its usefulness. Going from such a system to a limitation of payment according to pathology is much less acceptable for Belgian physicians, because they consider it a loss of freedom of care and protest the idea of being controlled, evaluated and penalized for financial reasons rather than medical criteria. The new financing system will completely change the relationship between physicians and hospital managers. Today, physicians' acts are a source of revenue not only for physicians, but also for hospitals, and this grants physicians significant power on the hospital level.

Physicians are also one of the main actors (along with mutualities) in the financing decisions inside the INAMI and in the advisory committees at the Ministry of Public Health.

This could explain the resistance of physicians and hospital managers to a prospective payment system: first, it would place a limit on resources, and second, it would completely change the physician–manager relationship within hospitals. Because of this, the extension of an APDRG financing system in Belgium for medical fees and drugs can only be done "politically" very gradually. A first step toward implementation for medical fees was enacted in 2004 with the reform of "amounts of references," which penalizes hospitals that have mean expenditures higher than a lump sum for services (clinical biology, radiology and internal medicine services) for the lowest levels of severity (levels one and two) for twenty-eight APRDRGs. Hospital budgets for drugs were brought into accordance with APRDRGs in July of 2006. A list of drugs not included in the budget was defined to avoid any risk to quality of care. Special payment will be provided for these outliers.

APRDRGs – a basis for case-based payment, or criteria to calibrate budgets?

It is impossible to take into account all of the factors that may impact the treatment and costs for each patient. Because of this uncertainty, there will always be some variation in mean expenditures according to casemix and other factors of the prospective financing system. It is difficult to evaluate this variation, which is in part due to the characteristics of the patient, as well as to efficiency and quality of care. It is for this reason that physicians in Belgium often argue for payment by pathology, based on guidelines. However, this can be applied only for a very few highly standardized medical procedures, and only if there is no co-morbidity.

Precision of expenditure means APRDRG, even by level of severity, is often very weak. Therefore, while prospective payment by admission based on APRDRGs limits risk of overconsumption, it creates risk in that some hospitals may not receive enough money to provide appropriate care for certain patients. For this reason, APRDRGs are not a good tool for financing by patient or admission, but only for the calibration of a global hospital budget. This allows for a more acceptable share of risk across patients and across APRDRGs.

A mixed financing system, partially prospective and partially retrospective, is another way to share risk between financing authorities and hospitals: retrospective special payments for outliers, financing for specific functions (emergency care, research, teaching, etc.), and exclusion of some pathologies from the prospective payment system (e.g. psychiatry) can be used. In Belgium, thanks to the fee for services system, it is also possible to share risk, by acts or by drugs, between the financing authorities and the hospital. This is already in effect for clinical biology, and will be for drugs in the near future; for both, prospective payment according to APRDRG can be applied only on 50 to 70 per cent of the fees. The complementary percentage continues to be financed by acts or drugs. This system allows maintenance of an information system linked to actual use of resources, which can be very useful in evaluating quality of care, cost shifting, etc.

In summary, APRDRGs are actually used for financing LOS (45 percent of hospital financing) and drugs for all acute hospitals in Belgium, and will be progressively used in the financing of other medical services. Prospective payment is based on mean LOS or lump sum by admission according to APRDRG and level of severity. The extension of casemix applications to all acute care hospitals has been both a bottom-up process, due to the initiatives of some universities and hospitals to implement APDRGs and to define their possible uses, and a top-down approach enacted by successive governments. The two key factors that allowed the acceptance of the case-mix by physicians and hospital administrators were their initial involvement in research projects that demonstrated the superiority of APDRGs compared to other systems in explaining resource use and the payment of coders in all hospitals provided they had been trained appropriately in the coding rules issued by the ministry.

DRGs: Objectives

The initial and main objective of the Belgian government has been financial reform from a fee for services system to a payment system based on casemix. Another objective was the use of internal management and benchmarking. However, this second purpose is generally incorporated into, and often to the extent that, the casemix system is used for financing. The quality of care was also mentioned, to encourage linkage of local data sets to the minimum basic data set. Another field of interest concerns epidemiological studies: comparisons of frequencies of diseases in the MBDS national sample to other data sources (national cancer register, Monica register for acute myocardial infarction, etc.), and an atlas showing geographical variation in the distribution of inpatient diseases and surgical procedures. The Ministry regularly provides feedback to hospitals, allowing them to compare their data to the national data.

Technicalities

The MBDS in Belgium has been developed according to European recommendations. The ICD–9–CM code was chosen. Versions are updated every two years, following the American, as well as DRG grouper, modifications. Belgium decided not to use ICD–10 in order to avoid mapping biases in the use of DRG groupers. The Ministry of Public Health has developed, jointly with several universities, computer programs to check data errors and inconsistencies, taking into account the coding rules edited by an expert group working for the Ministry of Health and comparing different sources of data, such as INAMI billing codes and ICD–9–CM codes. Interpretations are edited on the web in answer to coding questions asked by various hospitals. Clinicians are involved in the MBDS data collection through the content of their medical reports to general practitioners. In some hospitals, coding is done within departments, but the majority of hospitals utilize an editing process by trained coders in a centralized medical records department, often with the help of coding tools.

The ministry has also developed, in collaboration with scientific experts, program data auditing methods to combat fraud. These include a statistical overview of the situation, looking particularly at hospitals that suddenly have heavy diagnoses or a jump in very short stays for certain APRDRGs, and a re-encoding process of medical reports selected at random in order to compare results from the inspection to those of the hospital.

Assessment of the application of DRGs in Belgium

The impact of the implementation of prospective payment for LOS in Belgium was studied in 1995 using a database that included all acute hospitals from 1991–8, according to the comprehensive overview of expected effects of a shift toward prospective payment done by Coulam and Gaumer (1991). We observed a continuation of the slowdown of LOS across the whole period, except for a slight acceleration in 1995. The decrease is bigger in hospitals that were penalized by the reform, and for older patients.

The effect on older patients can be explained by better organization of hospital discharges (more quickly sent home or to nursing care, improved linkages to ambulatory services and care).

A shift toward prospective payment creates an incentive to increase the number of admissions. In Belgium, the number of classical admissions was stable before the reform. It increased significantly (2 percent) in 1995 and subsequent years, not including one-day surgery, which, over the period from 1995–8, rose sharply (42 percent). Another possible effect is growth in hospital expenditures not submitted for prospective payment, such as (in Belgium) medical fees. The data show that the growth in hospital expenditures related to medical services did in fact increase after the reform. At this stage, the new financing system did not allow for cost saving on total service expenditures, and may even have produced higher rates of total expenditures.

One of the most commonly cited consequences of implementing a prospective payment system is the change in casemix. Hospitals have a strong incentive to improve coding or to "up-code" to increase reimbursement. We measured the change in the level of severity by determining the percentage changes in the average number of affected systems by patient. The average severity was stable until 1994, then experienced a dramatic increase in the three years following (+7 percent over the three years). The most plausible interpretation of the increase in severity is the coding effect.

The objective of prospective payment is to reduce inefficiencies. However, hospitals may be prompted to shorten stays to such an extent that it could become detrimental to patient care. According to APRDRG and level of severity, mortality rates declined steadily over the complete period, but the rate of decline decreases after the reform. Some underestimation of post-reform mortality rates may occur; as LOS decreases, more patients may be dying at home or in nursing homes. On the other hand, our data may be biased by coding changes, as lower-severity patients may be classified at a more severe level in the APRDRG. As for readmissions, we observed a significant (3.45 percent) increase in 1995, while readmissions had been quite stable in the previous years. This could be a sign of poorer quality of treatment, but also could reflect splitting of hospital stays.

Another effect of prospective payment can be "cream skimming," or preferred risk selection. Hospitals may distinguish several groups of individuals with different expected costs within a risk group for which the risk adjusted per capita is the same, to select the most profitable ones and deny care to the others. One study using a large set of sixty-one Belgian hospitals shows the impact of severity and social factors on LOS, taking into account

APRDRG, age, and geriatric profile. It illuminates the problem of risk selection if social factors or severity of cases are ignored or not given enough weight in the financing formula. This selection can be direct, or indirect through hospitals' specialization in the more profitable specialties or patients. Further research has analyzed the impact of social factors related to APRDRG on use of resources, based on social data collected by the mutuality, and a corrective factor will be applied to hospital budgets to take into account this impact of social factors on LOS. A hospital survey was also distributed after the reform to assess the number of references for medical services in twenty-eight APRDRGs. The survey shows that the small impact of the hospital financing reforms resulted in the disinterest of physicians and managers. Physician and hospital reactions have focused more on ways to bypass the reform (medical tests conducted pre- and post-hospital stay) than on improving efficiency.

In summary, implementing an APRDRG payment system resulted in a slight decrease in LOS, a large increase in severity, a sharp increase in readmission, an increase in growth of total expenditures, a slowdown in the decline of mortality rates, a risk of selection bias, and a risk of "bypass" of the reform. The prospective payment by APRDRGs enables pathology-based clarification of hospital production and can induce studies on decreasing costs based on the resources provided in the treatment of the patient. It also can result in "escape" or "bypass" strategies by hospitals, and is not a guarantee of cost containment, efficiency improvement or quality of care. It can favor adverse selection and impair accessibility to care if certain factors (social, severity, etc.) are not taken into account. It appears to be an irreversible process, but it should be made clear that such reform needs to be as global as possible to avoid cost shifting and adverse selection. Evaluation programs for quality, outcomes, admissions and readmissions must be set up, and guidelines developed in order to allow evaluations based on clinical criteria. Greater attention to quality problems and evaluation is one positive effect of the prospective financing reform. As is often the case in the health care sector, introduction of efficiency incentives must be stringently regulated in order to avoid adverse effects.

New trends

To improve data collection, computer programs to check data input have been provided to hospitals by the Ministry of Public Health. Data transfer will be done through the web, beginning in 2006.

To supplement the medical record summaries, it appeared necessary to analyze more specific data sets in nursing, psychiatry and emergency care. Research projects are also devoted to intensive care (SAPI score), geriatric and rehabilitation units, and casemix tools. The question of episodes of care is also very important. Additional research has taken into account hospital stay and all billed data (visits, diagnostic tests, drugs, etc.) prior to and following hospital stay. However, the lack of diagnosis data in ambulatory care remains. The inclusion of such data is still experimental (except for day cases), given its large volume. A follow up study of clinical guidelines is also planned.

Standards have been developed for data transfer, using XML, and a new law is in discussion regarding secure access to patient data through a federal portal to a network of health services (Be-Health Project). Data warehousing is used to facilitate feedback to users.

The rapid development of the EPR (electronic patient records) system in Belgium offers new possibilities for collecting and checking data. Problem lists are recommended as a way to summarize the content of the record. They could be used to ascertain data comprehensiveness. More uniform medical language could also help select diagnoses and procedures in texts automatically. It has been advised that an indicator of a "new" diagnosis should be added.

In conclusion, APRDRGs are a useful tool for the clarification of hospital production. Their implementation favors the development of quality evaluation and cost effectiveness research. Their use in prospective financing opens many questions, and will require continued new developments.

8 | DRGs in Germany: Introduction of a comprehensive, prospective DRG payment system by 2009

Günter Neubauer and Florian Pfister

(1) The system of hospital care provision in Germany: An overview

To understand the discussion about the DRG payment system, it is helpful to give a short overview of the German system of providing hospital services. We will do this in a graphical way. In Figure 8.1 three modules determine the structure: first, the module of the providers which are the hospitals, second, the module of demand which is subdivided into a financing and a consuming element, third, the module of co-ordinating supply and demand. The co-ordinating module again, is computed out of two elements: planning by the states ('Länder') and the reimbursement system.

Demand

We begin with a brief explanation of the demand side. Demand is based on the needs of the population, which depend on several demographic factors. Some import figures are illustrated in Table 8.1.

Health care in Germany is based on the principle of social insurance rooted in the time of Bismarck, enacted in 1883.

By the year 2050, dramatic challenges are expected. The population will decrease by 10 million; people older than sixty-five will increase by about 15 million. At the moment the health expenditures of the last group are financed at a share of 50 percent by the younger generation, which will itself dwindle by about 20 million. This scenario makes all politicians nervous.

Will the current social health insurance system (SHI) be able to manage this problem?

Financing

On the financing side, sickness funds are the sustaining pillar of the system. In the beginning, only blue collar employees were mandated to join sickness funds. Company based sickness funds ('Betriebskrankenkassen') were started prior to local organised sickness funds ('Ortskrankenkassen'). In the 1920s, white collar workers became mandatorily insured. They were free to join an existing sickness fund or could fulfill their mandate by remaining in one of the existing private insurances specialising in white collar employees.

In 1996 all the mandatorily insured – 90 percent of the population – received the right of free choice among all sickness funds. This was the beginning of competition inside the SHI. As the contribution rates are strictly related to the salaries, and family dependents without their own salary are co-insured free, sickness funds collect different volumes of contributions according to labour income and family status. In a competitive world, sickness funds with high social burdens are losing because their contribution rates are high, and mobile and flexible contributors will move to sickness funds with low rates.

To compensate for these unequal conditions, a risk adjustment fund was established. About 15 percent of all contributions are reallocated by this fund.

Around the beginning of the discussion to introduce free choice for the insured, sickness funds acted and reacted with a concentration of the funds. From 1,200 independent funds in 1992, the number declined to 260 in 2005 and this process is still ongoing.

The privately insured represent 10 percent of the population, and an additional 10 percent have supplementary private insurance for amenities the sickness fund will not cover.

At the moment 300,000 inhabitants have no coverage at all. Most of them had been privately insured and lost their job, so the employer no longer pays 50 percent of the rate and they cannot afford to pay 100 percent. Nevertheless, in case of illness social assistance has to cover the costs of treatment in case of need.

The sickness funds are semi-public institutions and are mandated to reimburse the providers. The two big players on the provider side are the hospitals through the state hospital associations and the panel physicians that are – via regional associations – contractors of the SHI and obliged to treat all mandatorily insured. Although the mandatorily insured patients have no direct access to hospitals, the regional panel physician associations are powerful, and they negotiate the mode and volume of reimbursement with the regional associations of sickness funds.

A 1989 law obligates sickness funds to limit their expenditures strictly to the volume of their annual contributions, to avoid higher contribution rates which imply an increase of labour costs by the fringe benefits.

Supply

Hospital services are offered by 2,197 (2003) hospitals with 541,901 beds. 40 percent of the hospitals and 60 percent of the beds are owned by public institutions (i.e. municipalities and the state), 40 percent of hospitals with 30 percent of beds are run by charities and 20 percent of the hospitals with 10 percent of the beds are private for-profit hospitals. Since 1992, the market has been restructured in favour of private for-profit hospitals (see Figure 8.7). Hospital physicians and nurses are employees. Only 5 percent of physicians are visiting physicians with their own offices. In public hospitals the contracts of physicians often cannot be terminated, in private hospitals tariffs of personnel are more flexible, although contracted within tariffs.

The heads of departments usually have the right to receive private payment, meaning that privately insured patients have to pay them directly. These payments often exceed the salary of other physicians by three to six times. Hospitals are beginning to cancel private payment and charge the private patients directly. Under these new arrangements, physicians receive a share from the hospital.

The remuneration of office-based panel physicians follows a per capita formula. The different regional sickness associations negotiate the per capita volume with the regional association of panel doctors. The regional association of panel doctors distributes the collected money in a fee for service mode to their members. The consequence: If services increase faster than the total volume, fees per service go down.

For hospitals, panel physicians are the most important 'bed fillers'. As social insured patients have no direct access to hospitals – emergency cases exempted – 70 to 80 percent of the patients are referred by panel physicians. So hospitals offer networks to the panel physicians, while they also urge politicians to open hospitals for direct access. In the last reform in 2004, hospitals could allow more direct access.

Co-ordination

In our context, the co-ordinating module in Figure 8.1 is the most important.

On the one hand, co-ordination is done by the sixteen states; each state developed a hospital plan in which all necessary hospital capacity including number of beds per department is determined according to the planned provision. Investments in plan hospitals are financed out of taxes via the states. The Hospital Financing Law of 1972 says all big economic investments have to be financed by the states. Due to the present financial weaknesses of the states, the publicly financed investment rate of 5 percent of all expenditures is only half or even less of the required amount.

On the other hand, sickness funds negotiate as a group with a single plan hospital using a performance-based flexible budget; capital costs are excluded as these are financed by the states. Budgets have not been cost-based since 1995. Up to the introduction of DRGs in 2004–5, the number of bed-days delivered had been the most important performance unit (see Table 8.1). Since then the volume of cost weight has been subject to

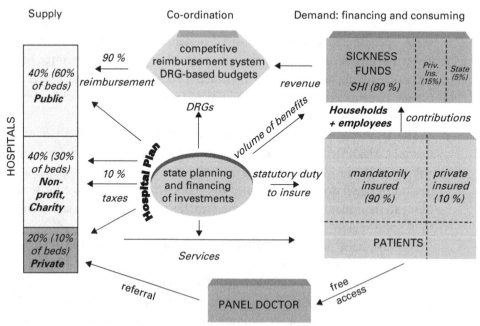

Source: Author's illustration

Figure 8.1   System of hospital care provision in Germany

Table 8.1 General demographic and health data (2004 if not otherwise stated)

General demographics		Health sector	
Population	82,431,390 (July 2005 est.)	Total health expenditure as % of GDP	10.9 (2002)
Life Expectancy	78.65 years	Physicians per 1,000	3.62
Pop. 65+ years	18.9 %	Gov. exp. on health as % of total exp.	78.5 (2002)
Child mortality per 1,000 (2003)	4.5	Bed occupancy rate	77.6 % (2003)
Fertility rate	1.39 children	Beds per 1,000 population	6.57 (2003)
GDP per capita in PPP	$28,700	Hospitals (acute only)	2,197 (2003)

Source: WHO 2005

negotiation. To constrain hospital expenditures, sickness funds are fixed by the law of stability which says expenditures must not exceed contribution volume per year. So hospitals have a cap on their budget according to stable contribution rates. If hospitals exceed this volume by treating more patients than contracted, reimbursement falls down to 35 percent of the 'normal' price of a DRG.

Competition enters into the system because the reduction of length of stay (LOS) overcompensates the increase of patients, which leads to an overcapacity of hospital beds.

Figure 8.2 shows trends which are observed worldwide. In Germany, these trends caused competition for patients, as an occupancy rate under 75 percent will result in a reduction in the budget. Hospital competition is mainly a quality competition in the direction of referring physicians and patients. To contain unit costs by improving efficiency, several hospital reforms have been launched. All hospital reforms since 1972 suffered the dilemma that the first chamber of parliament ('Bundestag') can only decide on the reimbursement system. The second chamber ('Bundesrat') is responsible for the state planning module; and has to agree in those instances when a reform of the reimbursement module will impact the state module (see Figure 8.1). Up to now, states have not been willing to give up hospital planning and investment financing, which is not consistent with a competitive reimbursement system. So hospitals have a so-called dualistic financing system. Current costs are reimbursed via DRGs by the sickness funds. Investments or capital costs are financed by the states. All plan

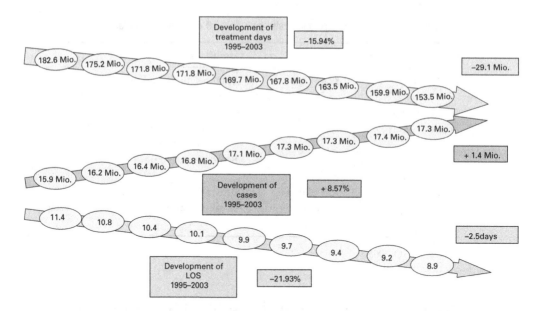

Source: Federal Statistical Office (Fachserie 12) 2005

Figure 8.2   Length of stay, number of patients, and hospital days from 1993–2003

hospitals are entitled to receive a negotiated budget via the sickness funds. Only the cost weights are subject to hospital negotiations over the budget. The base rate is negotiated at state level.

Where no agreement is reached, an arbitration board has to decide. Both sides, hospital and sickness funds, can appeal to a court as *ultima ratio*.

With this background it will be easier to understand the process of hospital reform in Germany. Since 1972, all reforms have been focused on the reimbursement module. The direction of all reforms aimed for intensified competition. Nevertheless, the state module of hospital planning and investment regulating survived. As of 2005, the governing coalition had a good chance to harmonise the reimbursement module and the state module and, by this, improve efficiency.

(2) The prehistory of DRGs

In *The Migration of Managerial Innovation*, published in 1993, the author contributed a chapter headlined 'Germany – an outsider in the DRG

Table 8.2 Modules of the current DRG-reimbursement system

Units of reimbursement	Mode of valuation	Flexible units
Volume of DRG casemix Negotiated between single hospital and sickness funds occupying 5% or more beds	*Base rate of state* Negotiated by state hospital associations or sickness funds	*Additional payments to DRGs (Zusatzentgelte)* Outliers, psychiatric patients, nurse schools

Source: Author's illustration

Table 8.3 German system of reimbursement from 1995–2004

Units of reimbursement	Mode of valuation	Flexible units
73 surgical patient groups 147 treatment complexes	Negotiated payments	Trimming points
Departmental *per diem* rates Basic *per diem* rate	Evaluated by costs based on a budget	Nursing schools; exceeding and undershooting budget lines

Source: Weibler, Zieres, p. 23, 2005

Development'. At that time there was a discussion in Germany about a reform of the hospital reimbursement system. The objective had been to establish a performance-oriented instead of a cost-based reimbursement system. As a result, a mixed system was introduced in 1995/6. About 80 surgical patient groups (following the Patient Management Category grouping system) and 220 treatment complexes (Sonderentgelte) were used alongside *per diem* rates differentiated according to the departments and basic *per diem* rates for general services. The first two reimbursement units have been evaluated by negotiation. The latter were still based on costs. Table 8.3 gives an overview.

All reimbursement units were embedded in a flexible budget. This meant that if a hospital increased its unit of reimbursement, the exceeding units were paid only 35 percent of the 'normal' value. However, if a hospital provided fewer units of reimbursement than negotiated, it received 65 percent of the 'normal' for covering fixed costs. Training for nurses was reimbursed outside the budget. These rules are also used in the DRG-based budgeting system.

It had been planned to increase the share of negotiated payments in the following years and to reduce cost-based reimbursement. But this failed mainly because of the resistance of the medical profession and the German Hospital Association. Also, the Health Ministry hesitated, trusting more in hospital budgeting than performance payments. Nevertheless, in these years hospitals had to learn how to code patients by means of diagnosis and procedures. The tenth version of the ICD code has been established and a procedure code has been introduced on the basis of the International Code of Procedures in Medicine (ICPM). Both codes, the ICD–10 and the ICPM, in a revised edition, are still in use for the G-DRG system.

In 1998 Germany experienced a fundamental change in its political agenda: the former liberal–conservative government was replaced by a social democratic–Green government. The Conservative health minister was replaced by a Green health minister. This political change and the recognition that a stepwise introduction of a new reimbursement system had proved to be impossible led to the political decision to change the old reimbursement system to the DRG system.

(3) The way to the DRG decision

With the political change in 1998, the administration of the Health Ministry also changed. The new administration was in favour of a comprehensive case-based hospital reimbursement system. The question was what kind of scheme to implement. At that time the eight municipal hospitals of the City of Hamburg tested the AP-DRG system with the purpose of an internal reallocation of resources. The responsible sickness funds urged the city to save an overall amount of €100 million within three years (Lohmann 2000, p. 190). To find out which hospitals were less efficient and could save money, the AP-DRGs were applied. At the same time, the 3M company began to lobby for AP-DRGs. Several hospital managers, health fund administrators and other decision makers were invited to visit the US to see DRGs at work. The Hamburg hospital test was probably the most important. It demonstrated that AP-DRGs were practical, coding was possible by a mapping system and the results helped to save money.

However, the German parliament did not decide which DRG system should be introduced, but commissioned the Federal Hospital Association and the seven federal associations of the sickness funds plus the association of private insurances to find out which DRG system was best suited to the German system. The associations were due to report in the first six months of 2000. Four DRG systems were in focus: the AP-DRG, as favourite, the

Table 8.4 Indicators of hospital efficiency in the year 2003 (*2002)

	Length of stay in days acute care	Number of acute care beds per 1,000	Hospital costs per patient in $	Health expenditure per capita in $
Germany	9.2*	6.6*	1,073	2,971$
France	5.6	3.8	1,196	2,832$
UK	6.7	3.7	–	–
USA	5.7	2.8	1,526	5,551$

Source: German Hospital Association 2005, OECD Health Data 2005

French GHM, the Austrian LKF and the Australian AR-DRG (Neubauer 2000). After six months of intense discussions, the Australian AR-DRG was chosen. One important reason for this was that the Australian government offered the system for a low fee, without any further conditions for future German system developments.

(4) Expectations of the DRG system

The main political hope was to increase hospital efficiency and by this contain the cost of health expenditure. It was decided that LOS should be shortened, and bed capacity reduced. By international standards, in Germany, the length of stay in hospitals is rather high as is the number of beds per 1,000 inhabitants. However, the cost per patient is modest.

The private, for-profit hospitals have mainly supported the DRG introduction. They expected that their better management would help them overtake public hospitals. The public hospitals were afraid of DRGs, fearing that they might lose out to more efficient hospitals in a defined process of convergence. Sickness funds and private insurance also put expectations on a fair reallocation of their expenditures by improved performance, transparency and efficiency. The majority of hospital employees, namely physicians and nurses, resisted DRGs. They were afraid of more bureaucracy by coding and grouping, and less time for patients. Physicians were afraid that hospital services would be cut back and that they would lose autonomy to management. Nurses were afraid of losing their jobs because of shorter LOS.

Hospital managers were divided into a small but outspoken 'pro' group and a silent, larger 'contra' group. The pro-managers saw the chance to

Table 8.5 The four phases of introducing DRGs in Germany from 2000–2009

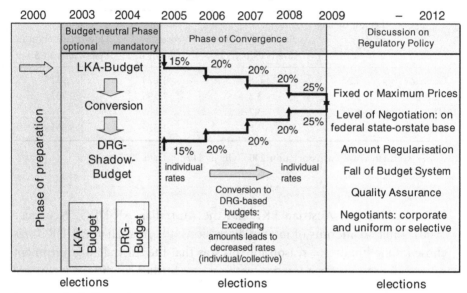

Source: Author's illustration

improve internal process management by controlling patient treatments. Until this point, insured and patients were not aware of any changes to the system. By August 2005, however, they saw the first positive effects. All hospitals had to publish DRG-based quality reports on their home pages. This is discussed later in the chapter.

(5) Phases of introduction

The process of introduction took place in a four-phase process (see Table 8.5). The first phase began in 2000 and ended in 2002–3, and was the preparatory phase in which the selected DRG system was adapted to the German hospital situation. Most important, the Australian procedure code had to be mapped with the German procedure code – the OPS 301 – which is based on ICPM. The second important step was the development of a cost calculation system for computing the relative cost weights. In 2001, single hospitals had used the Australian grouper to make first tests. In 2002, hospital physicians began to discuss the quality of AR-DRGs and to formulate requirements for adequate grouping. In 2002, the Institute for calculating DRG cost weights (InEK) was founded by the Hospital Association and the sickness funds. Coding is done by the German Institute of Medicine Informatics (DIMDI), which is associated with the Health Ministry.

At the end of 2002, the first version of a German DRG system was born. It included 650 DRGs, half of which are differentiated in up to three degrees of severity. The cost calculation was based on data from about 100 out of 2,100 hospitals. These participated voluntarily and were probably not representative. No university hospital was included in the sample.

The budget-neutral phase 2002–2003–2004

In 2002–3, all hospitals were given the option to group their patients using G-DRGs and national cost weights. The sickness funds could already use the DRG data to negotiate DRG-based budgets which should have had the same amount of revenue as the old reimbursement system. About 700 hospitals used the DRG system. For those hospitals that turned to DRG budgeting, hospital-specific base rates have been calculated. Simply described, the given hospital budget has been divided by the volume of cost weights to determine a hospital-specific cost index. The hospital-specific base rates neutralised any economic impact of DRGs. But the difference in the base rates showed the hospitals whether they would be winning or losing if the base rates were merged.

For this reason, a number of hospitals lobbied for improvements in grouping and costing. During 2003, a second version of the G-DRG was prepared. Approximately 100 new defined and calculated DRGs came out of these proposals and requests for improvement. The 'extra payments' ('Zusatzentgelte'), can be added to specific DRGs, for example, special drugs or medical devices which are not normally used. Several university hospitals took part in DRG cost calculations and delivered data to the InEK. While DIMDI had to define appropriate ICD and OPS codes, InEK had to calculate the absolute average costs for the old and new DRGs and to determine the relative cost weights. The cost data that were used described costs in about 130 hospitals with approximately 15 percent of all patients in 2002 and were collected and computed by InEK for use in 2004. This time lag reduced the diffusion of the DRG system, but could be compensated by a hospital-specific base rate. In the year 2004 all plan hospitals were obliged to negotiate DRG budgets with the sickness funds. About 1,500 hospitals did so. Thus, for the majority of hospitals, the specific base rates were known at the beginning of 2004. These base rates were used to calculate the rates for the 2005 convergence phase.

The convergence phase 2005–2009

In the reform of 2000, it was decided to introduce levelled base rates for each Bundesland (state). This resulted in sixteen different base rates; however, the law stipulates that a nationwide base rate must be introduced in the long term. Initially, a two-year convergence period was planned for 2005–6. However, when recording and comparing the differences between individual hospital base rates, it was clear that more time was necessary to reduce actual staffing costs and to improve the G-DRG system. Statistical results showed that variations in base rates are correlated with the hospital supply function. University hospitals and big community hospitals have the upper base rates, basic hospitals have the lower.

In 2004, there was a short discussion about whether there should be different base rates for the three defined provision levels (see Figure 8.3) or if the time for the convergence phase should be extended. The sickness funds and the basic hospital group opposed the proposal of differing base rates, the maximum level hospitals and some state health ministers favoured it. As a compromise, it was decided to postpone the convergence to 2009 and to limit the loss of hospitals to a maximum of 1 percent per year. So, some hospitals may not come down to the average base rate until 2009.

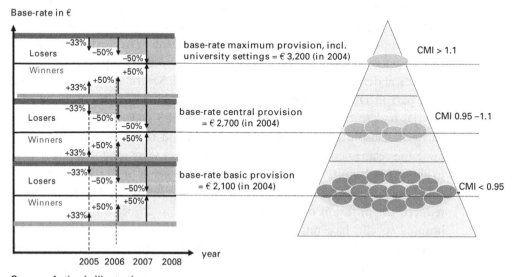

Source: Author's illustration

Figure 8.3   The alternative: differentiated base rates per provision level

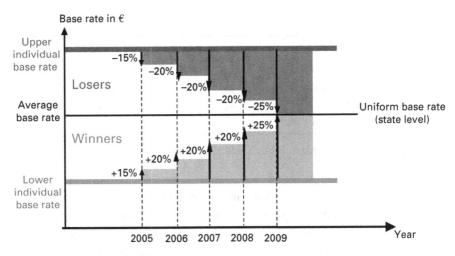

Source: Author's illustration

Figure 8.4   The decided convergence phase 2005–9

(6) The development of the German DRG system

In 2002–3, the Australian DRG system was introduced in German hospitals. Up to that point, procedure codes had been mapped to the German procedure codes (OPS), so German hospitals could use the grouping system with Australian cost weights. From 2004, a German DRG system was available, with its own grouping system and German cost weights. Table 8.6 describes the changes between 2003 and 2006.

The number of DRGs increased rapidly from 664 in 2003 (the Australian system counts 642) to 954 in 2006. The added DRGs are mostly splits of existing DRGs by age, innovation and intensive care which are provided in hospitals of maximum provision level. In 2004, so called 'additional payments' were created. These will be paid on top of a DRG for expensive drugs or blood products used. Blood products are differentiated according to the necessary dose, so a further splitting of up to fifteen doses is possible; these splits are not counted as additional payments. Again university hospitals are favoured because additional payments are outside the calculation for the hospital base rates. Separate cost weights are calculated for attending physicians. Attending physicians will be remunerated out of the panel physician fund, so 'attending' DRGs are calculated without the attending

Table 8.6 Development of the German DRG system

	2003	2004	2005	2006
DRGs total	664	824	878	954
DRGs attending physicians	642	739	762	748
Basic DRGs	411	471	614	578
Additional payments	–	26	71	83

Source: Schlottmann, Fahlenbrach, Köhler and Simon 2005, p. 847

physician services. These attending DRGs vary only with their cost weights: coding and grouping are not different. Private insurance also uses DRG reimbursement for hospital services. They pay additionally for private rooms and the individual services of the chief physician.

The German DRG system is defined as a learning system, which means that every year there will be a revision of the grouping system and a recalculation of all cost weights. New DRGs can be defined, but not calculated because of a lack of valid data. The reimbursement for innovative products can primarily be negotiated between single hospitals and the health funds for a maximum of three years. After that time, the innovation has to become part of the DRG system.

(7) Impact of the DRGs: A first evaluation

It is too early to analyse the impact of the DRGs in Germany because statistically reliable and valid results are not yet available, therefore only the first observed impacts will be described.

Internal hospital effects

The first internal effect has been caused by coding of patients. Many hospitals established new jobs for medical controllers, who have to control the grouping process. Medical controllers are trained as physicians, often with additional postgraduate management training. They also have to train the coding physicians to do it in a DRG context. Although it is not regulated, in some hospitals physicians themselves do the coding, while others employ specially trained coders.

A second early effect has been DRG benchmarking. Initially, the dominant provider of DRG grouping and analysing software for benchmarking

Table 8.7 Variation of base rates in 2004

	Base rates		
Variation	Lowest	Medium	Highest
States	€2,579	€2,579 (unweighted)	€3,157
All hospitals	€961	€2,623 national average	€6,200

Source: Krankenhausreport 2005

was the 3M Company Health Information System (HIS). Today, several providers share the market and HIS has lost its dominance.

Benchmarking has resulted in a lot of effort to restructure hospital processes; standardised clinical pathways are established in many hospitals and the length of stay has been reduced. In the decade 1991–2001, the length of stay was reduced by 3.8 days (12.5 to 8.7): from 2001–4, the reduction is two days (8.7 to 6.9) (Weibler and Zieres 2005, p. 75).

The intended reimbursement system with a standardised base rate forced hospitals to calculate and control their own base rate. The variation between the specific base rates of hospitals (about €1,600) is considerable. This is the same on a state level, as Table 8.7 demonstrates.

The base rate is negotiated at state level; individual hospital base rates are calculated using individual hospital costs.

Under the pressure of the convergence phase, hospitals are controlling principally personnel costs. The emphasis has been to shift employees into cheaper tariff zones. For example, public hospitals must use public institutions which pay higher tariffs for private cleaning, house maintenance and others in the view of hospitals. Outsourcing supplementary services helps to lower personnel costs. In a sense, we are observing an 'internal privatisation'.

Another tactic to reduce the hospital base rate within a defined budget is to increase the CMI and/or the number of patients. From an economic point of view, a higher volume of patients by number or CMI means an increase of (budget) efficiency under the constraint of a given budget.

Figure 8.5 shows the development of CMI, which depends on selective coding of diagnosis and procedure.

An increase in the CMI is not inducing higher expenditures because of a budget constraint according to the stability law, but it does affect the distribution of resources between hospitals. A transgression of budget leads to a sharp decrease in price per DRG (i.e. 35 percent of the 'normal' payment).

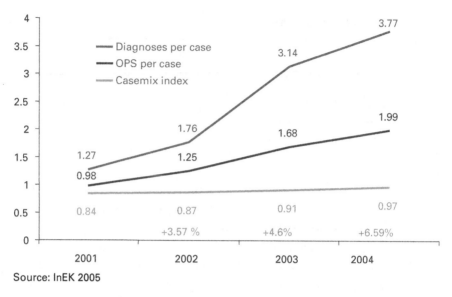

Source: InEK 2005

Figure 8.5   Development of CMI from 2001 to 2005

We will discuss the development of the number of patients later. We simply note here that the number is declining because patients have been moved to day surgery which is (still) outside DRG reimbursement.

Effects on the hospital system

The hospital system has undergone a period of remarkable change: private (for-profit) hospitals are overtaking public hospitals. This process began in the early 1990s and is gaining speed with the introduction of DRGs.

Figure 8.6 makes it clear that public hospitals are the losers and for-profit hospitals are the winners. The next figure is even more convincing. It shows the development of the revenues of patients from the four biggest hospital chains compared with the total market development.

The graph also indicates an increase since the year 2000, when DRGs were introduced and communities hurried to sell their hospitals to a private hospital chain. For historical reasons, this process has been more intense in the 'Neue Länder' than in the 'Alte Länder'.

Besides privatisation, co-operation is another reaction of hospitals. Community hospitals are unified inside the community limits and are rapidly starting to co-operate beyond the limits.

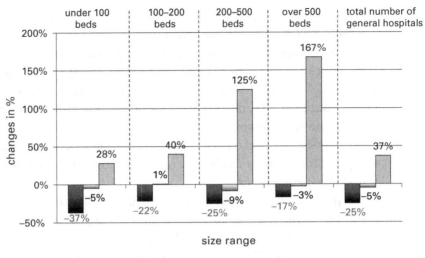

Source: Author's illustration

Figure 8.6 Winners and losers in the hospital restructuring process 1993–2003

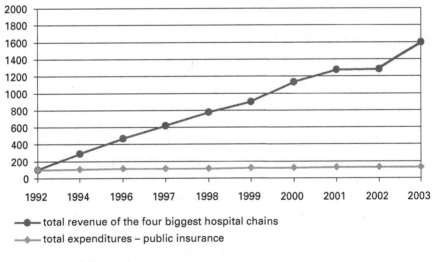

Source: Author's illustration

Figure 8.7 The winners: the four biggest hospital chains 1992–2003 (1992 = 100)

Not-for-profit hospitals begin to imitate private hospital chains; they do not buy and sell hospitals but merge.

Public hospitals pursue two goals by co-operation and merging: the first is to reduce the intensity of local competition, the second is specialisation and cost reduction. As a consequence, the hospital market has become more highly concentrated, and this has caught the attention of the monopoly commission in Germany.

In 2004–5, three take-overs of public hospitals by private chains were stopped. One of those received permission subject to restriction, and one was stopped completely.

All hospitals have experienced a stagnation of patient numbers since 2004. The main cause is an increase in day surgery, which is defined by sickness funds, the Federal Hospital Association and the Federal Association of the Contracted Physicians (which represents office-based specialists). Hospitals that are losing patient days by the reduction of LOS and stagnating patient numbers are trying to compensate for these losses by opening ambulatory care facilities. Generally ambulatory care is the monopoly of the office-based physicians, and is defended by them zealously. Nevertheless, hospitals have succeeded in entering this market in a small way, and they hope to increase their access.

Effects on neighbouring providers

Reduction of LOS motivates the hospitals to co-operate with all post-hospital services, mainly medical rehabilitation, home nursing and, less importantly, nursing homes and hospices.

As of September 2005, there were about 300 co-operation contracts between hospitals, rehabilitation clinics and sickness funds relating to so-called 'integrated care contracts'. These are supported by the sickness funds outside of budgeting, so it is attractive for all providers.

Hospitals seem to have focused their activities on their core competence – diagnostic and therapeutic procedures combined with hospital beds. Activities like administration, accommodation, house maintenance, rehabilitation and others are shifted to co-operating partners. Figure 8.8 describes this development.

Figure 8.8 starts with a ten-day hospital stay and describes the trend that we observe in Germany after the introduction of DRGs. LOS in hospitals goes down and patients are referred earlier to the different hospital partners. These providers see a shift of services, but sickness funds are not willing to

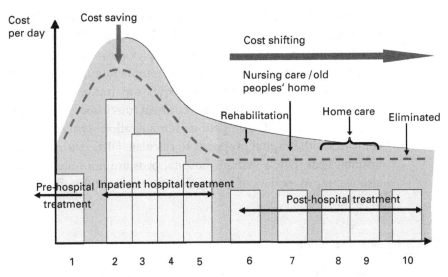

Source: Author's illustration

Figure 8.8   Integrated care: cost saving versus cost shifting

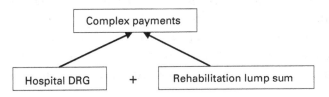

Source: Author's illustration

Figure 8.9   Complex lump-sum payments

raise the reimbursement. Hospitals are saving costs by shifting services to other providers. Within integrated care this shifting process is neutralised by various kinds of integrated reimbursement. One of the most common forms is the so called 'complex lump-sum payments' which Figure 8.9 roughly outlines.

Complex payments are protecting sickness funds against added demands of the providers and force providers to optimise the process of patient care among themselves. One effect of complex payments is an opening discussion about 'rehabilitation patient groups'. The objective is to build a rehab patient grouping system which will be consistent with DRGs in a way which facilitates the calculation of complex payments.

Similar trends are observed in the remuneration system of office-based specialists. Their remuneration schedule was transferred to a more global schedule in 2005. The new government discussed going further in the direction of a DRG-compatible remuneration system. This discussion coincides with hospital proposals to calculate DRGs with and without use of hospital beds. DRGs without hospital beds are not only one-day cases but also include more days of treatment. The results of this discussion remain to be seen.

Effects on sickness funds

From the beginning, sickness funds supported the introduction of DRGs as much as possible. They have always advocated a simple and transparent hospital reimbursement system. By changing from *per diem* rates to DRGs, the financing burden is also reallocated on the side of sickness funds. Funds which have less severe patients with relatively long LOS profit by DRGs and *vice versa*. One indicator for a long stay is the age of the patients; as LOS is reduced sharply, sickness funds with older insured are profiting. Effects in the long term are changing as different DRGs are calculated and used. For example, hip replacements are frequent and well-calculated DRGs; sickness funds which have a higher at risk patient membership pay more. As the DRG calculations are revised every year, effects can change quite fast.

To avoid cost shifting, sickness funds also push ahead integrated care and integrated reimbursement forms, as discussed earlier. Generally, the DRGs encourage sickness funds to engage in selective contracting, as DRGs produce transparency of quality, volume of specific DRGs and economic efficiency. Selective contracting is used in the system of integrated care while collective bargaining is still the dominant way of budgeting.

Enhanced quality assurance is an indirect effect of DRGs. On the one hand, minimum numbers of treatments per DRG in cases such as organ transplants and knee replacement have been introduced. The self-governing bodies are mandated to enlarge the use of DRGs step-by-step. On the other hand, hospitals are obliged to publish a quality report regularly on their websites. Thus, referring physicians and referred patients can have access to a lot of information before entering a hospital.

Effects on patients

DRGs and their effects are not really discussed to any great extent in the media in Germany. DRGs are judged as topics for specialists. Physician complaints about a lack of staff and equipment are discussed only indirectly. But this may change, when the convergence phase moves forward. Patients are concerned about the closure of small rural hospitals. Again DRGs are only indirectly involved in the discussion, although they are the major impulse to reorganise hospital care.

The mandatory quality reports of hospitals available on the internet are receiving more attention. Elective patients are very likely to visit the home pages of the hospitals they are to be admitted to. Besides a general description of the hospital facilities and the personnel, the number of treatments per DRG is the most important item. At the moment, the thirty most frequent DRGs in the hospital and the ten most frequent DRGs per department must be published. However, hospitals are free to publish more.

Sickness funds support their members by offering hospital navigators, which help a patient to find a convenient hospital near to their home. In this way, quality and competition are growing and improving. The next steps will be to deliver more outcome indicators like mortality rates and similar data.

Patients are not aware of the price of services. Patients still have to pay €10 per day up to twenty days in the same year independent of the 'price' of a hospital. Patients do not select hospitals based on their price–performance relationship. Patients are only assessing the quality performance. This view will need to be corrected in the long run.

Table 8.8 summarises our results and gives an overview without valuing the various effects.

(8) Outlook

DRGs give a lot of impulses to the total health care system of Germany. But it is difficult to separate the effects of DRGs from independent medical and economic trends. In most cases, DRGs are accelerating developments, which is very helpful in the complicated interest-group-driven health care system. Today in Germany, DRGs are accepted by all important groups. The discussion is now focused on the details and on long-term development.

Table 8.8 Overview of the different effects of DRGs in Germany

Effects	Grouping system	Reimbursement system	Flexible components
Hospital internal	Improvement of coding Medical controlling Clinical pathways Benchmarking Length of stay	Cost controlling CMI increasing Number of cases Lowering of tariffs Outsourcing	Shifting activities to flexible components
Hospital system	Privatisation Horizontal cooperation Increased ambulatory care		
Neighbouring providers	Cost shifting Integrated care Concentration on core competencies Integrated reimbursement Rehabilitation patient groups DRG with/without bed		
Sickness funds	Reallocation of cost burden Selective contracting Quality assurance Minimum number of treatments		
Patients	Quality transparency Selective choice of hospital Reduction of rural hospitals		

Source: Author's illustration

It is not yet apparent whether there will be a more market-oriented hospital system or one which is more state-regulated. Today, market forces seem to prevail. But without a revision of the financing system, especially a separation of health care expenditure from labour costs, market forces cannot bring acceptable results.

REFERENCES

Lohmann, H. (2000) Die Zukunft hat schon begonnen. *Forum für Gesellschaftspolitik* July/August.

Neubauer, G. (1993) Germany: An Outsider in DRG Development. In Kimberly, J.R., de Pouvourville, G. and Associates, *The Migration of Managerial Innovation*. San Francisco: Jossey Bass.

(1998) Kriterien zur Bewertung und Auswahl eines Krankenhaus-Vergütungssystems. *Das Krankenhaus* October.

(1998) Systematische Bewertung der wichtigsten Vorschläge zur Weiterentwicklung der Krankenhausvergütung. *Das Krankenhaus* November.

(2000) Schritte zur Einführung der DRG-Pauschale in Deutschland. In Bläsing, J.P. (ed), *Die lernende Organisation* Ulm: Ton-Verlag.

(2001) Reduktion der Verweildauer durch DRGs. *Das Krankenhaus.*

(2003) Hospital Care System in Germany. *Die BKK* August.

(2003) Zur ökonomischen Steuerung der Krankenhausversorgung unter DRG-Fallspauschalen. *Krankenhausreport.*

(2004) *DRGs in Orthopädie und Unfallchirurgie.*

(2004) *Verlängerung der DRG-Einführungsphase – Keine sachgerechte Lösung. Qualität und Evidenz.*

(2005) Teilstationäre DRGs: Spalten-, Zeilen-, oder Abschlagslösung? *Das Krankenhaus.*

(2005) G-DRG – Vergütungssystem für den Gesundheitsmarkt. *Management Handbuch* December.

Neubauer, G. and Ujlaky, R. (2005) Einführung und Entwicklung der DRGs in Deutschland. In Beck, Goldschmidt, Greulich, Kalbitzer, Schmid and Thiele (eds.), *Management Handbuch* December.

Neubauer, G. and Zelle, B. (2000) Finanzierungs- und Vergütungssysteme. In Eichhorn, P., Seelos, H. J. and Graf Schulenburg, J. (eds.), *Krankenhausmanagement.*

OECD Health Data 2005.

Schlottmann, N., Fahlenbrach, C., Köhler, N. and Simon C. (2005) G-DRG-System 2006: Ein erster Überblick aus medizinischer Sicht. *Das Krankenhaus* October.

Weibler, U. and Zieres, G. (2005) *Diagnosis Related Groups (DRGs).* Nierstein.

9 Casemix in Switzerland

Hervé Guillain

Introduction

Switzerland has a very decentralized health care system the main characteristics of which are described below.

Private health insurance is the dominant form of basic coverage. Since the adoption of a new Health Insurance Law in 1994, purchase of a health insurance policy is mandatory and coverage is thus universal. The benefits package included in the basic coverage is the same for everyone, premiums being neither risk-related nor income-related, but vary from area (canton) to area and from sickness fund to sickness fund. At least once a year beneficiaries can change the sickness fund they want to be a member of, without any restriction (i.e. whatever their age, sex, health status, place of residence, etc.). Subsidies are available to people with low socio-economic status to help them with the payment of their premiums.

Sickness funds pay for all treatments, except those covered by the Swiss accident assurance fund, which is an independent, non-profit company under public law.

Additional health insurance for benefits not included in the basic coverage may be purchased (e.g. for homeopathy, acupuncture or inpatient treatment in a private, for-profit clinic). Premiums are then risk-related and are not regulated by the Health Insurance Law of 1994. Between one-quarter and one-third of the population buy an additional health insurance policy. It must be noted that such a policy may not cover deductibles and co-payments related to the basic package of benefits.

In the ambulatory sector, physicians and other health professionals (nurses, physical and occupational therapists, etc.) work in privately owned facilities (solo or group practice) and are paid by sickness funds on a fee-for-service basis. Since 2004 all physicians in private practice have been paid according to TarMed, a national tariff which replaced all the tariffs that previously applied in the cantons. Services provided in hospital outpatient clinics are also reimbursed according to TarMed.

The majority of Swiss hospitals are either publicly owned or private, not-for-profit facilities receiving state subsidies. Private, for-profit clinics specialize in elective surgery, maternity care and uncomplicated medical treatment. Their number varies greatly from canton to canton.

There is currently a wide variety of financing systems in the hospital sector because of the great autonomy of the cantons. In some of them a traditional *per diem* payment system is still in place, in others All Patient Diagnosis Related Groups (AP-DRGs) have been, or are being introduced, and in others some local funding rules are used.

One constraint must be respected in all cantons because it is stipulated in the 1994 Health Insurance Law: costs for inpatient treatment in public hospitals or state-subsidized hospitals must be covered both by the state and the sickness funds and the latter do not have to reimburse more than half of the costs related to the care provided to patients (sickness funds must not pay for teaching and research).

Cantonal authorities and sickness funds organize themselves in different ways to finance hospitals. They may transfer money into a common account managed by an independent institution responsible for financing hospitals or they may pay for inpatient stays separately.

Since the federal state does not have much power with respect to health care services, the major players in the Swiss health care arena are the Conference of the Cantonal Ministers of Public Health, the Association of Hospitals, the Association of Sickness Funds, the Swiss Accident Assurance Fund and the Medical Association. No important change in the Swiss health care system can be made without a consensus among these players.

A brief history of the introduction of casemix in Switzerland

In Switzerland the interest in casemix started soon after the introduction of DRGs in the United States. In 1984 a study was launched by the University of Lausanne's Institut universitaire de médecine sociale et préventive (IUMSP) and the public health service of the canton of Vaud, with the support of the cantons of Bern, Fribourg, Geneva, Jura, Neuchâtel, Soleure,

Tessin and Valais. The authors of this study examined the possibility of using casemix tools for different purposes including hospital planning, benchmarking, internal management and funding. The results were published in French in 1989 and in German in 1990. They represent a milestone in the history of casemix in Switzerland, even if the recommendations made by the authors didn't lead to any concrete change before the mid 1990s. Moreover, this study is the only research project conducted to evaluate if and how casemix could be introduced in Switzerland.[1], [2]

Who was involved?

The early adopters are to be found among health economists and public health researchers, some working in universities and others in state agencies or para-public institutions such as the former Swiss Institute for Public Health (Schweizerisches Institut für Gesundheitswesen – Institut suisse de la santé publique). A number of cantonal authorities interested in the use of casemix tools gave their support to the study previously mentioned and participated in its steering committee.

However, for many years none of the major institutions or stakeholders of the Swiss health care system became involved in activities aiming at implementing casemix tools. The discussions about DRGs and related topics took place among individuals who were interested in them, and no formal decision regarding their implementation in the country was made. There was almost no political desire to use DRGs on a national level.

In 1989 those who wanted to promote casemix in the country founded an association called "PCS Switzerland" (PCS stands for Patient Classification Systems). Since then this association has been publishing a newsletter for its members and other interested persons and organizing debates and conferences on various topics related to DRGs.

Under the name "APDRG Switzerland" a group was created in 1997 by people representing about twenty hospitals, health administrations from a few of the cantons, a handful of insurers and the Swiss Medical Association (FMH – Federatio Medicorum Helveticorum). The main objectives of this private entity were, on the one hand, to find software (called "grouper") that could process the data routinely collected in Swiss hospitals and make it available to those who wanted to start using DRGs and, on the other hand, to set the rules to be applied by hospitals in cantons where the health authorities were willing to implement a casemix-based financing system.

What were the drivers?

The early adopters of casemix tools were mainly interested in their use for health services planning and management as well as benchmarking. For example, in the study launched in Lausanne in 1984, DRGs were used to predict the number of beds needed in a hospital.

The emphasis switched progressively to casemix-based funding and by the mid 1990s the main objective was to replace the *per diem* payment system by a prospective payment system. As in many countries, the rise of health care expenditure in Switzerland led to the search for payment systems that would promote cost-effectiveness and equity in resource allocation among providers. It became obvious that *per diem* rates had to be abolished because of the wrong incentives they provided.

Today there is a will to "pay for services and not for the walls inside which they are delivered," meaning that money must follow the patient and be proportionate to her or his needs. To reach this goal the implementation of casemix tools is required.

Furthermore, there is a growing demand for more transparency and accountability in all areas of the health care sector. In particular, hospitals are increasingly faced with questions about the relationship between their budget, the services they provide and the type of patients they admit. How do you justify the amount of money you spend to treat your patients? Are your patients usually as sick as you claim? How do you compare with other facilities? Without casemix tools it is impossible to answer such questions.

Amazingly, sickness funds, which would probably be those for whom DRGs would be most useful and advantageous, never argued strongly in favor of their introduction. They have always been afraid that a casemix-based funding system would imply an increase in the amount of money they have to reimburse to the hospitals. They request that any change in the financing mechanisms be "cost neutral," (i.e. that it does not force them to pay more as long as the basic coverage remains unchanged). Furthermore, because of the weaknesses of the risk adjustment system put in place to compensate sickness funds for enrolling sicker people, some sickness funds fear that DRGs will make them lose money.

Implementation

This group named "APDRG Switzerland" had to find software that allowed hospitalizations to be classified according to the variables of the discharge summary that each Swiss hospital is required to establish for every hospitalization. In this discharge summary, diagnoses are coded according to ICD–10 and procedures according to ICD–9–CM Vol. 3 (also called CHOP in Switzerland).

As there was no software which could handle the Swiss discharge summaries, the group which had decided to introduce DRGs in Switzerland either had to invent one, or negotiate the adaptation of existing software to the characteristics of the data routinely collected in Swiss hospitals. The second solution was selected because the development of software specific to Switzerland would have been very costly and represented a disproportionate task, bearing in mind the small number of potential users. The company 3M HIS produced "AP-DRG Version 12 adapted for Switzerland," the adaptation consisting primarily of regrouping hospitalizations according to the diagnostic codes originating from ICD–10 instead of ICD–9–CM. The advantage of AP-DRGs was that they take better account of the complexity of cases than do Medicare DRGs and they do not have too many groups (Version 12 of the AP-DRGs includes 641 groups). A more sophisticated classification (APR-DRG, for example) would have been significantly more difficult to adapt to ICD–10 and would not have been of great use, given that at the time of selecting AP-DRGs, medical coding was of a poor quality in most Swiss hospitals.

Despite its weak financial means, the group "APDRG Switzerland" succeeded in collecting and handling data essential to the calculation of the cost-weights applicable to stays in acute care hospitals in Switzerland. The first version of these cost-weights was published at the end of 1998, the second in 1999, the third in 2001 and the fourth appeared in May 2003.

As Switzerland is a very federalist country, particularly in the field of health care services, in the year 2002 casemix funding based on AP-DRGs started in two cantons only, the one (Zurich) in the German-speaking part, the other (Vaud) in the French-speaking part of the country. Zurich and Vaud played a pioneering role in the diffusion of casemix in the country and were progressively followed by other cantons.

The current situation

The uses of casemix

AP-DRGs are mainly used for benchmarking and funding. In several cantons studies were conducted to compare hospitals in terms of length of stay, number and type of outliers as well as overall caseload. The results of these studies are not in the public domain.

In 2004 the Swiss Federal Statistical Office (www.statistics.admin.ch) published an analysis of the data collected in all Swiss hospitals. Each hospital stay was assigned to an AP-DRG and, using the cost-weights calculated by the group "APDRG Switzerland," the casemix index of each acute care facility was computed. As mentioned by the authors of this study, the results they obtained must be interpreted cautiously because the quality of the data varies from hospital to hospital. However, since the introduction of AP-DRGs coding is improving every year, the usefulness of casemix tools to compare hospitals will certainly increase.

Extensions of casemix

AP-DRGs are used in an increasing number of cantons to finance acute care hospitals. By 2006 they will be implemented in about two-thirds of the cantons. In some of them their use will be restricted to patients covered by a specific type of insurance, in others they will be used for all hospitalizations. Moreover, depending on the canton, AP-DRGs are used only for adjusting hospital budgets according to their overall caseload or, alternatively, for paying for each stay separately (as in a hotel).

AP-DRGs are used only for financing or paying for acute somatic in-patient care. No funding for rehabilitation, psychiatric, primary or long-term care is based on them. In 2002 there was an attempt in the canton of Vaud to use them to cover same-day surgery carried out in outpatient clinics, but it caused a lot of difficulties because there were large differences between the cost of some treatments and their reimbursement. The following year AP-DRGs were replaced with a fee-for-service payment for outpatient care. It must be noted that the cause of the problems encountered does not lie in AP-DRGs, but in the way they were adapted for the payment for outpatient services.

A few projects are underway to explore the feasibility of a casemix-based funding system for rehabilitation stays, but such a funding will not be implemented, at least on a large scale, for several years. Currently the preoccupation is rather on separating rehabilitation from acute care stays: the average length of stay for a number of hospitals is higher than expected because in these facilities there is no clear distinction between hospitalizations for acute care and those for rehabilitation.

Technical issues

A new release of the AP-DRG grouper is provided every year by the company 3M HIS, to take into account the annual changes made to ICD–9–CM Vol. 3. The group "APDRG Switzerland" takes care of the contacts with 3M HIS and deals with all aspects related with the grouper. It also collects data from hospitals where cost-per-patient is available and calculates cost-weights, of which a new version is usually published every other year.

The diagnostic and procedure classifications (ICD–10 and ICD–9–CM Vol. 3) are maintained by the Swiss Federal Statistical Office. Since these are not local ones, the financial and human resources needed for their maintenance are small. An expert committee meets a few times a year to discuss the changes in these classifications, to establish coding guidelines and to answer questions related to them.

Since 1998 hospitals have been legally obliged to provide a uniform discharge summary for each admitted patient. Hospitals are organized in various ways to produce this discharge summary. The medical records may be abstracted and coded by the physician who is in charge of the patient or by professional coders (who may be nurses, medical assistants or physicians). Abstraction and coding may be centralized in a medical record department or done in each ward of the hospital. A general trend can nevertheless be observed: coding is done more and more in medical record departments by professional coders. In small hospitals it may even be outsourced and done remotely by consultants specializing in this field.

The discharge summaries are sent to the Swiss Federal Statistical Office, where they are recorded in databases that may not be freely accessed. Their use is limited by a law stipulating that the identity not only of the patients, but also of the facility in which they are admitted, must not be known. Researchers and other interested people can obtain data from the Swiss Federal Statistical Office, but these data are always aggregated in such a way that any comparison between hospitals is impossible. Such a comparison can be made only if each hospital concerned formally agrees with it.

Impact, debates, controversies

Since AP-DRGs were only introduced in 2002, it is too early to draw conclusions about their impact on the Swiss health care system. Moreover, they were first implemented in two cantons only.

Nevertheless, changes are already perceived in those hospitals which are now under a casemix-based financing system. Discharge planning is improving, as well as the communication between acute care facilities, nursing homes and home care services. As a result, the average length of stay is decreasing at a rate higher than in the previous years.

The mentality of hospital managers is changing. Payment by AP-DRGs make them behave more like entrepreneurs who have to compare the cost of their products with the revenues they get from their sale. There is an increasing interest for activity-based costing or patient costing and the number of hospitals where data on the cost of each stay is available is rising. Many hospitals are changing the way they organize data collection, coding and billing. Coding has been compulsory since 1998, but almost nobody cared about it before the beginning of the introduction of AP-DRGs. Now it is a major preoccupation that should lead to an improvement in several areas such as epidemiology, clinical research, health statistics, etc.

Two categories of people who did not really speak to each other are now talking more and more together: clinicians and economists. They realize that a hospital will survive only if there is a dialog between them and if they exchange their views, even though these may be sometimes quite different!

There is a consensus that specific measures must be taken when implementing casemix-based funding. One of them is the monitoring of the quality of coding. So far this is the only area where some evidence of the impact of AP-DRGs has been gathered. Coding audits have been conducted in several regions and the results of some of them are publicly available. In 2004, a study on hospitalizations in the year 2003 was carried out in the canton of Vaud, where 2,561 medical records from fourteen hospitals were recoded to evaluate how precisely they were initially coded. The number of records reviewed in each hospital varied between 146 and 313, depending on the size of the hospital (the number of admissions per hospital ranged between 709 and 30,411). After recoding, the AP-DRG assignment was modified in 234 records out of 2,561 (i.e. a 9.1% error rate). A statistical analysis was made to estimate whether the reimbursement of all stays in each hospital would be lower or higher ("upcoding" or "downcoding") if medical records had been coded by the auditors. Confidence intervals were calculated and showed that there was neither upcoding nor downcoding in thirteen out of fourteen hospitals. In one hospital there was a statistically significant difference in the casemix computed before and after recoding; coding errors made in this hospital led to a reimbursement that was lower than expected.

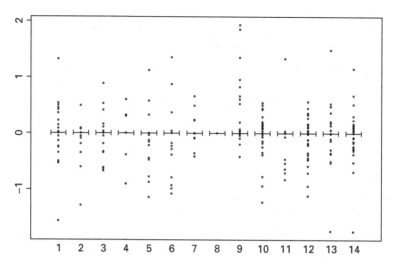

Figure 9.1   Differences in reimbursement before and after recoding

Figure 9.1 shows for each hospital (*x* axis) the difference in reimbursement on a relative scale (*y* axis) before and after recoding. Each dot represents a medical record. A positive value means that reimbursement would be higher after recoding.

In hospital No. 9 the reimbursement of all stays would be higher if codes assigned by the auditors were taken into account. In all other hospitals there is no statistically significant difference.

The study described here demonstrates that coding errors made in the hospitals where audits took place do not aim to increase their revenues. These results are important because sickness funds and, to a lesser extent cantonal authorities, fear that hospitals cheat and charge more than they are allowed to. So far this has not been observed, but it is planned that audits should be conducted on a regular basis in all cantons where AP-DRGs are implemented.

Despite the results presented here, there is a lack of trust between payers and providers. In addition to audits conducted by independent coders, sickness funds have started to hire coders whose job it is to verify the codes assigned by the hospital when a bill is considered to be dubious. This double checking is a waste of resources.

There is also a consensus that readmissions must be monitored because hospitals may try to split stays to increase revenues. This monitoring is not systematically carried out yet, but the tools needed for that purpose are already available. In the Swiss hospital discharge dataset there is a field containing an anonymous identifier that allows for the search for any readmission of the concerned patient, be it in the same facility or in any other hospital in the country. The Swiss Federal Statistical Office therefore has the possibility to compute readmission rates for each hospital, but, as previously mentioned, the law prevents their publication or communication to any third party.

Readmission rates may increase not only because stays are split to increase revenues, but also because patients are discharged too early or are not treated appropriately. Therefore a distinction must be made between the rate of all readmissions and the rate of potentially avoidable readmissions. These can be used to detect problems related to the quality of care provided to patients. As there are fears that this quality may decrease with the implementation of AP-DRGs, research is being conducted to define an algorithm with which potentially avoidable readmissions can be identified and separated. A first report was published in 2002 (Halfon, P., Eggli, Y., van Melle, G., Chevalier, J., Wasserfallen, J. B. and Burnand, B. Measuring potentially avoidable hospital readmissions. *J Clin Epid* (2002) 55:573–87).

Indicators other than readmission rates are progressively implemented, such as nosocomial infections, pressure ulcers, returns to operating room and patient satisfaction. Under the name "Verein Outcome" (www. vereinoutcome.ch) a major initiative was undertaken in the canton of Zurich to introduce the use of quality indicators in all public hospitals and to promote benchmarking with these indicators.

Perspectives

New areas of development

In April 2004 an association called "SwissDRG" (www.swissdrg.org) was created by the five most important actors in the Swiss health care system: the Conference of the Cantonal Ministers of Public Health (www.gdk-cds. ch), the Association of Hospitals (www.hplus.ch), the Association of Sickness Funds (www.santesuisse.ch), the Swiss Accident Assurance Fund (www.suva.ch) and the Medical Association (www.fmh.ch). The goal of SwissDRG is the implementation on a national level of a casemix-based financing system for all acute care hospitals. The project is underway and four working groups have been formed to deal with all aspects of such a system (choice of a patient classification system, creation of a national database to compute cost-weights, establishment of reimbursement rules and maintenance of the future Swiss casemix system).

Using data from Swiss hospitals several classifications were evaluated and compared to the AP-DRGs currently used. The assessment included APR-DRGs (3M HIS), AR-DRGs (Australia), G-DRGs (Germany), IR-DRGs (3M HIS), LDF (Austria) and SQLape (a classification developed by a Swiss researcher). From a statistical point of view none of these classifications could be considered as better than the others. The members of SwissDRG decided to retain either G-DRGs or IR-DRGs as potential models on which future Swiss DRGs would be built. It is planned that a national casemix-based system be subsequently put in place between 2006 and 2010.

After the start of the SwissDRG project discussions took place in the Swiss APDRG group about the continuation of its activities. It was decided that the group would become an association of users of AP-DRGs that will be dissolved only when Swiss DRGs are actually implemented. As a result, in December 2004 the group APDRG Switzerland was replaced with an association bearing the same name (www.apdrgsuisse.ch) whose aim was to provide the support needed by the cantons where AP-DRGs had been or would be introduced while waiting for the future Swiss DRGs. In particular, this association is in charge of computing the cost-weights used for hospital funding.

Messages for new adopters

The implementation of casemix in Switzerland is a much slower process than in many other developed countries, but it shows that in a country with a decentralized health care system casemix-based financing can coexist with other types of hospital financing mechanisms and be introduced gradually. The creation of the SwissDRG association is a sign that this process will not be reversed and will eventually end up in a national casemix-based funding.

The lessons learned in the cantons where AP-DRGs have already been implemented will certainly help to prevent errors when Swiss DRGs are introduced. Several problems encountered in the area of coding and cost-weight computing have shown the importance of establishing clear and comprehensive coding guidelines as well as costing guidelines. Moreover, since some inconsistencies between coding rules and grouping algorithms are causing difficulties in the assignment of a number of hospital stays, a new type of collaboration will be required in order to iron out these difficulties.

Limits to casemix

AP-DRGs have been introduced by a group of motivated people without any legal or political change on a national level. In this context a major weakness is the lack of an authority that coordinates the regional implementations. For example, nobody could prevent sickness funds from using, simultaneously, different versions of cost-weights in different cantons. One canton even threatened to use cost-weights other than those published by APDRG Switzerland. This, of course contradicts the goal of achieving better transparency in the Swiss health care system. These will fade when Swiss DRGs are introduced.

The current lack of a national casemix office is also an issue. By law the Swiss Federal Statistical Office is responsible for the maintenance of the diagnostic and procedure classifications (ICD–10 and CHOP), but it is not obliged to take into consideration the impact of coding guidelines on the assignment of hospital stays by the AP-DRG grouper. The advent of Swiss DRGs will change this situation and it is planned that a national casemix office be created to deal both with coding and grouping issues.

A basic principle of casemix-based funding is that a stay assigned to a given group is paid according the mean cost of all stays in this group. Therefore, very often the amount billed for each individual stay does not match its observed cost, especially in groups with low homogeneity for costs. When all stays of a large hospital are billed to the same payer, differences between cost and reimbursement of each individual stay are not problematic because they even out. To fix a budget on the basis of casemix is easier and makes more sense than to bill each individual stay to different payers. In Switzerland there are many sickness funds and consequently stays are billed to many different payers, some of whom are at risk of paying much more or much less than the cost actually generated by their patients, in particularly if the size of the sickness fund is small. Swiss DRGs are expected to be very homogeneous in terms of cost and it is likely that the future national casemix-based financing system will be quite complex and include rules for additional payments to narrow the gap between cost and reimbursement. If this is the case, the incentives to provide cost-effective care will, of course, be weaker.

NOTES

[1] Paccaud F., Schenker L. (eds) (1989) *DRG. (Diagnosis Related Groups) – Perspectives d'utilisation*. Paris: Masson.
[2] (1990) *DRG Diagnosis Related Groups – Gültigkeit, Brauchbarkeit, Anwendungsmöglichkeiten*. Bern: Hans Huber.

10 The first decade of casemix in Italy

Paolo Tedeschi

The Italian National Health System: Structure, funding and evolution

The introduction of a casemix system in Italy is quite symbiotic with the evolution of its National Health Care System (SSN – Servizio Sanitario Nazionale), first created in 1978 and then reshaped in the 1990s through a process of institutional and financial decentralization (from state to regions[1]), combined with a delegation of managerial autonomy to the lower levels of health care provision and payment. Previously, until 1992, the system was basically administered by local municipalities following an ideal of democratic participation and local control, but often with a bureaucratic and inefficient use of resources (Donatini *et al.* 2001).

In 1978, the SSN replaced a system of health insurance funds in order to provide the entire population with uniform and comprehensive care, on the basis of both payroll and general taxation and according to the constitutional principle of 'solidarity and freedom of choice for the patient' (mainly concerning the provider and settings of care). In terms of figures, 2005 Italian health care public expenditures were €95 billion in current prices, equal to 6.4 percent of GDP, but growing to 8.4 percent with private out-of-pocket spending (OECD 2006), serving a population of 57.3 million (meaning a public per-capita expenditure of €1,828). In 2004, hospitals[2] absorbed, on average, 48 percent of public expenditures, 12 percent of outpatient services, and 6 percent of primary care. Italy is characterized by a low fertility rate (1.3 in 2004) and a large proportion of elderly people (18.6 percent of the total population is above sixty-five). Under thirty-five, accidents and other injuries are the main causes of death; over thirty-five, the main causes of death are cardiovascular diseases and cancer.

In terms of institutional architecture, the SSN has been designed as "multi-tiered" (Fattore 1999), with the central government initially in charge of financing and administration, regional governments dedicated to fund allocation, and the local level for payment and provision of care. The local level is embodied by 171 local health authorities, named ASLs – Aziende Sanitarie Locali,[3] and 95 independent public hospital trusts, called AOs – Aziende Ospedaliere. Research/teaching hospitals[4] and APPs – accredited private hospitals[5] (for-profit or not-for-profit) complete the hospital supply for both inpatient and outpatient services. In order to act as providers of the SSN, private hospitals have to obtain accreditation from regions and negotiate provisional agreements. In particular, each ASL is responsible, on a territorial basis, for assessing needs and for local health status by providing a full range of direct services, from preventative and primary care, to community services (nursing, residential, and day care), up to secondary general hospitals (delivered through 538 local hospitals), or by reimbursing care provided to its residents by other AOs or APPs.

Regarding health service features, Italy has a high ratio of physicians (4.3 per 1,000 people vs. EU average of 3.3 and OECD of 2.9). In 2004, the SSN had 646,050 employees, 108,500 of which were physicians, and 214,000 nurses. All employees have civil servant status, though physicians may also practice privately (under certain conditions). Primary care is provided by 47,061 independent family doctors and 7,416 pediatricians, mainly paid on capitation, and responsible for referring patients, with some limited gatekeeping. Drugs are distributed through a network of retail pharmacies, while dental and ophthalmic care is basically provided privately.

Until 1992, the system was financed on the basis of actual expenditures, with funds allocated from the state (tax-collector) to regions and then to USL – literally Local Health Units (later ASLs), which at that time also managed all hospitals (no autonomous trusts – AOs – yet existed). Without any cost containment incentives, most USLs overspent their budgets, forcing the central government to cover deficits. Following major SSN reforms in 1992–3 and 1999, regions progressively acquired legislative and planning power over health care, as well as partial fiscal autonomy,[6] so that some observers tended to consider regions as "parent companies with their own subsidiaries" (Anessi Pessina et al. 2004); indeed, regions can now appoint general managers of ASLs and AOs, provide them with goals and guidelines, and fund their expenditures with capitated budgets. In the words of Jommi and Fattore (2003), regionalization implies that Italy's twenty-one regional governments have been given the opportunity to introduce different organizational and funding models "to achieve an acceptable combination of equity, efficiency, freedom of choice and cost containment;" consequently, through regionalization, managerialism and quasi-markets, ASLs and AOs gained more discretion over their affairs, but also started to be kept accountable for improving performance and meeting higher standards. However, the Italian quasi-market proved to be imperfect, as AOs and APPs are paid on the basis of their activities (DRGs for inpatient and fee-for-service for outpatient services), but with two significant limitations: on one side, "regional caps" on expenditure, on the other, "patients' freedom of choice," which often transforms ASLs from "empowered purchasers" into "third-party payers." For such reasons, rather than internal markets, many speak of "governed competition" (France and Taroni 2005).

Moving forward, in 2001 a new constitutional law was passed promoting further power-shifting to regions, which are now fully accountable for all deficits. However, the process of decentralization is proceeding at differing paces, depending on regional capabilities. This could lead to the risk of further increasing the traditional north–south "health-care provision divide," especially since the Italian version of the quasi-market adopts the rule of "money follows the patient," meaning more resources potentially drained from the relatively limited availability of the south for payments attracted to the north.[7] Moreover, since regions are more independent, differentiation in health care organization has emerged, ranging from: first, the "ASL-centered model" (receiving most of the regional funds, delivering directly or reimbursing health care provided externally to its residents), second, the "purchaser–provider split model" (e.g. only in the Lombardia region, where ASLs act as purchasers from both public and private hospitals), and third, the opposite 'region-centered model' (with the role of the purchaser directly exerted by the region, holding all resources and paying both ASLs and hospitals according to delivery of care).

At the end of this process, which was not dismantled by the different political governments in office through the 1990s, responsibility for health care is shared by two actors: the state, which sets major goals through a National Health Plan and defines the so-called LEAs – "Essential Levels of Care" – meaning national standards of care[8] (Torbica and Fattore 2005), and regions, which have great autonomy for the organization and management of the supply system, as well as financial responsibility, though significant "interregional differentials" exist in terms of services and accessibility (France *et al.* 2005).

The introduction of casemix in Italy

The 1992 reform, in a scenario of political and financial crisis, did "set the agenda" to replace "retrospective reimbursements" with "prospective payment systems" (Anessi Pessina *et al.* 2004); the set-up of the SSN was marketed as a way to avoid previous troubles (e.g. by fixing the level of health care spending outside the system), giving full responsibility to the central government and later on to regions, instead of municipalities. Even under these new circumstances, the state had limited power over the USLs, which in turn resulted in their being too vertically integrated and only subject to local political influence (France and Taroni 2005).

Moreover, at the beginning of 1990s, the Italian political party system lost its legitimacy through illicit fundraising scandals, which led to two technical governments. This "window of opportunity" was completed by an economic crisis (the exit of Italy from the European monetary system), which allowed two consecutive prime ministers, Giuliano Amato and Carlo Azeglio Ciampi, to exploit the situation with massive tax increases and expenditure cuts equivalent to 6 percent of GDP. The health care reforms of the 1990s therefore reflected the general goal of ensuring both macro-economic stabilization and microeconomic efficiency.

Since 1994, capitation (for regions and ASLs) and activity-related funding (for AOs and APPs) have become the main "financial levers" for managing regional health care systems. In particular, it appears that Italy adopted a form of internal market from England and a diagnosis-related casemix system from the United States, probably representing a good case of "path-dependent health policy," in which the cost of reversing existing models was unacceptable (e.g. prior health insurance funds facing bankruptcy). Other observers point out that the advent in 1994 of hospital prospective payment systems represents an exemplary case of policy transfer, based on the experience of a comparable country (the US), but largely adapted and transformed, especially at regional level (Arcangeli *et al.* 2004). Indeed, as some hospital services proved difficult or inappropriate to fund using DRGs (e.g. emergencies, transplants, intensive care, etc.), the Italian regions sought new complementary funding channels, such as: additional fee-for-service financing (e.g. to reward specialized services), functional financing (e.g. lump sums to promote outpatient services vs. inpatient) or extraordinary financing (e.g. to promote investments, enhance efficiency, etc.). A "pure" financial system based on casemix was thus transformed into

Table 10.1 Health care funding channels adopted by five Italian regions in 2000

Region	Capitation (covers DRGs)	Regional Direct Funding	Activity Related Funding	Functional (lump-sum)	Extra-ordinary Funding	Not Classifi-able	Total
Lombardia	83.6%	0.7%	0%	4%	4.3%	7.4%	100%
Veneto	77.9%	8.9%	0%	3.7%	1.2%	8.3%	100%
Toscana	90.7%	1.4%	0%	4.4%	1.9%	1.6%	100%
Marche	84.9%	1.6%	0%	5.4%	6.2%	2%	100%
Sicilia	62.8%	0.5%	18.7%	10.6%	1.1%	6.2%	100%

Source: Adapted from Anessi Pessina *et al.* 2004

a "mixed" system, with regional variations in terms of financial sources (an example for several Italian regions is reported in Table 10.1).

The introduction of a casemix system was then set by a Ministry Decree of 1994, and by January 1, 1995, all Italian hospitals (public and APP) were progressively shifted to a DRG-based financial system (which has been implemented, as a matter of fact, with several differentiations among regions, regarding both disease classification schemes and DRG classification versions – see the technical appendix for details). On this point, from January 1, 2006, all regions should finally adopt a unique disease classification system (Italian 2002 version of ICD–9–CM), which implies also a shift to a new DRG classification system (nineteenth revision).

The Decree of 1994 had introduced a set of "general criteria for the definition of tariffs" developed in collaboration with various medical professional associations. Such a law was anticipated by some debate, enhanced mainly by a circumscribed "think-tank community" from institutions such as the Istituto Superiore di Sanità,[9] but also including researchers, civil servants, hospital managers, health policy analysts, public health researchers, and health economist scholars. In 1991, the Department of Planning of the Ministry of Health launched a project named "ROD" ("Raggruppamenti Omogenei di Diagnosi" / homogeneous grouping of diagnoses), aimed at studying patient discharges from a sample of Italian hospitals; this project actually made RODs the official Italian name for DRGs. The process was also driven at the regional level, particularly involving the Emilia-Romagna, Lombardia and Friuli Venezia Giulia regions (Falcitelli and Langiano 2004; Nonis 2003), and was later amplified by both medical schools (e.g. the Catholic University in Rome, etc.) and public institutions born in the mid-1990s (e.g. the National Agency for Regional Health Services, the

Regional Health Agencies of Emilia Romagna, Tuscany, etc.) and also by universities with traditions in health economics and management (e.g. Public University of Milan, Bocconi University, etc.). In terms of external influences, as pointed out by France and Taroni (2005), there happened to be an authorized translation of the 1989 British White Paper Working for the Patients (Istituto di Studi delle Regioni, 1990) accompanied by a volume of essays by Italian health economists and policy analysts (France 1990); an appraisal of Swedish public competition was also translated into Italian (Saltman and von Otter 1999). Finally, the Ministry of Health "informally" hired a consulting firm that had also assisted the UK Department of Health.

Goals, debates and SSN evolution under the casemix system

As previously stated, the main rationale for introducing a casemix system derived from major changes in the delivery of health services mandated by the reform of 1992. By introducing a "quasi-market perspective," the goal was to control the growth of hospitalization costs, making hospitals more accountable for their productivity (e.g. shifting patients to more cost-effective settings).

Before the introduction of casemix systems and DRGs, when funding was based on actual expenditures, the general attention was concentrated on factors and costs used for service delivery. By paying according to a casemix system, the idea was to shift attention from expenditures to production (e.g. volume, quality, patient casemix). Therefore, a system describing hospital production, linking clinical practice with resource consumption, without losing professional autonomy, was considered valuable.

Of course, criticisms were instantly raised concerning patient-skimming opportunities, accelerated hospital discharges, manipulations according to tariff differentials (e.g. DRG creep), inappropriate patient severity, and variability. However, given the existing external circumstances in Italy at the time, the political will was to adopt DRGs as a good compromise between scientific precision and technical feasibility, acknowledging also the limits and problems experienced by other countries. Some think that the introduction of DRGs was itself a success, as it challenged the hospital system to research better productivity and efficiency from the inside: hospitals were urged to measure their activities to improve their ability to manage margins between costs and tariffs. From this perspective, as the DRG system was adjusted according to the limited hospital casemix and cost information available, the game proved to be not so much on a "level playing field;" public organizations happened to be penalized because of the wider range of services, the more severe casemix usually experienced, and the reduced flexibility in managing personnel and other goods (Taroni 1996). Some hospitals, especially APPs, decided to exploit or develop some medical specializations according to tariff differentials (e.g. a boom of cardiac and neurological surgeries was experienced by some Italian regions in the second half of the 1990s).

Looking backward, Italy must acknowledge that the introduction of competition in health care was likely not thought through well enough in advance. What happened in the second half of the 1990s was a process of pragmatic "learning by doing," mainly involving ASLs, AOs, APPs, and later on regions, experiencing the potential of new tools (e.g. planning, service level agreements, rewarding systems based on DRGs), but also the negative effects associated with economic conveniences (e.g. increase of volume for unnecessary services, excessive early hospital discharges, etc.). This process enhanced a move towards regional "governed competition models" (Anessi Pessina *et al.* 2004), with the adoption of top-down controls in terms of expenditure caps on hospitals (e.g. by object, such as supplies, or by function, such as inpatient), funding ceilings (e.g. billed services proportionally reduced when exceeding a limit), funding targets (e.g. billed services might exceed targets, but fees decrease with volumes), bilateral contracts (e.g. between an ASL and providers on volume, mix, price, waiting times, quality). Some regions, especially those that introduced their own fee schedules, such as Lombardia, also activated systematic utilization reviews, with sampling controls on medical records for inpatient and outpatient services (focusing on high-margin DRGs, shorter or longer than average stays, sharp changes in DRG frequencies, repeated hospitalizations), leading to periodic revisions of regional tariffs and, in some cases, to denied payments for inappropriate services. However, increases in efficiency and productivity were also achieved through hospital reorganizations by reducing length of stay and using day care.

Moreover, as France and Taroni (2005) observe, the overall environment of policymaking changed significantly in the second half of the 1990s, with a new electoral system bringing in regional presidents directly elected by popular vote, and thus more accountable for public services. It was at this time that clashes occurred between Rosy Bindi, the "center-left coalition" Minister of Health at the time, and some regions on how to interpret managerialism and competition in health systems. This became evident when, in 1997, the "center-right coalition" regional government of Lombardia, lead by Roberto Formigoni, passed a law for a total separation of providers (e.g. hospitals) from purchasers (e.g. ASLs), with the aim of creating a real internal market: for the first time since 1978, a different institutional scenario was conceived (as normally ASLs concentrate both provision and purchase of care). Under these circumstances, a new SSN reform was passed in 1999, borrowing again from the UK (e.g. White Paper The New NHS, Department of Health 1998), with the goal of reviewing somehow the "cost-paring mentality" and the risk of "democratic deficit" in the governance of health organizations brought in by the previous 1992 reform; the ideal was to promote clinical governance balanced by a tighter control over medical professions (e.g. through a new compulsory continuous educational program for doctors, called ECM – Educazione Continua in Medicina).

Finally, in 2000 and 2001 the process of decentralization and regional fiscal autonomy moved a step forward under the new "center-right coalition" national government, though with growing ambiguities. On one side, the devolution process pressed ahead (with new reforms); on the other, national legislation still interfered in areas of regional responsibility, limiting managerial autonomy of ASLs and AOs as cost containment was again an imperative. Regions indeed have become powerful in managing health systems, but also must ensure financial accountability (which implies the risk of local tax increases, co-payments, delisting of benefits, and cost containment). Consequently, the evolution of the casemix system in Italy nowadays appears to depend more on negotiations between the national government and the regions, especially at the permanent conference for state–regions relationships,[10] and less from laws passed by the Parliament or the Ministry of Health. Regions have indeed had the time to mature as institutions; their social learning and policy transfer capabilities have improved, though with visible differences in terms of implementation.

The relevance of shifting Italian hospitals to a casemix system also relates to the fact that the SSN had long been dominated by the hospital sector; however, in 1996 a national program for bed closure was launched (with the national standard on beds for acute care falling from 11 to 4.5 per 1,000 population between 1975 and 2001), the goal being to enhance efficiency while at the same time ensuring patient choice among a plurality of public and private providers. But few hospitals had accounting and information systems that were complementary to prospective payment systems, so very often regions applied DRGs only to inpatient services and day care provided by autonomous AOs and APPs, but not necessarily to internal hospitals directly managed by ASLs. Most of the regions set their tariffs according to national references calculated using cost data from a sample of eight public hospitals, those of the earlier national ROD project (France *et al.* 2005). Indeed, the previously available information system, managed by the Italian National Institute for Statistics (ISTAT), was not designed to provide data on costs, but only for hospital aggregated discharges and length of stays. To overcome this gap, a new information system based on SDO – "scheda di dimissione ospedaliera" (medical discharge report) – had to be implemented both at the regional and public/private provider levels, according to new national standards (set by two Ministry Decrees of 1991 and 1993). As there was little historical need for patient or insurance company billing, hospital information systems did not display data at the required patient level.

Despite such technical problems, regions were free to decide how to finance (e.g. DRGs or fee-for-service) the main categories of hospitals, but within tariffs defined at national level. The choice of the American framework for the casemix system represented the lack of reliable data, both of an accounting and clinical nature, as well as of cultural limitations in managing patient classifications. For such reasons, discussions arose around the clinical consistency of casemixes, while issues of tariffs compared to costs were quite often amazingly dismissed by adopting national values and applying American weights in order to obtain average costs for hospitalizations. Only in some cases did regions start to track hospitalization costs (especially if costs were high), so that the underdevelopment of cost analyses still represents one of the major limitations to system equity and distributive efficiency within the Italian SSN (Taroni 2003; 2004).

National tariffs therefore represented financial references for both regional hospitalizations and interregional patient mobility. Substantial differences among regional tariffs appeared through time (ranging from +16 to −30 percent of national rates). According to Guccio (2005), regional tariffs might differ in terms of construction, scope of application, hospital structure, and control systems, leading to a set of differentiated models (see Table 10.2). Indeed, only five regions developed their own regional tariffs, though almost all regions varied national tariffs according to the typology of hospitals (e.g. public or private), service configurations (e.g. with or without an emergency department), activities (e.g. research, teaching, casemix width and complexity), or by excluding from prospective payment systems activities with costs unrelated to volume (e.g. organ transplants).

Table 10.2 Main features of DRG tariffs adopted by Italian regions (2004)

Regions	Year of introduction, reference to national DRG list (yes/no)	Number of DRGs, Grouper version, last update	% of abatement applied to national tariffs	Distinction of reimbursement by type of hospital, service, or specialization	Use of financial ceilings	Tariffs abatement for over-production	Regulation on non-appropriate DRGs
Abruzzo	1996, yes	489, n.10, 1999	–20%	No	No	No	Tbd
Basilicata	1997, yes	489, n.10, 1999	0%	Yes (private –20%)	Yes	No	Limitations and financial cuts
Calabria	1995, yes	489, n.10, 1999	–12%	No	Yes	Yes	Limitations and financial cuts
Campania	1995, yes	489, n.10, 2000–2001	0%	Yes (3 categories of public and 3 for private hospitals)	Yes	Only private H.	Limitations and financial cuts
Emilia-Romagna	1996, no	492, n.14, 2001–2	n/a.	Yes (2 groups with or without emergencies)	Yes	Yes	Limitations
Friuli Venezia Giulia	1995, yes	489, n.10, 2002	0%	Yes (2 groups with or no emerg. and research)	Yes	Only private H.	Limitations
Lazio	1995, yes	489, n.10, 2000	3%	No	Yes	Yes	Limitations and financial cuts
Liguria	1995, yes	489, n.10, 2002	0%	Yes (public and private hospitals and children's hospitals)	Yes	Yes	Tbd

Lombardia	1995, no	492, n.19, 2005	n.a.	Yes (3 tariffs: base for H. with emerg., +5% with high spec., −3% without emerg. or high spec.)	Yes	Limitations and financial cuts
Marche	1995, yes	492, n.14, 2002	0%	Yes (2 groups: AOs, private and second H.)	Yes	Limitations
Molise	1995, yes	489, n.10, 1999	0%	Yes (2 groups: all public H, −15% for private H.)	Yes	Limitations
P.A. Bolzano	1995, yes	489, n.10, n/a.	0%	Yes (4 categories from +33% to −5% according to hospital and DRG)	Yes	Tbd
P.A. Trento	1997, yes	489, n.10, n/a.	0%	Yes (according to hospital, from −6% to +16%)	No	Limitations
Piemonte	1995, yes	492, n.14, 2002	n/a.	Yes (public H. from +5.5% to 9%, private from 0% to −15%)	Only private H.	Limitations
Puglia	1995, yes	489, n.10, 2000	−10%	Yes (4 categories of hospitals, based on specialties)	Only private H.	Limitations and financial cuts
Sardegna	1995, yes	489, n.10, 2001	−5%	No	Yes	Limitations
Sicilia	1995, no	489, n.10, 2002	n/a.	Yes (6 categories of H. based on casemix and org. complexity)	Yes	Limitations and financial cuts

Table 10.2 *(cont.)*

Regions	Year of introduction, reference to national DRG list (yes/no)	Number of DRGs, Grouper version, last update	% of abatement applied to national tariffs	Distinction of reimbursement by type of hospital, service, or specialization	Use of financial ceilings	Tariffs abatement for over-production	Regulation on non-appropriate DRGs
Toscana	1995, no	492, n.14, 2005	n/a.	Yes (2 tariffs based on DRG weights)	Yes	Yes	Limitations and financial cuts
Umbria	1995, yes	489, n.10. n/a.	−10%	No	Yes	Yes	Limitations
Veneto	1995, no	492, n.14, 2001	n/a.	No	Yes	Yes	Limitations
Valle d'Aosta	1995, yes	489, n.10, n/a.	0%	No	No	No	Limitations

Source: Adapted from Guccio (2005), based on 2003 data from the National Agency for Regional Health Services.

A vast majority of regions also regulated DRGs considered inappropriate through limitations or by cutting tariffs. But in general what emerged is a differentiation in the use and modulation of regional tariffs, reflecting political evaluations or local lobbying capabilities. Recently, Pelliccia (2004) observed that more regions have started to review tariffs on the basis of real costs, especially because, since 2001, pressure is growing to reduce inappropriate hospitalizations. Moreover, in the words of Taroni (2004), if the three major components of a casemix system (classification of diseases, grouping systems, and weights and tariffs) are not constantly updated, technological innovations are likely to be excluded (as managers have to leverage on partial tools, whereas clinicians might perceive DRGs as more of a threat than an assessment tool). An example of this happened in 2002 with drug eluting stents, which caused different reactions: Lombardia created three new DRGs to encourage utilization, Emilia Romagna applied increased tariffs and established a regional registry to monitor effectiveness, and other regions did not review their policies, thus limiting the diffusion of the technology.

More generally, the choice for a casemix system in Italy reflected a political will to contribute to the decentralization of the SSN; by funding according to DRGs, financial risk is transferred to hospitals, which are inevitably transformed into "residual claimants," facing the challenge of managing unitary costs versus predetermined tariffs, and/or exploiting economies of scale and areas of expertise to leverage higher margins (Arcangeli and France 2004). By the end of the 1990s, this had become a paradox for the SSN. On the one hand, hospitals had improved their efficiency and productivity (as will be discussed below), but at the same time, the majority of regions began to accumulate significant deficits, mainly because of worsening Italian economic conditions and debatable political choices, such as: elimination of co-payments on drugs (2001), followed by a partial reintroduction (in eleven regions), of extensions in public coverage of costly drugs and more generous personnel contracts (1999–2000). From this perspective, more regions are increasingly governing their "quasi-markets," reducing the autonomy of providers and encouraging cross-organizational cooperation (e.g. among similar services of ASLs and AOs).

This sort of "policy reversal" is probably also due to the push for hospital specialization enhanced by prospective payment systems. Nowadays, more regions are trying to encourage networking among providers, based on complementarities of hospital supply rather than pure competition, with the final goal being to place some responsibility for regional system performance on providers, while preserving results achieved in terms of individual efficiency and accountability.

Characteristics of the Italian casemix system

From the SSN point of view, the casemix system for inpatient hospital services was introduced with the aim of putting pressure on hospitals and improving equity in fund allocation, as payments referring to the same DRG are based on a tariff derived from the average cost of hospitalizations for the same diagnosis. This scenario should also have induced competition among providers, leading to better service quality and possibly cost containment.

An overview of major technical issues can help to understand other features of the Italian casemix system. In particular, Italian DRGs can be considered to have a number of benefits, especially after they were used to redefine the national standards for hospital care; this is true mainly for surgical DRGs, while medical ones define economic constraints based on discrimination of the appropriateness of diagnoses for hospitalization. The structure of the Italian casemix system was then initially built on a national list of 489 mutually exclusive DRGs (both surgical and medical) grouped in 25 MDCs (Major Diagnostic Categories – see Table 10.3). Some regional lists display 492 DRGs. As already pointed out, diagnoses and procedures are encoded as ICD–9–CM codes. However, since January 1, 2006, with the shift to the 2002 Italian version of ICD–9–CM and the nineteenth revision of the DRG classification system, the total number of DRGs has grown to 523.

On the basis of this casemix structure and the Ministry Decree of 1994, which introduced DRGs, it is possible to specify the articulation of tariffs applied in the Italian SSN (see Table 10.4). In this regard, while the central government is still responsible for defining classification systems, national tariffs, and criteria for regional fees, regions can articulate weights, tariffs by provider, financial ceilings, rules of abatement, and additional funding. For example, although being one of the regions that invested more heavily in the development of activity-based funding, Lombardia currently uses additional funding for emergency call centers, patient transportation (helicopter and transfer of newborns included), emergency departments, intensive care services, services for extended burns and toxic poisoning, organ transplantation centers, tissue banks, research, teaching and education for

Table 10.3 Overview of twenty-five MDCs and number of DRGs included (1994)

MDC	Description	Number of DRGs		
		Surgical	Medical	Other
Pre-MDC	Liver, bone marrow transplantation, tracheotomy	4		
24 (Pre-MDC)	Multiple trauma	3	1	
25 (Pre-MDC)	HIV infections	1	4	
1	Diseases and disorders of the nervous system	8	27	
2	Diseases and disorders of the eye	6	7	
3	Diseases and disorders of the ear, nose, mouth, and throat	15	11	
4	Diseases and disorders of the respiratory system	3	26	
5	Diseases and disorders of the circulatory system	19	25	
6	Diseases and disorders of the digestive system	23	17	
7	Diseases and disorders of the hepatobiliary system and pancreas	11	17	
8	Diseases and disorders of the musculoskeletal system and connective tissue	28	22	
9	Diseases and disorders of the skin, subcutaneous tissue, and breast	14	14	
10	Endocrine, nutritional, and metabolic diseases and disorders	9	8	
11	Diseases and disorders of the kidney and urinary tract	14	18	
12	Diseases and disorders of the male reproductive system	12	7	
13	Diseases and disorders of the female reproductive system	13	4	
14	Pregnancy and childbirth	6	9	
15	Newborns			7
16	Diseases and disorders of the blood and blood-forming organs	3	5	
17	Myeloproliferative diseases and disorders	6	9	2
18	Infectious and parasitic disorders	1	8	
19	Mental diseases and disorders	1	8	

Table 10.3 (*cont.*)

MDC	Description	Number of DRGs		
		Surgical	Medical	Other
20	Alcohol/drug use and alcohol/drug use induced organic mental disorders			5
21	Trauma and poisoning	5	12	
22	Burns	3	2	1
23	Factors that impact health status and demand for health care services	1	6	
	Residuals			5
TOTAL	489	211	258	20

auxiliary health care personnel (e.g. nurses and technicians). In addition, it grants lump sums for specialized centers on tuberculosis, hemophilia, cancer, eating disorders, and epilepsy.

The 1994 Decree also established that regional tariffs were to be calculated according to "standard production cost",[11] adjusted for hospital general costs,[12] "thus adopting a full costing approach, but without taking into account the variability of costs on the basis of volume". Finally, the Decree also proposed a list of DRG-specific weights, equivalent to those used in the USA HCFA Grouper Version 10, which had to be updated annually by regions on the basis of cost data acquired from regional hospitals (in case of technical problems, they were allowed to define regional DRG weights according to national standards). In practical terms, each DRG was assigned to a weight (also called "score point"), or relative value, that expressed the cost of a specific set of patients compared to the average cost of admissions (equal to the unit in origin): as the base unit of a score point has an economic monetary value, the final tariff is derived by multiplying such a value with the relative weight of the DRG (Cantù and Palucci 2004). Tariffs were therefore expected to cover total costs of hospitalization using a grid of values based on the concept of "cost per point" of an Adjusted National Standardized Payment (PNSA – "Pagamento Nazionale Standardizzato Aggiustato"). History since 1994 has shown that, because of the initial lack of analytical data regarding both resource consumption and relative unit costs, as well as clinical characteristics, regions demonstrated limited capabilities to update weights and tariffs, thus freezing the situation at the initial national cost sampling effort, at least up to 1997 (see technical appendix).

Table 10.4 Current articulation of Italian hospital services referred to casemix system and tariffs

Type of service	Standard of hospitalization	Unit of payment
Inpatient ordinary regime for acute care	Ordinary admissions of 1 day	Per-case DRG tariff
	Ordinary admissions (from 2 days to outlier)	Per-case DRG tariff
	Extraordinary admissions (with length of stay above cut-off value by single DRG)	Per-case DRG tariff + ('days in excess from cut-off' x 'daily tariff' reduced by 52%, since 09/12/06)
	Ordinary long-term admissions	Per-day tariff (up to 60 days, then reduced by 40%)
Day hospital regime for acute care	One day access	Per-case DRG tariff (for surgery), per-case MDC tariff (for medical treatments)
	Cycle of programmed accesses within one diagnosis	'Number of accesses' x 'DRG rates'
Inpatient and day hospital rehabilitation regime	Ordinary admission or daily access	Per-day tariff uniform for all cases inside a particular MDC (up to 60 days, then reduced by 40%)
Residential regime and semi-residential (nursing homes)	Ordinary long-term admission	Per-day tariff, only health care component (up to 60 days, then reduced by 60%)
Psychiatric care (inpatient, residential, outpatient)	Ordinary admissions or outpatient services	In general terms follows rules for inpatient and outpatient tariffs
Outpatient specialist care regime (emergency care included)	Unit of service or access	Per-unit tariff
Patient transportation regime	Unit of transport	Per-unit tariff[1]
Thermal care regime	Unit of treatment cycle	Per-treatment tariff

Sources: Elaborated on the basis of Taroni (1996), Pelliccia (2004), Fattore and Torbica (2004).

[1] There is no publicly available data on the methodology applied in defining those tariffs; prior to the issue in 1996 of a national list for outpatient services, some sort of cost assessment was conducted on a limited number of providers. This cost assessment utilized a gross costing approach to evaluate total costs for ambulatory care services to be allocated to different specialty areas and then to specific services.

In general terms, hospitals received a tariff for every ordinary hospitalization of more than one day, while admissions for rehabilitation or long-term care were paid according to the length of stay. In the case of ordinary admission longer than a threshold, an additional *per diem* rate was to be applied. Moreover, in 1995 the Ministry of Health issued a set of guidelines for the implementation of DRGs, giving regions two options: either to adopt the national tariffs (with the opportunity to lower them as much as 20 percent) or to develop their own tariffs by assessing regional hospital costs (replicating the full costing national approach or adopting a simplified procedure based on the calculation of full costs for a limited set of DRGs, in order to derive an indicative historical cost per 'DRG point' to be used as a calculation base for other DRGs). However, only five of the twenty-one regions developed their own tariffs on the basis of some kind of cost assessment; the majority adopted the national fees, which were updated only in 1997 (and then in 2006), with an update of weights and values. In summary, characteristics of casemix systems and DRG tariffs vary extensively across Italian regions.

In 1996, a national list of specialized outpatient public services was also issued in terms of: a positive list of services (inclusive of clinical laboratory and diagnostics imaging, generally without specific links to clinical conditions), a positive list of services available only for specific clinical–diagnostic indications and limited to special patient categories, and a negative list of specialist care not covered by SSN. Regions were allowed to set up their own rates (using national rates as a maximum), as well as to deliver additional services for which they were to be financially responsible. Since its approval in 1996, the national fee schedule has not been updated; all regions, however, have been continuously updating their own tariffs.

Finally, another technical issue concerns patient interregional mobility, which is not negligible and reflects a constitutional right, meaning that regions are required to pay for treatments provided to their residents elsewhere (called passive mobility), but, in turn, can receive payments for health care provision to patients coming from other regions (active mobility). Payment flows include a wide spectrum of services: inpatient and outpatient care, primary care, pharmaceuticals, and patient transportation (including helicopter transfer). In relation to inpatient services, special agreements now apply for compensation. Since July 1, 2003, a so-called "uniform tariff" (TUC – "tariffa unica convenzionata") applies to hospital treatments provided outside the region of residence. This tariff is DRG-specific and is equivalent to the national fees of 1997. Specific adjustments apply to: DRGs classified as "high complexity cases" (national fees are increased by 10 percent), DRGs defined as "at high risk of being inappropriate" (−25 percent for medical DRGs and −50 percent for surgical), and transplantation (special tariffs apply). Tariffs might also differ in consideration of a list of specialized centers (likely to attract patients and rewarded with an additional 5 percent) and for being a teaching hospital (7 percent increase).

The definition of a uniform tariff was urged by at least three factors: the need to compensate for equity deficits among regions, the political will to decrease patient mobility for low-complexity cases, and finally, the demand for rationalization in the interregional compensation process (which can take years, with potential perverse retrospective effects on regional balance sheets).

The situation in 2006

As previously discussed, a casemix system has been introduced in Italy with the aim to enhance hospital productivity and master cost-effectiveness. This choice is connected to the evolution of the Italian SSN and the redefinition of institutional roles; the central government is responsible for ensuring funding to the regions (based on capitation) and supervising and monitoring the provision of the benefits specified with LEAs, while regions are responsible for the organization of health care services, and are accountable for financial performance (including deficits or provision of additional services on the basis of regional own resources).

The general framework is characterized by the need to balance equity with economic sustainability across Italian regions; in particular, as regional funding is based on capitation, it implies the risk of financing the existing system on the basis of historical costs (and efficiency levels), thus implicitly following a "policy of first under-financing the SSN and then periodically covering regional deficits" (France et al. 2005). Moreover, Italy appears to be quite peculiar because of the high contiguity between third-party payers (regions, ASLs) and providers (again ASLs, but also AOs), which leaves some ambiguity on the final sharing of financial risk (e.g. the region is accountable, but performance is driven by ASLs). For such reasons, transfers based on capitation are still complemented by other means[13] (e.g. to address priorities or high-cost services; see Table 10.5).

In this scenario, hospital services receive funding derived from the capitation allocated to ASLs and within casemix provisional annual budgets. The rule applies to all public and private hospital budgets. The move to a casemix system therefore had two main implications for

Table 10.5 Financial flows leading to funding based on casemix systems

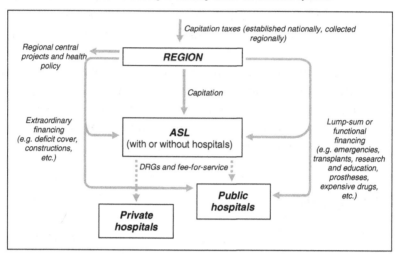

hospitals: it shifted the financial system from real costs to a prospective system, and it changed the financial source from the binomial "state-region" to "region-ASL." Since then, ASLs have become the final "purchasers" and have to negotiate yearly with internal or external hospitals the number and casemix of admissions (surgical and medical), waiting lists, quality standards, etc. Indeed, because the SSN is essentially a single payer, all patients are included in the new financing scheme. Hospital tariffs are intended to cover full costs of hospitalization, including medical consultations and other staff and pharmaceutical costs, though specific services receive ad hoc funding (e.g. emergencies, transplantations, etc.). Moreover, to complete the scenario, capitation is also used for paying primary care and other services provided by health districts (the territorial articulation of ASLs), such as vaccinations, home care assistance, familial support, mental health, etc.

Concerning hospital budgets, internal planning usually does not reflect the external financial channels but is articulated according to productive factors: activities (e.g. number of admissions, length of stay, casemix, patient severity, etc.), goods and services (e.g. sanitary and not sanitary), intermediate services (e.g. lab, diagnostics), personnel (e.g. medical and non-medical), and investments (e.g. technologies, research projects). Therefore, hospital central staff ensure the combination between external sources and internal planning. Very often medical appraisals are connected to budgets that might refer directly or indirectly to DRGs, so that financial incentives are likely to be connected to personal or organizational objectives expressed using casemix tools. The same logic applies to utilization reviews and internal or external benchmarking.

Specific activities such as medicines, prostheses, research, and teaching receive particular attention and are ruled differently, with further differentiations at regional levels:

- Expensive drugs (e.g. for chemotherapy) or drugs dispensed through outpatient services or home-care assistance, to ensure care continuity, might be comprised within DRGs or be financed on a real-cost basis (e.g. list of drugs by specialty or disease, called "File F," defined by a central agency of the Ministry of Health, called AIFA[14]). In general, on this subject there is complex legislation regulating drugs, both within hospitals and outside (e.g. primary care), according to cost-effectiveness principles and administrative rules. Some regions exert rigorous controls through permanent observation, others just sampling controls; hospitals usually try to abide by the rules, with the support of internal pharmacists and administrative staff, because misuse could endanger financial ceilings or contracts negotiated with ASLs or regions.

- Access to prosthetics, orthopedic and technical aids in the SSN is differentiated according to three lists of devices: List One includes technical appliances which require a prescription from a specialist, an authorization from the ASL of residence and a final implant by a trained technician (e.g. prosthetics and orthotics); List Two contains technical aids which do not require particular implants (e.g. aid for self-care and protection, home adaptation aids); and List Three, goods that are directly purchased by ASLs and provided to patients (e.g. respiratory curative aids). If a need arises in a hospital, the ASL is required to respond within five days. In both cases, if the ASL does not respond in due time, the authorization is considered to be conceded; prosthetics are therefore paid according to reimbursement tariffs under specific rules (e.g. cochlear implantations must be authorized). Finally, a Ministry Decree of 2005 introduced a national classification with the aim of grouping medical devices according to similarity of use (thus adopting a multi-layer sorting in main categories, anatomical or functional groups, and final typologies, which is intended to foster a common language for devices, monitoring of consumption and accidents, and possibly development of detailed reference prices).

- Research and teaching activities usually receive complementary funding according to the nature and status of the hospital: for example, tariffs applied to hospitalizations within the thirteen university teaching hospitals run by the SSN are increased by 8 percent, whereas medical staff might be remunerated by the region or the Ministry of Education and Research.

In Italy, DRGs also proved to be useful for hospital planning, as they allow the combination of quantitative matters (volume) with qualitative issues (casemix) and economic values, thus increasing hospital awareness about economic effects of decision making, cost, and margin control. In this regard, Cantù and Palucci (2004) conducted research on the 29 AOs of the Lombardia region, which highlighted that DRGs improved the capabilities of analyzing hospital activity through the identification of final products, and the construction of indicators for performance measurement.

Indeed, the shift to DRGs did increase the economic accountability of Lombard hospitals: fifteen out of twenty-nine AOs shifted to full costing schemes to know the value of intermediate services, manage expectations from high and low margin units, and compare standard production costs to relative tariffs. The attention was mainly on economic indicators, with eighteen out of twenty-nine AOs using economic values to define responsibilities for organizational units in terms of costs, margins, volumes, operational efficiency, casemix proximal severity (DRG average weight or casemix index[15]), and, in a limited number of hospitals, also in terms of revenue (e.g. DRG absolute value, DRG average value,[16] DRG average weight[17]). Some hospitals tried to push indicators harder to measure things such as: hospitalizations by single DRG, repeated admissions by DRG, performance index,[18] bed rotation,[19] percentage of surgical DRGs, percentage of 0 to 1 day admissions, percentage of outlier admissions, ALOs by DRG point, and day-hospital index.[20] The initial trend was therefore to address the issue of performance measurement by using economic and monetary values, rather than organizational, clinical, or multidimensional issues (as nowadays some hospitals try to do, by using tools such as balanced score cards or six-sigma methodologies). However, 13 AOs were involved in the definition and measurement of patient pathways to improve hospital processes. Finally, quality indicators in terms of value delivered to patients and impact on health status were not often used; usually quality coincided more with indicators such as correct coding, patient perceived satisfaction, reduced waiting lists, and staff participation in training. More emphasis, starting from the region, is now placed on indicators of appropriateness, but mainly because inappropriate treatments are not reimbursed: indicators vary from repeated hospitalizations, admissions above outlier value, percentage of patients discharged from surgical units with a medical DRG, admissions of one day, long hospitalizations in acute care units, and number of unplanned day treatments.

As in the Lombard example, Italian hospitals did use DRGs for managerial purposes quite extensively, with the risk of transferring great expectations onto casemix tools. There also appear to be some limitations: the classification process allows homogeneous classes of hospitalizations, it is usually behind medical practices, and it might reflect the American hospital context too much. Moreover, as hospital volumes in the future are not expected to increase, additional non-economic measurement systems are required to control appropriateness, quality, social and health care integration, and patient pathways. These last considerations highlight the need for quality, consistency and reliability in hospital activity and cost data. In Italy, coding errors were a severe problem for some years, even more pervasive than the phenomenon of DRG creep; indeed, according to Di Loreto and Spolarore (2004), in 1996, 22 percent of the 10,000,000 hospital discharge forms had coding errors, while in 2001, the percentage dropped to 5 percent of more than 12,000,000 discharges. Quality improvements are also observable in terms of average number of diagnoses and interventions by discharge form; in 1996, 1.9 diagnoses and about 1.5 interventions by form were reported, while in 2001, the number increased to 2.1 diagnoses and 1.9 interventions.

Concerning the maintenance of the casemix system, it has been mostly delegated to regions, though in 2000 a national technical group was nominated at the ministerial level to monitor and suggest updates, in particular concerning the review of ICD–9–CM, a new retrieval and analysis of hospital data on costs (in order to start up a tariff redefinition), and, finally, the experimentation of APR and APG classification systems (Gruppo tecnico 2001). In 2002, another ministerial research study was coordinated by the pediatric teaching hospital Bambin Gesù of Rome, with the participation of sixteen other Italian hospitals, which led to a review of classification systems for patients less than eighteen years of age. Such examples enable a consideration about critical areas of casemix systems experienced in Italy. On one side, there are under-financed medical areas (neonatology and pediatrics, major pathologies treated in intensive care, such as neurological or neurosurgery, and oncology, but also psychiatric rehabilitation, some orthopaedic treatments, and trauma). On the other, casemix systems might also end up concentrating on too many clinical episodes in one specific "DRG garbage can" (e.g. DRG 55 for otorhinolaryngology). In addition, the attention and capabilities for continuous reviews of casemix systems and DRG tariffs, whether a deliberate political choice or not, were demonstrated to be insufficient.

In general, coding procedures in Italian hospitals have been centralized to medical record staff, usually working for the hospital medical director (reporting to the general manager), and following data flow requirements defined nationally (SDO hospital discharge form) and, in some cases, also regionally. There are of course exceptions, in which coding is practiced directly at the ward or hospital service unit level by physicians (e.g. Valduce hospital of Como, one of the eight hospitals in the initial national ROD project). Usually data on public and private provider activity must be sent to ASLs and/or regions according to periodic defined "information debt" procedures, to allow for controls and, afterwards, for final payment managed by ASLs according to patients' residency. When the process implies hospitals outside regional boundaries, the timing and rules of compensation among regions are slower and subject to other cross-check procedures (though, as described previously, the introduction of a uniform tariff across regions was helpful).

Impact, debates, controversies

The introduction of DRGs in Italy raised concerns similar to other countries (Louis *et al.* 1999). Will cost-cutting incentives also affect needed care (besides eliminating unnecessary or marginally beneficial care)? Will reductions in length of stay or in the use of specific services lead to worsened patient outcomes, such as increased severity of illness at discharge, increased readmissions, or higher mortality rates? Nonis (2003) reports that "incredibly, Italy has been able to digest DRGs!" But many do think that the DRG revolution tried to "change everything by changing nothing," or, as Taroni (2003) observes, it certainly reshaped the power balance inside hospitals, diminishing the influence of clinicians in favor of professionalized bureaucrats.

In order to provide an assessment of the Italian experience in using a casemix system and its potential irreversibility (as argued, for example, by Falcitelli, 2004), an impact analysis on hospital performance can be discussed (Table 10.6).

Table 10.6 Changes in Italian hospital provision (1994–2003), public and private

Key factors	1994	1995	1996	1997	1998	1999	2000	2001	2002	2003
Ordinary admissions	5,226,591	7,539,381	9,024,892	9,120,856	9,838,940	9,626,154	9,299,266	9,158,604	8,878,778	8,339,745
% change		44.3%	19.7%	1.1%	7.9%	−2.2%	−3.4%	−1.5%	−3%	−6.1%
Day-hospital admissions	517,457	1,055,073	1,394,407	1,744,752	2,324,135	2,461,534	2,627,610	3,041,774	3,302,957	3,816,750
% change		103.9%	32.2%	25.1%	33.2%	5.9%	6.7%	15.8%	8.5%	15.6%
ALOS (days)	8.9	8.1	7.6	7.2	7.1	7	6.9	6.8	6.5	6.7
Number of ordinary beds	–	–	290,539	276,161	262,065	254,625	234,203	226,996	216,934	199,869
Number of beds for day-hospital	–	–	18,962	21,199	21,629	24,811	23,781	24,010	25,634	28,048
Total days of hospitalization	–	–	–	88,794,932	88,009,005	85,811,850	82,484,479	81,425,592	80,393,353	78,450,940
Total DRG average weight	0.79	0.81	0.81	1.04	1.05	1.09	1.11	1.14	1.18	1.22
Medical DRG/ surgical DRG	–	–	–	–	2.3	2.1	1.9	1.8	1.7	1.68
Num. of days in DH/days for ordinary admission	2.8	4.8	5.4	7.6	9.3	1,2	11.8	13.4	15.1	17.0
Num. of incorrect hospital discharges	33.9	33.3	20.3	17.8	16.3	5.3	4.5	5	5.9	5.67

Source: Adapted from Cantù *et al.* (2004), Cerbo and Langiano (2004), Pelliccia (2004) and Ministry of Health data.

Starting from available numbers, the introduction of DRGs affected hospital provision and productivity; concerning capabilities, the total number of beds for acute care was reduced (−23 percent from 1998 to 2004, especially in public hospitals), while beds for day care were increased (+27 percent in the same period, especially among APPs, with +149.3 percent, compared to +14.3 percent in public). In terms of productivity, the number of admissions increased (+16.9 percent overall from 1996 to 2002, meaning +13.4 percent for public hospitals and +46.8 percent for APPs), but with differences among types of hospitalizations: for example, admissions for acute care diminished overall by 1.6 percent (though public hospitals reduced by −5.85 percent and APPs increased by 30.6 percent), whereas day cases increased by 136.9 percent (+128.3 percent in public hospitals and +325.6 percent for APPs). In addition, ALOS fell from 8.9 days in 1994 to 6.7 in 2003; the mortality index during hospitalizations or after 30 days did not deteriorate, occupancy rates of hospital beds did not change significantly, and hospital transfers of patients remained limited (in 2002, less than 1.5 percent of total admissions).

The performance of the Italian hospital sector under a casemix system appears, therefore, to be affected by two major factors. On one side, it was affected by structural interventions such as cuts in public beds, which was quite differentiated among regions, although with some clustering trends: according to Cerbo and Langiano (2004), from 1996–2002, Abruzzo cut as much as 26 percent of its beds, nine other regions cut from 15 to 23 percent, and the remaining regions, about 10 percent. On the other side, productivity gains were enhanced by rationalizations in hospital functioning. Symptomatic in that sense appears to be the change in ALOS practiced by APPs; in 1996 they displayed 8.5 days, compared to 7.5 in public hospitals (which still resented the previous funding system based on length of stay); in 2002, the numbers had reversed, to 5.7 for APPs and 6.9 for public.

Besides such numbers, further evaluations would require cost performance data, which is not easy to either obtain or compare due to regional heterogeneity in terms of casemixes and tariffs. Without a real opportunity to read costs systematically, it becomes problematic to assess improvements in terms of operational efficiency, especially taking into consideration that hospital expenses from 1995–2002 grew by 54.2 percent (+52.9 percent in public, +61.1 percent in APPs).

However, more recently a ministerial analysis of Italian hospital costs has been conducted with the aim of assessing the impact of factors such as number of beds, research and teaching activities, and specialized emergency

Table 10.7 Cost distribution in a sample of 42 public and 16 private Italian hospitals (2000)

Cost category	Average value in % for public hospitals	Average value in % for private hospitals
Nursing assistance and sojourn services	24.68	16.94
Operating rooms	6.03	7.96
Drugs	6.79	3.47
Radiology	4.54	8.07
Laboratory	5.37	4.38
Medical devices and prostheses	6.50	10.44
Rehabilitation therapies	0.54	0.83
Clinical services (e.g. emergencies, delivery rooms, anaesthesia, etc.)	5.42	4.59
Intensive care	3.23	4.92
Medical personnel	17.10	13.07
General and administrative costs	19.80	25.34

Source: Adapted from Adduce and Lorenzoni (2004).

units. The research analyzed two samplings (one made of forty-two public hospitals, a second of sixteen APPs) for a total of 596,996 admissions in 2000. According to Adduce and Lorenzoni (2004), it highlighted that the average cost per case was €3,308 in public hospitals and €2,680 in private ones (the differential mainly depending on research and teaching activities, though private hospitals had a higher casemix index of 3.34 percent). In particular, the distribution of costs also reveals interesting differentials between public and private hospitals (Table 10.7), for instance, on nursing assistance, medical personnel, general costs, medical devices and prostheses, radiology, and drugs.

Regarding quality performance, some additional insights might be derived from analyzing variations in DRG rankings by frequency (Table 10.8). As expected, the only constant through time is natural birth, while the great reduction of "garbage-can DRGs" (e.g. 468, 470) reflects major improvements in coding. More generally, surgical DRGs improve (e.g. 39, 371, 359, 222, 209, 198, and 119), while medical ones decrease (e.g. 183, 243, 133, 134, 369, 254, 284, and 324), and finally, DRGs with low clinical complexity are reduced as well (e.g. 183, 184, and 243).

On the basis of another study of thirty-two hospitals in the Friuli Venezia Giulia region (in the northeast of Italy), Louis *et al.* (1999) concluded that the incentives of DRGs in Italy encouraged the use of day care and

Table 10.8 Comparison in DRG ranking by frequency (ordinary admissions, 1994–2001)

DRG	Cases		Ranking							
	1994	2001	1994	1995	1996	1997	1998	1999	2000	2001
373 – Natural birth without complications	169,342	322,962	1	1	1	1	1	1	1	1
371 – Caesarian section	–	160,440	30	11	10	8	7	6	5	5
183 – Esophagus > 18 years	114,546	176,610	2	2	2	3	3	3	3	4
184 – Esophagus < 17 years	48,780	107,940	20	14	12	13	12	11	13	13
243 – Back pains	100,334	129,732	3	4	4	4	5	5	6	7
39 – Intervention on eye crystalline	86,587	229,316	4	3	3	2	2	2	2	2
127 – Cardiac insufficiency and shock	–	177,276	25	9	5	5	6	4	4	3
410 – Chemotherapy	–	129,732	>30	>30	>30	17	17	13	10	6
133 – Arteriosclerosis	74,471	–	5	19	28	>30	49	60	>60	>60
470 – Non-attributable to other DRG	73,195	–	6	10	>30	21	>60	>60	>60	>60
467 – Other factors affecting health	69,583	–	7	>30	>30	>30	>60	33	32	>60
162 – Inguinal hernia intervention	62,670	111,936	8	5	6	6	9	8	8	12
134 – Hypertension	61,738	83,585	9	8	8	9	11	14	16	17
88 – Chronic obstructive pulmonary disease	61,591	112,739	10	6	7	7	8	7	7	11
222 – Intervention on the knee	–	113,958	>30	>30	22	16	15	12	12	10
359 – Intervention on the uterus	–	116,911	23	16	13	12	14	10	11	9
369 – Menstrual difficulties and disorders of the female reproductive system	59,399	–	11	20	21	27	36	39	45	45

82 – Respiratory neoplasies	59,006	–	12	17	17	22	29	27	30	27
381 – Abortion with hysterectomy	57,925	88,166	13	7	9	10	13	15	15	16
14 – Cerebrovascular diseases	56,274	118,730	14	12	11	11	10	9	9	8
254 – Fractures of arm and leg, except foot	56,272	–	15	13	15	19	>60	23	25	>60
430 – Psychosis	53,893	99,224	16	15	14	14	16	16	14	14
468 – Extended surgical intervention unrelated to main diagnosis	52,370	–	17	>30	>30	>30	>60	>60	>60	>60
284 – Minor diseases of skin	51,923		18	22	25	>30	33	35	41	51
324 – Urinary calcolosys	50,054	–	19	18	16	15	18	20	22	24
209 – Intervention on major articulation and reimplantation	–	97,686	>30	>30	>30	>30	23	18	17	15
198 – Cholecystectomy	–	79,178	>30	29	24	26	24	22	21	18
139 – Arrhythmia	–	78,092	24	24	26	24	22	21	20	19
119 – Stripping of veins	–	76,339	>30	23	20	18	19	19	19	20

Source: Adapted from Adduce and Lorenzoni (2004).

discouraged the use of acute beds, as from 1993–6, significant decreases in admission rates, mean length of stay, and days of care rates were reported for nine major medical conditions,[21] with few significant differences in mortality rates.

Moreover, some argue that improvements over time in quality and reliability of hospital information make it advisable to use only post-1998 data (France *et al.* 2005), when hospitals were finally able to manage discharge information correctly. Indeed, between 1998 and 2002, the SSN bed capacity fell by 15 percent (−18.9 percent in AOs and −13.4 percent in APPs), admissions dropped by 4.4 percent (inpatient hospitalizations by −10 percent), and length of stay by 5.6 percent, while day cases tripled from 6.7 percent to 28.7 percent. As already pointed out, APPs behaved differently in terms of length of stay (shorter), admission rates (higher), and indeed, as a final consequence, revenues of the private hospital sector increased in that period by 43.9 percent (though limited by automatic tariff reduction mechanisms) compared to the 26.9 percent increase experienced by public hospitals (Cerbo and Langiano 2004).

Besides such considerations, other observers, such as Arcangeli *et al.* (2004), argue that the debate on casemix systems has not been supported by enough evidence on the effects of DRGs in terms of volume and service type variations, delivery patterns, quality of care, and financial impact, so that it is possible to wonder whether the expected results were actually achieved. However, casemix tools have proved to be a powerful policy tool influencing regional and hospital behaviors, though they require maintenance and updates in order to keep pace with changes in treatment practice, new technologies, and new delivery patterns. France *et al.* (2004) add that the effects of introducing prospective payment systems in a single-payer health care system remain uncertain; in Italy the financial system covers a continuum, from hospitals directly managed by ASLs, to independent hospitals (AOs), to private for-profit or not-for-profit players with contractual relationships with purchasers (APPs). Of course, moving from public to private providers, incentives associated with casemixes and tariffs increase. Italian policy makers (e.g. regions) reacted by introducing restrictive production budgets, financial targets, and tariff reduction, which probably helped to protect hospitals' allocative efficiency, but not necessarily operational efficiency.

This phenomenon also produced effects in terms of equity, co-payments, and waiting lists. Regarding equity, attention has focused more on horizontal and geographic access to care than vertical equity (as in Italy income plays a considerable influence in the use of private specialist care). There-fore, hospital tariffs confirmed existing inequities, such as the smaller bed stock and poorer endowment of medical equipment in southern regions. Concerning co-payments on drugs and ambulatory care, considering that exemptions have been quite liberal by income, age, and health status, they have had a limited impact on access, but served more to change the public–private expenditure mix in favor of the latter. Waiting lists became a public issue in later years, and regulation focused its attention on specialist con-sultations and diagnostic tests by imposing a maximum waiting time. Regions proved to be able to manage access to diagnostics, but performed poorly for specialist visits (the introduction of clinical priority rating sys-tems helped; tough inefficient services and doctor dual practices are still diffused).

Finally, other insights can be derived from the 2005 edition of the ministerial report on hospital activities according to hospital discharge data (see Table 10.9).

In terms of 2002–3 trends, hospitalizations for acute care diminished by 4.9 percent, day cases were augmented by 8.19 percent, and overall admissions were reduced by 1.08 percent. Average length of stay went up, to 6.7 days, while the casemix index continued to increase to an average weight of 1.22. Shifts in admissions (with ordinary hospitalizations falling from 72.3 percent in 2002 to 70.5 percent in 2003 and, simultaneously, day cases increasing from 27.7 to 29.5 percent) and dynamics in the medical to surgical DRG ratio (from 2.3 in 1998 to 1.68 in 2003) also confirm the ongoing attempt to improve quality and reposition the delivery of care.

Perspectives on the future of casemix systems in Italy

Italians are living longer and with fewer functional limitations compared to some other major European countries (OECD 2005), but they report a low level of satisfaction with SSN performance, which appears to, since about a decade ago, be in a 'perennial financial and identity crisis' (France et al. 2005). Spending is a serious matter, given the European budgetary and debt standards, leading to open conflicts between national and regional governments. In such a scenario, the general perception is that DRGs are not in discussion, though the game has not been fair among regions and hospitals, and therefore many observers ask for cost monitoring,

Table 10.9 Hospital discharges and days of hospitalization (2001–3)

Type of activity	2001		2002		2003		Δ% 2002–3	
	Discharges	Days	Discharges	Days	Discharges	Days	Discharges	Days
Ord. adm. for acute care	9,158,928	62,275,391	8,878,595	59,449,206	8,443,471	56,594,442	−4.9	−4.8
Day cases for acute care	3,042,564	8,370,923	3,302,961	9,004,920	3,573,384	9,633,887	8.19	6.98
Rehabilitation – ord. adm.	246,896	6,177,128	252,309	6,619,688	260,914	6,882,002	3.41	3.96
Rehabilitation – day cases	55,030	549,349	51,573	594,680	53,598	642,332	3.93	8.01
Long-term care	80,422	2,752,131	88,103	2,821,328	94,273	2,867,366	7	1.63
Newborn	354,382	1,258,257	369,760	1,285,532	378,248	1,287,674	2.3	0.17
Total	12,938,222	81,383,179	12,943,301	79,775,354	12,803,888	77,907,703	−1.08	−2.34

Source: Ministerial annual report on hospital activities (2005).

improvements of casemix systems, and tariff reviews; looking backward, the introduction of DRGs has contributed to an increase in the already existent interregional diversity in the supply mix. From this perspective, some recent independent studies launched a provocation by analyzing costs by geographic area of the sixty most frequent DRGs (absorbing 51 percent of total admissions). As examples, a new birth delivery in Emilia Romagna had a tariff of €697, in the province of Trento it was €1,727, and in Calabria €1,310; a hospitalization for diabetes in Friuli Venezia Giulia cost €3,108, in Veneto €1,766, and in Sardegna €2,067. Therefore, under the assumption that lower costs mean better efficiency, if all regions were to adopt the lower tariffs or average tariffs weighted by residents, the SSN in 2002 would have saved as much as €5 billion out of its €22.5 billion public hospital expenditure, especially since 25–30 percent of hospital admissions were evaluated as being inappropriate anyway (Observatory for the Elderly 2005).

A second perspective regarding casemix system refinement and maintenance was that failure to update classification systems proved to be a major shortcoming of the Italian prospective payment system. This weakness has become even more serious, since DRGs are also used to define public benefits (e.g. through the negative list of DRGs associated with LEAs). This leads to some considerations about the need to complement casemix systems with additional features or tools able to enhance quality monitoring and evaluation of the severity and complexity of illness; during the 1990s, Italy had already assisted in a debate regarding the use of disease staging techniques (Taroni 1996), APR-DRGs, and PRUO (revision protocol of hospital use).

For instance, disease staging defines severity of illness based on clinical definitions, rather than on the use of resources, and it has been used in Italy to evaluate the appropriateness of hospital admissions. One example comes from the Emilia Romagna region, where disease staging has been used to assess the appropriateness of admissions corresponding to a list of sixty-seven DRGs (Donatini *et al.* 2005); the analysis highlighted that inappropriateness was more likely for medical DRGs than surgical, it was more concentrated in private hospitals than in public, and, overall, there also existed a small share of tardive DRGs which could have been intercepted before hospitalization.

PRUO systems, derived from the American AEP (Appropriateness Evaluation Protocol), enable analyses of organizational appropriateness independent of diagnosis, to be able to improve hospital activities; for example, it has been used in the Friuli Venezia Giulia region to link economic incentives to reduction of hospital admissions. This experience showed that by setting appropriate hospital targets and regular controls, it is possible to exploit the potential of prospective payment systems while preserving quality of care (Lattuada *et al.* 2002).

Concerning APR-DRG, Lorenzoni (2000), for example, conducted a study of fifteen hospitals to test the feasibility and validity of using such systems in Italy. The analysis involved a panel of clinicians and administrators and allowed the identification of the major strengths of the system, when compared to HCFA-DRG, such as the focus on an "all-patient" population, the use of age at admission and birth weight as classification variables of cases, the possibility of differentiating patient groups by severity of illness, and the definition of a risk adjustment model for in-hospital mortality, but also weaknesses, such as the high number of final groups (1,530 in Revision 12), the inclusion of complication of care in the subclass assignment process, and the dependence of the system on multiple co-morbidities to assign severity levels. The utilization of the APR-DRG system to measure casemix proved to be very useful in the process of understanding aspects of resource consumption and quality of care within Italian hospitals, though the performance of the system is highly dependent on the quality of the administrative data. In particular, when used for comparison among facilities, a refined system may enlarge differences due only to the specificity and accuracy of the abstracting and coding process. The Piemonte region explored the complexity of patient casemix for 2001–2 hospitalizations on the basis of APR-DRG in order to assess hospital needs according to pathologies actually treated; the study showed that, while admissions were reduced by 9 percent and day cases increased by 12 percent, the average weight per case went up by more than 3 percent, confirming the regional objective to both shift treatments to more cost-effective settings while improving responses to complex pathologies (De Filippis *et al.* 2004).

The debate and research about ways of refining casemix systems highlights a shared wish of many Italian health policy thinkers: addressing organizational appropriateness as the next frontier and challenge of hospital management, in order to also fully exploit the prospective payment system as a tool of clinical governance and improvement. This could help to confirm whether a reduction in absolute terms of inappropriate admissions really generates final net benefits (e.g. from 2001–3, ordinary admissions on the list of forty-three inappropriate DRGs were diminished by 8 percent, while day cases increased by 33 percent, but what is the final evaluation?). In general terms, Pelliccia (2004) highlighted that the need to master current

Italian hospital costs has become something that cannot be avoided in order to defend the credibility of DRGs. Moreover, casemix systems must be improved and reviewed to increase unmet clinical representation (e.g. oncology, psychiatry, paediatrics, rare diseases), change the payment scheme for rehabilitation, reduce incentives associated with medical day cases, and weight clinical severity to correspond to single DRGs.

From what is publicly known, this issue began to be addressed in 2003 by the Ministry of Health, with the idea of reconstructing the "basic bricks" of the health care system, along with the redefinition of a new national information system able to combine data on costs and quality. In this perspective, regions have been involved on matters such as: evolution of the national DRG system, measurements of appropriateness and outcome, measurement of costs, public health and personal clinical records. Concerning the casemix system, the expectation is the definition of a new data set for hospital discharges capable of tracking services, clinical issues and resource consumption.

Inevitably, the implementation of DRGs in Italy presents some highlights, and some grey areas. For example, have the results associated with the introduction of DRGs been achieved so far? Certainly the Italian hospital system did improve its efficiency in terms of the cost-effective provision of care, appropriateness, and management techniques (accounting and measurement systems, budgeting, and reporting systems). However some concerns were raised about the consistency of repeated admissions, and the conflict between the need to control expenses and the natural mission to improve health status and maintenance. The absence of reliable data on hospital costs limits the ability of serious assessments to go beyond organizational impact, especially in terms of whether there was improvement in quality of care. Moreover, the fact that casemix systems, tariffs, and control systems have been poorly updated (nationally only in 1997 and 2006) implies that interregional differences and variations might cover significant differences in ratios between costs and tariffs.

As Arcangeli et al. (2004) put it, there is a need to expand the scope and improve the use of DRGs (e.g. small hospitals still managed by ASL and financed under capitation instead of DRGs, outpatient services, long-term care) in order to be able to perform utilization reviews, benchmarking of resources and outcome measurements, evaluations of mortality rates, implementation of clinical pathways, and proper performance measurement. Indeed, continuity of care requires casemix systems able to reason not just in terms of admission and discharge, but also for full disease episodes (and their complexity or severity rate). Otherwise, the risk is that financial constraints over resources will again overcome "cost-effective thinking" as is likely to happen with the 2006 tariff review, which is expected to increase fees associated with seventy DRGs of high specialty by 10 percent, while maintaining other tariffs unchanged (meaning an overall increase of tariffs by 2 percent since 1997). Additionally, unlike in the past, the new national tariffs will represent the maximum applicable tariffs (and not just references for regional scales), so that regions already above those levels will have to lower values or pay the differential with their own resources. From this perspective, the introduction of innovation in medical practice and technology remains a critical issue, as very often it requires "a management by exception process" at the regional level, which could lead to additional reimbursement upon hospital request and on top of DRGs tariffs, health technology assessments through research, or national funding before adopting innovation.

Generally speaking, there are also ideas of extending the use of casemix systems; Italian nursing home care has been an area of demand, as have rehabilitation, geriatrics, and psychiatry, along with the request to embed DRGs into patient pathways and disease management programs involving home care and some primary care services. However, it is advisable that such expansion happens in the context of better internal and external controls; casemix systems are in theory neutral tools, but if they are not complemented by other instruments able to align demand for health care with provision, the Italian SSN is likely to continue to suffer inequities in terms of access, quality of care, and patient mobility. Indeed, as in many countries, ruling and managing hospitals in Italy is a challenging issue, also complicated by the fact that providers are multi-level in terms of governance (e.g. managed centrally, by regions, independent or subordinate to ASLs), multidimensional in terms of activities and medical specialties (e.g. levels of care, research, teaching), multi-proprietary in terms of interests (e.g. according to public or private status), meaning that it is inconceivable to try to control them by acting only on the supply side without any orientation and management of demand. In other words, besides the financial tool to be used (DRGs, for instance), if a purchasing power cannot be expressed, it will remain difficult to shape responses according to needs and, therefore, the game is at risk of remaining in favor of the providers (Tedeschi and Tozzi 2004).

However, innovations in Italy frequently follow moments of crisis; the reforms in the 1990s tried to address some of the most enduring problems of the system. But the goal of transforming the highly integrated ASLs into a system of internal markets has been partially realized (France *et al.* 2005). Moreover, unlike HMOs or PPOs in the USA, residents are automatically enrolled at birth in ASLs, meaning that freedom of choice is limited to the provider; consequently, the purchasing role of ASL has mostly been relegated to third-party payer. For these reasons, a general recent trend (Jommi *et al.* 2001) has been a greater centralization in the governance of regional systems, with several corrections to opportunistic behaviors from hospitals, substituting financial targets with statutory contracts, increasing the use of discretionary funding (e.g. lump sums for priorities), tightening control over the allocations, and differentiating tariffs (e.g. lower ones for private or rural hospitals).

In conclusion, casemix systems and related DRGs tariffs are likely to remain in the Italian health care system, especially as the full potential of prospective payment systems has been to a significant extent exploited. Indeed, fine tuning of classification and tariffs has been mostly ex post, in order to correct behaviors and cover deficits rather than to shape provision according to priorities (quality!) and evolving health needs. DRGs were initially implemented as a financial system, but have quickly become a managerial tool with organizational consequences for hospital activities; by linking hospitalizations with internal objectives and external funding, regions and hospital managers have a powerful tool to influence professional behaviors, although internal and external controls are required to ensure that the game is "win–win" in favor of patients, with fair recognition for the professionals, instead of "win–lose" or, even worse, "lose–lose" nightmares. Casemixes and DRGs can therefore be a truly managerial lever leading to innovation, especially when clinical and financial issues are taken into account and properly balanced.

NOTES

1. Each one of the twenty regions is a distinct institutional and administrative layer with its own elected council (Consiglio Regionale) and executive government (Giunta Regionale). Other administrative layers are the 103 provinces and the 8,101 local municipalities.
2. Hospital care is mainly delivered by public structures (59 percent of the total, accounting for 86 percent of discharges).
3. Literally public local enterprises, meaning a public independent entity with its own balance sheets, run by a general manager (appointed by a region) who is accountable for

performance and has to apply private-sector management techniques (Jommi *et al.* 2001). Previously ASLs were called USLs (literally local health units), basically managed by a board controlled by municipalities.

4. Research hospitals comprise a network of thirteen public university policlinics, twenty-three public and twenty-nine private institutes for scientific care and treatment. Such hospitals all carry out, (though with a different mix) research, teaching, and care activities.

5. In 2002, private for-profit hospitals accounted for 38.1 percent of total hospitals, private non-profit (mainly Church-owned) for 2.9 percent; jointly they manage 13.8 percent of total national bed stock.

6. Complemented, at least up to 2011, by a national solidarity fund to compensate for cross-regional differences in fiscal capacity.

7. The regional mobility rate of patients accounted for 7.5 percent of total hospital discharges in 2000, 7.7 percent in 2001–2, and 7.9 percent in 2003. In the same years, the mobility rate for day cases was 6.6 percent in 2000, 6.7 percent in 2001–2, 6.6 percent in 2003, and 7.2 percent in 2004 (Ministry of Health).

8. LEAs (Livelli Essenziali di Assistenza), introduced in 2001–2, are expressed in terms of both a positive list of benefits, to be ensured, and a negative list of ambulatory services (e.g. cosmetic surgery), diagnostics (e.g. excimer laser surgery) and hospital treatments (e.g. a list of inappropriate hospital admissions corresponding to forty-three DRGs), for which regions are supposed to provide alternative services in day or ambulatory care (see technical appendix for details). In 2000, the forty-three DRGs absorbed 25.83 percent of total discharges (with a mix of 75.53 percent in ordinary admissions and 24.7 percent in day cases); in 2003, they were down at 23.7 percent (with a mix of 53.71 percent in ordinary admissions and 46.29 percent in day cases – ASSR 2002, 2005). In addition, the SSN also displays a positive and negative list of drugs in the National Pharmaceutical Formulary.

9. The Superior Institute of Health is the main public technical–scientific central institute of the SSN; founded in 1934, it provides services ranging from research to consulting, training, and controls mainly related to public health.

10. The Conference was set up in 1988. For what concerns health care, since 2000 it has assumed greater importance in terms of being an institutional body for the negotiation of major topics (e.g. national SSN planning and projects, national standards of care, national budget, fund allocation, deficit coverage, professional contracts and ruling, etc.).

11. Standard production costs were to be set on the amount of resources consumed for providing a specific service, on the basis of market prices (acquisition costs) in the previous year (eventually adjusted for inflation). The cost components to be included were specified in terms of: personnel directly involved, materials and supplies directly used, depreciation cost of medical equipment, overhead cost of the service production unit or department.

12. Meaning a proportion of hospital general overheads (e.g. general services and technologies, building maintenance, energy, etc.).

13. According to a 2003 research study by the National Agency for Health Services (ASSR), ten Italian regions use functional funding: Piemonte (university and teaching, emergencies, regional priorities), Lombardia (emergencies, teaching, transplants, high-specialty rehabilitation), Veneto (emergencies, intensive care, infectious diseases,

transplants, teaching, high cost specialties), Liguria (emergencies, specialized hospitals), Emilia Romagna (transplants and special projects), Lazio (emergencies), Puglia (transplants, emergencies, rare diseases), Basilicata (emergencies, transplants, reanimation, intensive care, home care), Calabria (emergencies, helicopter transfers, intensive care, blood), Sardegna (emergencies, transplants, intensive care, severe burns).

14. AIFA (Agenzia Italiana del Farmaco) is the central agency on pharmaceuticals, created in 2004 to replace different services and commissions of the Ministry of Health.

15. Casemix index (CMI) is calculated as the ratio between the casemix complexity treated by a hospital and the casemix complexity of a hospital sampling (if a hospital CMI is > 1, then its casemix is considered as superior to standard, independent of efficiency, though casemix complexity affects other indicators, such as average length of stay, admissions turnover and costs).

16. DRG average value represents the casemix average complexity on the basis of regional tariffs, weighing short and outlier hospitalizations.

17. DRG average weight represents the casemix average complexity treated by a hospital.

18. Performance Index is the ratio between ALOS standardized by casemix and ALOS by reference to express operational efficiency; when values are > 1, ALOS standardized by casemix (the performance) is considered to be worse than the standard.

19. Bed rotation: measures the number of admissions by bed by dividing the number of admissions by the number of beds.

20. Day hospital index is the percentage of day hospital over total hospital activities.

21. Reflected by DRGs for: appendicitis, diabetes mellitus, colorectal cancer, cholecystitis, bronchitis/chronic obstructive pulmonary disease, bacterial pneumonia, coronary artery disease, cerebrovascular disease, and hip fracture.

REFERENCES

Adduce, A., Lorenzoni, L. (2004), Metodologia e primi risultati di un'indagine ministeriale sui costi delle prestazioni di ricovero ospedaliero, *Politiche sanitarie*, 5(4) 158–72.

Agenzia per i Servizi Sanitari Regionali (ASSR) (2002), Analisi dell'appropriatezza per 43 DRG ospedalieri, Monitor – Elementi di analisi e osservazione del sistema salute, Anno 1 Numero 1.

(2005), DRG ad alto rischio di inappropriatezza – Anno 2003, Monitor – Elementi di analisi e osservazione del sistema salute, Anno IV Numero 14.

Agnello, M., Merlino, L., Zocchetti, C. (2003), DRG in Lombardia, in Nonis, M., Lerario, A. M. (eds.), *DRG: valutazione e finanziamento degli ospedali- Esperienze nazionali e politiche delle regioni in Italia*.

Anessi Pessina, E. (2000), Il sistema di budget, in Casati, G. (a cura di), *Programmazione e controllo di gestione nelle aziende sanitarie*, McGraw-Hill, Milan.

Anessi Pessina, E., Cantù, E., Jommi, C. (2001), New funding arrangements in the Italian National Health Service, *International Journal of Health Planning and Management*, 16 (4): 347–68.

(2004), Phasing out market mechanisms in the Italian National Health Service, *Public Money & Management*, 5, 309–16.

Arcangeli, A., Falcitelli, N., Langiano, T. (2004), I primi dieci anni dei DRG in Italia, *Politiche sanitarie*, 5(4) 155–7.

Arcangeli, A., France, G. (2004), La logica del nuovo sistema di remunerazione dell'attività ospedaliera, in Falcitelli, N., Langiano, T. (eds.), *Politiche innovative nel SSN: i primi dieci anni dei DRG in Italia*, Il Mulino.

Bevan, G., France, G., Taroni F. (1992), Dolce Vita: Inside Italy's SSN. *The Health Services Journal* (27 February): 20–23.

Cantu, E., Carbone, C., Lecci, F. (2004), La struttura del SSN italiano, in Anessi Pessina, E., Cantu, E. (eds.), *L'aziendalizzazione della sanità in Italia – Rapporto OASI*, EGEA.

Cantu, E., Jommi, C. (2003), I sistemi di finanziamento e di controllo della spesa in cinque regioni: un aggiornamento al 2003, in Anessi Pessina, E., Cantu, E. (ed.), *L'aziendalizzazione della sanità in Italia – Rapporto OASI*, pp. 168–92, EGEA.

Cantu, E., Palucci, G. (2004), L'uso dei DRG nei sistemi di gestione delle Aziende ospedaliere lombarde, in Anessi Pessina, E., Cantu, E. (eds.), *L'aziendalizzazione della sanità in Italia – Rapporto OASI*, pp. 523–38, EGEA.

Caselli, R., Lomuto, C., Pisani, E. (1999), Valorizzazione dei processi di assistenza ospedaliera classificati in DRGs, *Mecosan*, 8(29) 93–100.

Cerbo, M., Langiano, T. (2004), L'impatto a livello nazionale del sistema di remunerazione, in Falcitelli, N., Langiano, T. (eds.), *Politiche innovative nel SSN: i primi dieci anni dei DRG in Italia*, Il Mulino, Bologna.

De Filippis, G., Pia, M., Di Maio, A. (2004), Sulla complessità dei ricoveri ospedalieri in regione Piemonte: un'analisi per mezzo degli Apr-Drg e delle linee di produzione, *Politiche sanitarie*, 5(4) 197–206.

Degli Esposti, G., Roversi, E., Palmieri, M., Serio, R. M. (1996), Matrici di mobilità per DRGs: analisi descrittiva ed applicazioni per la programmazione e le politiche sanitarie regionali, *Mecosan* 5(19), pp. 52–63.

Del Favero, A., Barro, G. (1996), Health Services: An Italian Market. *The Lancet* 348: 167–75.

Di Loreto, P., Spolaore, P. (2004), L'evoluzione del sistema nelle politiche regionali, in Falcitelli, N., Langiano, T., (ed.) *Politiche innovative nel SSN: i primi dieci anni dei DRG in Italia*, Il Mulino, Bologna.

Donatiti, A., Fiorini, M., Louis, D. (2005), Disease staging e valutazione dell'appropriatezza dei ricoveri ospedalieri nella Regione Emilia Romagna, in Guccio, C., Pignataro, G., Rizzo, I. (eds.) *Finanziamento e valutazione dei servizi ospedalieri*, FrancoAngeli, Milano.

Donatini, A., Rico, A., D'Ambrosio, M. G., Lo Scalzo, A., Orzella, L., Cicchetti, A., Profili, S. (2001), Healthcare systems in transition: Italy, in Rico, A., Cetani, C. (eds.), *European Observatory on Health Care Systems*, www.observatory.dk.

Falcitelli, N., Langiano, T. (eds.) (2004), *Politiche innovative nel SSN: i primi dieci anni dei DRG in Italia*, Il Mulino, Bologna.

Fattore, G. (1999), Cost containment and reforms in the Italian SSN, in Mossialos, E., Le Grand, J. (eds.), *Health Care and Cost Containment in the European Union*, Ashgate, Aldershot.

Fattore, G., Torbica, A. (2004), Health service benefit catalogues in Italy – Country report Italy, Health Basket project (Commission's 6th Framework programme – grant: SP21–CT–2004–501588, European Health Management Association), Bocconi University.

France G. (1990), Al servizio dei pazienti. Il Libro Bianco sulla riforma del Servizio Sanitario Britannico. Una valutazione italiana, Quaderni per la ricerca – Serie Studi No. 20, Istituto di Studi delle Regioni, Roma.

(2004), Standard nazionali e devoluzione: una prima cognizione, *Politiche sanitarie*, pp. 3–15, 5(1) gennaio–marzo.

France, G., Taroni, F. (2005), The evolution of health policy making in Italy, *Journal of Health Politics, Policy and Law*, 30(1)–(2) February–April, 169–87.

France, G., Taroni, F., Donatini A. (2005), The Italian Health-care System, *Health Economics* 14, 187–202.

Gruppo tecnico (2001), DM 22/06/00, L'aggiornamento del sistema di remunerazione delle prestazioni di assistenza ospedaliera nell'ambito del SSN, *Tendenze nuove*, 2–3.

Guccio, C. (2005), Le politiche di riforma organizzativa ed istituzionale nel sistema ospedaliero italiano, in Guccio, C., Pignataro, G., Rizzo, I. (eds.), *Finanziamento e valutazione dei servizi ospedalieri*, FrancoAngeli, Milan.

Istituto di Studi delle Regioni (1990), Al servizio dei pazienti. Il Libro Bianco sulla riforma del Servizio Sanitario Britannico, Quaderni per la ricerca – Serie Documentazione No. 8, Rome.

Jommi, C. (2000), I meccanismi regionali di finanziamento delle Aziende sanitarie, in Anessi Pessina, E., Cantu, E. (ed.), *L'aziendalizzazione della sanità in Italia – Rapporto OASI*, pp. 71–92, EGEA, Milan.

Jommi, C., Fattore, G. (2003), Regionalization and drugs cost-sharing in the Italian SSN, *Euro Observer*, 3: 1–4.

Langiano, T. (ed.) (1997), *DRG: Strategie, valutazione, monitoraggio*, Il Pensiero Scientifico Editore, Rome.

Lattuada, L., Burba, I., Stiore, F. (2000), I controlli sull'attività di ricovero in Friuli Venezia Giulia, *Tendenze nuove*, 1.

Lega, F. (1999), Il sistema DRGs: aspetti introduttivi, Materials of SDA Bocconi Masters in Sanitary Management.

Lorenzoni, L. (2000), Use of APR-DRG in Fifteen Italian Hospitals, *CASEMIX*, 2(4) December 31.

Louis, D., Braga, M., Cicchetti, A., Rabinowitz, C., Laine, C., Gonnella, J., Yuen, E. (1999), Impact of a DRG-based Hospital Financing System on Quality and Outcomes of Care in Italy, *Health Services Research*, April.

Ministero della Salute (2005), Rapporto annuale sull'attività di ricovero ospedaliero – Dati SDO 2003, Direzione generale programmazione sanitaria, 27 June.

Observatory for the elderly (Osservatorio Terza Età) (2005), La spesa sanitaria nazionale: analisi ed ipotesi di contenimento, *Ageing & Society*.

OECD (2006), OECD Health Data.

Oliver, A., Mossialos, E. (2005), European Health Systems Reforms: Looking Backward to See Forward? *Journal of Health Politics, Policy and Law*, 30 (1–2) February–April, 7–27.

Pelissero, G., Velo, D. (2004), *Competition in Health Systems – in Italy, in the EU, in the World*, Associazione Italiana Ospedalità Privata, Rome: AIOP.

Pelliccia L. (2004), Il punto sul sistema di pagamento a prestazione degli ospedali, *Politiche sanitarie*, 5(4), 173–83.

Saltman, R., von Otter, C. (1999), *Essays on Public Competition in the Healthcare Sector*, Formez, Rome.

Spandonaro, F., Pennini, F. S., Atella, V. (2004), Criteri per l'allocazione regionale delle risorse per la sanità: riflessioni sul caso italiano, *Politiche sanitarie*, 5(1), gennaio–marzo 27–32.

Taroni, F. (1996), *DRG/ROD e nuovo sistema di finanziamento degli ospedali*. Il Pensiero Scientifico Editore, Rome.

Tedeschi, P. (2004), Governo della domanda e sistemi sanitari regionali, in Tozzi, V., Tedeschi, P. (eds.), *Il governo della domanda. Tutela della salute, committenza, programmazione-acquisto-controllo*, McGraw-Hill, Milan.

  (2004), Le système de santé italien: décentralisation au niveau régional, *Gestions Hospitalières*, 440, November, 679–84.

Tedeschi, P., Tozzi, V. (eds.) (2004), *Il governo della domanda. Tutela della salute, programmazione-acquisto-controllo*, McGraw-Hill, Milan.

Torbica, A., Fattore, G. (2005), The essential levels of care in Italy: When being explicit serves the devolution of powers, *The European Journal of Health Economics*, online issue of 29 October, Springer-Verlag GmbH .

Vagnoni, E., Crimi, G. (1996), Il sistema di finanziamento delle aziende ospedaliere attraverso i DRGs. Una soluzione analoga in riabilitazione, *Mecosan*, 5(17), 50–58.

Vichi, M. (1996), Alcune note operative sull'applicazione dei DRG, *Mecosan*, 5(20), 79–84.

Casemix development and implementation in Australia

Stephen J. Duckett

Introduction

Australia, with a population of around 20 million, is a federation consisting of six states (the largest, New South Wales, accounting for about 33 per cent of the population, the second largest, Victoria, accounting for a further 25 per cent of the population) and two territories. Casemix development in Australia has been shaped by the design of the Australian health care system, Australia's federal constitution, and the division of responsibilities between the Commonwealth government and the states. Australia has a universal health insurance system providing for public funding for access to hospital and medical care, complemented by private health insurance which provides insurance against the costs of access to private hospital care and ancillary services (such as physiotherapy, dental). About 40 per cent of hospital admissions occur in private hospitals.

Funding of public hospital care is shared between the Commonwealth and state governments, but states have operational responsibility for public hospitals. This mix of Commonwealth and state shared responsibility and public and private sectors means that the organisational arrangements of health care in Australia are quite complex.

Private health insurance organisations negotiate contracts with private hospitals to minimise out-of-pocket costs for their contributors. In some circumstances these contractual arrangements involve casemix-based payments to private hospitals (see Willcox 2005 for a discussion of these payments).

The relationship between the Commonwealth and the states is governed by the Australian Health Care Agreements, which are negotiated every five years (see Duckett 2004 for an outline of negotiation issues surrounding the 2003–2008 Australian Healthcare Agreements). The Australian Health

Care Agreements provide for significant grants from the Commonwealth to the states, and that the states will ensure that all Australian citizens and permanent residents will be able to obtain public hospital care (inpatient and outpatient) without any direct charge. Commonwealth grants to the states cover about 50 per cent of the cost of public hospital care. State governments are, however, autonomous with respect to hospital services and so funding arrangements for public hospital care and hospital governance arrangements vary substantially across states (see Rix *et al.* 2005 for a discussion of contemporary state organisational arrangements).

The Commonwealth universal health insurance scheme, Medicare, provides rebates for the costs of medical services, both in the community (for general practitioners and specialists) and for private patients in either public or private hospitals. Medical costs of public patients in public hospitals are not covered by these insurance arrangements, but are covered by state government funding arrangements for those hospitals.

History of casemix development

Australia has a long history of casemix development. A pivotal role was played by George Palmer, then Professor of Health Administration at the University of New South Wales, who was an early proponent of the use of casemix measures in Australia. Palmer maintained close contacts with developments in health services research in the United States. During his 1970 Fulbright Senior Fellowship, Palmer met with Fetter and Thompson of Yale University, who were in the early stages of developing what came to be known as Diagnosis Related Groups (DRGs). Palmer subsequently spent sabbatical leave from the University of New South Wales as a Visiting Professor at Yale University in 1982 and 1987 (Turner and Short 1999). In 1981 Palmer received a significant grant from the Commonwealth Department of Health to analyse Australian computerised discharge datasets and to group these data to the then prevalent US version of DRGs. This work provided evidence that the US casemix grouper could be used to assign Australian inpatient data to DRGs.

Palmer persuaded the then Health Commission of Victoria to invest in a research programme grouping Victorian hospital inpatient discharge data to US DRGs and estimating inpatient costs by DRG using the 'Yale cost model'. Palmer's initial work led to further Victorian work routinely grouping and reporting on hospital activity, and comparing length of stay performance of public hospitals in terms of DRGs, and also developing patient-level costing for DRGs. Victoria was the first Australian state to embrace DRGs as a method of measuring hospital activity. Although the author was initially sceptical about the benefits of using DRGs (Duckett 1985), Palmer's work and a subsequent, more thorough, examination of the use of DRGs in Europe and North America (Duckett 1986) converted the author into an advocate. I was able to use my bureaucratic position to develop capacity and understanding of DRGs and their use within the Health Commission and its successors. Palmer was also a consultant to the South Australian Health Commission and provided analytical support for casemix development in that state.

Palmer continued as a consultant to Victoria for a number of years, grouping and analysing Victorian data with the Health Department Victoria publishing the output. This work showed significant differences in practice patterns between the US and Victoria. Further, in contrast to the US, Australian coding guidelines allowed same-day cases to be counted as admissions, leading to further anomalies in comparisons with US practice. Although the US DRGs provided a good base for measuring hospital inpatient activity, this Victorian work provided the analytical evidence for the development of an Australian version of DRGs to become the national standard. Work on developing an Australian modification to US DRGs began to be seen as an important precursor for DRG use in Australia, particularly in gaining greater acceptance from clinicians.

In parallel with developments in Victoria and South Australia, the Commonwealth, as part of the 1988–1993 Australian Health Care Agreements (then know as 'Medicare' Agreements), proposed a casemix development programme which provided funding for projects that would:

(i)   assist in the development of state-wide morbidity systems (specifically using the International Classification of Diseases, Ninth Revision, Clinical Modification (ICD–9–CM) or its replacement for diagnosis and procedure coding;

(ii) assist in the development of hospital cost systems based on morbidity data;

(iii) assess the applicability of cost-based casemix systems within a hospital or hospitals;

(iv) develop pilot cost-based casemix systems that could be adopted by the states and the territories.

A substantial proportion of the funding under the Agreements was allocated to individual research and development projects in hospitals and other settings throughout Australia. This, further strengthened by large annual conferences bringing together researchers and practitioners, led to creation of a 'casemix community' of people who were enthusiastic about the potential to use casemix to describe, analyse or fund health care activity. This 'community' was broad and 'multidisciplinary' and included a significant minority of medical clinicians, the latter providing a cadre of casemix advocates within a range of specialties and hospitals. It also provided a pool to populate the various casemix advisory committees at state and national levels. The breadth of involvement created a constituency which helped to ensure that casemix measures quickly developed credibility and influential supporters. Funding under the casemix development programme was also provided for educational programmes and, importantly, for the development of an Australian DRG classification and grouper. Victoria used a large proportion of its funding to provide the infrastructure for hospital patient-level costing systems.

Classification development

The first Australian DRG classification system ('Australian National DRGs', AN-DRGs) was developed by 1993 based on the use of ICD–9–CM to code diagnoses and procedures. Part of the commitment in the development process was that the classification system would be updated on a regular basis to recognise the changes in clinical practice. The Australian DRG system has been refined over time and the Australian National DRG classification has now evolved into the Australian Refined DRG (AR-DRG) classification based on coding in ICD–10 (www.health.gov.au/casemix). The current classification (AR-DRG Version 5.1) has 665 groups, fully described in a three-volume definitions manual.

Responsibility for development

The DRG classification system is a national one in the sense that classification development is led nationally by the Commonwealth Department of Health and Ageing. The classification development process is not simply a centralised bureaucratic one, but has extensive involvement of practising clinicians, principally medical practitioners. A formal consultative committee, the Casemix Clinical Committee of Australia, provides clinical advice on classification issues and other casemix matters to the Commonwealth Department. This Committee is responsible for liaising with clinicians and professional bodies on casemix issues: the key task of the Casemix Clinical Committee is to ensure that the final casemix classification system is clinically meaningful.

The approach to defining the classification involves a multi-stage process using a national dataset of information on patients treated in a range of hospitals. The database includes data on patient separations (discharges, deaths and transfer) with full ICD–10 diagnosis codes, an Australian developed procedure coding system, demographic data, length of stay and, for the most recent version of DRGs, cost data.

One of the major developments in the Australian casemix classification system since its inception has been the development of sophisticated algorithms to estimate the impact that secondary and additional diagnoses will have on resource utilisation. In the AR-DRG system, every recorded diagnosis is evaluated to estimate its impact on resource utilisation and every diagnosis is taken into account in DRG assignment. Each diagnosis is assigned a rank (known as a 'complication and co-morbidity level'). The value of the rank is between 0–3 for medical episodes and 0–4 for surgical and neonatal episodes. A code of zero indicates that the diagnosis does not represent a complication or co-morbidity, forms part of the definition of the adjacent DRG, or that the complication or co-morbidity is closely related to the principal diagnosis. A code of 1 indicates a minor complication or co-morbidity, 2 moderate, 3 severe and 4 catastrophic. Each additional diagnosis thus has a complication or co-morbidity level assigned to it. Various combinations of these levels can be synthesised into a summary patient-level measure (known as the 'patient clinical complexity level', PCCL) that takes into account all the additional diagnoses for that admission. For example, two diagnosis codes ranked at level 2 are summarised into a single overall PCCL measure of 3. These overall summary measures are then used as part of the splitting procedures for defining individual DRGs.

A set of statistical rules has been developed as part of the casemix classification development process. The rules ensure that the casemix system is resource homogeneous according to robust statistical criteria. The current criteria provide that new DRGs can only be created by splitting an existing DRG:
- when the national size of the DRGs contains at least 250 cases and at least 10 per cent of the original group cases; and
- there should be improved homogeneity, with a reduction in variance (in length of stay) of at least 5 per cent.

The statistical process is reviewed by a clinical committee to ensure that the splits both at the adjacent DRG level and at the individual DRG level are clinically meaningful. The statistical criteria ensure that the process yields a high level of explanation.

Each DRG in the AR-DRG system is described using a standard alphanumeric code. The first alpha-numeric character indicates the broad group (usually MDC) to which a DRG belongs. The second and third digits indicate the adjacent DRG (codes ranges from 0–39 indicating surgical partition, 40–59 other, 60–99 medical). The fourth and final digit is a letter indicator that distinguishes the individual DRG: an alphabetical ordering based on resource consumption with 'A' being the DRG with the highest resource use within the surgical partition of the adjacent DRG. If the DRG is not split on resource use, the letter Z is used.

Casemix funding

A most significant development occurred in Victoria in 1993–4 when casemix moved from a discussion topic to the forefront of policy: the Victorian government adopted casemix measures as the basis for allocating public hospital budgets. A number of other states, most notably South Australia, followed Victoria's lead and even the smaller states and territories, with too few hospitals for an effective casemix allocation system (e.g. with no within-state peer groups), began using the rhetoric of 'casemix funding' (Duckett 1998). Victoria now has more than ten years' experience in casemix allocation – the longest in Australia.

The initial design of Victoria's casemix funding system has been described elsewhere (Duckett 1995) but in summary, it involved a number of key elements:

- DRG standardized activity was used as the basis for determining inpatient budgets.
- A fixed and variable model of funding was used: each hospital was allocated a 'base grant' based on historic activity levels and had access to a 'variable payment' up to a negotiated hospital-specific activity cap.
- Cases in excess of the activity cap were counted towards marginal payments from an 'additional throughput pool' of funding. Each quarter, payments would be available to hospitals from this, payment per case depending on the amount of money in the pool and the hospital's relative contribution to the total number of cases above the activity caps across all eligible hospitals.

- Access to the 'additional throughput pool' was conditional on meeting elective surgery waiting list targets.
- Most other hospital activity (e.g. in emergency departments and outpatient clinics) was funded on a block grant basis based on historic recorded expenditure in these areas.

The initial design of the system was consistent with optimal hospital pricing strategies involving a mix of fixed and variable payments (Ellis and McGuire 1986). The capped nature of the funding regime means that it should more accurately be described as casemix allocation, in the sense that it is a method of allocating a fixed state-wide budget pie rather than casemix 'funding', which connotes a more open-ended system. In the decade following implementation, casemix measures were developed for hospital outpatients, rehabilitation and emergency department activity. These areas of hospital activity became funded on an activity basis, with the amount of hospital funding allocated as a historically based block grant concomitantly declining.

Hospital funding was not increased in line with hospital cost inflation during the early years of casemix allocation and as a result, there was significant under-funding of hospitals, with their financial positions being maintained essentially through run down of capital and other non-recurrent solutions.

Design of price and regulatory systems needs to recognise adverse selection and moral hazard (Laffont and Tirole 1993). In addition to pricing policy, the Victorian casemix funding policy incorporated a number of 'regulatory changes' and monitoring systems designed to complement the pricing policies to facilitate an effective response to adverse selection and moral hazard, and to address other policy goals of government. Essentially the Victorian casemix funding innovation included an array of complementary instruments to achieve the espoused objectives and minimise unintended consequences.

The most prominent of the regulatory strategies was designed to ensure that the budget reduction did not lead to increases in patient waiting (Street and Duckett 1996). This was effected through a condition on access to the 'additional throughput pool', that the hospital had no 'Category 1' patients waiting for elective surgery for more than thirty days. This access-focused strategy was abolished after a year and replaced by a series of bonuses and penalties for a number of access indicators. These have evolved over time, and in the contemporary version of the policy (2004–5) involve penalties for failing to meet targets in the following areas:

- percentage of time on hospital bypass;
- percentage of emergency patients who are not admitted to an inpatient bed within twelve hours;

- percentage of category 1 elective patients not admitted within thirty days;
- average waiting time of category 2 elective patients on the waiting list;
- number of hospital-initiated postponements per 100 waiting list admissions; and
- total number of patients on the elective surgery waiting list.

The quantum of the penalty for each target is specified and, in any one quarter, failure to meet all targets could cost a hospital up to the equivalent of treating 400–500 patients or about A$1 million.

Within Victoria's casemix system, legitimate adverse selection, essentially identified as systematic within DRG variation beyond the hospital's control, was principally dealt with by special grants (known as specified grants); the classic example was an additional payment for the prison ward at one of the major teaching hospitals. The main risk from moral hazard was perceived as 'up coding', and an independent random sample coding audit was introduced to mitigate this risk.

The introduction of casemix funding in Victoria had a dramatic effect on hospital funding policy in Australia. The speed of the Victorian implementation (over a five-month period) and its perceived early success (Duckett 1995), led other states to emulate the policy (e.g. South Australia in 1994–5) and to a number of states describing their funding arrangements in casemix terms, even though the reality of their allocation basis was still essentially historic or hospital specific.

New South Wales was the only major state to eschewed casemix funding. It placed emphasis on an alternative funding paradigm and allocation of risks: area funding with allocations to areas being based on the weighted population served by the area. Although the rhetoric in New South Wales was funding from the area to the hospitals 'informed' by casemix measures, reporting arrangements did not facilitate comparisons of hospital performance, nor were there serious attempts to decompose hospital activity and measure and standardize the full range of hospital products (e.g. outpatients, teaching and research). The differences in funding policy between the two states thus provide a natural experiment that allows for comparison of trends on key variables, to allow an evaluation of the impact of casemix funding in Victoria.

An evaluation of the Victorian experience

Table 11.1 shows data for before and after policy implementation in Victoria and comparative data for New South Wales on measures of

Table 11.1 Selected comparative statistics, public hospitals, NSW and Victoria, 1989–1990–2002–2003

	Average cost / weighted separation (A$)		Public hospital separations / per thousand population		Percentage same day separations		Mean diagnosis codes per separation		Mean procedure codes per separation, separations with procedures	
	NSW	Vic	NSW	Vic	NSW	Vic	NSW	Vic	NSW	Vic
1989–90	2,389	1,796	165.6	140.5						
1990–91			167.1	148.2						
1991–92	2,299	2,468	168.6	155.9	28.0	31.3	2.1	1.9	1.5	1.4
1992–93			181.6	156.3	31.0	33.1	2.3	2.3	1.6	1.5
1993–94	3,251	3,221	199.4	177.0	31.0	37.0	2.4	2.3	1.6	1.5
1994–95	3,342	2,832	205.2	190.1	36.3	41.6	2.6	2.5	1.6	1.6
1995–96	2,975	2,245	202.7	191.8	37.3	43.4	2.7	2.6	1.6	1.6
1996–97	2,586	2,353	198.1	196.4	39.2	44.8	2.8	2.7	1.8	1.8
1997–98	2,637	2,462	202.0	200.7	40.2	46.3	3.0	3.0	2.0	2.0
1998–99	2,766	2,413	192.1	199.4	40.6	48.2	3.2	3.0	1.8	1.8
1999–2000	2,812	2,529	185.5	203.1	40.7	49.9	3.2	3.0	1.9	1.8
2000–01	2,886	2,801	181.7	204.5	40.8	51.4	3.0	2.7	2.4	2.2
2001–02	3,010	3,117	188.2	222.5	41.9	53.1	3.7	2.7	2.3	2.2
2002–03	3,283	3,285	190.2	231.3	43.0	54.3	2.9	2.7	2.5	2.3

efficiency and utilization. Nationally consistent data are not available for each year of the early period covered by the table. Although the basis for national statistics changed over this period (cost data prior to 1996–7 are not casemix adjusted; cost data for 1989–90 and 1991–2 incorporate an adjustment for outpatient activity) there is no reason to believe that this changed the relativities for the two states.

The average cost per weighted separation immediately prior to the introduction of casemix funding was about 7 per cent higher in Victoria compared to New South Wales ('separation' is the technical term in Australia for a death, discharge or transfer from hospital). This disparity was part of the justification for the significant funding cuts applied in the early years of casemix implementation.

The effect of the budget cuts can be seen in the relativities for average cost per separation over the next few years. Victoria's public hospitals moved quickly from a position of being more expensive than those in New South Wales, to being substantially cheaper (by 25 per cent in 1995–6) with the cost difference easing up to 1999–2000. 1999 marked the return of a Labor government, which recognised that the previous government's budget cuts had probably gone too far and reinvested in the hospital system, possibly over-correcting, with average cost per separation in 2001–2 in Victoria being marginally higher than New South Wales. The two states came back into parity in 2002–3.

In terms of activity, public hospitals in Victoria provided fewer separations per 1,000 population than their New South Wales counterparts before the implementation of the casemix funding policy. Separations from Victorian public hospitals increased dramatically over the ensuing decade: from 1992–3 to 2002–3 there was a 48 per cent increase in public hospital separations per 1,000 population in Victoria, compared to a 5 per cent increase in New South Wales. Most of the Victorian growth was in same-day separations. Patients admitted and discharged on the same day can be counted in official separation statistics in Australia and, because the admission decision involves a clinical judgment, decisions about whether to count a patient as a same-day separation (rather than an outpatient attendance or as a Commonwealth-funded private case) can be manipulated according to where cost is minimized or avoided or revenue is maximized. Under a state casemix funding policy, same-day outpatient attendances generate revenue; under alternative policies, there is no marginal revenue for these patients, so there is no incentive to count these patients against state-funded revenue streams and hence there is a greater incentive to shift activity to Commonwealth funding sources. This might explain the pattern in New South Wales, where public hospital separations per 1,000 population declined from the mid-1990s.

In line with contemporary clinical practice, the percentage of same day separations increased in New South Wales, but plateaued in the mid-1990s. In contrast, same-day separations in Victoria increased much more dramatically and have shown no sign of plateauing. Over the period 1992–3 to 2002–3, overnight separations per 1,000 population in New South Wales and Victoria decreased by 11 and 1 per cent respectively, but same-day separations increased by 73 and 157 per cent. If one assumes that all of the Victorian excess proportion of same-day activity is nominal (i.e. reclassification), then Victoria's public hospital separation rate would be 205 per 1,000, approximately equal to the peak New South Wales rate. The trend in separation rates suggests that public hospitals in Victoria may well have succumbed to moral hazard by maximizing same-day separations to garner additional revenue. This is despite the fact that Victorian funding policy guidelines have adopted separate same-day budget caps since 1994–5.

Obviously a casemix funding system encourages hospitals to place more attention on ensuring that separations are properly coded and creates the moral hazard of overcoding; in Victoria the mitigation strategy included a state-wide coding audit. Table 11.1, above, includes information on 'coding depth': the mean diagnosis codes per separation and the mean procedure codes per separation for those cases with procedures. Both measures reveal increased coding depth in both states over time. Over the period 1992–3 to 2002–3, mean diagnosis codes per separation increased at approximately the same rate (by 37 per cent in New South Wales and 42 per cent in Victoria); the increase in procedure codes per separation was almost identical (65 per cent in New South Wales and 67 per cent in Victoria). However, it is important to consider these results in the context of the much higher proportion of same-day separations in Victoria. Same-day separations could normally be expected to be lower acuity with fewer diagnosis and separation codes per separation and consequently, the Victorian measures of coding depth ought to be somewhat lower than those in New South Wales. Although this is the case, the differences are small and not commensurate with the significant differences in same-day proportions, suggesting possible overcoding in Victoria, but a definitive conclusion in this regard cannot be drawn from the available national data.

Victoria's casemix policy placed strong incentives on hospitals to ensure that all patients classified as Category 1 for elective surgery were treated within thirty days, and this did happen. Although a number of jurisdictions have developed sophisticated algorithms for waiting list categorisation (Hadorn 2003), this has not been the case in Victoria where categorisation still relies on a surgeon's unconstrained clinical judgment. This creates a further risk of moral hazard, allowing hospitals to meet waiting list / time targets through re-categorisation. Since the introduction of the casemix policy, Category 2, the number of patients waiting longer than ninety days, has generally increased. The result of the casemix funding policy should thus be described as a significant success in terms of recorded Category 1 patients being treated within the acceptable clinical time, meeting a political need about publicly released waiting time data. However, the reduction in Category 1 patient waiting may have occurred by shifts in categorization practices as much as improved waiting times for access to elective surgery.

Lessons for other jurisdictions

The Victorian experience with allocating budgets on the basis of casemix is a significant one and probably provides the most useful lessons to other countries from the Australian casemix development experiences. Victorian public hospitals have now been subject to this funding regime for more than ten years, across governments of significantly different political persuasions. Although health policy is not directly transferable across political borders because of the path dependency of policy innovation (Tuohy 1999), the Victorian experience can provide lessons that other jurisdictions contemplating funding reform could take into account in policy design.

Casemix funding, or more accurately casemix allocation, is possible in a public, cash-limited system

Victoria's implementation was one of the early experiences of public system prospective payment internationally, within a fixed annual allocation for hospital services. The fact that the casemix policy has been sustained over a decade is therefore significant in itself. Health policy, like management, is subject to fads and fashions (Marmor 2004) and policy survival in a turbulent political environment is an achievement.

There are a number of attributes of the policy that facilitated its retention, most notably that casemix allocation changed the balance of power in the health care system from strong, independent hospitals who were able to blame government for all their financial ills, to one where government was able to sheet home to hospitals the responsibility for poor financial performance. This, of course, relied on the price set by government being seen as legitimate. Individual hospitals did not have the political power to challenge the overall price even though, in retrospect after a change of government, it was acknowledged as being manifestly inadequate (Auditor-General of Victoria 1998). The changed political dynamic resulting from the changed balance of power was obviously attractive to policy makers of both political persuasions.

Another politically attractive feature of the policy was that it changed the dynamic of hospital responses to budget reductions. Hospitals were no longer able to reduce services to patients to solve budget problems. Because hospitals were rewarded on the basis of activity, simple activity reductions were no longer a viable budget strategy. The fact that there was a promulgated benchmark price set by the regulator also helped to focus hospital management attention on efficiency improvements. The extent to which efficiency improvements were delivered was, of course, a function of the management's capacity and skill, and the extent to which the price placed pressure on their viability.

The data on average cost per separation in Table 11.1 show that a casemix-based allocation system can be used to drive significant efficiency changes in a hospital system, and this is also clearly a political attraction. However, the experience in growth in costs under the Victorian Labor government shows that the allocation basis *per se* does not drive efficiency, but rather it is a neutral instrument that can be used to allocate any level of funding. What a casemix allocation system does do, however, is to ensure that all hospitals are treated equally in such a system and that inefficient hospitals are not rewarded by being funded at higher levels for treating a case that is treated on a less costly basis at a more efficient hospital.

Although casemix was implemented at the zenith of the political power of the Liberal state government, it was continued by a minority Labor government six years later, thus demonstrating that technically rational policies can survive a change of government. Moving from a negotiated or political basis for budget setting to a technically rational one changed the system fundamentally. As outlined above, the policy was not only about efficiency, but also incorporated incentives for achievement of other policy goals, in particular about access. The fact that the policy could be used to achieve these goals strengthened its political salience. The high degree of transparency and technical rationality of the policy probably contributed to its bipartisan acceptance.

In a democratic community with locally elected politicians, political pressures will always exist. The casemix allocation policy and its high degree of transparency meant that political pressures could be channelled, but not eliminated. This increased transparency somewhat reduced the scope for special pleading and special deals, although it did not entirely eliminate special pleading. The casemix funding policy changed the nature of special pleading and framed its discourse to one about adverse selection and within-DRG variation rather than an unmeasurable espoused public or community benefit.

Transition to the new budget system could be staged and managed, transaction costs could be limited, but the way implementation anomalies are handled is important

The implementation process of casemix funding, led by the author, has been discussed elsewhere (Lin and Duckett 1997) but it had a number of key attributes that facilitated the transition to the new system:

- it built on the long history of provision of casemix information to hospitals by the Health Department;
- it co-opted leading hospital managers (primarily through those who had argued consistently in the past that there should be more rewards for efficiency);
- it involved key clinician leaders who were able to articulate a number of weaknesses in the initial design of the new funding system and arrange for focused consultation with relevant clinical leaders (e.g. to develop improved funding arrangements for dialysis);
- it incorporated wide consultation and information provision to the hospital system more broadly;
- the implementation team recognised the issue of adverse selection, and identified and addressed anomalies. Such recognition did not undermine the principles or counteract the incentives involved in the overall policy and was co-ordinated in a transparent way;
- the transition was phased (over a two-year period) through 'compensation grants';
- the transition was staged over a number of elements of the budget, starting where measurement difficulties had been resolved or minimised and slowly widening the ambit of activity-based funding using available data.

Implementation involved increased transparency in terms of the budgets for hospitals and how they were set. The higher transparency contributed to building support for the new policy, as all hospitals were seen to be facing the same levels of pain. Although less efficient hospitals were required to achieve greater levels of savings, this was seen as equitable. The transparency was accompanied by a government-wide deregulatory overlay (Alford and O'Neill 1994, Costar and Economoce 1994) where the funding department initially attempted to reduce micro-management of the agencies, to place greater emphasis on hospital performance and autonomy, consistent with the then prevalent public policy view of emphasis on 'steering, not rowing' (Osborne and Gaebler 1992).

The rhetoric accompanying policy change is an important component of implementation

The implementation of 'casemix funding' was more than simply the introduction of a new set of financial incentives: it involved significant shift in the funder's rhetoric. The 'hortatory' aspects of public policy have long been recognised (Edelman 1988) and the language used in the Victorian policy change was as much part of the casemix intervention as the financial levers themselves. The policy launch was prominent in the media, bureaucrats and ministers emphasised the new language of efficiency and highlighted the importance of hospital activity for hospital revenue. This in turn carried through to intra-hospital management discourse and strategies. To some extent all of the staff of hospitals (medical, nursing and general) became aware that performance in terms of efficiency at ward level or in terms of decisions about length of stay and the number of tests ordered, had an impact on the overall financial position of the hospital. A number of professions within hospitals changed their status relativity: discharge planning and management of coding achieved a new level of prominence.

The government quest for improved hospital efficiency was generally favourably received in the media, changing the power balance of the public discourse from the previous situation where budget cuts had generally been seen to affect service quality and access adversely. There was strident political rhetoric and invective about hospital failure and the 'hospital suicide list' from the Departmental Secretary (Head), who invited hospital management to 'hand the keys over' to the funding department in the event that they felt they could not manage in the new environment. This rhetoric probably contributed as much to managers' performance anxiety as the financial levers and the budget cuts.

Work (of bureaucrats) expands to fill the time available for completion (Parkinson 1965)

The team responsible for the design and implementation of casemix was quite small and worked quite intensively. No additional staff were appointed for the design and implementation phase, which meant that when this period was finished the team responsible for monitoring and managing the policy was roughly the same size as that involved in implementation.

Monitoring requires substantially less effort than design and implementation and, in line with Parkinson's Law, a bureaucratic industry grew of regularly updating the funding guidelines and funding policies. Changes have been made to the design of the system every year since implementation, and some of these reflected unfinished business. For example, as originally implemented the main activity measured was inpatients, with outpatients funded on an historic block grant. As credible methods of measuring outpatient activity were developed (see Jackson *et al.* 1995), these were implemented. Similarly, measures of rehabilitation activity were developed and an activity-based funding system was introduced.

However, the greatest focus of bureaucratic activity related to technical refinements. There was only occasional change to fundamental design elements of the system over the ten years. These technical refinements and updating became quite elegant and sophisticated, but created problems for management of the system as a whole. Medical practice changes and so price relativities need to be updated regularly. In the Victorian system this was undertaken annually using patient level cost data collected from the individual hospitals (Jackson 2001). The upside of updating relativities regularly is a short lead time between practice change and changes in price relativities. However, management behaviour change in the hospital sector is often slow. The regular changes in policy attenuated the policy (price) signals being sent. Without stability of pricing signals, an excess of costs over revenue in any year could be reversed in a subsequent year through changes in price relativities. This meant that managers could argue that they should not respond managerially to inefficiency as identified by a comparison of revenue and costs, because of perceived instability in revenue estimates. (The reality was that high volume DRGs exhibited little annual variation in price, but highly specialised, high cost, low volume DRGs did exhibit price variation). This instability in pricing signals thus undermined some of the key efficiency measures that the casemix funding policy was designed to address.

Bureaucratic activity in other areas also increased, with the introduction of more funding streams involving small projects which were the preserve of particular sub-units of the bureaucracy.

Long-term organizational change requires consistency of incentives over the longer term and needs to be credible, clear and consistently implemented

As indicated above, some of the strength of the casemix allocation policy was mitigated by the instability of payment rates and policies. There is thus clearly a tension in managing a casemix funding system between responding to changes in medical technology and practice and changed political priorities, on the one hand, and policy stability for sustained change on the other. The appropriate balance will vary over time. One of the strengths of Victoria's casemix policy was the clarity of its objectives and incentives. This meant that the policy was clearly understandable and the incentives were able to be clearly explained and understood.

The casemix policy was relatively complex in having multiple objectives (improving efficiency and reducing costs; reducing waiting lists; maintaining quality), but each strategy was linked to a specific instrument, the instruments being either pricing or regulatory in form. Thus, although the overall policy was initially framed about introducing payment per separation on the basis of casemix, all the pricing and regulatory strategies were important. These regulatory strategies also were able to evolve over time.

Prima facie the financial incentives were successful, delivering efficiency improvements and a significant budget cut. But the recorded savings in future budgets proved illusory. A panoply of short-term strategies were used to disguise the true underlying position of hospitals: hospitals were able to deal with recurrent funding problems by reducing capital assets, borrowing, or through assistance ('bail outs') by the funder. Hospitals were thus effectively able to operate at quite different efficiency levels (price per case) without management consequences. The efficiency incentives of casemix were thus mitigated and the policy undermined, and the policy lost some of its credibility. The newly elected Labor government provided a funds injection and strengthened its rhetoric about the consequences of failure, attempting to overcome a perception that poor financial performance would be dealt with by an injection of funds rather than management consequences.

Classificatory change is easier than organizational change – funders/purchasers need to ensure strong, continuous monitoring and auditing of key reported data

One of the aspects of moral hazard relates to gaming behaviour, including cost shifting, cream skimming, DRG creep, etc. (Duckett 1995). Casemix classifications can be manipulated, and evidence of this in Victoria is perhaps best seen in the rapid growth in same-day activity. In the early years, much of this same-day growth was probably through a reclassification of activity that was previously counted as outpatient or emergency department activity (or not counted at all) and became counted and classified as inpatient activity. This 'nominal' throughput growth was thus a significant element of hospital response to the new incentives and the budget cuts. Some of the monitoring activities of the department and the changes in policy that occurred over time were thus probably the regulator attempting to keep track and ahead of the regulated.

Trends in waiting lists/times also reveal an exposure to moral hazard. The lack of clear guidelines for categorisation and the absence of any centralised audit of waiting lists leaves open the suggestion that improvements in recorded waiting times for patients may not reflect real improvements in practice and patient experience.

Organisational and leadership change should be anticipated

The post-casemix funding environment in which hospital managers found themselves was significantly different from the pre-existing approach.

Managers had an advantage over the regulators in the pre-casemix negotiated funded environment as they would always know more about the idiosyncrasies of their hospital, and it was always possible for them to devise a 'special case' that distinguished their hospital from other hospitals. Budget cuts by government were portrayed as unfair and impacting adversely on patients. All the skills of negotiation in terms of use of the media and charm could be used by hospital managements to obtain a better deal for their hospital. In the more transparent and rational environment represented by the casemix funding arrangements, the nature of the management skill set had to change. There was now clearer and measurable accountability for hospital performance and poor financial results could not be simply blamed on a poor negotiation outcome and the venality of the funder. Managers needed to focus internally rather than externally. Financial directors also required new skills (and techniques) to monitor revenue closely and match costs and revenues to identify areas for efficiency improvement. These pressures led to an almost complete replacement of hospital management and financial directors over the two-year period post-implementation.

Because casemix funding specified a price per case rather than allowing price per case to vary on the basis of negotiation, this produced an exogenous method of determining whether a hospital was viable. This became particularly relevant in rural Victoria where, despite experiencing significant reductions in activity, hospitals had maintained budgets, effectively resulting in increased subsidies and increased subsidized costs per case. Although independent of the casemix decision, the fact that hospital viability was now measurable highlighted this issue and led to a number of closures of rural hospitals.

The new management pressures also called into focus whether the organisation of hospitals was appropriate. Management skills to function in the new environment were in short supply, and economies of scale in management roles were increasingly recognised. Acute hospitals did not always have functioning links with downstream providers, especially aged care services. Following a review, the Liberal government implemented a major restructure of hospitals in Melbourne, replacing single-site management with 'networks' responsible for multiple institutions. Similar changes also took place in rural Victoria. This restructure had a downside, creating further instability in the health system in Victoria and diverting attention from internal process improvement while leadership positions were determined.

Just as a different skill set was required amongst hospital management, so too a different skill set was required amongst the regulators, including skills such as understanding casemix and functioning in a technically rational environment.

The ability to effect organisational change was mitigated by the nature of the information systems in place within hospitals and the ability of hospital management to use such information effectively. Not all hospitals were able to monitor the revenue received by the hospital and associated costs at departmental level. Many hospitals did not have functioning information systems to provide the information necessary to be an efficient manager in the new environment. In the pre-casemix environment, detailed monitoring of costs within the hospital and assigning those costs to hospital casemix was not necessary nor, except in occasional circumstances, valued by hospital management. In the post-casemix environment, closer attention to hospital activity and the costs associated with particular types of cases and the way in which the hospital treated them, became much more important.

Once a framework of financial incentives and disincentives has been developed, price signals can be used (judiciously) to achieve emerging policy objectives. However, casemix policy should not be seen as the only policy instrument in the health sector and it needs to be complemented by other policy initiatives

Although there is clearly a balance here between stability and responsiveness, a more transparent pricing and regulatory framework, with inherent financial incentives, can be used to promote other policy goals. There can be pricing adjustments to achieve objectives about encouraging hospitals to pay more attention to primary and ambulatory care in their communities through price signals for chronic readmissions and ambulatory sensitive conditions (see www.health.vic.gov.au/healthstatus/acsc/). It may also be possible to use price signals to deal with allocative efficiency goals and to promote safety and quality goals.

The Victorian casemix policy addressed hospital efficiency and hospital access. It did not attempt to address a range of other issues in health policy (e.g. adequacy of primary care) nor indeed did it attempt to address all aspects of hospital policy (appropriateness of service mix). The casemix funding policy changes were, however, very high profile politically and bureaucratically. Initially the funding department acted as if pricing policy would fix most of the ills of the system; the Departmental Secretary, for example, derided hospital planning as unnecessary and inappropriate in the new environment. In his view efficiency considerations and patient choice would ensure an optimal configuration of the hospital system. This casemix *über alles* approach did not survive his term as Secretary, and a more balanced recognition that pricing policy is only one aspect of hospital policy subsequently prevailed.

Improving hospital efficiency had been the prime focus of Victorian hospital policy for some years prior to the introduction of casemix funding, which was generally seen as the principal way of addressing that policy goal. But over the ensuing years new policy issues emerged. The Quality of Australian Health Care Study (Wilson *et al.* 1995) brought issues of quality to the fore. Because efficiency was, in a sense, seen to be resolved in Victoria, hospital funding and efficiency issues no longer dominated the policy agenda to the same extent and issues such as hospital quality began to have higher salience and political and management attention.

Conclusion

A quarter of a century after Palmer's initial work, casemix measures are now embedded in Australian health policy. The second largest state in Australia, Victoria, uses casemix as the basis for allocating funds to its public hospitals. In most other states casemix measures are routinely used, either for funding purposes (e.g. in South Australia) or to compare efficiency between hospitals. At the national level, casemix is used to standardise hospital activity to compare performance of states, and is part of national routine reporting of hospital activity.

Using casemix measures to allocate funds to hospitals does not determine the level of funding to be paid per weighted case. In the longer term, politics will out. Casemix does not and cannot determine the long-term level of expenditure on the public hospital sector – this is determined by the political competition for funds with other government-funded sectors: education, public transport, police, etc. – not by the within-sector allocation mechanism, and is also determined by the politics of the overall levels of taxation that government is willing/able to levy. Equifinality is a key characteristic of systems (von Bertalanffy 1968) and thus it is no surprise that levels of expenditure in Victoria have returned to being similar to NSW – as the politics of balancing waiting lists, ambulance bypass and vocal clinicians against education and transport, etc., and the overall levels of taxation are probably about the same over the long term in both states.

The long-term outcomes of casemix allocation in Victoria appear to have been to:

- strengthen the role of policy makers versus individual hospitals;
- focus management (including clinician manager) attention on achieving activity targets as well as financial targets;
- enhance funding rationality and to make special pleading harder; and
- provide an incentive at the hospital level in Victoria for higher same-day activity rather than shifting this activity onto Commonwealth programmes.

Especially in casemix funding states, casemix measures are used within hospitals to track financial activity and in some cases are used as the basis for intra-hospital resource allocation. The development of casemix measures has also led to an increased awareness of the utility of the computerised hospital data sets, which are now also used for reporting on patient safety issues. Processes have been developed to update an Australian classification system

(ICD–10–AM), and the resource weights used for casemix to allow comparison of efficiency. All of this is now established infrastructure within Australia and casemix has quite clearly moved from the development stage to routine practice.

REFERENCES

Alford, J. and O'Neill, D. (eds) (1994) *The Contract State: Public Management and the Kennett Government*. Deakin University Press: Melbourne.

Auditor-General of Victoria (1998) *Acute Health Services under Casemix: A Case of Mixed Priorities. Special Report No. 56*. Victorian Government Printer: Melbourne (also www.audit.vic.gov.au/old/sr56/ags56cv.htm).

Bertalanffy, L. von (1968). *General System Theory: Foundations, Development, Applications*. George Braziller: New York.

Costar, B. and Economou, N. (1999) *The Kennett Revolution: Victorian Politics in the 1990s*. UNSW Press: Sydney.

Duckett S. J. (1985) 'If DRGs Are the Solution, What Is the Problem?' *Australian Health Review*, 8(1): 25–31.

   (1986) 'Diagnosis Related Groups: Towards a Constructive Application for Victoria', *Australian Health Review*, 9(2): 107–15.

   (1995) 'Hospital Payment Arrangements to Encourage Efficiency: The Case of Victoria, Australia', *Health Policy*, 34: 113–34.

   (1998) 'Casemix Funding for Acute Hospital Inpatient Services in Australia', *Medical Journal of Australia*, 169(Supplement, 19 October): S17–S21.

   (2004) 'The Australian Health Care Agreements 2003–2008', *Australia and New Zealand Health Policy*, 1(5).

Edelman, M. (1988) *Constructing the Political Spectacle*. The University of Chicago Press: Chicago.

Ellis, R. P. and McGuire, T. G. (1986) 'Provider Behavior under Prospective Reimbursement', *Journal of Health Economics*, 5: 129–51.

Hadorn, D. and Steering Committee of the Western Canada Waiting List Project (2003) 'Setting Priorities on Waiting Lists: Point-count Systems as Linear Models', *J Health Serv Res Policy*, 8(1): 48–53.

Jackson, T. (2001) 'Using Computerised Patient-level Costing Data for Setting DRG Weights: The Victorian (Australia) Cost Weight Studies', *Health Policy*, 56: 149–63.

Jackson, T., Sevil, P., Tate, R. and Collard, K. (1995) *The Development of Relative Resource Weights for Non-admitted Patients*. National Centre for Health Program Evaluation, Monash University: Fairfield.

Laffont, J.-J. and Tirole, J. (1993) *A Theory of Incentives in Procurement and Regulation*. MIT Press: Cambridge, Mass.

Lin, V. and Duckett, S. J. (1997) 'Structural Interests and Organisational Dimensions of Health System Reform'. In *Health Policy in Australia*, H. Gardner (ed.) Oxford University Press: Melbourne, pp. 64–80.

Marmor, T. (2004) *Fads in Medical Care Management and Policy.* The Nuffield Trust: London.

Osborne, D. and Gaebler, T. (1992) *Reinventing Government: How the Entrepreneurial Spirit is Transforming the Public Sector.* Addison-Wesley: Reading, Mass.

Parkinson, C. N. (1965) *Parkinson's Law or The Pursuit of Progress.* Penguin Books: Harmondsworth, Middlesex.

Rix, M., A. Owen, *et al.* (2005) '(Re)form with Substance? Restructuring and Governance in the Australian Health System 2004–2005', *Australia and New Zealand Health Policy*, 2(19).

Russell, L. B. (1989) *Medicare's New Hospital Payment System: Is it Working?* The Brookings Institution: Washington, D.C.

Street, A. and Duckett, S. (1996) 'Are Waiting Lists Inevitable?' *Health Policy*, 36: 1–15.

Tuohy, C. H. (1999) *Accidental Logics: The Dynamics of Change in the Health Care Arena in the United States, Britain, and Canada.* Oxford University Press: New York.

Turner, L. and Short, S. D. (1999) 'George Rupert Palmer – DRG Carrier and Champion', *Australian Health Review*, 22(2) 86–102.

Victorian Dept of Human Services (2000) *Ministerial Review of Health Care Networks – Final Report.*

Willcox, S. (2005) 'Buying Best Value Health Care: Evolution of Purchasing among Australian Private Health Insurers', *Australia and New Zealand Health Policy*, 2(1): 6. Available at: www.anzhealthpolicy.com/content/2/1/6.

Wilson, R. M., Runciman, W. B., Gibberd, R. W., Harrison, B. T., Newby, L. and Hamilton, J. D. (1995) 'The Quality in Australian Health Care Study', *MJA*, 163 (6 November): 458–71.

Young, D. W. and Saltman, R. B. (1985) *The Hospital Power Equilibrium: Physician Behaviour and Cost Control.* Baltimore: Johns Hopkins University Press.

12 Diagnosis procedure combination: The Japanese approach to casemix

Shinya Matsuda MD, PhD, FFPHM

Introduction

Japan's universal health insurance system, which covers a population of 122 million people, is divided according to workplace and living place. The type of company you work for determines the insurance society to which you belong and the financial contribution you must make. Although thousands of independent societies exist, they are all integrated into a uniform framework mandated by the national government. The Japanese health system is based on fee-for-service reimbursement under a uniform national price schedule. Health insurance funds (both public and semi-public) collect premiums from their insured and reimburse the cost for medical facilities according to the type and volume of services provided (Figure 12.1). The health insurance scheme is categorized into three basic groups according to age and employment status: Employees' Medical Insurance scheme (EMI) for employees and their dependants; the National Health Insurance scheme (NHI) for the self-employed, farmers, retired and their dependants, and a special pooling fund for the elderly. Every Japanese citizen is covered by one of these schemes. Because the system is portable, Japanese residents can receive medical services at any medical facility with a modest co-payment (30 percent in general, and 10 percent for the aged).

Today the health insurance scheme is an important infrastructure supporting the Japanese people. However, while the socio-economic structure is facing large and rapid changes due to an ageing population, an increase in the numbers of working women, and a transformation in the working environment and industrial structure, the people's awareness and social values are also changing rapidly. For example, a neoliberal way of thinking is becoming dominant, instead of the socio-democratic norm.

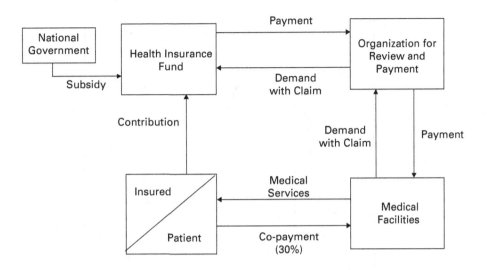

Note: Co-payment is set for 10% in the case of aged patient

Figure 12.1 Structure of social medical insurance scheme

As shown in Table 12.1, how to cope with the increasing health insurance burden is becoming increasingly important. The following topics are under discussion: the creation of a new health insurance scheme for the aged, a re-evaluation of the scope of public health insurance benefits to make the payment system more cost-efficient, and the introduction of a disease management scheme to differentiate between the functions of different medical facilities. A more detailed explanation of the health system in Japan by this author is available elsewhere (Matsuda 2004).

History of the introduction of casemix systems in Japan

As explained above, the health care system in Japan is facing serious financial difficulties due to a rapidly ageing population and costly innovations in medical technology. To maintain Japan's health insurance scheme, the system must become more efficient. Objective data are needed, to implement any changes. Unfortunately, a database which evaluates the performance of medical institutions has not been developed. Japan has very detailed claims data, which contain information on diagnosis, procedures conducted, and drugs prescribed. However, claims data are not

Table 12.1 Total medical expenditure in Japan, 1965–2003

	Total Medical Expenditures (TME)		Per capita TME (Thousand yen)	National Income (NI)		TME/NI	TME for the aged		Per capita TME for the aged (thousand yen)	TME for the aged/TME (%)
	Total (billion yen)	Increasing rate (%)		Total (billion yen)	Increasing rate (%)		Total (billion yen)	Increasing rate (%)		
1955	238.8	11.0	2.7	6973.3		3.42%				
1965	1122.4	19.5	11.4	26827.0	11.5	4.18%				
1975	6477.9	20.4	57.9	123990.7	10.2	5.22%	866.6	30.3	184	13.38%
1985	16015.9	6.1	132.3	261089.0	7.4	6.13%	4067.3	12.7	499	25.40%
1995	26957.7	4.5	214.7	374277.5	0.1	7.20%	8915.2	9.3	752	33.07%
1996	28454.2	5.6	226.1	386793.7	3.3	7.36%	9723.2	9.1	782	34.17%
1997	28914.9	1.6	229.2	391341.1	1.2	7.39%	10278.6	5.7	790	35.55%
1998	29582.3	2.3	233.9	379264.4	− 3.1	7.80%	10893.2	6.0	801	36.82%
1999	30701.9	3.8	242.3	373340.3	− 1.6	8.22%	11804.0	8.4	832	38.45%
2000	30141.8	− 1.8	237.5	379065.9	1.5	7.95%	11199.7	− 5.1	758	37.16%
2001	31099.8	3.2	244.3	368374.2	− 2.8	8.44%	11656.0	4.1	757	37.48%
2002	30950.7	− 0.5	242.9	362118.3	− 1.7	8.55%	11730.0	0.6	737	37.90%
2003	31537.5	1.9	247.1	368659.1	1.8	8.55%	11652.3	− 0.7	753	36.95%

standardized and are not held in an electronic format, so these data have not been fully utilized to formulate health policy. One of the main purposes of the DPC project is to implement a standardized electronic claim system.

Since the late 1990s, the Ministry of Health, Labor and Welfare (MHLW) and its affiliated research institute (the Institute of Health Economics and Policy: IHEP) have been researching the feasibility of a casemix classification system as a tool of standardized medical profiling. Several existing types of casemix classification, such as HCFA-DRG, AP-DRG, APR-DRG, and an early version of the Japanese original casemix system were tested. For example, the IHEP report indicated relatively positive results for the use of DRG in Japan (IHEP 2000). The R^2 of each DRG for average length of stay (ALOS) was as follows:

- HCFA-DRG: all cases (0.29), surgical cases (0.37), medical cases (0.25);
- AP-DRG: all cases (0.30), surgical cases (0.38), medical cases (0.26);
- APR-DRG: all cases (0.29), surgical cases (0.37), medical cases (0.25).

From these results, the IHEP report concluded that the DRG approach is applicable to the Japanese hospital system and that AP-DRG would represent a sound starting point for the development of a DRG system in Japan. As the comparative study proceeded, however, there was some resistance from those in the medical profession. They were accustomed to fee-for-service (FFS) reimbursement and were afraid that the casemix approach might curtail their freedom to practice. The physicians thought that the existing casemix classification systems were not precise enough to reflect their practice patterns correctly, but they also recognized the necessity for casemix profiling to improve the transparency of medical decisions and processes to their patients and insurers. An original classification system was needed, one that was compatible with practice patterns in Japan and at the same time allowed comparative benchmarking both within the country and against the systems of other countries.

To identify alternatives, between 1997 and 1998, the DRG applications in the UK (HRG), France (GHM), Sweden (Nord DRG), Belgium (AP-DRG), Portugal (HCFA-DRG), Austria (LDF), Germany (FP/SE) and the Netherlands (DBC) were studied intensively. On the basis of this research, a decision was made to develop the new casemix system as a profiling tool of medical services under a PMC-like principle. This was heavily influenced by the French and Austrian approach to casemix application for regional health planning and the Belgian and UK approach based on incremental development.

In 2001, the Japanese casemix research team (the DPC Project team) was organized to develop the Japanese casemix system. Dr. Yajima (former senior advisor, Health Economics Division, MHLW) designated the author of this chapter as the chief researcher for this project. He created the core research team (CRT), which included the author, Prof. Imanaka (Kyoto University; health economist), Prof. Hashimoto (Tokyo University; epidemiologist, cardiologist), Dr. Fushimi (Tokyo Medical and Dental University; nephrologist, specialist of medical information), Dr. Kuwabara (Kyoto University; surgeon, epidemiologist), Mr. Ishikawa (National Cancer Center; epidemiologist, specialist of information science), Mr. Anan (Kyushu National Medical Center; clinical coder), Mr. Horiguchi (Tokyo University; economist), Mrs. Ueda (Sendai National Medical Center; clinical coder) and Dr. Enami (former Deputy Director, Health Economics Division, MHLW). The CRT met weekly for discussion and data analysis to establish the Japanese casemix classification and implement it as a tool for payment in 2003.

Classification development

To create a new casemix system that was suitable for Japan, eight research groups were organized under the CRT. The CRT has responsibility for data handling, developing the database and reporting. The eight research groups are: DPC grouping logic; costing; health economics research; information systems; coding; quality of care; and hospital management. For DPC grouping, the need for collaboration with specialist physician associations was recognized, and twenty-one specialty associations were invited to join a working group to establish the Japanese casemix system – Diagnosis Procedure Combination (DPC).

The basic idea for constructing the casemix systems moved beyond DRGs. Because Japanese medical professionals required a more process-oriented system, a PMC-like approach was adopted. The key classification is diagnosis and then other types of procedure are considered to decide a group. The first step of development is to construct a definition table (Table 12.2). The first column is a diagnosis – this corresponds to a group of pathologies. In this case, "malignancy, stomach" contains gastric cancer (C16$), and carcinoma in situ (e.g. D002). In the second step, a series of medical procedures is listed based on expert judgment by the physician's panel. Finally, other situations such as co-morbidities and complications are

Table 12.2 An example of DPC definition table (stomach, malignancy 060020)

Base DPC	Diagnosis	ICD–10	Surgical Procedure	JPC	Adjuvant therapy 1	JPC	Adjuvant therapy 2	JPC	CC	ICD–10	Severity
Stomach, Malignancy	Carcinoma, Stomach	C16$	Total gasterectomy	K6572			CVH	G005	Renal failure	N18$	
	Carcinoma insitu	D002	Partial gasterectomy by Brawn procedure	K6552			Chemotherapy		Cardiac failure	I50$	
				K662			Radiation		. . . . . .	. . . . . .	
			. . . .	. . . . . .			Ventilator	J045$			

Table 12.3 Major diagnosis category of DPC

01	Diseases and disorders of the nervous system
02	Diseases and disorders of the eye
03	Diseases and disorders of the ear, nose, mouth and throat
04	Diseases and disorders of the respiratory system
05	Diseases and disorders of the circulatory system
06	Diseases and disorders of the digestive and hepatobiliary system
07	Diseases and disorders of the musculoskeletal system and connective tissues
08	Diseases and disorders of the skin and subcutaneous tissue
09	Diseases and disorders of the breast
10	Endocrine, nutritional and metabolic diseases and disorders
11	Diseases and disorders of the kidney, urinary tract and male reproductive system
12	Diseases and disorders of the female reproductive system
13	Diseases and disorders of the blood and blood forming organs and immunological disorders
14	New borns and other neonates with conditions originating in the perinatal
15	Diseases and disorders of childhood not covered by other MDC
16	Diseases and disorders not covered by other MDC

listed. Based on this definition table, the research team analyzed the actual data and constructed the DPC groups.

Based on the data from eighty-two specialist hospitals (eighty university hospitals and two national centers), DPC Version 3 was established in 2002. The new classification is composed of 2,552 groups under sixteen MDCs (Table 12.3). Based on DPC Version 3, payment of hospital fees to the eighty-two specialist function hospitals started in April 2003.

Structure of the DPC code

In a DPC algorithm, diagnosis, procedure, and co-morbidity/complications are three key variables for classification. Additional information (e.g. birth weight in the case of neonatal intensive care) is also referred to in some groups. Diagnosis and co-morbidity/complications were coded using the ICD–10 coding scheme. In the Japanese Code, procedures are defined in the fee schedule of the national health insurance system. DPC Version 3 is composed of eight parts as shown in Figure 12.2.

The first code is the Major Diagnosis Category and DPC serial number, which corresponds to ICD–10. The second code indicates the type of admission. The third code indicates age and birth weight. The fourth indicates existence and types of surgical procedures. The fifth and sixth indicate the existence of additional procedures and adjuvant therapy such as chemotherapy, immunotherapy and radiotherapy. The seventh indicates the existence of co-morbidity/complications. Finally, the eighth is the code for severity. Although the eight components are the prototype of the classification structure, it should be noted that they are for profiling only and all of the components are not necessarily used for the reimbursement schedule.

Traditionally, the method of payment used in the Japanese health insurance scheme has been fee-for-service (FFS). Health information

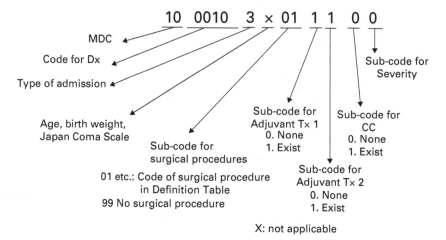

Figure 12.2 Structure of DPC

companies adapted to this scheme and developed their computer systems around it. Using tariff tabled data, a receipt (claim sheet) for each patient is produced for reimbursement. This is then sent to the payers' insurance scheme. All procedures, drugs and devices for reimbursement are registered for each patient on a daily basis using a standard code. By using this FFS-based data, a DPC can be allocated to the RDDL (Receipt Data Download) system. This system is used not only for acute inpatient services, but also for chronic inpatient services and ambulatory care. This is why DPC can be used for all categories of medical services.

Another innovative system is the code finder, which was developed by Prof. Ohe of Tokyo University. This converts a diagnosis into ICD–10 code. By combining the RDDL system and code finder, an appropriate DPC code can be determined for each patient relatively easily. The dictionary of diagnosis is constantly updated, which is reflected in the code finder. Using these basic infrastructures, DPC for payment could be introduced within a relatively short period of time (two years from development to application for payment).

Reimbursement system based on DPC

The Japanese DPC-based reimbursement scheme is quite different from other countries. The payment for hospitals has two components: the DPC component and the fee-for-service component. DPC corresponds to the "so-called" hospital fee, which comprises hotel fee, pharmaceuticals and supplies used on wards, lab. tests, radiological examinations, and any procedures cheaper than ¥10,000 (US$100). FFS corresponds to tariffs for surgical procedures and anesthesia, pharmaceuticals, equipment used in operating theatres, and procedures that cost more than ¥10,000 (US$100). For the DPC component, a *per diem* payment schedule is set for each DPC group.

Table 12.4 shows an example of a "DPC 0600203x01000x (Malignancy, Stomach, Total gasterectomy, No additional procedure, No CC)." For each group, the standard *per diem* payment is defined, and three periods are set for reimbursement: Period I, Period II and Upper limit for DPC-based payment (Figure 12.3). These correspond to the 25 percentile-day, ALOS day and ALOS+2SD day, respectively. Up to Period I, *per diem*

Table 12.4 An example of a DPC definition table for reimbursement

No. of DPC	Name of DPC	Surgical Procedure	Ad Tx 1	Ad Tx 2	CC	Severity	LOC(days) I	LOC(days) II	Points Under I	Points Between I and II	Points Over II	Upper limit for DPC based
0600203x01000x	Stomach, Malignancy	Total gasterectomy	None	None	None		15	29	2,939	2,172	1,846	45

ICD–10
C16$
D002

Japanese procedure code
K6572

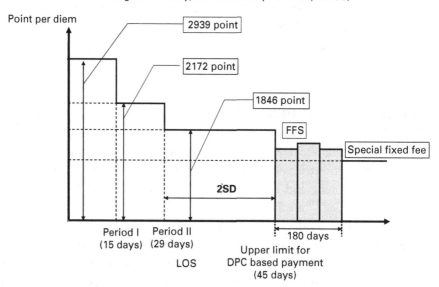

DPC 0600203x01000x (Malignancy, Stomach, Total gasterectomy, No additional procedure, No CC)

Point per diem

2939 point

2172 point

1846 point

FFS

Special fixed fee

2SD

Period I   Period II
(15 days) (29 days)

180 days

LOS   Upper limit for
DPC based payment
(45 days)

Figure 12.3 An example of DPC-based payment for hospital

payment is set at 15 percent more than standard *per diem* payment. Furthermore, the hospital coefficient is calculated for each facility according to its function and characteristics. From period II to upper limit day, *per diem* payment is set at 15 percent less than the standard payment. A reduced FFS payment scheme will be applied after upper limit day. In the average case of DPC 0600203 × 1000x, the DPC component is responsible for about 50 percent of total payment, and the rest is paid by FFS.

The calculation of DPC-based payment is extremely complicated, so all hospital information systems must be computerized. The DPC-based hospital computer system for reimbursement is based on the former FFS-based tariff calculation system.

Refinement of DPC

During the first year's implementation for payment in 2003, the DPC project team gathered additional information to refine the classifications. In the 2003 study, the treatment of secondary procedures (i.e. secondary surgery, chemotherapy, radiotherapy, etc.) and CCs was re-evaluated. The results were discussed within each of the twenty-one clinical groups with DPC core research team members. After many recommendations and proposals, Version 3.1 of DPC was finally established and applied to any payments made after April 2004.

DPC Version 3.1 is comprised of 3,067 groups under sixteen MDCs. From 2004 the hospitals that were paid by DPC expanded to another sixty-two hospitals, with both public and private facilities. Besides these DPC-based payment hospitals, another 200 (both public and private) participated in the program without DPC-based payment. These are known as "DPC preparation hospitals."

In 2008, DPC Version 3.3 was introduced. This is made up of 2,345 groups. In April 2006, 360 hospitals were paid by the new DPC Version 3.2 and another 372 hospitals became "DPC preparation hospitals." Currently DPC-related data are collected from more than 1,500 acute care hospitals, (about 450,000 beds). Data are continuously analyzed by the DPC research team for further refinement. Another major revision of the classification is anticipated in the near future.

DPC-based cost analysis project

Providers have long held the view that the current FFS tariff table does not reflect the real cost of medical services. As each DPC price is determined by the average cost based on the current tariff table, the validity of the DPC is also questioned. To answer its critics, the DPC costing manual was developed in 2002 after two years' intensive research activity. Using this manual, twenty-eight university hospitals tried to estimate the cost of each DPC in 2003. Although the results were positively evaluated by participant hospitals, several points needed further refinement. For example, the method for computing overheads had to be fine-tuned, so it could apply to all hospitals, as did the evaluation and determination of research and education costs.

In 2004, the costing study was extended to another 112 hospitals (private and public), and in 2006 this increased to more than 200 hospitals. To facilitate data collection, special computer software has been developed, which is used in every hospital.

Evaluation of the DPC system

Efficient use of health resources

The main purpose of DPC implementation is to make Japan's health system sustainable: in other words, to make it more efficient. The DPC-based lump-sum payment should result in a more efficient organization of the system. In fact the ALOS for DPC-based hospitals has decreased from 20.4 (2002) to 17.6 days (2005). This can be broken down into: the decrease in ALOS of each DPC, the changes in patient mix of each hospital and the interaction of the two factors. Our analysis has suggested that the two-day reduction is due to a decrease in ALOS of each DPC, and that another two days are due to the interaction effect. The composition of casemix has changed with more cases of longer ALOS. This suggests that the DPC hospitals have begun to accept more severe cases and to treat them with shorter LOS.

As shown in Table 12.5, for most of the DPCs, resource consumption was reduced for all items after the DPC-based payment was introduced. According to the results of our investigation, this has not been effected by a drop in the standard of patient care.

Patient choice

In 2001, the MHLW launched its three main principles for future health reform: respect for patient choice and information, realization of an effective and high-quality care delivery system; and the construction of a reliable health system.

Table 12.5 Changes in resource consumption after the introduction of DPC between 2002 and 2003 (an example for "DPC 0600203x01000x (Malignancy, Stomach, Total gasterectomy, No additional procedure, No CC)": 82 hospitals)

	Year	N	Mean	SD	P	Coefficient of variance
Total charged cost	2002	753	146813.7	35240.4	0.000	0.24
(FFS base)	2003	592	139942.6	34459.8		0.25
Lab. test cost	2002	753	11979.6	5134.2	0.000	0.43
	2003	592	10980.5	4698.6		0.43
Rad. exam. cost	2002	753	6321.0	4614.7	0.000	0.73
	2003	592	5417.7	3956.5		0.73
Pharmaceutical	2002	753	1020.7	1653.3	0.076	1.62
cost (oral)	2003	592	857.1	1697.9		1.98
Pharmaceutical	2002	753	6127.6	8814.3	0.002	1.44
cost (injection)	2003	592	4923.7	5656.3		1.15
Surgical procedure	2002	753	70869.6	10123.2	0.692	0.14
cost	2003	592	71101.7	11347.1		0.16
Length of stay	2002	753	27.9	12.3	0.000	0.44
	2003	592	25.4	11.3		0.44
Pre-operation LOS	2002	752	9.7	9.0	0.000	0.93
	2003	585	7.8	7.0		0.92
Post-operation	2002	752	17.8	7.6	0.001	0.43
LOS	2003	585	16.4	7.1		0.43

10 points = 1 US$

It is expected that DPC-based information on hospitals will be important for patient choice. Compared with other casemix classification systems, DPC contains more clinical information behind the classification code, such as disease staging, ADL, outcome, and clinical severities such as NYHA score / Killips score, etc. Thus it is possible to construct various clinical indicators from a DPC data set. This information will be extremely useful to both patients and insurers.

Quality assurance program

As shown in Table 12.5, in most DPC groups there has been a significant decrease in resource use. There was concern that DPC-based bundle payments might mean poor patient care. To evaluate the effect of this kind of bundle-type payment on the resource consumption in acute inpatient care and its quality, the DPC scientific committee was organized under the Central Social Medicine Council of MHLW. The committee has conducted research on the following subjects: readmission (rate and reasons), changes in resource consumption, generic drug use, reasons for changes in resource consumption, use of clinical pathways, patient satisfaction, and staff satisfaction.

According to the results of a questionnaire, major reasons for the reduction in resource consumption included: an increase in the use of generic drugs and devices, the introduction of clinical pathways, and the transfer of lab. tests and radiological examinations to outpatients. All related studies have shown that the standard of care has not been compromised, despite this decrease in resource consumption.

Readmission rates have increased from 7.7 to 9.7 percent from 2002 to 2004. According to the official investigation into these rates, planned readmissions, such as chemotherapy and radiotherapy account for most of the increase.

The research results mentioned above concluded that after the introduction of DPC-based payment, resource use has been rationalized with little adverse effect. Compared with other countries, ALOS in Japan is still longer, and the use of generic drugs and supplies is limited, even though their use has been increasing. In theory, however, too strong an incentive for cost containment may lead to under-treatment. A system is needed to prevent possible adverse effects and to ensure quality care. A DPC-based benchmarking system is being constructed for this purpose. In this system, each participant hospital is required to send its basic data electronically (with a high level of security). After the treatment of data by the working team, each hospital can compare its outcomes with the national average and best practice hospitals for a series of indicators, such as ALOS, pre-operation ALOS, resource use based on charged cost and real cost, readmission rate, various type of clinical indicators (crude mortality rate and the risk-adjusted mortality rate for each DPC level, numbers of each procedure, etc.). The user can analyze the DPC data with the OLAP tool as shown in Figure 12.4. This DPC-based benchmarking system is expected to function as a framework to promote quality of care and scientific management in Japan.

Future perspectives

Japanese patients demand better quality care at a reasonable price. As the Japanese health system ensures total free access for the patient, it is very difficult to regulate increase in expenditures. To balance the quality and cost

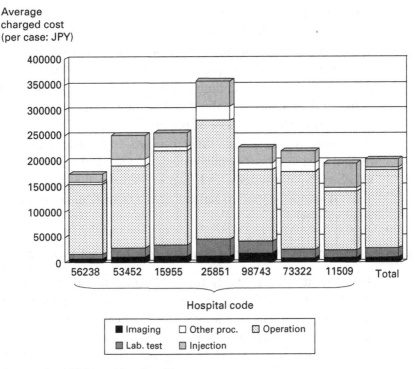

Average
charged cost
(per case: JPY)

Figure 12.4 An example of DPC-based benchmarking

of medical services, providers, payers and patients need a common language.

One of the most important missions of our research project is to ameliorate the transparency of hospital activities, to make hospital services measurable, and then to prepare a common basis for discussion about health reform. It is the first time in the history of Japanese health policy that the data shown in this chapter have been systematically established and made available to the public. Using these DPC-related data, the performance of hospital services can be objectively analyzed. Standardization, transparency and accountability are the keywords of the DPC project.

International comparison

Faced with the economic difficulty of paying for the social security fund, the payers' organization has tried to make each medical service cheaper, claiming that the Japanese tariff table is too expensive. However, the providers' side has been claiming that the Japanese tariff for medical services is much cheaper than that in other developed countries. For this reason, there has been a long debate (or war!) about the price of medical services in the Central Social Medical Insurance Council. The introduction of DPC opens up the possibility for the international comparative study of medical services. For example, our preliminary study revealed that the Japanese DPC tariff of "Major joint and limb reattachment procedures of lower extremity (without doctor's fee)" is about half of the US DRG, but almost twice that of Germany. The high price of imported artificial joints in Japan is one of the reasons for these wide differences. As DPC gathers all kinds of information used in other casemix systems, it is relatively easy to transform DPC to other casemix systems and then to compare the price of each casemix. These data can be used to rationalize the tariff table from the international point of view.

Incremental approach for next step – from *per diem* payment to per case payment

The current system adopts the DPC-based *per diem* payment for acute inpatient services. The main reason for this is a wide variation in ALOS among the hospitals. If the per case payment criterion is applied in this situation, some hospitals are no longer viable, so a cross-over period would be needed. After publishing the profiling data of LOS and cost, DPC-based hospitals have began to compare performances and standardize their activities. As a result, the difference in cost between hospitals was reduced, and the insurers recommended that the payment system should be changed from *per diem* to per case to make the system simpler and more efficient.

This fact-based incremental approach is one of the key factors for the success of DPC implementation. The "big bang" approach does not suit Japanese culture.

Extension of DPC grouping for other medical services

The extension of DPC use to other areas such as middle- and long-term inpatient and ambulatory services is also intensively studied, and Dr. Fushimi, a member of the DPC core research team, has already succeeded in applying DPC logic to a wide range of patient data and has estimated disease profiles at national and local levels.

Due to high variability within patient type, it is relatively difficult to introduce the DPC-based bundle-type payment for ambulatory services, and currently there is no plan to adopt DPC for the payment of outpatient services. However, DPC logic can be applied to ambulatory care to estimate total medical expenditure at macro level. Using this kind of data, the sector budgets or expenditure objectives for medical services can be discussed.

The extension of DPC logic to psychiatric care, rehabilitation services and chronic inpatient services has also been intensively studied by the DPC core research team. Z and R codes are now included in the DPC definition table, as is necessary information such as nursing care and an ADL score.

DPC innovation in hospital management

At the beginning of the DPC project in 2001, the main targets for DPC use were those in charge of hospital management. According to Japanese medical law, a hospital director must be a medical doctor. However, there is little systematic academic training in hospital management in Japan. For this reason, a more scientific approach to hospital management has not been developed here, compared to other countries, such as the USA. The status of non-medical personnel in hospital management has been relatively low in Japanese hospital culture. To change this a number of seminars on DPC data handling and management have been organized. With the introduction of DPC use, hospital managers have begun to play a pivotal role in their hospitals. Using national data, each hospital can detect problems that need to be solved in its cost structure and clinical performance.

The regional disease structure data that were constructed by Dr. Fushimi will allow each hospital to conduct situational analyses such as SWOT analysis (as shown in Figure 12.5). Using DPC-based disease structure data, each hospital can calculate the market share for MDC level, base DPC level and full code (14 digits) level. This figure corresponds to an analysis of the external environment when cross-referenced with an analysis of the internal environment, so each hospital can conduct a SWOT analysis and establish its future strategy.

Using this framework the development of a DPC-related Balanced Score Card is also ongoing under our research program. Numerous seminars on DPC-based management have been held by various organizations, such as hospital associations and private companies. DPC has become one of the hottest issues in medical journals, and is seen as a tool for real innovation in hospital management.

Without specialists in hospital management, it is very difficult to construct a meaningful strategy for the future. However, there are some charismatic DPC managers from DPC hospitals – Mr. Masaki (Kumamoto

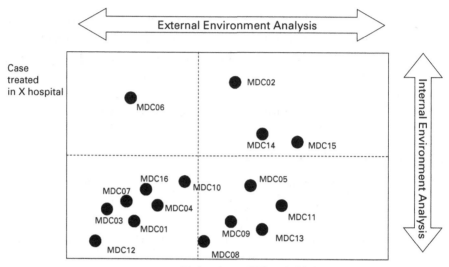

Figure 12.5 DPC and SWOT analysis

Saisei-kai hospital), Mr. Anan (Kyushu Medical Center) and Mr. Maruyama (St-Maria Hospital) whose seminars always attract large audiences.

Challenge for further development – DPC as a tool for health reform

Of course not everyone agrees about the general use of DPC. For example, the Japanese Medical Association is very cautious about it, because it will have a deep impact on the quality of care and on distribution of medical expenditure between acute inpatient and other medical services. Hospital associations are also very cautious about the possibility of strengthening the cost-containment policy through DPC-based bundle-type payments.

In 2006, plans were announced for a large-scale reform of the health insurance system. From 2007, the post-war baby boomers start to enter retirement age. This demographic change will have a huge impact on Japan's social insurance scheme. According to an MHLW estimate, those aged sixty-five and over will comprise 30 percent of the population and spend 70 percent of the health insurance budget by 2027. At that time, the contribution rate for social security will be 34 percent of the total revenue of Japanese citizens. However, it remains to be seen if they are willing to accept this level of contribution.

Furthermore, the neoliberal way of thinking is becoming prevalant in Japanese society under the current Liberal Democratic government, so the socio-democratic system in place today may not continue, as social change continues apace in Japanese society.

The health insurance scheme has been an important cornerstone of Japanese society. If the principle erodes, the safety of society will decline and social costs will increase, so steps must be taken to ensure that the current Japanese health system can be sustained. For example, MHLW intends to control the increase of medical expenditure using health promotion campaigns.

To make citizens aware of the importance of a healthy life style, objective data are needed to demonstrate the burden that disease places on the health insurance scheme. The use of DPC allows the financial cost of preventative activities and/or disease management programs to be estimated. This task is, of course, very difficult, but very challenging and fascinating. This is the mission of our DPC project.

REFERENCES

IHEP (2000). *Report on a Survey of the Introduction of DRGs in Major European Countries.* Tokyo: IHEP.

IHEP (2000). *Report on Studies concerning the Applicability of US DRG for the Japanese Health System.* Tokyo: IHEP.

Matsuda, S. (2004). Health Status and its Influence on Health Policy in Japan. *Journal of Economics and Medicine*, 22 (1–2) 5–14.

(2004). Health Insurance System in Japan. *Journal of Economics and Medicine*, 22 (1–2) 15–26.

(2004). Health Promotion Policy in Japan. *Journal of Economics and Medicine* 22 (1–2) 39–48.

(2004). Re-organization of the Japanese Hospital System. *Journal of Economics and Medicine*, 22 (1–2) 69–78.

13 Casemix in Singapore

Chien Earn Lee, MD and Eng Kok Lim, MD

Background

Singapore is a country with a total land area of 699 sq. km (434 sq. miles). The total population is about 4.35 million, with a resident population of 3.55 million in 2005. Singapore has a relatively young population, with only 8.3 percent of the population above 65.

The state of health in Singapore is good by international standards. The infant mortality rate in 2005 stands at 2.1 per 1,000 live births, while average life expectancy is 79.7 years. The leading causes of morbidity and mortality are currently the major non-communicable diseases, with cancer, stroke and cardiovascular disease accounting for approximately 60 percent of all deaths in 2005.

In 2005, Singapore spent about S$7.6 billion, or 3.8 percent of GDP, on healthcare, of which government expenditure on health services was S$1.8 billion, or 0.9 percent of GDP.

Healthcare system

Singapore has a hybrid system of healthcare delivery. The government manages the public healthcare system, while private hospitals and general practitioners comprise the private healthcare system. Private practitioners provide 80 percent of the primary healthcare services, while the public sector polyclinics provide the remaining 20 percent. For the more costly secondary and tertiary hospital care, it is the reverse, with 80 percent of hospital care being provided by the public sector and the remaining 20 percent by the private sector.[1] Patients are free to choose providers within this dual healthcare delivery system.

Healthcare financing

The Singapore healthcare delivery system is based on individual responsibility coupled with government subsidies to keep basic healthcare affordable. Government subsidies are only available for the public sector polyclinics and hospitals.

Patients are expected to pay a portion of the cost of the medical services they use, and to pay more when they demand a higher level of service. For example, in public sector hospitals, class C patients receive an 80 percent subsidy, while class A patients pay full fees. The difference is in physical amenities – a class C patient is housed in a eight-bed cubicle, while a class A patient has a single room. Patients choose the ward class to which they wish to be admitted.

Individuals are encouraged to take responsibility for their own health by saving for medical expenses. Under the Medisave scheme (introduced in 1984), every working person is required by law to set aside 6–8 percent of his income into a personal Medisave account, which can be used to pay for hospitalization expenses incurred by the employee and immediate family members. MediShield, a catastrophic illness insurance scheme introduced in 1990, is designed to help individuals meet medical expenses resulting from major or prolonged illnesses. Medifund, an endowment fund set up by the government, acts as a safety net of last resort for those who are truly indigent. Therefore, no Singaporean will be denied access to the healthcare system or turned away by a public hospital due to inability to pay.

The median waiting time for elective surgery is around one week. Patients requiring emergency or urgent surgery are always admitted immediately.

Casemix implementation

The Ministry of Health began monitoring the development of casemix in countries such as the United States and Australia in the early 1990s. The implementation of casemix in Singapore, however, started in earnest in 1997.

Objectives of implementing casemix

One of the Ministry of Health's key objectives in implementing casemix was to facilitate the fairer allocation of resources (e.g. for the provision of funding (subvention) to public sector hospitals). Prior to the introduction of casemix, hospital outputs were described in terms of length of stay (LOS) and table of surgical procedures (TOSP). Funding on a *per diem* basis was rather unsatisfactory, as the resource requirements for one day of hospitalization can range from purely board and lodging (for those under observation or who are recuperating) to intensive care services. Casemix-based funding seeks to address this anomaly. Instead of a flat rate applied across the board, use of casemix allows the Ministry of Health to better target the increase in specific DRGs where additional resources are required.

In addition to its use as a funding tool, the Ministry of Health had also intended casemix to be used as a tool for improving clinical quality by facilitating meaningful comparisons of cost, quality and access, in particular cost efficiency (i.e. input/output) and cost effectiveness (i.e. input/outcome) studies.

Funding formula

The essential features of the casemix funding system in Singapore are:
- Acute inpatient or day surgery inlier episodes in subsidized wards would be subvented on a per-DRG basis.
- For a minority of cases, there may be reasons for patients to be hospitalized beyond the expected LOS. Such patients, or outliers, are funded on a per-DRG basis, with additional high outlier *per diem* beyond the high trim point.
- Sub-acute patient services, such as rehabilitation, are funded separately on a *per diem* basis.
- A standard set of cost weights will apply across all hospitals.
- Other hospital activities, such as teaching and research, continue to be funded separately. These funds are not to be used for clinical service.
- Some programs, such as transplantation, renal dialysis, health screening and cardiac rehabilitation, would also be funded separately with fixed grants. These are termed program funding.

It should be noted, however, that casemix implementation only affected the way the Ministry of Health funded public sector hospitals. It did not directly affect how the hospitals charged their patients or how they paid their clinicians. Hospitals continued to charge patients on a fee-for-service basis. As doctors in the public sector hospitals are employees of these hospitals, they continued to be paid in accordance with the respective hospitals' remuneration schemes.

Managing the transition

The Ministry of Health started using casemix to fund day surgery and inpatient services in public hospitals and national centers providing acute care services in October 1999. Casemix implementation in Singapore can be characterized as a top-down initiative (championed by top management, including the Minister for Health and the Permanent Secretary) with an inclusive and pragmatic approach. The main "vehicle" driving this change was the Casemix Taskforce, chaired by the Deputy Secretary (Health). This was made up of senior management of the Ministry of Health, CEOs and senior clinicians from the public sector hospitals, and supported by the Casemix Project Office of the Ministry of Health.

Several committees were formed to drive specific areas. These included Ministry of Health committees such as the:

- Committee on Quality of Care, to ensure that quality of care was not compromised;
- Casemix Finance and Information Management Workgroup;
- Public Communications and Patient Feedback Survey Workgroups, to assess patients' perception of the care that they received before and after casemix implementation; and
- Clinical Coders Forum, to guide the development of clinical coders.

The Clinical Classification Committee (CCC) was also formed to assess the suitability of the DRG system for Singapore. The CCC was supported by seventeen specialty committees to examine each Major Diagnostic Category. Members of these committees were appointed by Ministry of Health senior management and generally welcomed the invitation to represent their respective specialty and institution in shaping the development of casemix in Singapore.

A program for the education and training of doctors was also developed to ensure that clinicians understood the nature, implications and impact of casemix classification and funding. The program included "roadshows," a casemix website, a newsletter ("Casemix Matters") handbooks, and even a casemix video.

Public sector hospitals had also set up their own implementation workgroups to prepare for the implementation of casemix. Although provision was made for a private hospital casemix group, this workgroup was not activated, as this initial phase of implementation affected only public sector acute hospitals. Attempting to implement casemix as a measurement tool in the private sector, which does not receive funding from the Ministry of

Health, would have been challenging and would potentially have diffused our energies, as the private sector would not see any direct benefits from adopting casemix.

The organization chart for the various workgroups is shown in Figure 13.1.

Through all these committees and workgroups, most (if not all) of the key decision makers were involved in one way or another in casemix implementation. Decisions were arrived at by open discussion and consensus.

Key concerns that surfaced included a possible reduction in the overall healthcare budget, as this was the experience in several other countries when casemix-based financing was implemented. The Ministry of Health assured hospital management and clinicians that the healthcare budget would not be cut – government healthcare expenditures (excluding capital expenditures) actually increased by nearly 15 percent[2] from FY1999 to FY2000.[3] The Ministry reiterated that hospitals would be allowed to retain their efficiency gains. Casemix would be used, not to cut resources, but to better allocate them to where they were most needed.

The Ministry of Health also recognized that some hospitals would need time to adjust to the new funding formula. These hospitals may, as a result of the re-allocation of resources, suffer a shortfall in revenue from subvention during the transition period. To allow services to continue without disruption to the public, and at the same level of quality, a transitional top-up grant for the first year of casemix implementation was devised.

Some pediatricians and geriatricians had raised concerns that casemix systems placed those treating children and the elderly at a disadvantage, as they were likely to consume more resources than the general population. The Ministry of Health conducted a study which found that, at both the DRG and the global levels, subvention was pegged at the appropriate level (i.e. total subvention versus total cost) for these two groups of patients (below twelve and above sixty-five). This was not, however, the case at the inter-departmental level. In hospitals where less severe cases within the DRG were managed elsewhere (e.g. general medicine departments), pediatric and geriatric departments did suffer deficits as a result of casemix-based funding.

These findings were communicated to hospital management and clinicians, and efforts were undertaken to find better ways to distribute the subvention from the Ministry of Health to the respective departments. Options such as better severity splits (and administrative splits) to DRGs were considered.[4] This is still an ongoing endeavour.

Technical considerations

Choice of casemix system

As a country starting out on its casemix journey, Singapore was faced with two main options: develop its own system from scratch or adopt an existing system. The first option was not considered to be feasible by the Ministry of Health. It would have incurred substantial resources in terms of manpower, time and effort when there were already extensively researched systems available. The Ministry thus proceeded to consider systems that might be appropriate for its local needs.

After studying various casemix systems around the world, the Ministry decided to adopt Version 3.1 of the Australian National Diagnosis Related Group (or AN-DRG) classification system. This decision was based on several factors. First, the AN-DRG classification system was a mature and robust system. The Ministry was aware, at that stage, of potential new systems that were likely to be introduced soon. It decided however, as its initial venture into casemix, to go with a tried and tested system. Second, it could benefit from the extensive Australian research and experience in implementing AN-DRG. Third, the geographical proximity and close professional links between Singapore and Australia would facilitate the implementation and acceptance of AN-DRG.

Ensuring data accuracy

The primary objective of implementing casemix funding is to ensure equitable funding and resource allocation in the public acute hospitals. This in turn depends to a great extent on the accuracy of casemix data submitted by the hospitals. Wrongly coded data would affect the calculation of resource weights, as well as the subvention that the hospital receives (i.e. "GIGO (garbage-in, garbage-out) subvention)."

The Ministry had, as such, adopted a National Data Quality Assurance Framework. This framework uses a three-pronged approach to ensure data quality and integrity:

- Establishing Singapore coding and clinical documentation standards. Singapore uses the Australian coding standards with local modifications to local practice patterns.
- Regular audits of coding data. The Ministry conducted external coding audits with auditors from Australia and New Zealand. Hospital administrators are also expected to establish an internal coding audit framework for their respective hospitals.

- Professionalization of clinical coders. The Ministry developed a Code of Ethics and national competency assessment and accreditation system for clinical coders.

Pilot run

Casemix was first introduced in public sector hospitals through a pilot run in May 1998 involving one of the general hospitals and one tertiary center. The pilot run was then extended to all other (eleven in total) acute care public hospitals and tertiary referral institutions, starting October 1, 1998.

The objectives of the pilot run were threefold. First, it served to identify early operational issues in implementing casemix coding at the hospital level. As it had been decided that it was more manageable and feasible for coding to be performed by professional coders instead of clinicians, there was an urgent need to recruit and train adequate clinical coders.

The hospitals and institutions sought to minimize the learning curve by recruiting non-practicing doctors, nurses and those with some degree of medical knowledge as clinical coders. In addition, several hospitals recruited people with health information management training to provide leadership and guidance to the new coders.

The Ministry of Health also helped to jumpstart clinical coding by acquiring the DRG encoder–grouper software for all public hospitals. This enabled the newly recruited coders to code more efficiently, as the ICD–9–CM and DRG algorithms were already incorporated into the encoder grouper. In addition, the Ministry arranged for external consultants from Australia and New Zealand to come and train the hospital coders.

Another key operational issue addressed as part of the pilot run was the setting up of the necessary information technology (IT) infrastructure to facilitate the submission of casemix data from the hospitals to the Ministry of Health. The key challenge was the lack of a common platform for data submission. Although most hospitals were already using enterprise resource management (ERM) software from the same company, they had made adjustments to fit their own needs so that data transmission to a central system was not possible. The lack of a standard data set across hospitals was also an issue that needed to be resolved. Initial attempts to address these issues, such as submissions using Microsoft Access, were found to be unsatisfactory. As the hospital needed to re-enter patient particulars (e.g. demographics, etc.), transcription errors were common.

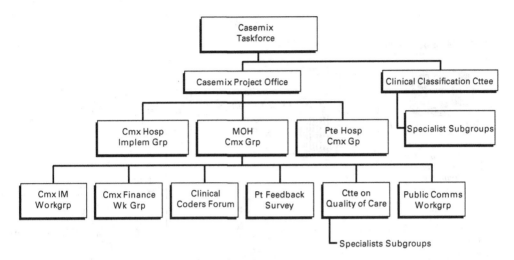

Figure 13.1 Casemix implementation: key drivers

The Ministry collaborated with the hospitals' information services departments to develop the Casemix and Subvention (C&S) System (see Figure 13.2). This system provides seamless integration between the hospital's existing IT systems, allows self-edits of erroneous records and generates automated reports. The system took two years to implement and involved extensive consultation and troubleshooting.

The second objective of the pilot period was to obtain casemix data for derivation of resource weights. Data from the pilot run were also used for the Clinical Classification Committee (CCC), comprising senior clinicians, for the first review of the AN-DRG Version 3.1 classification system in May 1999 (described above). During the pilot period, two parallel systems were in operation: hospitals were funded under the old system, but inpatient and day surgery cases were classified using AN-DRG Version 3.1. This allowed simulations of potential gains and losses by individual hospitals when casemix went "live," the third objective of the pilot run.

Other initiatives

Quality of care

One concern of casemix implementation is that providers may trade off cost against quality of care. Patients may then end up being discharged prematurely "quicker and sicker." To address these concerns, the Ministry of Health instituted the National Medical Audit Programme (NMAP) in 1998, prior to the implementation of casemix. As part of the NMAP, all acute

IT Infrastructure

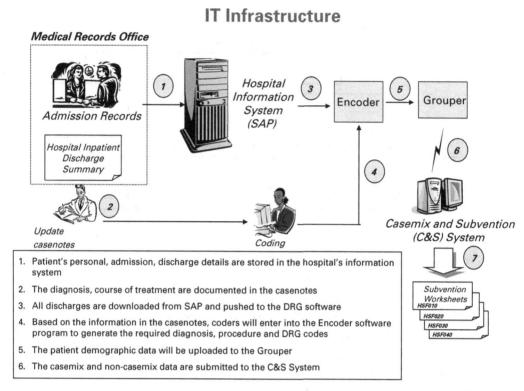

Figure 13.2 IT infrastructure

hospitals are required to submit on a regular basis a set of seven hospital-wide clinical performance indicators, adapted from the Maryland Quality Indicator Project (QIP), to the Ministry. These indicators include inpatient and perioperative mortality rates, unscheduled readmissions, unscheduled returns to the operating room, and unscheduled admissions following ambulatory procedures. These indicators did not show any deterioration in the quality of care post-casemix implementation.

Progress thus far

Improving cost consciousness

Casemix-based funding has led to greater cost-consciousness in public sector hospitals. Prior to its introduction, cost data was only available at the service (e.g. X-ray, ward, etc.) level. As casemix required patient-level cost data in order to compute the subvention for each DRG, it provided the impetus for hospitals to develop robust patient-level costing systems that enabled them to determine the cost for the whole episode of care. All hospitals are currently using such systems.

The introduction of casemix provided an opportunity for hospitals to compare their costs using a common unit of measurement. Several hospitals initiated utilization management programs[5] to optimize the use of resources. Casemix data was also used in designing disease management programs.[6] One key impetus for such comparisons occurred in 2003, when the Ministry of Health began using casemix data to publish the average bills of seventy common conditions, by hospital, on its internet website. Hospitals that found themselves to be outliers undertook reviews to reduce their costs without compromising quality.[7]

One of the key lessons from this exercise was that hospitals with the lowest cost per unit of service (e.g. laboratory test, ward charge, etc.) do not necessarily have the lowest cost for a particular admission if these services are used inappropriately. For example, a hospital with the cheapest non-standard drug would still be more expensive than another hospital that uses generic drugs.

Enhancing system efficiencies

While casemix is a useful tool in improving technical efficiency (i.e. in choosing the most cost effective options in managing a particular admission) it needs to be supplemented with other mechanisms to promote systems efficiencies (i.e. addressing questions such as, does the patient need to be admitted? or, could this patient have been better managed in the community? or even, could the disease have been prevented in the first place?).

The Ministry of Health thus moved to a hybrid funding system in 2005, in which the top seventy day surgery and inpatient conditions (e.g. cataract surgery etc., for which outcomes can be more easily monitored) are funded on a piece rate basis using casemix, while other services, including primary care services, are funded on a global budget basis. This allows the Ministry and the hospitals to 'drill down' into common conditions and extract maximum efficiency gains, while at the same time encouraging providers to consider innovative models of care for other conditions (in particular, chronic diseases, where the emphasis should be on prevention, early detection and integrated care within the community).

Areas for further study and action

Casemix-based funding can potentially promote care that is more patient-centered, rather than department- or specialty-centered, by encouraging hospital departments to adopt a collaborative approach to managing costs of entire episodes of care (e.g. total knee replacement) rather than just components of care (e.g. surgery, rehabilitation, radiological and lab. tests, etc.). However, this potential is yet to be fully realized.

One of the key enablers of this process would be to review the way the financial performance of each department or specialty is reported. Incentive systems should be structured so as to encourage more inter-departmental collaboration instead of competition.

Existing casemix systems need to be enhanced to better adjust for severity. Improved severity adjustments would facilitate comparisons of outcome. This would open up new possibilities for the application of casemix in cost effectiveness studies. There is also a need to develop casemix systems that are able to follow patients across time and services by multiple providers rather than just at the episode or encounter level.

As DRGs work on the principle of the "Law of Large Numbers" – with a sufficient number of cases, the distribution of cases would assume a normal distribution – they work well at higher levels of aggregation (e.g. at the hospital and especially at the national level). They are less effective at lower levels of disaggregation (e.g. the departmental or even the individual physician level), as the smaller number of cases means that one or more outliers can potentially skew the averages significantly. Therefore, hospitals that wish to examine resource utilization at lower levels of aggregation must develop supplementary mechanisms using additional variables, such as patient functional status.[8]

Conclusion

Within the space of slightly more than five years, Singapore has moved from a non-casemix subvention system to one where DRGs are utilized for funding, utilization management, and public reporting of hospital bill averages. Singapore adopted a pragmatic "adopt and adapt" approach in implementing casemix. More time was spent on the adapting stage, as ultimately the usefulness and/or value of a casemix system depends more on how it is used than which system is utilized.

The key success factors included strong political will and leadership, with extensive consultation and involvement such that, even if there were disagreements, there were no surprises in terms of last minute changes etc. The fact that casemix was implemented without changing clinician remuneration, budget cuts, or hospital billing systems also contributed to its rapid deployment in the public sector.

NOTES

1. There are thirteen public sector hospitals and thirteen private sector hospitals. However, the private hospitals are much smaller in size compared to the public sector hospitals.
2. Subsidies for acute healthcare services. MOH Information Paper 2004/3.
3. Casemix-based funding was implemented in mid-FY1999.
4. Splitting DRGs for Administrative and Clinical Purposes; C. E. Lee, E. K. Lim; Paper presented at the 18th Patient Classification Systems/Europe (PSC/E) Conference 2002.
5. Utilisation Management: A Cluster's Perspective; Y. J. Lim, H. Y. Tai; Paper presented at Casemix Conference Singapore 2004.
6. Using casemix and DRG data to design the National Healthcare Group Chronic Heart Failure Disease Management Programme; M. P. H. S. Toh, H. N. Tan; Paper presented at Casemix Conference Singapore 2004.
7. Evaluating the Effects of Transparency on Hospital Bills; W. Yeo, E. K. Lim, S. Chowdhury, W. Y. Mok; Paper presented at 22nd Patient Classification Systems/ International (PSC/I) Conference 2006.
8. Casemix in Singapore – Five years on; E. K. Lim, C. E. Lee; *Annals Academy of Medicine Singapore*, 33(5), September 2004.

14 Experiences with the application of the DRG principle in Hungary

Dr. Júlia Nagy, Csaba Dózsa, and Dr. Imre Boncz

A brief description of the Hungarian health care system

With the political changes in 1990, the Hungarian health care system changed from a Soviet-type health care system to the *Bismarckian traditions of compulsory national health insurance* similar to many other East European countries. After 1990, the responsibility for maintaining all levels of health care services was transferred from central to local government with a few exceptions (universities, national medical institutes).

Responsibility for the financing of health care services was given to the National Health Insurance Fund (NHIF), the only insurance fund in Hungary, and performance-related financing was introduced. As a general rule, *NHIF finances the running costs*, while coverage of capital costs is the duty of the owner of the health care institute, usually local government.

Most of the health care budget comes from *contributions*. Employees pay a contribution of 4 per cent of their gross income, and employers pay 11 per cent, without an income ceiling. In 1996 a "health tax" was introduced, which was a fixed, lump sum amount (currently 3,450 Ft/month/employee (approx. US$18.50); average income in Hungary is about US$600/month). This health tax is expected to be eliminated in the future. Although currently only about 38 per cent of the total Hungarian population pay health insurance contributions, the rest (pensioners, children, the unemployed, etc.) also receive health insurance coverage and are entitled to health care services. Until 1998, health insurance contributions were collected by the NHIF Administration; since 1999, they have been collected by the Tax Office (State Tax Authority). Approximately 57 per cent of total health expenditure is covered by health insurance contributions, 13 per cent from the central budget (general taxation), and 26 per cent from out-of-pocket payments.

Most general practitioners (GPs) are private entrepreneurs that have a contract with the NHIF. The largest portion of their revenue (64 per cent) comes from the capitation fee, adjusted for age, with a special point system for different age groups. The second largest source of GP revenue is the fixed fee (19 per cent), which, as the name suggests, covers the fixed fees of the GP, such as heating, cleaning, etc. The fixed fee varies according to the type of practice (adult, child, or mixed) and the number of patients involved in the practice. The third part of financing is a supplementary fee (5 per cent), which equalizes the differences in practice location (capital or large city, village, covering more than one village, or on the outskirts). GPs receive reimbursement for being on duty (11 per cent), and a case fee for cases not registered on their list (5 per cent). They act as gatekeepers to specialist care.

With regard to outpatient care in Hungary, a fee-for-service financing system is used. Medical procedures are listed according to the ICPM WHO code system. To keep within budgetary limits, until June 2000 there was a floating-rate system in the fee-for-service financing of outpatient care, with monthly changes in the Hungarian forint value of one performance point. In July 2000, this floating system was abolished.

Since 1993, acute inpatient care has been financed through the implementation of an American Diagnosis Related Groups (DRG)-like system, with the Hungarian term: "Homogén Betegségcsoportok," (further referred to here as DRG). This DRG-like financing system is not a pilot study in selected hospitals or regions, it covers all Hungarian acute hospitals. Physicians are reimbursed indirectly; they receive the usual salary payment, but there are several other payment methods, which depend on the type of contract between the physician and the health provider.

The Hungarian health care system is described in detail elsewhere [1].

In the drug reimbursement system, many reimbursement options and techniques are used to subsidize drug prices (normative reimbursement categories: 90, 70, and 50 per cent, fixed, and 0 per cent reimbursement; maximum reimbursement for special diseases: 100 per cent and 90 per cent; maximum reimbursement for the socially handicapped (100 per cent); reimbursement by special permit; reimbursement by special budget; no reimbursement). A detailed description of the Hungarian drug pricing and reimbursement system can be found elsewhere [2].

There are a large number of private health providers in the Hungarian health care system. Besides special enterprising operations of GPs, which are general, several outpatient units are also private, mainly in the area of modern technologies. There are only a few private providers for inpatient care.

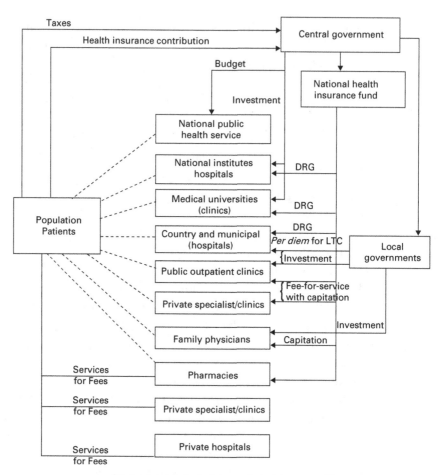

Figure 14.1 Flow of financing in the Hungarian health care system
Source: OECD Health Data 2004 [3]

A brief history of the introduction of casemix systems in Hungary

In 1986, the viability of a casemix classification method for health care provision began to be discussed in Hungary. The Hungarian hospital reimbursement system was based on a so-called input reimbursement system. The annual resource allocation for hospital care was granted based on the previous budget and modified by the inflation rate and changes in capacity (new departments, new beds), independent from actual activity levels. Hospitals created the budget plan, and after planning and discussion, local governments as payers defined the final budget. Hospitals were reimbursed on a monthly basis.

The drawbacks of this input system were already being strongly felt. Disparities had arisen in the supply structure of hospital care and in reimbursement. The treatment paths of patients were long; the route to the appropriate care was via a strictly enforced system of referrals. This represented a considerable waste of time and resources. In addition, there were several problems in determining an appropriate budget because, although in the latter years of that period some performance data were available, such as the number of patients treated and the number of different diagnoses, there was no data for health resource allocation.

Due to the reimbursement methods, the financial status of hospitals, quality of care, and accessibility were very different and unequal. Demand was growing for health care activities and performance to be measurable and appraisable.

The initial purpose of embarking on casemix development was to motivate fundamental transformation of the financing of active inpatient care, and to implement cost-efficiency and cost containment rationally. As was the case in other countries, Hungary was struggling with how to allocate the necessary resources rationally, and more productively, to health care service providers. One of the greatest obstacles to this change was the shortage of information regarding the internal utilization of resources within hospitals, and the nature of the actual activities performed. No cost calculations were prepared for health care services. In practical terms, based on the limited data available, it was not possible to judge what resources had been expended, in what manner, and with what result, and how the structure and treatment processes could be modified. In this situation, accounting for the advances in health care information technology, the casemix-type system promised a solution that could bring results.

The main objectives of modifying the hospital financing system were defined by health policy:

- patients are only to be admitted to a hospital for necessary treatment;
- only those services that cannot be provided efficiently elsewhere are to be provided by the hospital;
- patients are to receive treatment at the appropriate location and should receive the appropriate standard of treatment;
- hospital cases are to be treated cost-effectively following admission (reduction in nursing time, adherence to specified nursing times, omission of unnecessary tests);

- a basic requirement is that there should be no significant regional or other discrepancies in the availability of treatment;
- financing limitations are to be realistic.

The DRG system was also expected to assist in solving other problems in the field of hospital care; as average length of stay could be reduced, technical cost-effectiveness and allocation cost-effectiveness of treatment could also improve. Hospital cases that no longer required active care should be transferred from active hospital care to chronic hospital care in due course. It was necessary to reduce the number of hospital cases in favor of outpatient care. The structure of the hospital network could be more responsive to needs and real utilizations. The fairness of financing could be increased, by employing a system of performance-linked norms.

The preconditions for developing a DRG-like reimbursement system were very favorable by that time. The major data processing that would be required was already in operation at the national level. From 1974 onwards, the Ministry of Health regularly gathered and evaluated an approximate 10 per cent sample of the "minimal database" of inpatient care. In the early years, data were received by the central processing unit in paper form; later on, an increasing number of health care units provided the information electronically. IT applications were introduced at the larger hospitals in clinical, diagnostic, and economic management systems. Many hospitals used IT systems for admissions, recording medical data, and financial operations.

The main international code systems were also applied systematically for the purposes of managing health care documentation.

Doctors were familiar with the ICD and ICPM coding systems issued by the WHO for the classification of diseases and medical interventions. In the minimal dataset system, reports on surgical interventions were based on these coding systems. A large number of basic conditions necessary for the development of a DRG system were already available. Only the cost calculation data, needed to determine the cost-weights of the case groups, was not available at the beginning.

The first actions toward modernization started prior to the major political changes, were supported by economic and medical experts interested in technological innovations, and developed from there.

The adaptation of DRGs for use in Hungary began with a survey of resource consumption, and treatment path assessment. For a period of six months in 1986, and for the purposes of evaluation, a study was made of the most important areas of clinical care in a single hospital. This was intended to form the basis of a wider-ranging study involving several hospitals, to determine the types, characteristics, and cost requirements of hospital cases, and to define the classification algorithms.

Between 1987 and 1991, data were collected from an ever-wider range of sources. More than eighteen hospitals participated in the study. Medical universities and national health institutes also contributed data. The cost assessments and analyses, and the Hungarian grouping algorithm, were completed.

In the initial development period there were no opportunities to actively exploit international relationships, hold professional consultations, or involve specialists from abroad. Studies published in specialist literature represented the only reference point in the local development of casemix. However, the DRG principle appeared so rational and applicable that it could be feasibly implemented even through the creation of a Hungarian development base.

In 1992 – with the exception of a few special institutes, such as military hospitals – all general hospitals, universities, and national institutes introduced the IT systems necessary to operate the system and commenced the casemix assessment.

Casemix-based financing was introduced from July 1, 1993, for all active hospital events in Hungary.

Unlike other countries, where the first initiatives to develop a casemix system usually originated from universities and research institutes, in Hungary, the Ministry of Health played a key role. The development project in Hungary began very shortly after the first US application of the system. A major contributing factor to this unusual circumstance was the fact that, at this very early stage, the medical and economic universities concerned did not establish units of health economics as a scientific discipline, and had no independent faculties, professions, or training schemes. The first to show an interest in developing casemix were the universities of medical sciences. Today, a large and comprehensive health care economics and management training system has emerged, which also provides a grounding in casemix.

The casemix development was carried out by the Information Centre for Health Care in the Ministry of Health (GYÓGYINFOK). At that time GYÓGYINFOK was responsible for performing research, methodology and coordination related to health care IT, and also carried out data processing at national level.

This IT institute was established in 1973, and was intended to play a leading role in developing and distributing the computer models that could be recommended to health care service providers. GYÓGYINFOK possessed the technical resources and the experience needed to ensure the necessary professional resources for application of the casemix system.

Four key factors were instrumental in the successful and rapid development of casemix in Hungary. It seemed that, in Hungary, casemix development always reached an appropriate stage at a fortuitous time to government support and made it possible for the next step to be taken. Political changes were also a factor, mainly owing to the fact that all participants in the process of change wanted to alter their situation. When the demand for change arose at the same time, a need for performance appraisal had emerged; for all intents and purposes a system that fulfilled expectations was ready to be introduced. A further important motivating factor was the need to provide the population with health care using extremely limited resources.

Health policy makers played a *decisive, proactive* role in the process, and their commitment, both prior to the political changes and immediately afterward, enabled them to make the most important decisions: development had to begin, resources had to be provided for this and for the related IT development, and the decision to modify the reimbursement system was also decided.

The system's *workability* was ensured by the fact that the initial IT development stages had already taken place, the new technology had been incorporated into the health care system, and a national institute capable of coordinating the work and implementing the development was already up and running.

Its *acceptance* was facilitated by the fact that service providers had faith in a system of proportional resource allocation, which was fairer than the previous input financing system, and which made it possible to obtain financial revenue commensurate with performance, in accordance with predetermined rules and without the need for negotiation or other special procedures.

Its *professional background* was guaranteed by the involvement of medical specialists. In Hungary, every medical specialization had its own national institute, as well as a Medical Specialist Collegiate-Board. The specialists representing them assisted in defining the bases of a classification system and checking the calculations.

By that time, the DRG system was subject to a lot of debate in the health care sector. The entire development process, and all its results, were subjected to public professional scrutiny, thereby exposing all associated problems. Information was disclosed systematically, and continuous relationships maintained, both within the hospitals and the wider medical community.

The DRG system satisfies a fundamental management requirement: never before had a measurement system existed that was able to express, so precisely and accurately, the tasks of the hospital, its responsibilities with respect to patient care, and its performance. The main questions under debate were markedly different in the various phases of development and application.

The fundamental questions under debate were several important points of reimbursement: whether the DRG system or fee-for-services reimbursement was preferable; whether reimbursements should be uniform nationwide, or consideration should be given to levels of progressiveness; whether all treatment was to be financed based on the DRG system, or if there would be exceptions; what proportion of the total reimbursement should be DRG-based and what proportion should remain as input or fixed reimbursement; whether the cost-weights of DRGs would be determined based on surveys, or in accordance with medical protocols; and what adaptation strategy was to be applied to ensure that the modification of the reimbursement system did not cause futher problems in provision or cost containment.

In the first phase of development, the suitability of the system's fundamental principle was without question. For the majority of hospitals, any system that was capable of expressing performance was better than the current system.

Later on – citing international practices – there was strong opposition from those who supported the introduction of fee-for-service reimbursement.

Physicians supported fee-for-service reimbursement, for both outpatient and inpatient care. The result of the debate was negative, not only because of the very limited health budget, but also due to the well-known problems of that type of reimbursement system. The main argument was the limited budget.

Previously, Hungary had no tradition of offering independent payments to physicians. Also, the plan was to create clear incentives within the new system. Considering the US experience, with independent payment for doctors, seemed to lead to a different center for incentives. The original Hungarian model was one-channel payment, covering every necessary cost, including investment cost, operational cost, and physicians' salaries.

No significant debates arose with respect to the technical implementation. The coding regulations were established and computer systems developed with a focus on patient admission tasks. Various training schemes were held for doctors, computer data processors, and management. Less serious debates arose surrounding the ambitious expectations (integrated online systems) that were expressed. Finally – rationally – the introduction of complex IT systems was not incorporated into the DRG system launch.

Debates arose with regard to quality requirements. Problems described in foreign specialist literature were also debated. Serious differences of opinion arose regarding the methodology for determining the cost-weights. The debate was general. Mainly, the medical experts of different players offered to use medical protocols. There were few attempts to calculate the cost-weight based on protocols. Studies showed clearly, in every case, that cost-weight was higher than resource-consumption surveys, due to the experts maximizing the resources required and not calculating different needs and different patient paths; nor did they have knowledge of the real utilization rates of different services etc. The argument continues to this day. The experience gained over the course of applying the system made it apparent that the benefits of both approaches can be combined.

There were also disputes regarding the uniform base rate for the same cases. There was a strong demand for a higher base rate to be established in the case of national institutes and universities. The paradox of this situation is that the first studies already showed that the cost of one discharge adjusted by casemix (case with 1.00 cost-weight) at the universities was in line with the national average, while certain small municipal hospitals often provided the same care at much higher cost levels.

There is still debate about these issues, but in certain matters, practical experience and results have clarified which combination of the various principles yields the appropriate results. The elements of the current reimbursement system give a good reflection of the rational solutions developed in the possession of a deeper knowledge of the interrelated factors of hospital care, and which help to improve the financing system not as a compromise, but based on strict rationality.

The circumstances of the early phases of development were a decisive factor in the fact that today Hungary applies an independent casemix classification system, which, however, based on its classification criteria and structure, is classed as a DRG-type system.

The initial stage of development – as we have already mentioned – coincided with a change of political regime in Hungary. During this period there were not yet any functioning relationships providing the opportunity to study, and directly adopt, the US grouping system. The Hungarian version was prepared based on examples gleaned from specialist literature. This stage of development also determined the future of hospital casemix classification. During the formulation of the first version, the technology and methodological background that was created ensured the opportunity for the development of an independent classification system.

The main arguments in favor of developing a Hungarian system were that Hungary had traditionally used the ICD–9 version for coding diseases, and the American ICD–9–CM was not in use.

In this period, an adaptation of the WHO ICPM system for the coding of interventions was already in use. At the time, in order for statistical issues in Hungary to be comparable with those of other countries, it was decided to utilize the WHO coding system for all health documentation. Of course, several modifications were necessary to continue its use to the present day. An established method – more detailed than the US minimal hospital data-set – was used to define the characteristics of hospital cases and describe the condition of treated patients.

The Hungarian cost structure was, and still is, different from the cost structures of developed countries. Labor costs are relatively low, while other health care expenditures (e.g. medicines, medical devices) are relatively high when compared to other countries.

It was expected that a locally developed version would make it possible for the reimbursement system to support Hungarian health policy goals, including the strategy for adopting the new health care technologies (e.g. separate groups for higher-cost, newly subsidized and cost-effective health care technologies).

The use of an appropriate grouping system does not rule out the possibility of Hungarian data being used in international comparisons, since the coding systems used for the minimal hospital data set are compatible with the system of terms used internationally.

In light of the above arguments, the necessity of a locally developed system has not recently been called into question. The demand for international data comparison is high. As early as 1993, in cooperation with St-Etienne University in France, and in 1997–8, with the support of USAID and within the framework of a State Collaboration Project supported directly by USAID, evaluations and comparative studies with the American grouping system were conducted. These results were used to refine the Hungarian DRG system.

The launch of casemix development was clearly motivated by its application in the area of reimbursement. Health policy makers sought a rational financing method, which, replacing the traditional input financing system, would ensure the cost-effectiveness of treatment, bring the allocation of resources into line with performance (money follows the patient), and provide incentives to improve care (based on quality and quantity criteria), while ensuring the sustainability of available resources.

From the beginning, it was obvious that for health policy makers, the casemix system also served other objectives besides financing. For example, it could be used to support health care planning, quality control, the definition and evaluation of quality indicators, measurement of treatment results, epidemiological studies, and needs assessment.

Following the development of the system, its multi-purpose application was implemented. It was incorporated into all related tasks, and has become an accepted, everyday comparative tool and regulatory device.

The application of the system for financing purposes began nationwide on July 1, 1993, and extended to all active inpatient care positions.

In order to ensure safety during the transition and sufficient time for adaptation, the first DRG-based reimbursement system included special regulations. There were nationally uniform dataset and data submission standards and uniform classification. At the national level, the reimbursement parameters and cost-weights were the same for every hospital.

At the beginning of DRG implementation, the base rate differed from hospital to hospital. The initial base rate was calculated using the total budget for a certain hospital in the basic period (1992) divided by the number of discharges adjusted by casemix in that hospital (1992). The result of that calculation was the initial base rate for a hospital for the next year. It took several years of adaptation to eliminate the disparities in hospital base rates that existed in the initial years. Besides this, to comply with cost containment issues, the hospital base rate changed monthly in line with changing activity (i.e. it was announced retrospectively).

To ensure hospital viability, it was decided that hospital revenues could not be less than 0.66 per cent of the previous financing amount. The reimbursement fees only covered operating costs. Investment costs were funded from other sources.

Operating costs also extended to cover the costs of physicians. For extremely expensive new health technologies, supplementary reimbursement methods were applied.

Under the DRG system, it is possible to spread the various risks of reimbursement (higher number of cases, more seriously ill patients, relatively higher-cost treatment) that can arise as a result of how reimbursement amounts are determined. At the national level, the active hospital sector had a closed budget. The annual closed budget was divided into twelve equal amounts. Each month, the total output of the active hospital sector was calculated using the DRG system. Based on a hospital's base rate and output, the monthly reimbursement was calculated. But, due to the closed monthly budget, by considering the amount and total activity of the hospital sector, the monthly base-rate modification factor was calculated. It meant the reimbursement was based on real activity with many modification factors. (Later the system was simplified with a national predefined base rate.)

Remaining within national budgets, the financial risk for any increase in the number and cases with higher cost-weight was transferred to the community of hospitals, although those hospitals that increased their activity could increase their payments. The Hungarian model of risk-sharing attempted to allocate risk according to how the players (hospitals, community of hospitals, National Health Insurance Fund) were able to handle the factors.

Risk was allocated to the community of hospitals and the National Health Insurance Fund when inpatient cases with the coding were higher, and risk was on the provider side when resource usage for certain individual cases was higher than the cost-weight.

The first version of DRGs used for reimbursement was very similar to the American HCFA DRG version, comprising main groups and a major diagnostic category for each organ system. It differentiated between surgical and non-surgical events. In several cases it took into account related diseases and age.

The benefits of applying casemix are also obvious to the hospitals. Besides their application for financing purposes, DRGs also had a profound impact on the evolution of hospital performance and cost control. Through its use in internal incentives systems, it transformed internal performance and cost-settlement systems. Initially, the institutions participating in the adaptation experiments, and later all inpatient institutions, began applying casemix evaluation methods, both in the area of control and in the development of their internal settlement and incentives systems.

The current situation

Today we have full DRG-based reimbursement, excluding investment cost. Before this was achieved, we went through a transition period. After the implementation, taking into account the ramifications of the system and adhering to the basic principles and regulations, several modifications were made to both the classification and the financing systems. The system's application became increasingly widespread, with a growing number of health care services reimbursed with the help of the DRG system.

The classification system actually used groups hospital cases into about 800 groups. The DRG (called HBCS in Hungary) system comprises groups that are developed on an ongoing basis. The system currently applied retains the basic HBCS classification system. However, within this, several refinements have been made, which, through an improved understanding of the nature of hospital treatment, have made it possible to better adapt the system to medical principles and challenges.

In addition to the definition of the main groups, the development of the first version of the DRG system was also assisted by statistical assessments, which ensure the homogeneity of medical criteria and resource requirements of the cases. The value of this basic methodological rule was borne out over time. However, besides this, the following classification modifications took place, also taking into consideration the consequences of over-coding.

Several ICD–10 codes are for diseases defined as acceptable main causes for admittance to active hospital care, and others are not included among those diseases.

The secondary diseases are additional classification criteria for moderately serious hospital cases only. There is no rationale for differentiating very severe diseases according to their secondary diseases, since they are usually accompanied by serious complications. Nor is it advisable to differentiate minor illnesses based on their complications, since, in the course of care provision, their treatment cannot represent or cause any significant risks for more resource needs.

There are numerous criteria and preclusions for the accounting of secondary diseases as grouping factors. Here it should also be noted that certain illnesses which are also defined as being among secondary diseases cannot be acceptable as grouping factors.

The list of very serious secondary diseases is limited. Only those cases with genuinely severe outcomes are included among the diseases that could be considered as classification criteria. DRGs with major co-morbidity can only be accounted for if therapeutic interventions (confirming procedures) are performed that entail life support, carried out in intensive care units.

The present system uses the ICF (International Classification of Functioning) coding system for determining the patient's condition in the case of chronic hospital care.

Table 14.1 Characteristics of the official versions issued to date

Version	Period of availability	Main characteristics
HBCS 1.0	July 1, 1993–June 30, 1994	The first Hungarian DRG-like version. No general correspondence between operations and ICD code
HBCS 2.0	July 1, 1994–February 28, 1997	The operations and ICD codes correspond to each other. From January 1, 1996, application of ICD–10
HBCS 3.0	March 1, 1997–September 30, 1997	Changes in the number of groups and the process of classifying very serious, complicated cases
HBCS 3.1	October 1, 1997–March 31, 1998	Changes in upper day limit, according to the application of guarantee rule
HBCS 3.2	April 1, 1998 to April 30, 1999	New groups in the fields of cardiac surgery, hematology, and pulmonology
HBCS 4.0	May 1, 1999–May 31, 2000	The version with some very distinctive Hungarian characteristics, where some grouping rules are not based on foreign DRG systems
HBCS 4.1	June 1, 2000–March 31, 2001	New groups in the field of short-term cases and emergency cases
HBCS 4.3	April 1, 2001–January 31, 2004	Decrease in the number of groups of smaller diseases with attached disease. New groups according to age groups in child-care and in some groups for adults
HBCS 5.0	February 1, 2004–November 30, 2005	Changes in DRG weights due to an increase in public sector wages of 50% on average. Preference of disease groups with operations (surgery, urology, gynecology)
HBCS 5.1.	December 1, 2005	New groups for chemotherapy based on reimbursement medical protocol and new groups for minor surgery to harmonize the reimbursement fee with outpatient's payment.

In a few cases, more cost-proportionate financing is ensured by taking into account supplementary HBCS (e.g. IVIG treatments), as well as multiple interventions.

In several HBCS groups, confirming procedures were also taken into consideration as the grouping factors of a higher resource-needs, higher standard of treatment. The system contains special groups for emergency cases requiring acute treatment over a short period. For events on the borderline between outpatient and inpatient treatment, special low-value HBCS groups were defined. These new considerations were added to the homogeneity criteria of the groups. In addition to professional and cost-effectiveness considerations, the current groups are also homogeneous in terms of the minimum requirements for treatment, based on the treatment competencies, and the expected patient's path, based on the "guarantee" criteria.

A feature unique to the current Hungarian system is that, in the individual hospital care groups, the classification also takes into consideration the treatment set out in medical protocols. For the time being, this principle is only applied in one specialist area, chemotherapy. Around 300 medical protocols have been created for solid tumor treatments, taking into account the indication and the chemotherapeutic active ingredients, which are financed in twelve types of HBCS groups. The groups are only homogeneous in terms of their cost requirement; the other parameters differ from one protocol to another. The statistical principle (calculation of cost-weight, classification of groups regarding main diagnosis, secondary diagnosis, main treatment, and other grouping factors) can be combined with a protocol-based principle (treatment according to strict medical treatment regulations and procedures) in all those cases where the medical requirements have been clarified in a "medical reimbursement protocol" and the indication has been underpinned with a cost-effectiveness study. This evolution is summarized in Table 14.1.

The extension of casemix systems in Hungary

The DRG system is widely used for reimbursement for active hospital care, including special care. The use of the casemix system in active hospital care can be regarded as 100 per cent (nationwide coverage), since the data are gathered, processed and classified at a basic level for all treatments financed within the social insurance system. The financing of active inpatient treatment – with the exception of the previously mentioned supplementary financing – takes place under the DRG system.

Essentially, the Hungarian system covers the treatment of inpatients admitted for more than 24 hours, but also includes several special provision forms between inpatient and outpatient care.

DRG reimbursement covers "one-day" surgery. The one-day surgery or clinic represents a treatment event where the length of the hospital stay is usually less than one day. The exceptions are where the patient's condition or other illnesses make a longer period of hospital treatment necessary. Longer

Table 14.2 Cost content of the Hungarian HBCS: average cost distribution of 1,000 HBCS cost-weights

Cost content of medical and accommodation services for average hospital cases (investment cost excluded)	Per cent (%)
Medical services	
1.1 Drug	11.55
Diagnostic and therapeutic services	
1.2.1 Histological tests	0.38
1.2.2 X-ray, ultrasound examinations	3.11
1.2.3 Gastrointestinal endoscopy	0.15
1.2.4 Laboratory test	2.58
1.2.5 Surgeries	11.12
1.2.6 Implants	2.21
1.2.7 Physiotherapy	0.46
1.2.8 Radiotherapy	0.04
1.2.9 EEG	0.03
1.2.10 EKG	0.20
1.2.11 Other diagnostic services	1.54
1.2.12 Psychiatric activities	0.52
1.2.13 Other therapeutic services	2.23
1.2.14 Special medical materials	0.76
1.2 Diagnostic and therapeutic services total	25.33
1.3 Other physician's activities at department	12.23
1 Medical activities total (1.1+1.2+1.3)	49.11
Nursing activities	
2.1 Staff	11.13
2.2 Nursing materials	4.75
2.3 Other nursing cost	0.14
2 Nursing activities total	16.02
Other departmental cost	
3.1 Staff	0.80
3.2 Materials, others	2.66
3 Other departmental cost total	3.46
4 Medical and nursing activities total (1+2+3)	68.58
Accommodation services (hotel)	
5.1 Staff	4.53
5.2 Non-medical materials	1.59
Ancillary services	
5.3.1 Maintenance	1.39
5.3.2 Energy, gas, water, heating, etc.	2.88

Table 14.2 (*cont.*)

Cost content of medical and accommodation services for average hospital cases (investment cost excluded)	Per cent (%)
5.3.3 Laundry, sewing, etc.	1.82
5.3.4 Central sterilization	0.89
5.3.5 Dietary services	5.37
5.3.6 Others	4.14
5.3 Ancillary services total	16.81
5 Accommodation services total	22.93
6 Total cost of medical, nursing and accommodation services (4+5)	91.52
7 Overhead cost for central management	8.48
8 Total cost (6+7)	100.00%

Source: National Health Insurance Fund Administration

periods of hospital treatment are obviously not prohibited in these cases, but the reimbursement fee is the same regardless of the length of the stay.

For the financing of brief emergency cases (generally requiring treatment that lasts more than six, but less than twenty-four hours), special DRG groups exist (so-called emergency care groups).

The purpose of the emergency subsystem is to ensure that hospital treatment for cases that are generally less major, but which give cause for alarm, is accounted for and classified in cost-proportionately financed groups rather than as longer-term inpatient treatment.

The system also covers certain 'serial treatments' by outpatient units. Characteristically anti-tumor therapies (chemotherapy, radiation therapy) – depending on the condition of patients and the availability of service providers – may also be provided in outpatient care, or, in the course of a given treatment process, therapy commenced in the framework of inpatient care may be replaced with ambulatory treatment. All of these treatments are documented and reimbursed within the same HBCS system.

(It was partly this extension of coverage by DRGs which caused an increase in the number of hospital cases.)

The current system does not yet cover rehabilitation, although the preparations for the development of a chronic DRG system have been made. In chronic care, which includes rehabilitation, financing is currently based on a daily fee. The amount of the daily fee is calculated using a multiplier that differs for each task group.

Reimbursement parameters are uniform for every Hungarian hospital

Cost-weights in Hungary are nationally uniform (Table 14.2). The duration trim-points for each group are determined taking the guarantee criteria into consideration. In the case of chemotherapy, the guarantee accords with the requirements of the protocol. National base rates are uniform and predetermined. The predictability of the system has increased substantially. The base rates no longer change on a monthly basis, but are announced in advance for longer periods.

The basic fee does not currently cover equipment amortization costs, just operating costs. However, it does provide cover for physician payments.

Regulation of reimbursement parameters

In 1998, an important advance was made when the Minister for Health regulated, in a decree, the system for the calculating the fees for DRGs and other health care services, and for modifying other financing parameters.

Based on the experience gained in the course of determining fees in previous years, the regulations specified the uniform and transparent methodology for calculation, the standards and procedural rules, and the organizations involved in the implementation of tasks and the preparation of decisions and the role that they play.

In Hungary, an established system exists for the maintenance of DRG parameters. It is a strategic objective: to create the role of health insurance

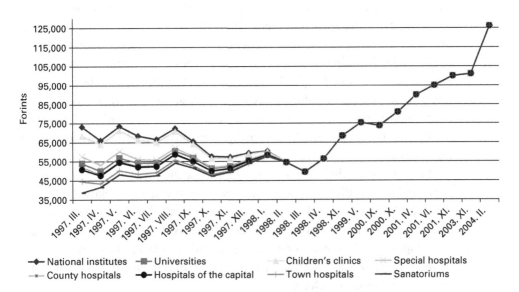

Figure 14.2 Closing the gap between base rates of different hospital groups

purchaser, so that openness, transparency, controlability, and cost-efficiency can be guaranteed when determining the reimbursement parameters of health care services, and thus the parameters and groups of the DRG system. The process of updating the financing fee parameters of health care services is regulated by the Minister's Decree on the statutory regulation of professional code systems and the maintenance of financing parameters.

There are different players (the National Health Insurance Fund Administration (OEP), professional organizations, national institutes, medical collegiate boards, Ministry of Health Refinement Working Committee on Reimbursement Parameters) involved in preparation and decision processes regarding reimbursement parameters.

The task of determining financing fee parameters is closely related to other areas of health care regulation. The most important related areas are determining minimum professional requirements and the acceptance of surplus capacities, including new health technologies, into coverage by the National Health Insurance Fund Administration.

Criteria to be fulfilled when performing maintenance tasks related to reimbursement parameters and DRG definitions include transparency with standardized, accepted methodology.

One of the most important data sources for the refinement of reimbursement parameters is a survey of the resource consumption of hospital cases. Usually this entails an itemized assessment of the services provided to patients, including medicine consumption, in respect of all medical services over a patient's total length of stay. The measurement unit is one hospitalization, including every departmental event. There are two versions of the survey. In one, within a certain period (usually two months), every discharge is included in the study. The other includes only certain types of hospitalizations. Usually, 5 per cent of the total hospitalization was observed (about 100,000 cases). (In several cases, the survey also covered the surgical services when each surgery event requiring hospitalization was also observed.) The number of hospitals involved in the study varied between eighteen and forty. This cost survey is a regular task for the system.

Hospitals provided other cost data regarding cost-centers (medical departments, ancillary services, management units, etc.). Based on these data, the DRG costs of the observed cases are calculated. Besides a homogeneity study, the development of the DRG classification algorithm entails the adoption of new health technologies, and the clarification and deletion of inappropriate classification criteria. The reimbursement parameters are issued in a Minister's Decree.

Basic reimbursement regulations

Full reimbursement is not payable if the length of stay of certain hospitalizations does not reach the lower trim-point, (e.g. if the patient was transferred to another hospital before the end of the normative length of stay specified for the DRG). A hospital case is one reimbursement case, regardless of the number of departmental events, except where treatment is provided over a sustained period (at least thirty days) in a chronic care unit between two active departmental events. Where the patients were readmitted prior to the upper trim-point, new reimbursements will not be settled, except for a few urgent, independent DRG groups (e.g. trauma, AMI, stroke, etc.). For those cases that continue beyond the upper trim-point (day-outliers), a limited daily fee is payable, the amount of which may not reach that of the lowest daily fee for chronic care. For very expensive hospital cases (cost-outliers) if the certified cost is more than five times the fee for the DRG group, then a supplementary fee is payable.

Several supplementary rules under DRG reimbursement

Some expensive devices and interventions come under itemized financing (e.g. organ transplants, the more costly vascular grafts, drug-emitting stents, etc.). (Previously, a few chemotherapy treatments also fell into this category. However, for the purposes of financing, these treatments are also managed within the DRG system.) New health care treatments (e.g. large joint prosthetics, coronary stents, hemodynamic dilatory catheters, etc.) are only included in this reimbursement category during a transition period. After a few years, they are incorporated into the main DRG financing system.

Chronic hemodialysis is reimbursed under a separate system, based on fee-for-service settlement; regardless of whether the patients are treated in hospitals or in outpatient care. Hospitals that provide a higher level of progressive treatment are entitled to receive supplementary fees. The differences in reimbursement between hospitals are basically created by the DRG settlement. The base rate and cost-weights are identical. Additionally, in recognition of the fact that a higher proportion of the more severe hospital cases within the same DRG group are admitted to university clinics and national institutes, these receive supplementary fees. However, these supplementary fees are based on total volume and case composition. No more than 1.5 per cent of the annual active hospital budget is allocated for this purpose.

An availability payment, which is also a small percentage of the annual active hospital budget, is given to provision units. These are more affected by random factors, which make it more difficult to plan and schedule treatments. Often, management has only limited means at its disposal to create the optimal operating conditions and utilization ratios, such as centers for infectious diseases, traumatology, and urgent care.

Ensuring adequate hospital care is also a central target of the present health policy. One of the most important and difficult problems associated with the provision of hospital care is how to optimize the quantity and content of hospital treatment by ensuring that certain forms of treatment are only given to patients with a genuine need.

One of the key factors in the efficient application of all output-oriented financing systems, and therefore the financing of inpatient treatment, is how to prevent unnecessary hospital admissions. However, this aim runs contrary to the incentive provided by output-financing systems to achieve the highest possible performance volumes.

The most flexible regulatory elements (i.e. those that adapt to actual treatment requirements) for the restriction of hospital care volumes have not yet been developed, but even the existing Hungarian system attempts to apply a few checks and controls.

Hungary controls hospital activity through the coverage procedure for new providers and services

This coverage procedure brings the volume, professional composition, and scope of activity of the facilities participating in the treatment into line with actual requirements. The entry of new health providers into public financing occurs within the framework of a restricted and regulated system, based on a tender issued by the insurance fund, or an independent application. In both cases, the actual health services needs of insured patients and the equalization of accessibility are key factors. The adoption of new health technology also takes place within a regulated procedure.

After several years of continuously increasing hospital-sector activity, there is now volume control through the setting of health provider performance limits, and using the digressive reimbursement of surplus volumes

The maximum total volume of already adopted capacities and services that may be settled for is specified for each individual hospital based on its 2003 activity. Within a given year, full base rate reimbursement cannot be provided above this. A digressive fee, proportional to the surplus performance, is payable. (In most cases, when a hospital generates +5 per cent activity, the reimbursed base rate is only 60 per cent of the total reimbursement fee, and in the next range (+5–10 per cent activity) it is just 30 per cent. In cases where there is NHIF acceptance of new capacity, a "volume" increase is possible.) In the system – with a few exceptions – restrictions on total volume are the norm. This is a relatively flexible means of restricting performance, as it pertains to total volume, not to the individual activities themselves. Within that specified volume, the hospitals can flexibly restructure their activities to focus on high-priority hospital care, and have special treatment management competency within the boundaries of the given budget. The annual case number for certain very costly or new health care technologies is restricted to service level. For very expensive health care technologies, the treatment's inclusion is decided based on strict selection criteria. This must be confirmed with supplementary medical information submitted in addition to the hospital base data. This is the only means of ensuring that the treatment is cost-effective.

There are also strong attempts to limit the unnecessary activity of hospitals with a managed care system

Over the past few years, a treatment management system has also been in operation within the health service on an experimental basis. Under this system, certain health care service providers undertook – within a per-capita financing system – the management of all services used by patients from a given general practitioner's catchment area, including hospital treatment. The treatment managers settle with the hospitals, as well as with the other cooperating health care service providers, in accordance with the rules of the HBCS system, while the documentation of performance usage takes place within the uniform nationwide performance settlement system, through the management of "virtual accounts." This experiment was also launched with the objective of optimizing the use of hospital resources.

Harmonization of reimbursement for outpatient and inpatient care is also a very important element to achieve the appropriate structure of care

Since the introduction of the DRG system, another focus for debate has been the means of achieving treatment procedures under which the necessary treatment is performed within the framework of outpatient medical care in less serious cases. One solution could be to harmonize the fees for outpatient and inpatient care. This would involve a considerable reduction in fees for certain low-value surgical procedures, while the fees for the same treatment in outpatient care would rise significantly. The fees for non-urgent hospital treatment, which did not require surgical intervention, were considerably reduced. This cut down on unnecessary treatment, without compromising the standard of care received by patients.

The DRG system has been supplemented with quality assurance elements

In Hungary, service providers need an operating license to provide health treatments. The operating license specifies a treatment level. The personnel and material conditions for providing the various levels of treatment are regulated for each profession.

It also regulates which DRG groups may be performed by the individual professions for each treatment level. This means that certain DRG groups may only be accounted for at a higher treatment level, or by service providers operating in a special professional field. (Simply meeting the quality requirements is not enough to receive financing. Service providers who possess an operating license must undergo a financing accreditation procedure to be allowed to settle with the health insurance fund for services performed.)

In certain cases, the competency and the necessary professional conditions of the treatment levels are determined at or within DRG level, by medical procedures.

Several quality indicators were established to analyze health care provision

One important advantage of using the DRG system is that the quality parameters of treatment can be evaluated using a minimum of data. In Hungary, programs have been launched with the aim of developing quality indicators [4, 5]. The values of certain treatment parameters have already been made public. The publication of the results sparked considerable media controversy. A problem was caused by the explanation of the indicator values, which pointed out that it is necessary to evaluate all of the factors involved in the treatment in order for both the medical profession and the patients to receive satisfactory information.

Development of disease treatment protocols

In the interest of providing quality care, improvements have also been made to professional standards, protocols, and recommendations. The Ministry of

Health published several medical protocols jointly with the Medical Collegiate Boards. These contained diagnostic and therapeutic recommendations for a given disease or group of diseases. When formulating the medical protocols, the results of technological assessment were also taken into consideration. Today, these protocols are in need of refinement. However, this provides an opportunity for well-controlled and properly evaluated treatment procedures to be developed with regard to the most significant hospital events. The medical protocols help to control the cost-weights and adjust the results of the cost survey.

The planning of the annual budget

The budget for inpatient care has been carried out under the DRG system for several years. Recently, large-scale regional development concepts have been unveiled. The casemix information was once again used in planning calculations and needs assessments.

Health care management training and health care IT training have been developed

The teaching of casemix skills constitutes a part of the syllabus. Initially, regular training courses were held for hospitals. These teaching materials have become part of the syllabuses of official training centres.

The appropriate local information system needed for payment is a basic requirement for the DRG reimbursement system

For the operation of the performance-based reimbursement scheme, the hospitals receive a free settlement program supported by the Ministry of Health. These bare-bones settlement programs are capable of gathering basic data, performing the logical verification of the submitted data, and presenting settlement results. Hospitals may use any program to perform settlement tasks, with the proviso that the data service must be performed in the manner (with regard to content and form) specified in the decree. The required technical form for submitting data is defined as the record communication standard. This is a special, regulated system of electronic communication used for the purposes of data provision, under which health care regulators determine, at statutory level, the mode, form, and content for the electronic provision of data by participants in the health system.

Hospitals submit their data for settlement on a monthly basis, on the tenth day following every given month. At the end of the second month following the given month, they receive financing based on their performance, after it has been centrally processed.

Within hospitals, data processing results related to the settlement of output are usually recorded in the patient admission systems. The majority of hospitals are networked. The basic unit of observation is the departmental case. In most hospitals, a person is designated in each department to ensure data accuracy. Nearly every hospital has a quality control department, the duties of which include control and correction of the minimal dataset needed for reimbursement. When it was introduced, the system was totally centralized, and trained health care workers were involved. Today, these specialists remain, but it is more common for this work to be primarily overseen by doctors. Decentralization is also typical; medical departments have taken on increased responsibility for data provision.

An unusual feature of the Hungarian system is the involvement of quality control businesses in data provision. Their role has not been positive in every respect. Initially, they conducted a study of error in data provision, as an external audit for hospital management. In the latter part of this study, support for over-coding was clearly afforded greater emphasis.

The DRG health care provision database is widely used

With the exception of personal data, everyone has access to the health care data. Hungary has strict data protection laws regarding access to health care data, yet at the same time regulations also stipulate that access must be provided to data gathered at the state's expense. The provision of data to certain public entities is free, with the content and deadlines of data provision regulated in a decree. For others, a data access fee is usually charged. DRG data are also widely used for health economics analysis [6]. Many scientific papers utilizing data based on the Hungarian DRG system have been published [7, 8, 9, 10, 11, 12, 13].

Impact, debates, controversies

Development of the DRG system began almost twenty years ago. For more than twelve years, it has been used continuously for the reimbursement of active inpatient care. The DRG system has lived up to expectations, since it is capable of precisely expressing the competencies of hospital care, is suitable for determining output, and can be linked to incentive rules in the interests of optimizing the use of resources or achieving professional goals.

However, in itself the DRG system is merely a classification system which attempts to express the characteristics of hospital involvement in health care. It is unequivocally capable of supporting many health care policy goals. It is not capable of solving all the problems of health care provision.

The DRG system plays a key role in expressing the differences between the various hospital care events, in terms of their expected cost requirement. It is also capable of expressing and fulfilling specific health policy goals and quality requirements. Thus, for example, if a health care system wishes to give preference to certain forms of care, these events can be separated in the classification, and their treatment encouraged by allocating higher fees etc. The DRG system can also be used to coordinate the process of care, since financing can be allocated not only to a single hospital care event, but also to a series of events. Much is also dependent on the type of financing system to which it is applied, and the nature of its relationship with the financing of other care levels.

In the last few years, health care provision has undergone several major changes, some of which – among other influences – resulted from the innovative role played by the DRG-based approach.

The role of DRGs was fundamental in the realization of basic health policy goals. One of the key factors when assessing any health care system is whether it is capable of satisfying the principles of cost-effectiveness, cost limitation, and fairness. The application of the DRG system has a number of proven strengths for achieving these goals.

The DRG system unambiguously supports *technical cost-effectiveness*, since, in effect, its fundamental principles already embody this requirement. The system provides the hospital with a financing budget for the treatment of specified case types, and the amount of the allocation does not change, even if the hospital operates with longer nursing times and higher resource usage.

Regarding *allocation cost-effectiveness*, it obviously cannot provide a complete solution, since the coordination of allocations between care levels also requires other types of regulation. However, the DRG system is able to successfully cooperate with other regulatory elements in the interests of allocating resources efficiently.

The DRG system is a suitable means of achieving *cost containment*. It is capable of providing far more flexible restrictions, which can be adapted to suit care requirements. The risk management problem that arises from changes to costs can be reduced to an acceptable level with DRG. It is also capable of imposing restrictions selectively. The DRG system is not cost limitation in itself, since it allocates budgetary funds depending on case type. In the Hungarian system, the risk of cost limitation by case type affects the service providers, while the risk of an increase in output owing to changes in patient numbers and the severity of cases affects the community of service providers within the closed fund.

The principle of fairness is supported by the fact that all patients have access to appropriate care, and patients with more serious conditions can also obtain the appropriate care. Access to services is also facilitated by the fundamental principle, independent of DRGs, that all hospitals are obliged to treat all residents within their catchment area, but patients are also free to choose an institute from outside their area.

As a result of the Hungarian application of the DRG system, quantifiable results have been achieved in hospital care

In the past ten years, the average length of active hospital care has decreased by at least 33 per cent. Parallel to this, the number of hospital beds in operation has fallen considerably, although there could still be further substantial reductions; the process is not yet complete. A political decision is also necessary for a further reduction in the number of beds.

The output of the hospital sector has increased dramatically. This is partly attributable to the incentive nature of the output financing of the DRG system.

The growth is concentrated in two main areas. The amount of spending on new, modern technologies rose considerably, as did the number of related cases (PTCA, anti-tumor therapies, laparoscopic procedures, implantation procedures, catheter operations, etc.). Besides modern treatments, the number of non-serious cases that are less likely to require hospital care has also risen. The refinements built into the regulations over the years have served as a global brake on the rise in hospital care. A successful strategy was provided by the Hungarian version of volume control, which curbed the upward trend in a flexible manner, relying on care management abilities. In the area of new, modern technologies, the professional monitoring and patient selection system currently being developed as a complementary system could guarantee compliance and cost-effectiveness. The identification and formulation of the optimal places and methods for care management could lead to significant advances.

The global output growth was accompanied by a global budgetary brake in the form of a significant decline, in real terms, in hospital budgets. It can be assumed that there is a close relationship between this and the fact that the DRG system has rendered hospital care manageable in a situation where the health care system has been subjected to major restrictions. This means that the budgetary cuts have not reduced access to services, modern technologies have been able to evolve, and patients have access to these new treatments. There are no waiting lists, with the exception of a few expensive treatments such as transplants, to which access is very limited. The only way to ensure this was for hospitals, spurred on by the incentives of the DRG system, to choose the path of increasing their output while utilizing resources more rationally. However, it should also be highlighted that all this took place disproportionately, to the detriment of HR incomes and through the abandonment of comfort requirements; this is not sustainable over the long term.

In the allocation of internal hospital resources – as confirmation of the above – major changes took place. Basic hospital care cost data proves that while hotel costs fell and medicine consumption ratios declined, the ratio of other diagnostic and therapeutic costs rose considerably in comparison to the base period. (This was largely attributable to technological innovation.)

The utilization of care became more balanced at the national level; the money follows the patient. The mobility of patients within the country is less restricted. The differences in usage that emerged between the areas are not primarily due to the means of financing, but result from care management problems.

The "redistribution" of health care tasks between hospitals took place at the beginning of the process. The national institutes and universities increased their output, to the detriment of Budapest, county, and municipal hospitals. This also improved access to the higher care levels for patients.

In the course of implementing the system, the phenomenon known as DRG creep was also strongly felt. However, opportunities for up-coding are limited. In the interests of reducing DRG creep, changes have been made to the coding regulations and classification system. The most serious system flaw – caused by unjustified, erroneous increases in output – occurred in this area, because a suitable control system was not developed in Hungary. Controls were slow to be implemented and problems with the system created the opportunity for up-coding in the expectation of securing extra revenue. However, up-coding is always easy to track and localize within the system.

Overall, the quality of patient care has not deteriorated. The avoidable mortality indicators of hospitals have not worsened. The premature discharge of patients, and lack of provision of necessary treatment and medicine has occurred. Although these phenomena are detrimental and to be avoided, they cannot be unambiguously attributed to the DRG system. A reduction in budgetary financing opportunities, accompanied by the introduction of other means of financing, could also aggravate these problems. In the Hungarian system – taking note of international experience – protective elements were incorporated in the interest of ensuring adequate care. One such element is the guarantee rule, which does not allow repeated financing in the case of returns made within a specified time frame. For this reason, the definition of quality care, minimum care requirements, the development of medical protocols, and the use of quality indicators are important regulatory elements.

The system has not improved consistently; in some cases, it has gone backward. One such regulatory problem was represented by a period of around eighteen months during which professional multipliers were introduced as a factor to modify national cost-weights. The basic fee differed from one hospital to another for a period of four years. Shortly after this, the basic fees were equalized over a one-year period, and financing became completely uniform.

The criteria for implementing a normative system were only partially fulfilled, since the basic fee does not cover long-term secured assets.

Recently there have been several problems which will require future investigation. One of the imported problems arose because of uncontrolled access. HBCS in themselves can only enhance efficient care following justified admissions. One cannot expect hospitals to limit unjustified admissions on their own. However, this has had an impact in spite of the fact that the funds for paying for hospital services are a closed system on the national level with fixed national monthly reimbursements and a monthly adjustment factor to ensure enforcement. As a result, the monthly adjustment factor causes a continuous decrease in base rates. The proportion of patient referrals by their own outpatient unit was high compared with other units. (For example, 33.85 per cent of total hospital cases initially, increasing to 36.93 per cent following implementation.)

The high rate of hospital care has been a problem for the health sector for some time. The reimbursement system for patients, as well as the peculiar internal interests of the hospital personnel, have not enabled the development of the necessary harmonization among possible forms of care, not

Table 14.3 Main characteristics of acute care in Hungary

	1995	2000	2003
Total number of hospital beds	92,603	83,430	79,832
Number of acute care hospital beds	76,367	64,836	60,433
Share of acute care beds from total number of beds	82.50%	77.70%	75.70%
Number of acute care hospital beds in operation per 10,000 population	74.4	64.7	60.4
Number of patients discharged from acute care wards	2.3m	2.4m	2.559m
Number of performed nursing days in acute care, in days	20.8m	17.3m	17m
Average length of stay in acute care, in days	8.9	7.1	6.65
Percentage occupancy rate of acute care beds	71.5	73.2	77.17

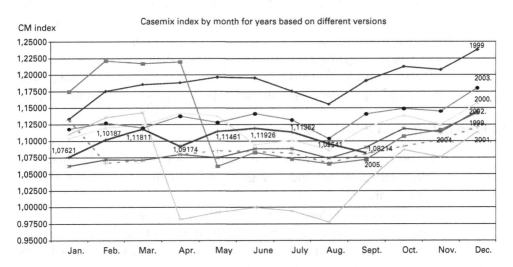

Figure 14.3 Monthly changes in the casemix index (CMI) in different years with different DRG versions. Some further aspects of the Hungarian DRG system are published elsewhere [14, 15, 16, 17, 18, 19, 20, 21].

only among outpatient specialist care, primary health care and inpatient care, but also between forms of social welfare services and hospital care. Patients are not required to make a co-payment for nursing care delivered at active or rehabilitation wards, whereas for nursing care delivered in special nursing homes, the obligatory co-payment to be made corresponds to a certain percentage of the minimum old-age pension. Hospital capacities are high, whereas bed occupancy rates are low, even with high utilization. Thus, the interests of patients and those of hospitals coincided. The implementation of the HBCS was not able to prevent this unfavorable trend.

In Hungary, the weak point of the system is the lack of adequate data control by NHIF. Additional efforts in this area will be necessary in the future.

The innovative role of the DRG system in the development of hospital management

The DRG system has prompted fundamental changes in hospital management. Previously, the role of management extended to the procurement of the resources necessary for providing care. However, managers did not possess a measurement tool suitable for the exact performance of their planning and management tasks.

As a result of the changes, hospital management has become more enterprising. The focus has shifted towards economic and professional control, the demand to provide care for as many patients as possible, and the requirement to remain within cost limitations. Internal settlement systems have been transformed, and an internal incentive system has emerged. Hospitals have developed quality assurance systems, adapted treatment protocols, and have undergone structural transformations. Departments have been established to implement controls, and IT has also taken on an important role.

The beneficial effect on patient care

The DRG system has eliminated regional disparities. All hospitals are entitled to the same fee, and they are expected to provide every patient with the same standard of services.

Reimbursement follows the patient, and this has increased the value of the patient to service providers. The treatment of as many patients as possible has become a key survival factor for service providers, which puts patients in a more favorable position. Patients are not generally refused admission. Patients from rural areas are frequently admitted to Budapest hospitals and national institutes. A competitive situation has emerged with respect to hospital care, in order to attract patients.

This is also corroborated by the fact that, as a result of the system, waiting lists have risen to a limited extent. This is also related to the fact that an informal incentive system continues to thrive.

A higher reimbursement fee is available for serious cases. This means that today there is more incentive to admit patients with serious conditions than under the previous system. Several factors affect access to certain hospital services: management of the patient's path, differences in physician knowledge, distance from hospital units, etc. Although the reimbursement follows the patient, the patient follows the capacity, and more capacity in certain regions could result in higher relative utilizations.

The impact of the DRG system on the health market

Important changes in the health care system were achieved by the implementation of the prospective reimbursement system based on DRGs, in that hospitals, instead of being "public institutions," started to operate as entrepreneurs within the conditions of the regulated health market with contract elements. They could emphasize several market elements. Thus, the amount of hospital turnover depends on their activities. This output-oriented system is a result of hospital choice, which replaced the restrictive rules of the previous system. Market goods, prices, and quality needs are defined, and access to these goods is regulated. The conditions are the same for public and private hospitals, when they have a contract with NHIF.

There were regular debates in the Hungarian health management literature on the experiences of the DRG system, which described both the achievements and the limitations of the adoption of DRG principles into the Hungarian setting [22, 23].

Perspectives for further development

Covering new health care areas by casemix: The focus of further modernization

Casemix development has continued. Preparations are under way for the development of a classification system for chronic hospital care. The medical protocols have been prepared. Preliminary analyses have been conducted. However, the development process is not yet complete.

Casemix development has also started in the field of ambulatory care. In Hungary, service providers submit base data for the financing of outpatient care that is similar to that used in hospital care. The sets of data can also be managed together.

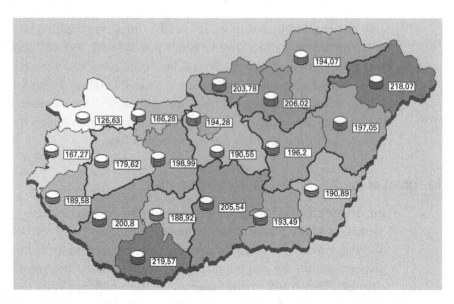

Figure 14.4 The activity (cumulative relative weight / 10,000 persons, by region, September 2005)

Casemix development could also migrate to classify the total episodes of health care or the patient group.

Adjustment of relative weight by required normative coverage for amortization is necessary for DRG systems to improve equipment utilization

Currently, HBC rates relate to operating costs, with development costs being channelled to the institutions from different sources and funds through different decision-making mechanisms based on different interests (from the municipalities owning the facilities, earmarked state funds, foundations, etc.). Efficiency requirements relate only to operating costs and do not involve assets and equipment. Currently, the procurement and placement of expensive machines and equipment are not properly influenced by the expected extent of utilization, possible exploitation, and efficient use. Therefore, the appropriate ways of addressing the issue of amortization need to change.

One of the challenges for casemix-based reimbursement is how to support new health technologies in a cost-effective way?

Many innovative health technologies introduced in recent years have resulted in increases in the health budget. HTA studies show clearly that new technologies are often cost-effective for selected patient groups, although in daily practice, they are often overused. Encouragment of the most cost-effective utilization of technology (DES, very expensive drugs for chemotherapy, etc.) is one of the major challenges for reimbursement. Health services are reimbursed based on output-oriented methods, such as the DRG-like reimbursement system for hospitals, fee-for-service for out-patient care, and capitation for GPs. Depending on the type, life-phase, and role of new health technologies in the total provision of care, different reimbursement strategies will be required to transfer these technologies into practice. The most interesting adjustment questions are how to combine the process of coverage and reimbursement policy, and how to clip interest among the different levels of care. Hungary established a regulated coverage process for new technologies, and there are several ongoing attempts to combine the process of coverage and the refinement of reimbursement parameters.

DRG as a casemix-like reimbursement method has helped ensure the viability of the health care system in Hungary

In acute inpatient care, the DRG principle as a new financing method has contributed to the successful survival of the Hungarian health care system. The introduction of new financing methods has been accompanied by a significant decrease in the financial resources allocated to health care financing.

REFERENCES

1. Boncz, I., Nagy, J., Sebestyén, A., Kőrösi, L. (2004) Financing of Health Care Services in Hungary. *European Journal of Health Economics*, 5(3): 252–8.
2. Gulácsi, L., Dávid, T., Dózsa, Cs. (2002) Pricing and Reimbursement of Drugs and Medical Devices in Hungary. *European Journal of Health Economics*, 3: 271–8.
3. OECD Health Data 2004. Paris: OECD.
4. Belicza, É., Balogh, Á., Szócska, M. (2001) Performance Indicators of Hospital Care: Evaluation of Acute Myocardial Infarction Patient Care. [In Hungarian: A kórházi ellátás minőségi indikátorai: az akut myocardialis infarctus kezelésének értékelése] *Orv Hetil*, 142 (21): 1003–9.
5. Belicza, É., Takács, E., Boncz, I. (2004) Development of an Indicator System for Evaluating the Quality of Health Care Services. [Indikátorrendszer kialakítása az egészségügyi szolgáltatások értékelésére] *Orvosi Hetilap*, 145(30): 1567–72.

6. Szende, Á., Mogyorósy, Z., Muszbek, N., Nagy, J., Pallos, G., Dózsa, C. (2002) Methodological Guidelines for Conducting Economic Evaluation of Healthcare Interventions in Hungary: A Hungarian Proposal for Methodology Standards. *European Journal of Health Economics*, 3: 196–202.

7. Sebestyén, A., Boncz, I., Dózsa, Cs., Nyárády, J. (2004) Cost Analysis of Peritrochanteric Fractures According to Types of Surgical Treatment and Progressive Care from the Viewpoint of Financial Providers. [In Hungarian: Trochantertáji törések ellátásának költségvizsgálata a műtéti eljárások és a progresszív ellátási szintek szerint finanszírozói szemszögből] *Orv Hetil*, 145(21): 1115–21.

8. Boncz, I., Sebestyén, A., Pál, M., Sándor, J., Ember, I. (2003) Health-economic Analysis of Cervical Cancer Screening. [In Hungarian: A méhnyakrák szűrések egészséggazdaságtani elemzése] *Orv Hetil*, 144(15): 713–17.

9. Csomós, Á., Hoffer, G., Fülesdi, B., Ludwig, E. (2005) The Incidence and Cost of Severe Sepsis in Intensive Care Units. [In Hungarian: A súlyos szepszis gyakorisága és kezelésének költsége intenzív osztályon] *Orv Hetil*, 146(29): 1543–7.

10. Boncz, I., Sebestyén, A., Börzsei, L., Nyárády, J. (2005) Market Share and Progressivity in Surgery According to the System of Diagnosis Related Groups (DRGs). *Eur Surg Res*, 37(S1): 19.

11. Sebestyén, A., Boncz, I., Börzsei, L., Nyárády, J. (2005) DRG-based Cost Analysis of Femur Neck Fractures in Patients with and without Complications using the Hungarian HBCS System. *Eur Surg Res*, 37(S1): 18.

12. Boncz, I., Sebestyén, A., Hoffer, G., Ember, I. (2004) First Results of the Hungarian Nation-wide Organized Breast Cancer Screening Program. *Anticancer Research*, 24(5D): 3440.

13. Boncz, I., Sebestyén, A., Dózsa, Cs., Pál, M., Nyárády, J. (2004) The Effect of the Implementation of Diagnosis Related Groups (DRGs) on Trauma Care in Hungary. *European Journal of Trauma*, 30(S1): 180–1.

14. Jávor, A., Bordás, I., Nagy, J. (1990) Introduction of the DRG System to Hungary. In: *Lecture Notes in Medical Informatics, Budapest*.

15. Bordás, I., Nagy, J. (1991) Measurement of Hospital Performance based on DRGs. [In Hungarian] *Egészségügyi Gazdasági Szemle*, 29: 37–49.

16. Nagy, J., Bordás, I., Weltner, J., Illés, S. (1997) Refinement of HBCS and the Results of New Versions Considering Homogeneity and Redistribution of Resources. 13th International PCS Europe Working Conference, Florence, Italy.

17. Kiss, Zs., Molnár, A., Dublinszki, P. (2005) Experiences with the Activity-Volume Controlled Financing System. [In Hungarian: A teljesítmény-volumen korláton alapuló finanszírozás tapasztalatai.] *Egészségügyi Gazdasági Szemle*, 43(1):

18. Fábián, T., Kincses, G. (1993) Critical Review of the Financing System of Prospective Payment / Diagnosis-Related Groups, based on experiences in the United States of America. [In Hungarian] *Orv Hetil*, 134(10): 523–6.

19. Kroneman, M., Nagy, J. (2001) Introducing DRG-based Financing in Hungary: A Study into the Relationship between Supply of Hospital Beds and Use of these Beds under Changing Institutional Circumstances. *Health Policy*, 55: 19–36.

20. Darago, L. Improving the DRG system in Hungary. *Stud Health Technol Inform*, 95: 818–23.

21. Darago, L. (2004) Caseview_HUN: Easy DRG Overview. *Stud Health Technol Inform*, 105: 182–9.

22. Boncz, I., Nagy, J. (2003) Ten Years of Experiences with the Adoption of the DRG Principle From a Financial Point of View [In Hungarian: A Homogén Betegségcsoportok (HBCS) rendszerének 10 éves tapasztalatai finanszírozói oldalról] *Egészségügyi Menedzsment*, 5(2): 21–7.

23. Dózsa, Cs. (2004) "Aggressive" DRG Policy in Hungary: Questions and Answers about the Function and Future of the DRG System [In Hungarian: "Agresszív" HBCS politika Magyarországon: kérdések és válaszok a HBCS rendszer működésével és jövőjével kapcsolatban]. *Informatika és Menedzsment az Egészségügyben (IME)*, 3(4): 14–20.

15 Casemix systems – past, present, and future: The Canadian experience

Sandra Mitchell and André Lalonde

Introduction

Canada, with a population of over 32 million, is a democratic federation consisting of ten provinces and three territories (spread over almost ten million square kilometers – comprised of very large rural / northern sparsely-populated regions).

Canada has a national health insurance program, often referred to as "Medicare," which is designed to ensure that all residents have reasonable access to *medically necessary hospital and physician services*, on a prepaid basis. Instead of having a single national plan, Canada has a national program, composed of thirteen interlocking provincial and territorial health insurance plans, all of which share certain common features and basic standards of coverage. Roles and responsibilities for Canada's health care system are shared between the federal and provincial / territorial governments.

While provincial and territorial governments are responsible for the actual management, organization and delivery of health services for their residents, the *Canada Health Act* (CHA), Canada's federal health insurance legislation, outlines five key principles that provinces and territories must meet through their health insurance plans to qualify for full federal funds under the Canada Health Transfer (CHT).

The CHA sets out the primary objective of Canadian health care policy, which is "*to protect, promote and restore the physical and mental well-being of residents of Canada and to facilitate reasonable access to health services without financial or other barriers.*"

Canada's health care spending was expected to reach $160 billion in 2007 (representing 10.7 percent of Canada's GDP), up from the $37 billion in 1984, when the *Canada Health Act* was introduced. A large part of this

Canada Health Act Principles

1. *Public administration:* Health insurance plans are administered and operated on a non-profit basis by a public authority responsible to provincial and territorial governments.
2. *Comprehensiveness:* Provincial and territorial health insurance plans must cover all health services insured under the Act (mostly physician and hospital services) and, where permitted, services rendered by other health care practitioners.
3. *Universality:* Every eligible resident of a province or territory is entitled to insured health services covered by the insurance plans. Residents are generally required to register with the plans in order to get coverage.
4. *Portability:* Residents receive coverage regardless of where they live and whether they move between provinces and territories. Coverage must be extended by the home province or territory for up to three months during the wait time for new coverage.
5. *Accessibility:* Provinces and territories must provide reasonable access to insured health services without discrimination on any basis, including ability to pay. This entitles residents to insured services in the location where services are provided, and as services are available.

increase is attributable to population growth, health sector inflation, increased use of health services, new drug therapies and the relative explosion in the use of new technologies. More than two-thirds (~70 percent) of Canada's total health spending comes from the public sector, while the remaining 30 percent relates to private sector spending, through private insurance programs and out-of-pocket expenses. While public programs in all jurisdictions cover a core set of services provided by physicians and hospitals (public funding for these services is 98 and 93 percent respectively), coverage for other types of care differs somewhat among provinces and territories in such areas as prescription drugs, dental services, home care services, non-hospital-based therapeutic services, etc. Hospital expenditures continue to make up the largest component of health care spending accounting for close to 30 percent of total health expenditure.

Over the last ten years or so, a variety of organizational delivery structures, accountability requirements, and funding models have emerged in Canada, with an increasing move towards the regionalization of health services and the use of population-based and/or casemix approaches to funding. This has resulted in an increased reliance by the provincial governments on casemix tools, methodologies, and case weights.

History of casemix development in Canada

Canadian Casemix Groups (CMG) were originally developed in the early 1980s as an adaptation of the American Diagnosis Related Groups (DRG) system, by the Hospital Medical Records Institute (HMRI), which later became the Canadian Institute for Health Information (CIHI). HMRI served as holder of the largest national database (Discharge Abstract Database) for hospital-based administrative data. Its services included the provision of monthly, quarterly and annual reports to hospitals and provincial/territorial ministries of health. The impetus to introduce the CMG methodology to Canada was identified by HMRI as a tool for utilization management that would allow hospitals to compare similar cases and length of stay patterns within and across facilities. The latter was accommodated via peer group comparative reports, based on facility bed size. The CMG methodology, designed for use with hospital acute care inpatient cases, was first introduced in Canada in 1983. Much of the adaptation process was directed at adjusting the DRG system that was built using ICD–9–CM codes, for use with the classification systems in use in Canada (i.e. the WHO version of ICD–9 and the Canadian Classification of (Diagnostic, Therapeutic, and Surgical) Procedures (CCP)). During the latter part of the 1980s, HMRI's redevelopment efforts were targeted towards creating a more "Canadian" version of CMG (to reflect differences in clinical patterns and hospital lengths of stay between both countries) using activity data from the Canadian Discharge Abstract Database (DAD). By 1987, the original CMG adaptation was also mapped back to ICD–9–CM and this methodology has since been applied to both coding systems as some provinces implemented the ICD–9–CM classification system.

HMRI's casemix experts (classification specialists, statisticians, methodologists, and analysts) under the guidance of a Physician Advisory Committee (PAC) led much of this development/adaptation work. PAC consisted of clinicians and researchers who provided expert clinical advice on classification and casemix issues. This group was supplemented by an RIW Technical Working Group (RIW TWG), which assumed responsibility for developing resource indicators such as Expected Length of Stay (ELOS) and Resource Intensity Weights (RIW), used to measure/estimate resource utilization and costs. The RIW methodology concept, introduced in 1987 (and later modified in the early 1990s) was based on the New York Service Intensity Weights (SIW).

About the Discharge Abstract Database

The Discharge Abstract Database (DAD) is a national database that contains information related to hospital inpatient and day surgery events. Currently, over four million records are submitted to the DAD annually. Inpatient records submitted to DAD represent 85 percent of all inpatient discharges in Canada. Each record in the DAD captures standard clinical, demographic and administrative data on a patient-specific basis. The database, in its present form, includes data from fiscal years 1979–80 to 2007–8.

The DAD was originally developed in 1963, in collaboration with the Ontario Hospital Association, the Ontario Medical Association, and the Ontario Ministry of Health, to collect data on hospital discharges in Ontario. Over time, it has expanded to provide national coverage (excluding hospitals in Quebec). Information from the DAD is widely used by health care facilities, ministries of health and researchers. Its primary uses are for system planning and evaluation, utilization management, research, and funding.

In 1993, ten years after the CMG methodology was introduced, CIHI introduced its Day Procedure Groups (DPG) methodology. The DPG methodology, developed to address the information needs of ambulatory care, was modeled on an American system, the Products of Ambulatory Surgery, and was adapted for use in Canada after careful evaluation and mapping between the two different classifications of procedures, CCP and ICD–9–CM. The DPG methodology was initially used to monitor day surgery procedures only, but advances in medical technology, changes in anesthesia use and techniques and the drive for lower cost service delivery have enabled the shift of several other types of procedures from the inpatient to the outpatient setting. In response to requests from hospitals and to assist the process of monitoring the transfer of cases from inpatient to outpatient surgery, a clinical review was conducted which resulted in certain CMG being designated as "May Not Require Hospitalization" (MNRH). This group of CMG represented a target population for a possible shift to outpatient services. Thus, the growing shift to ambulatory surgery could be evaluated by monitoring CMG and DPG in parallel. Presently, hospitals are more likely to make use of ambulatory care indicator reports, provided by CIHI, rather than relying on the MNRH data. In fact, the MNRH concept was discontinued with the introduction of the CMG + methodology in 2007.

In 1997, CIHI restructured its CMG methodology by introducing a complexity (Plx) overlay, and age group adjustments. While the actual number of CMG was reduced as part of this restructuring, each CMG was further refined with the addition of one of four complexity levels and one of three age groups.

In the mid-1990s, CIHI recognized the need for a more comprehensive methodology than DPG to fulfill the information needs of the ambulatory care setting. To this end, it undertook the development of a new ambulatory care grouping methodology, adapted from a methodology developed in the province of Alberta. This resulted in the introduction of the Comprehensive Ambulatory Classification System (CACS), which encompassed day surgery, emergency and ambulatory clinic services. The increasing demand for a comprehensive ambulatory grouping methodology reflects a change in the emphasis on information. Information about ambulatory services is no longer required primarily to evaluate the rate of transfer to this lower cost environment. Rather, ambulatory care has been acknowledged as a setting of choice for the delivery of a wide range of services and it has become increasingly important to have comprehensive information to manage this setting appropriately. The National Ambulatory Care Reporting System (NACRS), an administrative database and collection system, was created to enable the collection of data elements for CACS grouping purposes. The province of Ontario mandated the collection of NACRS data for day surgery cases, hospital emergency rooms, and select clinics, in 2001.

With the recent implementation of the Canadian modification of the *International Statistical Classification of Diseases and Related Health Problems – 10th Revision, Canada (ICD–10–CA)*, as well as the CIHI-developed *Canadian Classification of Health Interventions (CCI)*, CIHI has been actively engaged in redeveloping the above casemix methodologies so as to take full advantage of the increased clinical specificity provided by these new classifications. Furthermore, CIHI has also been actively involved in developing a number of other casemix methodologies to address the need of such health sectors as continuing care, rehabilitation services, home care and mental health. More details on CIHI's current casemix methodologies, as well as recent developmental work, are provided in subsequent sections of this chapter.

Responsibility for casemix development and maintenance

All nationally mandated casemix methodologies used in Canada are developed and/or maintained by the Canadian Institute for Health Information (CIHI). Created in 1994 by Canada's health ministers, CIHI is a federally chartered, but independent not-for-profit organization, responsible for coordinating the

About CIHI

CIHI serves as a focal point for collaboration among major health players – from provincial governments, regional health authorities and hospitals to the federal government, researchers and associations representing health care professionals. CIHI provides Canadians with essential statistics and analysis about their health and their health care system. CIHI's core functions include:

- identifying health information needs and priorities;
- conducting analysis and special studies and participating in / supporting health care system research;
- supporting the development of national health indicators;
- coordinating and promoting the development and maintenance of national health information standards (including minimum data sets, coding and classifications systems and grouping methodologies);
- developing and managing health databases and registries (CIHI currently maintains more than 20 national databases relating to health expenditures, health human resources and health services);
- funding and facilitating population health research and analysis, conducting policy analysis and developing policy options;
- providing appropriate access to health data;
- publishing reports and disseminating health information; and
- coordinating and conducting education sessions and conferences.

A sixteen-member Board of Directors governs CIHI. Its membership strikes a balance among the health sectors and regions in Canada. The Board provides strategic guidance to both CIHI and the Health Statistics Division at Statistics Canada. In addition, the Board maintains strong links with the Conference of Deputy Ministers of Health.

development and maintenance of an integrated health information system for Canada.

CIHI was originally created through a merger that brought together a number of programs, functions and activities from the Hospital Medical Records Institute (HMRI), the MIS Group, Health Canada (Health Information Division) and Statistics Canada (Health Statistics Division).

As noted previously, CIHI relies heavily on external advisors/experts to ensure that its casemix methodologies remain current and relevant to users. Over the last few years, CIHI has established a number of new committees and working groups to provide advice and guidance to its casemix team, as it pursues the redevelopment of its acute care grouping methodologies, and expands its activities beyond the acute care health sector. In addition to the ongoing work of its Casemix Advisory Group (CMAG), previously referred to as the RIW TWG, but with an expanded scope beyond acute care indicators, CIHI established a Grouper Redevelopment Advisory Committee (GRAC) to guide its redevelopment efforts for the CMG, DPG, and CACS methodologies. Supporting the efforts of these two groups is a newly established network of physicians and surgeons (in lieu of the standing PAC group that was disbanded in the late 1990s) which provides expert clinical advice on classification and casemix issues.

Casemix systems in use in Canada

This section describes all the casemix methodologies (and associated health resource indicators) used across the continuum of care in Canada, including inpatient and outpatient acute care, rehabilitation, long-term care, mental health and home care. Detailed information on CIHI's current redevelopment activities, most notably CMG+ that was launched nationally in April 2007, is provided later in this chapter. Before learning about the future methodologies, it is important to understand how they evolved, as this explains the key drivers for the evolution as well the crucial underlying data and technical concepts.

Casemix groups with complexity overlay (CMG/Plx)

Casemix Groups (or CMG) are the Canadian equivalent of the DRG system. Introduced in 1983, the CMG system adapted the ICD–9–CM-based DRG system to accommodate ICD–9/CCP classification systems. The creation of a Canadian grouping methodology stemmed from the fact that those involved in health care management wanted to:
(a) improve the comparability of national health care data;
(b) enhance the relationship between diagnoses and length of stay (LOS), especially secondary diagnoses that contribute to longer LOS; and
(c) provide a tool for utilization management based on Canadian health care data.

Since the CMG system was a direct adaptation of the DRG system, it shared the same body system approach as its first step to classifying cases. In fact, the Major Clinical Category (MCC) in the CMG system is essentially the same as the Major Diagnostic Category (MDC) structure in the DRG system. However, the similarities stopped there as different criteria were used to further subdivide cases.

Casemix Groups are based on the Canadian concept of the Most Responsible Diagnosis (MRDx). This is defined as the condition that was responsible for the greatest portion of the patient's length of stay and/or resource use. Similar to most DRG systems, the logic of the grouping methodology is structured around the assignment of an MCC that is analogous to an MDC used for DRG assignment. Grouping takes into account the presence of surgical interventions that the patient may have received. In earlier years, some groups were split on the basis of age and complicating or co-morbid conditions.

In 1997, CIHI introduced its complexity overlay (Plx). This identified diagnoses beyond the Most Responsible Diagnosis (MRDx) that had an influence on the patient's length of stay and resource use. "Plx" groups represented more homogeneous clusters of patients with similar clinical and resource utilization characteristics. Complexity levels were determined through the use of "grade list" diagnoses (co-morbidities) that combine within the medical or surgical partition of each MCC to influence the course of a patient's treatment. Complexity "grades" were established as: (A) life-threatening conditions; (B) conditions having important length of stay impact; (C) chronic disease; (D) debilitating conditions; and (P) psychiatric conditions associated with increased length of stay. Plx levels are derived from the combinations of the graded diagnoses into four levels: (1) no complexity; (2) complexity related to chronic conditions; (3) complexity related to serious/important conditions; (4) complexity related to potentially life-threatening conditions.

CIHI's process of data collection includes identification of diagnoses by diagnosis type. In addition to MRDx, diagnoses can be characterized as: Type 1 (Pre-Admit Co-morbidity), Type 2 (Post-Admit Co-morbidity), Type W, X, or Y (Patient Service Transfers) or Type 3 (Secondary Diagnosis). Secondary diagnoses do not influence complexity. The most recent (2003) CMG methodology had a total of 478 base-CMG groups, whereas the DRG system has between 321 and 367 base-DRG groups.

Together, Plx with age adjustment improve estimates of resources required to treat certain classes of patients – specifically the young, the elderly and the medically complex. These estimates are more sensitive than those previously available with respect to individual patient characteristics such as:

- the type and number of co-morbid conditions;
- the time of onset of co-morbid conditions;
- conditions affecting multiple body systems; and
- the patient's age group.

While CIHI did not make substantive changes to the CMG methodology following the introduction of the Plx overlay, it did produce annual updates to the associated resource indicators, including Expected Length Of Stay (ELOS) and Resource Intensity Weights (RIW). Discussion regarding CMG+, which was replaced by CMG/Plx in April 2007, is provided later in the chapter.

Day Procedure Groups (DPG)

The Day Procedure Groups (DPG) methodology is a national grouping methodology for hospital-based ambulatory care that focuses on the area of day surgery. The most up-to-date DPG methodology (prior to the implementation of the CCI refined version in April 2006), assigned cases to one of seventy-seven (77) mutually exclusive groups according to the principal or most significant procedure (based on CCI codes) recorded as part of a standard outpatient record or abstract. Cases assigned to the same DPG category represent similar clinical episodes and are intended to be homogeneous with respect to resource consumption.

Comprehensive Ambulatory Classification System (CACS)

The Comprehensive Ambulatory Care Classification System (CACS) is a national grouping methodology for ambulatory care patients which includes emergency departments, clinics and same-day surgery. The methodology (prior to the implementation of ICD–10–CA and CCI refined version in April 2006) consisted of over 400 clinically and resource homogeneous cells organized into nineteen Major Ambulatory Clusters (MAC) based on body system or functional grouping. In this methodology, patients are grouped according to main diagnosis, principal procedure, visit disposition and anesthetic technique data, collected via CIHI's National Ambulatory Care Reporting System (NACRS).

Resource Utilization Groups (RUG-III)

This methodology is applied to data submitted to CIHI's national Continuing Care Reporting System (CCRS), and is used to assign facility-based continuing care residents to one of forty-four resource utilization groups, based on clinical characteristics collected with the Resident Assessment Instrument (RAI) Minimum Data Set (MDS 2.0). The RUG-III methodology may be used to support facility, regional or provincial/territorial-level service planning and analysis of resource utilization in facility-based continuing care.

Resource Utilization Groups – home care (RUG–III–HC)

This methodology is applied to data submitted to CIHI's national Home Care Reporting System (HCRS), and is used to assign each home care resident assessment to one of twenty-three resource utilization groups, based on clinical characteristics collected with the Home Care Resident Assessment Instrument (RAI) Minimum Data Set. The RUG–III–HC grouping methodology may be used to support regional or provincial/territorial-level service planning and analysis of resource utilization in home care services.

System for Classification of Inpatient Psychiatry (SCIPP)

The System for Classification of Inpatient Psychiatry (SCIPP) is a *per diem*-based algorithm that has forty-seven patient groups as outputs. SCIPP was developed and tested with Version 1.0 of the MDS–MH and includes diagnostic, clinical scales and behavioral factors in differentiating the various patient groups. SCIPP has been cross-walked by researchers to Version 2.0 of the MDS–MH (i.e. the original SCIPP algorithm has been converted so that it can be applied to Version 2.0).

Rehabilitation Patient Groups (RPG)

In April 2008, CIHI implemented the Rehabilitation Patient Group (RPG) methodology developed for inpatient medical rehabilitation, which relies on data (i.e. patient diagnoses, functional status, length of stay (LOS), and social demographics) collected using the Functional Independence Measure (FIM^{TM}), developed as part of the Uniform Data System for Medical Rehabilitation (UDSMR). The FIM is a standard measure of the type and amount of human assistance required for a person to perform basic life activities. It contains eighteen items, each of which has seven explicitly defined performance levels and is the property of Uniform Data System for Medical Rehabilitation, a division of UB Foundation Activities, Inc. The FIM describes two dimensions of disability: one involving physical tasks, referred to as "motor," and the other involving communication and cognition, referred to as "cognitive." CIHI adopted this system for use with its national Rehabilitation Reporting System (NRS).

Resource indicators (used in CIHI grouping methodologies)

The following describes some of the key health resource indicators produced by CIHI for use with its various grouping methodologies. These include: Expected Length Of Stay (ELOS), Resource Intensity Weights (RIW), Ambulatory Care Weights (ACW), and Casemix Indices (CMI) values.

Length of stay (LOS) indicators (used only for the CMG/Plx methodology)

Every year, CIHI produces updated length of stay (LOS) indicators, which have been calculated using the most recent clinical activity data available from the Discharge Abstract Database (DAD). The LOS indicators represent an estimation or prediction of "typical" length of stay for all cases within the CMG, based on actual cases occurring during the reference period. Before the introduction of complexity, there was only a single value for all "typical" cases within each CMG. The predictive value used was simply the average length of stay (ALOS) for typical cases in that CMG. As a result, the ALOS was also the ELOS or expected length of stay.

In the complexity methodology, where age is found to be predictive of length of stay, the patient's age group (0–17, 18–69, 70+) is used to further refine the Plx group estimate of ELOS. Where a CMG is refined for both age and complexity, as many as twelve analytical groups or cells will result. These are referred to as APlx cells.

A trim point is calculated for each APlx cell, and this is used to identify cases as outliers if the patient's actual LOS is greater than this trim point. For atypical cases such as outliers, deaths, acute care transfers and sign-outs, complexity levels are assigned, but ELOS is not. Quarterly reports are available to each hospital, which summarize the experience of each case with respect to length of stay. The actual length of stay is compared to similar cases in the national database and comparisons are provided at various levels of aggregation, such as by doctor or patient service. Examples of how LOS reports are used are: review of bed utilization and LOS patterns; monitoring the allocation of beds to service/program areas; research and planning for future service requirements; and assigning expected date of discharge.

Resource Intensity Weights (RIW) (used for CMG/Plx and DPG methodologies)

The Resource Intensity Weight (RIW) methodology is a resource allocation methodology for estimating the costs of both acute inpatients and day surgery cases. The RIW is used to standardize the expression of hospital case volumes, recognizing that different patients represent different burdens on health care resources. After weighting, volumes can then be expressed in terms of "weighted cases." RIW are estimates of the resource intensity of particular cases relative to an average inpatient cost, and values are updated yearly.

RIW values are assigned to each analytical cell of the grouping methodologies (CMG, DPG, Plx) and are defined by a model of how case costs and ELOS vary by CMG, Plx level and age. The estimation procedures are specific for three different sets of cases: those with a course of treatment "typical" of the cases in the cell; those with "atypical" courses of treatment; and day procedures.

Typical cases are those with a LOS at or less than the trim point established for the cell. Atypical cases are defined as: deaths; transfers to or from other acute care institutions; voluntary sign-outs; and long-stay outliers. The patient LOS used to differentiate inliers from outliers is based on the patient's total LOS, including any days identified as alternate level of care (ALC). This acknowledges that non-acute days of stay generate costs, and therefore should be included in the estimation of RIW values.

Up until 1999, CIHI used an American database from the State of Maryland to calibrate its RIW values. This database contained information (including standardized charge data) on all inpatient and same-day surgery cases provided in the State of Maryland. Adjustments were made for hospital-specific factors, which affected patient charges. Hospital-specific factors include: teaching status; size; factor input prices; and the demographics of referral populations. These adjustments were made using a Hospital-Specific Relative Value (HSRV) method. This method removes these hospital-specific effects through iterative computations of population relative values from hospital specific estimates. Finally, the weights were adjusted for differences between Maryland average LOS and CIHI ELOS. This LOS adjustment relied on the separation of routine and ancillary (RA) charges that vary with length of stay from fixed charges that do not vary.

Since 1999, CIHI has completely abandoned the use of the Maryland charge database and has been using patient-specific costs collected from over forty health care facilities in the provinces of Ontario, Alberta, and British Columbia.

For the DPG calibration database, no LOS adjustments are made. With this database the first step was to compute the average charge by procedure, which was then weighted by the day procedure volumes from the most current CIHI fiscal year database. The weighted average of the mean charges by procedure was calculated for each DPG and each type of atypical case was calculated differently. As with the CMG RIW methodology, DPG RIW values are now calculated using only Canadian case cost data.

Ambulatory Cost Weights (ACW) (used for the CACS methodology)

The Ambulatory Cost Weights (ACW) methodology (prior to changes introduced in April 2006) is a relative resource allocation methodology for estimating ambulatory care case cost data (grouped using the CACS grouping methodology). These values are produced in a similar fashion as those for RIW, with the exception that ACW estimates are calculated relative to the average cost of a hemodialysis visit, and are currently not subject to any adjustments using the HSRV methodology.

Casemix Indices (CMI) (used for the RUG-III methodology)

Casemix Indices (CMI) are values reflecting the daily relative weight of resources used by an individual within each RUG-III group compared to a base resource level (the average resource use of the resident population). Each of the forty-four RUG-III groups has a unique CMI value, derived from time and motion studies and average wage rates. These values are updated on a yearly basis (based mostly on health professional wage rates data obtained from the province of Ontario).

Recent challenges

Impact of changes in classification systems (from ICD–9/CCP to ICD–10–CA/CCI)

Starting in April 2001, CIHI initiated a phased implementation of new diagnosis and intervention classification systems (ICD–10–CA and CCI). While the introduction of ICD–10–CA and CCI is expected to bring significant benefits through the use of classification systems that reflect current clinical knowledge and practices, its staggered implementation over a period of years posed a major challenge in terms of providing comparable data from year to year and across jurisdictions.

In an effort to achieve some comparability during the phased implementation, CIHI developed a modified ICD–9 based grouping methodology (using ICD–10–CA and CCI conversion codes), for use until such time as fully ICD–10–CA/CCI-based grouping methodologies could be developed.

Analysis of DAD data for the provinces having implemented ICD–10–CA and CCI in fiscal year 2001/2 indicated that the change in classification systems was causing shifts in the cases assigned to existing CMG and DPG, which was affecting the ability to conduct time-series analysis (at the CMG and DPG level), as well as creating some challenges in the use/interpretation of the associated resource indicators, such as RIW and ELOS.

To address this issue, CIHI undertook a detailed review of the codes used to convert data from ICD–10–CA/CCI to ICD–9/CCP or ICD–9–CM. As a result of this review, CIHI made a number of changes to the conversion codes used in these grouping methodologies. However, given that many of the shifts were due in large part to the structural changes and increased specificity of these new classification systems, the changes made to the conversion codes did not entirely address the shifts in the number of cases assigned to the CMG and DPG. Based on its analysis, CIHI undertook to provide clients with extensive documentation on the impacts arising due to the differences in classification systems and coding standards. CIHI also recalibrated the affected resource indicators, so as to ensure that these more accurately reflected the new "patient mix" introduced in these converted CMG and DPG methodologies. Finally, CIHI launched a project to totally redevelop its acute care grouping methodologies, using ICD–10–CA and CCI activity and cost data (see next section for details).

Variations in coding practices

At approximately the same time as CIHI identified issues relating to the use of its "converted" grouping methodologies, CIHI also identified increasing concerns that variation in coding practices in some hospitals was probably compromising the comparability and utility of the DAD data. To examine these concerns more closely, CIHI undertook an extensive analysis of several years of DAD data (going back to the introduction of its complexity overlay methodology). The analysis found large increases in the volume of grade list diagnoses reported by hospitals in Ontario and New Brunswick (since 1996–7). While much of the increase observed in New Brunswick appeared to be explainable through recent changes in their coding practices (New Brunswick had historically under-reported diagnoses), the same could not be said for Ontario. (Ontario, with its population of over 11 million, contributes more than 40 percent of the data found in the DAD, and is also a major contributor of patient-specific cost data that is used to calibrate RIW and to redevelop the new inpatient grouping methodology.) The Ontario increases had a major impact on case distribution by complexity level, weighted cases, and LOS performance.

The results of a two-year CIHI re-abstraction study also revealed higher than average rates of diagnosis discrepancies for some of the Ontario hospitals included in the sample.

The analysis also demonstrated that in addition to the increased coding and reporting of Types 1 (pre-admit) and 2 (post-admit) diagnoses in Ontario, the variation in reporting rates between hospitals had increased, and the comparability of this data between hospitals had been reduced. While the findings suggested that the changes in the Ontario data were at least partially a result of attempts by hospitals to maximize their RIW weighted cases for funding purposes (Ontario being one of the only provinces to provide additional financial incentives based on outputs, as measured by changes in weighted cases), this increase was not uniform across all peer groups, with teaching and large community hospitals being more susceptible to increased reporting. These observations led the Ontario Ministry of Health to decide that it would not use weighted cases based on CIHI's complexity levels for hospital funding purposes. Further, the Ontario Ministry of Health and Long-Term Care commissioned a reabstraction study of its case cost facilities to ensure that the activity data being used in the development of CIHI's new grouping methodology (CMG+) was reliable and valid.

These analyses, coupled with the recent CIHI DAD re-abstraction studies, helped CIHI to identify steps that needed to be taken to address variations in coding practices. Some of the actions initiated by CIHI since then include:

- the establishment of a national committee to develop recommendations to enhance/improve the overall quality of its DAD data;
- the release of enhanced rules relating to diagnosis typing;
- increased education of health records staff across the country;

- the implementation of more stringent monitoring of DAD submissions; and
- a comprehensive review and evaluation of the continued use of diagnosis typing in its new acute care inpatient grouping methodology.

Perspectives for the future

As previously noted, the implementation of ICD–10–CA and CCI across Canada necessitated the redevelopment of CIHI's acute care grouping methodologies, to take full and accurate advantage of the increased clinical and procedural specificity that these classification systems offer. To this end, CIHI launched a major initiative to redevelop its acute care grouping methodologies and associated resource indicators in the fall of 2003. The scope of this project included:

1. A complete redevelopment of the acute care inpatient grouping methodology (CMG/Plx), using ICD–10–CA and CCI activity and (patient-specific) cost data.
2. Refinement of the DPG and CACS grouping methodologies to make more effective use of the specificity of ICD–10–CA and CCI.
3. Refinement of the RIW, ACW and ELOS methodologies to allow for more consistent values and comparisons over time and across grouping methodologies.

Redevelopment of the acute care inpatient grouping methodology: CMG+

The process to develop the new methodologies involved the assignment of a project manager and early identification of select individuals with expertise in the CMG/Plx methodology and the new ICD–10–CA/CCI classification systems. Assistance from external experts and methodologists also provided the project team with guidance in developing the project plan and setting the direction for initial exploratory and analytical work.

During the early phase of this project, an extensive consultation process was held with both internal staff and external stakeholders/experts. This consultation served to clearly articulate the project objectives, deliverables and timelines. During this phase, a number of key activities were conducted:

- review of the literature on existing or emerging international acute care grouping methodologies;
- creation, dissemination and analysis of an electronic questionnaire targeted towards users of CMG/Plx methodologies;
- identification of collaborative opportunities;
- identification of potential conflicting initiatives; and
- review of all feedback and documentation received from internal or external stakeholders for proposed changes/enhancements to the current methodology.

During this period CIHI also established an extensive project management and advisory committee structure. The core project team was composed of casemix analysts and methodologists, classification specialists, and applications developers whose combined role was to assess the needs and constraints for the development of the new inpatient grouping methodology and conduct the required analyses to develop a new inpatient grouping methodology. Two external statisticians/methodologists were also recruited to provide guidance and direction to the project team.

A key success factor in the development of the ICD–10–CA/CCI grouping methodology was to ensure buy-in from CIHI stakeholders. This was facilitated by the creation of external committees whose members provided ongoing expertise to the process: the National Data Quality and CMG Redevelopment Steering Committee provided CIHI with guidance in accelerating the redevelopment of the acute care inpatient grouping methodology and resource indicators and recommended strategies to improve the validity of the underlying data. The Grouper Redevelopment Advisory Committee (GRAC) provided CIHI with expert advice and assisted in the development of the CMG+ acute care inpatient grouping methodology and related resource indicators. The Casemix Advisory Group (CMAG) provided CIHI with expert advice in the development and ongoing evolution of patient/client grouping and weighting methodologies used by CIHI. The CMAG also played a critical role in assessing the "fitness for use" of the clinical and costing data used to develop these methodologies and associated resource indicators.

Recognizing that the building of the ICD–10–CA/CCI grouping methodology was a rare opportunity, the project team undertook detailed exploratory analyses to determine which methodological approach would provide the most clinically meaningful and resource-homogeneous groups to represent the Canadian hospital patient population. Three different approaches were tested (the current (MRDx) approach, an intervention-driven approach, and a diagnosis-driven approach), over the course of approximately eight months. Data sources included all inpatient records from the FY2002/3 and FY2003/4 DAD (about 4.5 million records), as well as about 800,000 patient-specific case cost records from the provinces of Ontario, Alberta, and British Columbia.

In September 2004, following an extensive review of the findings, GRAC members unanimously endorsed the current approach which continues to involve the use of the Most Responsible Diagnosis to assign a patient case to a Major Clinical Category, as the preferred approach to grouping inpatient cases.

The current approach consistently outperformed the other approaches across the following criteria: clinical relevance; explanation of costs; logical hierarchy; transparency; and relevancy to the organization of hospitals. It was also felt that it represented the least amount of change from the present grouping methodology and would be more easily understood by users.

Notwithstanding this decision, the project team identified a number of enhancements to the new CMG+ grouping methodology, so as to improve its overall utility and relevance. Major changes are described below.

The current Major Clinical Category (MCC) concept remains essentially unchanged, but the structure has been streamlined, with the amalgamation of some MCCs (e.g. HIV MCC integrated into the Systemic Infections MCC). The Newborn and Neonates MCC will make use of the mother's gestational age in the assignment of CMG cells, and will incorporate an intervention-driven hierarchy, and will also use the presence of MCC-specific co-morbidities in the assignment of weights. In addition, refined age categories (newborns, neonates 0–7 days; and neonates 8–28 days) were introduced for this MCC.

The Pregnancy and Childbirth MCC will make use of the gestational age for the mother at admission and delivery times as a grouping variable in the next few years. Co-morbidities will also be factored in to the assignment of weights for this MCC.

CMG+ incorporates a new methodology that consists of five factors. These factors are applied following CMG assignment and are used in the assignment of the resource indicators, Resource Intensity Weight (RIW) and Expected Length of Stay (ELOS) values for each case. This replaces the Plx/Age overlay methodology of CMG/Plx.

The five factors are applied to the base CMG as applicable and consist of the following:

- age category;
- co-morbidity level;
- flagged intervention;
- intervention event;
- out of hospital intervention.

Table 15.1 Age categories based on cost and length of stay data

Newborn and neonate	Paediatric	Adult
Newborn	29–364 days	18–59 years
Neonate 0–7 days	1–7 years	60–79 years
Neonate 8–28 days	8–17 years	80 + years

Age category

Three new age categories have been created based on the analysis of both cost and LOS data. Within each category, there are three further age group splits.

Co-morbidity level

Given some of the data quality issues identified during recent data mining and re-abstraction studies, the project team needed to be cautious of how co-morbid diagnoses would be used in the new CMG+ methodology until such time as the quality of coding improved. To this end, the project team conducted comprehensive analyses to determine which diagnoses truly affected the use of resources (as measured by LOS and patient-specific cost data). This new co-morbidity factor methodology, which will no longer differentiate between type 1 (pre-admit) and type 2 (post-admit) diagnoses, will make use of a substantially reduced number of diagnoses (from the current Plx grade list). The MCC-specific Co-morbidity Factor code lists were developed based on clinical input, a predetermined resource threshold (as determined through regression modeling and analysis) and data quality performance determined via reabstraction inter-rate reliability testing. The Co-morbidity Factor lists also incorporate exclusions to account for pairs of codes that represent the same condition.

Co-morbidities are used to assign each patient to one of several Co-morbidity Factor Levels, each of which reflects the cumulative cost impact of these co-morbidities on the patient's stay.

Flagged intervention

This set of fourteen CCI intervention categories act as a flag to identify patients who are likely to consume significant resources; the interventions themselves are not necessarily costly. The Flagged Intervention Factor replaces the previous CMG methodology logic of grouping together certain cases deemed to be high cost (e.g. patients having undergone a tracheostomy intervention). By using an identified list of CCI interventions to factor in the higher cost of these patients, the patients can be grouped to a CMG that is clinically representative of the care received.

Intervention event

Cases with multiple intervention events may be more costly than those which involve only a single intervention event. For example, a return to the surgical suite after the initial intervention event may indicate a serious clinical condition and high resource consumption. Hence, the number of intervention events may provide an additional explanation of resources used in treating a patient, above and beyond that provided by the CMG, age, co-morbidity and flagged intervention factors.

Out of hospital intervention (OOH)

The facility where the patient is admitted as an inpatient does not incur the cost of this OOH intervention. For CMG+ 2007 when select *cardiac* interventions occur at another facility, a negative factor will be applied to adjust the RIW downward for the host facility. The ELOS value will not be adjusted.

National pilot of CMG+

In order to effectively support the April 2007 implementation of this new CMG+ methodology, a national pilot of CMG+ was conducted in August 2006, which provided the project team with a final external validation of the product. This pilot, involving ninety-one facilities from a representative sample of community, teaching, and pediatric facilities, in urban and rural settings from across the country, provided participants with an opportunity to preview the new CMG+ methodology and the factors that will affect the assignment of RIW and ELOS values (based on a review of their own fiscal 2005/6 facility data grouped using a draft version of the CMG+ methodology). Overall, participants indicated strong support for the new grouping methodology, citing the increased clinical relevance and transparency of the methodology as key success factors.

Since the CMG system is the de facto utilization/decision support tool for Canadian hospitals, it was essential that clients understood and felt comfortable with the new methodology and that it would serve as a better tool than the current CMG/Plx system for conducting impact analyses, analyzing and assigning resources, comparing activity within and across facilities and as a funding mechanism.

Statistical performance

The project team conducted an extensive system-wide analysis of the CMG+ methodology using fiscal 2004/5 data, including determining how well CMG+ explains the variance in resources. The CMG+ methodology R^2 results for cost and length of stay prove to be substantively better than that of CMG/Plx. When validated against all (i.e. typical and atypical) fiscal year 2004/5 cost records, the CMG+ methodology produced a cost R^2 of 60.4 percent, versus 41.2 percent for CMG/Plx. When validated against 2004/5 typical activity records as defined by CMG+, the CMG+ methodology produced a length of stay R^2 of 50.2 percent, versus 47.4 percent for CMG/Plx.

The project team also tested the reliability of the underlying data elements used for grouping to determine if the methodology was susceptible to the subjective application of coding standards. The introduction of the flagged intervention and intervention event components into the CMG+ methodology has reduced the reliance on co-morbidities. The flagged intervention component of CMG+ increases the cost R^2 by 26.3 percentage points (from 25 to 51.3 percent) after the CMG and age components (not co-morbidity) are taken into account. The co-morbidity component increases the cost R^2 by only 3.7 percentage points (from 56.7 to 60.4 percent) after all other components are taken into account.

Historically, grouping methodologies have been developed using two main approaches: clinical input and statistical analyses. The Grouper Redevelopment Project team strove to balance the statistical analyses with the clinical component. The expert advice and direction from members of the Grouper Redevelopment Advisory Committee (GRAC), the Grouper Redevelopment Clinical Panel and Clinical Working Groups ensured that an appropriate balance between these two approaches was maintained.

Refinement of the DPG and CACS grouping methodologies

The goal of this part of the project was to ensure that the current complement of CACS and DPG cells were populated with the appropriate ICD–10–CA and CCI codes. The original plan did not include changes to the actual grouping logic, however, once the code review process was initiated, it became clear that both the DPG and CACS methodologies would benefit greatly from some additional refinements. These consisted of the following changes:

- elimination of zero/low volume cells in both methodologies;
- improvements to the day surgery cells to make better use of the specificity found in the new CCI codes, as well as the anesthetic technique used in these cases which resulted in the creation of several new DPG cells (102 versus 77); and
- modification to the logic used to assign mental health and rehabilitation cases.

Once the modifications were made to the grouping methodologies, CIHI carried out an extensive clinical and stakeholder review and validation of the final grouping methodology (and associated ICD–10–CA and CCI codes). Implementation of these revised methodologies occurred in April 2006.

Refinement of existing RIW, ACW and ELOS methodologies

One of the objectives of the Grouper Redevelopment Project was to refine the methodologies used to calculate the resource indicators associated with the new acute care inpatient grouping methodology (i.e. Resource Intensity Weights (RIW) and Expected Length of Stay (ELOS)). The RIW and ELOS methodologies were updated to:

- incorporate the new CMG+ structure with the five factors; and
- refine the RIW and ELOS regression methodologies to provide improved and more stable resource indicators.

Resource intensity weights (RIW)

As discussed previously, the new CMG+ methodology introduces five new factors that replace the age/complexity overlay structure found in the CMG/ Plx methodology. These factors include: age group; co-morbidity level; flagged intervention; intervention events; and out of hospital intervention. The RIW and ELOS methodologies used in CMG+ are designed to incorporate these factors into the calculation of final RIW and ELOS values for each individual patient.

The first step is to apply the age group factor to a CMG's initial RIW value to create a base RIW for that CMG. The additional factors then contribute a multiplicative effect to those base RIW values.

The co-morbidity and intervention-based factors, which are found in less than 20 percent of cases, are indicators of patient cases that are likely to consume higher resources and experience extended lengths of stay and, as such, are considered to be good predictors of a patient's overall cost and length of stay.

In the CMG+ methodology, RIW values for all typical cases are rescaled such that the average RIW for all typical cases is 1.0000. RIW values for atypical cases (deaths, sign-outs and acute care transfers) and long-stay cases are calculated separately from the typical cases using different formulas. Atypical cost curves are used to adjust atypical cases for the observed LOS, depending on the case's atypical status.

Using the above process, RIW values are assigned to all cases. These values are to be used in the same fashion as in the CMG/Plx methodology: in reports, to calculate weighted cases, etc.

A new reporting variable has been created to help users understand the impact of the four co-morbidity and intervention factors on the RIW value assigned to cases. This variable, the Resource Intensity Level (RIL), is used to indicate the overall effect of all factors on a particular case. Non-factor cases will have an RIL of 1. Cases in the same CMG and age group with a greater resource use will have a higher RIL. For example, a case in a particular CMG and age group with a RIW that has doubled due to the impact of one or more of the factors will have an RIL of 2.

Expected length of stay (ELOS)

ELOS is now calculated using acute, rather than total, length of stay (i.e. Alternate Level of Care (ALC) days are not included as they were with CMG/Plx). Similar to the RIW methodology, ELOS regression models produce a base ELOS value for each CMG/age combination, and the base ELOS has multiplicative factor effects applied to it.

The ELOS estimation process also calculates trim points, which are used to identify long-stay cases. For factor cases, the base trim points are adjusted by the ELOS factors to recognize that these cases represent more complicated patient cases and usually have a longer stay in hospital. Long-stay cases are identified as those where total LOS is greater than the defined trim point.

Refinement of CACS and DPG weights

A decision was made to align the anchor point for both the inpatient and outpatient weights such that CIHI will no longer be producing ACW (anchored on the cost of a dialysis visit), but will instead produce RIW values (anchored on the average cost of an inpatient stay) for all CMG, DPG, and CACS cells. This approach will ensure that weights produced for these three different methodologies are directly comparable. This approach was implemented for the CACS and DPG methodologies in April 2006.

In addition to the extensive program of work described above, CIHI will also continue to develop, enhance and evolve the work relating to its other "non-acute care" grouping methodologies, such as RUG–III, RUG–HC, FIM-FRG, and SCIPP.

Conclusion

Over the course of its almost twenty years of experience in the field of casemix development, CIHI (and its predecessor organizations) has identified a number of factors that will be increasingly important if it is to remain successful in its mission to further the use and application of casemix tools in the Canadian health care environment. These include, among others:

Casemix systems must be dynamic and adapt quickly to changes in clinical and administrative practices. While CIHI has a very good track record in producing regular updates to its resource indicators, it will be increasingly important to adopt a similar rigorous process to update its grouping methodologies to reflect changes in practices. These changes, when they occur, have implications for users and they must be clearly understood and communicated in a timely manner.

Users should be closely involved in, and contribute to, the ongoing evolution of casemix systems. Users' provincial/territorial ministries of health, health regions/authorities and health care organizations can, and should, influence the ongoing evolution and enhancement of existing casemix tools. This can be achieved by communicating to CIHI any issues/concerns, identifying changes in clinical or administrative practices that may affect the existing grouping methodologies; and by improving the overall quality of the data being submitted to CIHI.

REFERENCES

1. Bartoli, H., Homan, C., Hatcher, J. and Yang, Q. (2005) *Inclusion of Intervention High-Cost Factors in an Acute Care Grouping Methodology.* Proceedings for the 22nd International Conference PCS/I . Slovenia, October.
2. Benoit, D., Skea, W. H. and Mitchell, S. (1999) *Developing Cost Weights with Limited Cost Data Experiences using Canadian Cost Data.* Proceedings of the Patient Classification System/Europe, International Working Conference 21–23 September.

3. Benoit, D., Sutherland, J. and Homan, C. (2002) *Refinements to the Comprehensive Ambulatory Care Classification System (CACS)*, Canadian Institute for Health Information, Ottawa.

4. Canadian Institute for Health Information (2003) *Coding Variations in the Discharge Abstract Database*, Ottawa.

5. Canadian Institute for Health Information (2003) *Coping with the Introduction of ICD–10–CA and CCI – Impact of New Classification Systems on the Assignment of Case Mix Groups / Day Procedure Groups Using Fiscal 2001–2002 Data*, Ottawa.

6. Canadian Institute for Health Information (2003) *Coping with the Introduction of ICD–10–CA and CCI – Impact of New Classification Systems on the Assignment of Case Mix Groups / Day Procedure Groups Using Fiscal 2002–2003 Data*, Ottawa.

7. Canadian Institute for Health Information (2004) *Acute Care Grouping Methodologies: From Diagnosis Related Groups to Case Mix Groups Redevelopment*, Ottawa.

8. Canadian Institute for Health Information (2004) *Diagnosis Typing: Current Canadian and International Practices*, Ottawa.

9. Canadian Institute for Health Information (2005) *Exploring the 70/30 Split: How Canada's Health Care System is Financed*, Ottawa.

10. Canadian Institute for Health Information (2005) *National Health Expenditure Trends, 1975–2007*, Ottawa.

11. Canadian Institute for Health Information (2006) About CIHI, www.cihi.ca, Ottawa.

12. Canadian Institute for Health Information (2006) Standards/Casemix, www.cihi.ca, Ottawa.

13. Canadian Institute for Health Information (2007) *CMG+ Directory 2007*, Ottawa, April.

14. Canadian Institute for Health Information (2007) *CMG+ Tool Kit: Transitioning to the New CMG+ Grouping Methodology (and Associated Health Resource Indicators) Fiscal 2007–2008*, Ottawa, March.

15. Gerson, D. and Hatcher, J. (2005) *Using Canadian Inpatient Activity and Cost Data to Develop Pediatric Age Groups for the New Acute Inpatient Grouping Methodology*. Proceedings for the 22nd International Conference PCS/I . Slovenia, October.

16. Hatcher, J. and Homan, C. (2004) *Evaluation of High-Level Business Rules in Redevelopment of the Canadian Acute-Care Inpatient Grouper*. Proceedings for the 21st International Conference PCS/E. Budapest, October.

17. Hatcher, J., Bartoli, H., Homan, C. and Yang, Q. (2005) *Analysis of Intervention Event Factors to Refine Cost Weights*. Proceedings for the 22nd International Conference PCS/I. Slovenia, October.

18. Hay Group, (2003) A Comparison of Selected Case Mix Groupers, Canadian Institute for Health Information, Ottawa.

19. Health Canada (2006) Canada Health Act – An Overview, www.hc-sc.gc.ca/hcs-sss/medi-assur/overview-apercu/index_e.html, Ottawa.

20. Health Canada (2006) Canada's Health Care System (Medicare), www.hc-sc.gc.ca/hcs-sss/medi-assur/index_e.html, Ottawa.

21. Homan, C. (2005) *Development of Neonatal Case Mix Groups within an Acute Inpatient Grouping Methodology*. Proceedings for the 22nd International Conference PCS/I. Slovenia, October.

22. Johnson, L. M., Richards, J., Pink, G. H. and Campbell, L. (1998) *Casemix Tools for Decision-Making in Health Care*, Canadian Institute for Health Information, Ottawa.

23. McKillop, I., Pink, G. H. and Johnson, L. M. (2001) *The Financial Management of Acute Care in Canada – A Review of Funding, Performance Monitoring and Reporting Practices.* Canadian Institute for Health Information, Ottawa.

24. Mitchell, S. (2004) *Building an Acute Care Inpatient Grouper: How and Why.* Proceedings for the 21st International Conference PCS/E. Budapest, October.

25. Mitchell, S. and Ladak, N. (2004) *Grouper Redevelopment: On Track.* The CHIMA Source. Toronto, Fall.

26. Ontario Ministry of Health and Long Term Care (2005) *Reabstraction Study of the Ontario Case Costing Facilities for Fiscal Years 2002/2003 and 2003/2004,* Toronto.

27. Riley, A., Bartoli, H., Horne, K., Coghlan, K. and Homan, C. (2004) *Creation and Application of Intervention Level of Invasiveness in the Redevelopment of the Canadian Acute Care Inpatient Grouper.* Proceedings for the 21st International Conference PCS/E. Budapest, October.

28. Sutherland, J. (2002) *Updating the Application of Case Mix Adjustments to Facility Based Long Term Care in Canada,* Canadian Institute for Health Information, Ottawa.

29. Sutherland, J., Mitchell, S. and Benoit, D. (2000) *The Impact of the Implementation of ICD–10–CA and CCI on Canadian Inpatient Grouping Methodologies,* Canadian Institute for Health Information, Ottawa.

30. Yeo, D., Hatcher, J., Yang, Q., Perry, M. and Perry, S. (2006) *Cost Weight Development for a New Multifactor Acute Care Inpatient Grouping Methodology.* Proceedings for the 23rd International Conference PCS/I Singapore, October.

16 Conclusions: The global diffusion of casemix

Thomas D'Aunno, John R. Kimberly, and
Gérard de Pouvourville

Introduction

The previous chapters have presented summaries of the adoption of patient classification systems (PCS) in fifteen countries around the globe, starting with the US in 1983 and continuing through to Germany in 2005. The purpose of this final chapter is to stand back from the details of each country's experience with patient classification systems and analyze patterns of convergence and divergence in these experiences. The chapters describe some similarities, but also a great deal of variation in the definition, goals, and purposes of PCS from one country to the next as well as in the processes by which these systems were adopted. These differences lead us to ask the following questions:

- Why do some nations use PCS extensively, including, for example, as a payment method for health care providers, while others rely relatively little on these systems?
- What accounts for variation in the difficulty and duration of adoption and implementation of PCS across nations?
- What accounts for variation in the timing of adoption? Why have some nations just begun to use PCS, while others have used them for more than twenty years?

Addressing these and related questions is important because the adoption and implementation of these systems remains incomplete both within and across nations. There may well be key lessons to be learned from examining adoption patterns, and these lessons can inform decision makers who are both current and potential users of this technology.

Similarly, health care systems around the world are now experimenting, or soon will be, with many new management technologies, aiming to improve system effectiveness and efficiency. Comparing the experiences of various countries with PCS may yield knowledge about what factors promote or inhibit the adoption of new management technologies in the health sector. Finally, we believe that understanding the adoption of a new management technology in a complex and turbulent setting, such as the health sector, can serve as a basis for understanding of the diffusion of management innovations more generally.

Of course, a large amount of literature on the adoption and diffusion of management innovations (e.g. Rogers 2003; Guler, Guillen and MacPherson 2002) already exists as does an earlier book on the diffusion of Diagnostic Related Groups (DRGs), the first PCS, from the US to Western Europe (Kimberly and de Pouvourville 1993). The account we develop below draws on this literature. We consider sociological, economic, political, and social–psychological factors that may account for the variation we observe in PCS adoption.

The chapter is divided into four sections. First, we discuss PCS as an innovation: what are its distinctive features and how might these affect its migration around the world? Second, we examine the variation in the adoption of PCS across nations (see Table 16.1 below), focusing on key dimensions of adoption, such as timing (early vs. late adopters); extent of PCS use (e.g. is PCS used for outpatient or only inpatient services?); difficulty and duration of adoption process (how long did adoption take?); differences in the uses of the systems; and differences in the origin of national PCS (primarily home-grown vs. primarily adopted from external sources). Third, we develop an analytic framework to account for PCS diffusion drawing on a range of relevant literature. And finally, the chapter concludes with a discussion of implications for policy makers, managers, and researchers in the health sector and other sectors as well.

Characteristics of PCS as an innovation

The social aspects of PCS

We begin by arguing that PCS, like all innovations, has both social and technical aspects (Callon 1987 and Latour 1987). Further, we argue that PCS is primarily a managerial, rather than a purely technical innovation and, as such, its social characteristics matter more for its use than its technical

Table 16.1 Variation in patient classification system adoption

Country	Year of adoption	Origin of system	Goals and purpose of the system	Difficulty and duration of adoption and implementation	Extent of system use
Australia	Exposure since 1981; 1993	Based on US model and adapted to Australian clinical practice data	Allocation of public hospital budgets; cost efficiency	*Easy* 5 months in State of Victoria; 2-year period staged implementation; casemix community	Inpatient hospital care, outpatient and emergency care
Belgium	1990 Implementation of ICD–9–CM coding 1995 adopted APR DRG	US model translated into French and Flemish	Financial comparisons; control of length of stay	*Difficult* Opposition from physicians	Inpatient hospital care; experiments/research projects with ER, nursing, psychiatric, ICU, geriatrics, rehabilitation and dependency services
Canada	1983 ICD–9–CM codes Late 1980s Canadian-specific version developed 1993 Day Procedure Groupings	Adjustment of US DRG system	Utilization management and financial, LOS comparisons; financial comparability of hospitals	*Easy* No delays or strong opposition	Inpatient, day surgery, ER, ambulatory care, home care, psychiatric care, functional abilities
Denmark	Late 1980s–early 1990s Pilot studies 1994 White Paper using NORD DRGs 2002 DkDRG implemented	Based on NORD DRGs, Danish-specific version developed	Productivity analysis of hospitals; financing; consumer free choice across country	*Moderate* System not used nationwide	All hospital activity

			Financing hospitals (recent goal)	Difficulty	Acute hospital care (medical, surgical and obstetrics)
France	1982–1989 US DRG research projects 1986 French DRG project–French grouper based on HCFA 1985 DRG system 1994 Implemented 1996 Full data 1998 Productivity report available 1997–1998 Discharge data recorded	US Yale systems, with adaptation and refinements	Financing hospitals (recent goal)	*Difficult* Conflicting policy, different payment rules for for-profit and non-profit providers	Acute hospital care (medical, surgical and obstetrics)
Germany	2005 DRGs introduced in phases, beginning in 2002; much preparation work completed earlier	Australian DRG system; Australian procedure code mapped to German code	Increase hospital efficiency; contain health spending; reduce length of stay	*Moderate* Change to DRGs was phased in; idea considered much earlier than 2002; stakeholders have varying views	All hospital activity
Hungary	1993 Adopted US DRG system (USAID project) 1999 Hungarian-specific system 2005 Adds reimbursement for chemotherapy and minor surgery	ICD–9 coding system	Financing of hospitals excluding investment costs	*Easy–Moderate* International literature scan, debate and engagement of stakeholders	Acute hospital care, ICF for long-term chronic care, same-day treatment, ER care, extended to chronic hospital care
Italy	1994 Capitation Act and related funding – Italian version of ICD–9–CM codes	Based on US model	Financial system to control growth of hospital costs, increase accountability for production	*Difficult* 1994–2002 choppy uptake, differences among regions in	Inpatient hospital activity; extends to nursing homes

Table 16.1 (*cont.*)

Country	Year of adoption	Origin of system	Goals and purpose of the system	Difficulty and duration of adoption and implementation	Extent of system use
Japan	2001 International scan and study for a casemix system 2003 Implemented for payment using ICD–10 codes	Influenced by French and Australian systems for regional health planning and Belgium and Britain for incremental development	Process oriented to reflect medical practice; hospital profiling and improved efficiency	*Moderate* Incremental rollout; strong IT system development, still opposition from physicians and hospitals diffusion and use / regional autonomy	Acute hospital care
Portugal	1984 Feasibility study to adapt US DRGs (USAID project with Yale) 1987 50% public hospitals 1990 90% public hospitals	US DRG system Maryland cost-weight system Input from Irish ICD–9 codes for ambulatory surgery	Rationalization of resource allocation for inpatient care production; hospital budgets; hospital comparisons; national tariffs for inpatient and ambulatory surgery	*Easy* But, at hospital level, limited analytic use	Acute hospital care including ambulatory surgery in public (NHS) hospitals
Singapore	1997 began assessing international experience 1999 Casemix introduced in public hospitals	Australian National DRG V. 3.1	Financing tool, expanded to cost efficiency and effectiveness	*Easy* Engagement of professionals, IT support and pilot coding training May 1998; full implementation in October 1998	Public hospitals only; covers acute care, utilization management, benchmarking for costs of inpatient stay

Country					
Sweden	Mid-1980s Benchmarking and cost analysis 1991 Payment system for acute inpatient care in 3 counties	NORD DRG (Swedish version). Based on HCFA-DRGs, 1995 version	Increase hospital productivity; support policy goal of patient free choice; funds follow the patient	*Moderate* 50% of all inpatient care is reimbursed under the NORD DRG system; administered by counties, 2 do not use DRG system; tiers of use, varies by location, size, type of service, analysis tools	Acute inpatient hospital care, excluding psychiatry; 2005 version adds mental health and day surgery services
Switzerland	1989–1990 Study on the applicability of DRGs to Swiss health care system 1989 Association formed to promote 1997 APDRG (a private association) formed to promote DRG use 2002 Funding of services in 2 cantons 2004 Swiss DRG group formed to implement national casemix based funding	Based on ICD–10 codes Software developed by 3M HIS	Contain costs by moving from *per diem* to prospective payment; benchmarking and funding	*Difficult* Federalist system, not supported by government; APDRG is a private group responsible for developing and implementing casemix and supporting IT systems; variable uptake among the Cantons	Acute somatic inpatient care; attempts failed to extend to outpatient treatment; exploring feasibility for rehabilitation services

Table 16.1 (*cont.*)

Country	Year of adoption	Origin of system	Goals and purpose of the system	Difficulty and duration of adoption and implementation	Extent of system use
United Kingdom	1981–late 1980s National Casemix Office 1991 English version of DRGs created 1991–1997 Health Care Resource Groups created HBG-Healthcare Budget Group, for primary diagnoses 2003 Payment by Results	Initially based on US DRG system, refined for UK practice situation	Increase transparency, reward efficiency, support patient choice for service location and focus on quality	1 April 2005 implementing Payment by Results, a prospective, casemix payment system. 60% of total NHS budget (most ambitious in terms of scope)	Acute inpatient, outpatient, emergency, adult critical care HRGs for pediatrics, chronic illness, specialized services and cancer
United States	1967 Yale University research project based on ICD codes of 10,000 diagnoses then organized into 383 diagnoses 1980–1982 72 hospitals in New Jersey came under DRG payment 1983 Congressional law using DRGs as payment for Medicare beneficiaries	Length of Stay as a standard measure; DRGs identified as the 'product of the hospital'	Forecast hospital costs Government health care budget control tool	*Moderate* 1980–1982 New Jersey hospitals 1983–1994 diffused to every region in the US 1991–2000 states using DRG-based payment systems	Inpatient care for Medicare beneficiaries (government sponsored health insurance for individuals over 65 years or disabled) 1992 prospective payment system 1997 extended to outpatient, skilled nursing, long-term care, home care and rehabilitation Current APR-DRGs development of refined DRGs to capture severity and risk of mortality

features. Specifically, the use of any type of PCS requires key actors in a health care system, especially hospital managers and clinicians, to change their behavior. Perhaps more importantly, the use of a PCS requires changes in interaction *between* actors both inside organizations (between hospital managers and physicians) and across organizational boundaries (public authorities, insurers, providers, professional organizations, and others).

Even for technical innovations, such as a CAT scanner, social factors matter a great deal (Barley 1986). Clearly, technical characteristics are the main drivers for technical innovation at the beginning of their diffusion, but if innovations do not fit with the social context in which they are supposed to diffuse, or if innovators are not able to convince social actors that the innovation may serve their interests, diffusion is not likely to occur.

Managerial innovations are thus relatively sensitive to the social context into which they are introduced, especially the power structure among actors. This is all the more true for PCS, which were introduced in health care systems with the aim of changing behavior. We discuss in detail below how social contexts seem to influence PCS diffusion.

Technical features of PCS

The main technical components of PCS consist of statistical methods and analyses that produce classification systems. Several distinctive features of PCS as a technology seem to promote its diffusion.

First, the relevance of DRGs for particular countries can be assessed empirically. Researchers and clinicians in any nation that considered using DRGs could gather data to determine the extent to which the classifications fit their circumstances. Such assessments could be used to counter critics who claimed that their patients and medical care differed from those of the US. Similarly, the ability to assess the fit of DRGs to local conditions empirically could counter a common and natural reaction to a new technology: "if it wasn't made here, it can't work here."

Empirical support for this argument seems very strong. Several nations (Australia, Hungary, Italy, Portugal, the UK, Canada) experimented with the US-developed DRGs and made adaptations to them as a result. Sweden, Denmark, and Norway worked together to develop a PCS for their region.

Another important feature of PCS to consider is that both the original technology for producing DRGs, including the computer-based "grouper," and revisions to the original, were available at reasonably low cost (Kimberly 1993). Of course, innovations that require less initial investment, and relatively little additional cost to revise, are more likely to be adopted.

Moreover, the developers provided consultation and technical assistance to potential users. Kimberly (1993) noted that Fetter and Thompson created a group of researchers and analysts at Yale University to provide a variety of services under contract. Under these contracts, potential users could receive help to assess: the feasibility of assigning DRG codes to patient data; hospital readiness to use such codes; and using the DRG-based cost and budgeting model for hospital payment. As one would expect, countries that worked closely with the Yale group were more likely to adopt the DRG approach (Norway, Portugal, France, Sweden, and England).

The ability to assess the fit of DRGs empirically is closely related to another of the system's key characteristics: DRGs are flexible and, provided one can collect and analyze the necessary data, they are easy to modify. Indeed, Fetter and Thompson (1980; 1991) developed the US-DRGs in 1984 and revised them in 1987. The fact that DRGs are relatively easy to modify also contributes to their acceptance, because advocates can use even minor changes strategically to "demonstrate" that a system has local relevance (e.g. as was the case in Japan).

More generally, the ability to adapt and refine DRGs reminds us that, in some important respects, they are as much an idea or set of principles as they are a technology, at least in the traditional sense of the term. They are also malleable enough to serve the interests of a variety of potential users. Indeed, the variation in their use described in the various country chapters makes this point quite clear.

As Kimberly (1993) observed, analysis of the adoption and diffusion of DRGs reveals the limitations of classic diffusion models. These models assume that innovations are relatively static in their form and substance and similar in their use from place to place (e.g. a CAT scanner). In the case of PCS, however, the innovation itself has changed and continues to change over time. The US, for example, continues to witness revisions to its system twenty years after its initial adoption.

Moreover, the use of PCS varies greatly from one nation to another. In particular, PCS has been used for health care planning, hospital management, utilization review, and payment. For example, Canada uses its PCS extensively for a wide variety of patient services (inpatient, acute care, ambulatory, chronic care), to pay providers, and monitor their use of resources. In contrast, in other nations, PCS are used in some locations (e.g. in one state) but not nationwide and they are used only to monitor the use of resources in hospitals. This variability suggests that a hallmark of PCS as a technology is that it can both be refined and used for a variety of purposes. In sum, the flexibility of the tool facilitates its adoption, but also its variability of use.

Finally, as we saw in Chapter 1, DRGs had been adopted as part of the prospective payment system in the US. This fact created interest in other countries and provided evidence that a new approach to controlling the cost of health care was feasible. Combined with the ability to adapt DRGs to local circumstances, their empirical foundation, their relatively low cost, and the availability of technical support for their use, the experience in the US was the principal driver of their spread to other countries.

Characterizing the migration of PCS

To understand why PCS have diffused to many nations, it is useful to characterize the variation in PCS and the processes that mark their adoption both across and within nations. Specifically, we examine a nation's adoption and implementation of PCS along two dimensions: the extent to which a PCS is used for: (1) multiple purposes, including as a payment mechanism and tool for monitoring resource use; and (2) multiple categories of patients and services (acute care, chronic care, ambulatory care).

Variation in PCS purposes and use for patients

As noted above, PCS vary importantly in their goals and purposes. The most ambitious goals are to use a PCS for both planning and paying an entire nationwide system of health care providers. Examples of countries with these goals are the US, Hungary, and Portugal; the UK, France, and Germany intend to join this group. In contrast, other nations have not made efforts to implement their PCS nationally (i.e. PCS use is at a local, regional, and hospital level). Examples of these countries include Australia and Sweden. Further, some nations use PCS for planning and cost containment, but not for paying hospitals or other providers; these nations include Singapore and Belgium.

Nations also vary in the extent to which they use classification systems for patients in various segments of their health care systems. All nations that we examined use their systems to classify patients in acute care hospitals, and almost all nations use PCS for patients in both public and private sector hospitals (exceptions include Portugal and Singapore whose PCS covers only public hospitals). Fewer nations, but still the majority, have extended PCS use to patients in non-acute care settings, including ambulatory care, emergency care, chronic and nursing home care, and psychiatric care.

Duration and difficulty of PCS adoption

Even among nations that now use PCS extensively, there has been variation in the duration and difficulty of PCS adoption and implementation. At one end of this continuum are nations such as Hungary, Singapore, Portugal, Australia, and Japan, where adoption and implementation proceeded relatively smoothly, though in some instances, such as Australia, it is important to note that PCS is not used nationwide to fund the provision of services. At the other end are nations where implementation took years to achieve (e.g. the US, France). Even some relatively small countries, as measured by GDP or population size, such as Belgium and Switzerland, have experienced long trial periods with PCS.

Timing of adoption

The earliest widespread use of PCS occurred, of course, in the US, while the most recent widespread use is in the largest economies of Europe: Germany, France, and the UK. Other early adopters include Belgium, Canada, Portugal, Australia, Denmark, and Sweden, though, as noted above, the use of PCS in the latter three countries remains limited.

Indeed, rather than consider the latter countries early "adopters" of PCS, it might be more accurate and useful to note that they were among the first to consider the use of PCS and analyzed and experimented with different versions of them. Among this group are Denmark, France, Sweden, Switzerland, and the UK (the latter, for example, established a National Casemix Office as early as 1981). In other words, we can identify this group both as early experimenters with the ideas of PCS, but also as late implementers of fully developed patient classification systems: for many years, these nations used PCS on a limited basis in terms of their purpose, geographic coverage, and the types of patients that they classified. We conclude that the fact that some countries (e.g. Switzerland, Australia, Sweden, Italy) have been involved in extensive trial periods both highlights the flexibility of PCS, and helps to explain their attractiveness.

Accounting for variation in the adoption of PCS

Overview

Most analyses of the adoption and diffusion of innovations begin with the now-classic S-curve model (Rogers 2003). In its most basic form, the

S-curve model has two major components: an early stage in which initial users adopt the new product, service, or technique, and a later stage in which potential adopters become converts to an innovation. The form of the S-curve, with time on one axis and the number of adopters on the other, reflects the fact that typically, relatively few members of a social system adopt an innovation when it is first introduced, and that over time, the rate of adoption generally increases until the number of potential adopters decreases and the rate slows down again (Guler *et al.* 2002). The point at which an innovation moves from initial and early adoption to reach larger numbers of potential adopters marks the inflection point in an S-curve. Early adopters are seen as innovators, while later adopters are seen as imitators, influenced by the behavior of their early-adopting counterparts.

Dynamics of the S-curve of diffusion

In the past two decades, researchers using institutional theory have elaborated on the innovation and imitation phases of the S-curve (Scott 2001). Institutional theorists argue that social systems and organizations typically resist changes in their practices, in part because the value of these practices is taken for granted. At the same time, social systems and organizations also resist change for political and material reasons: actors who gain power and resources from status-quo arrangements are reluctant to give them up.

This means that organizational practices that are in place and that are consistent with widely-held views are highly resistant to change. Such practices are, to a large extent, institutionalized. In turn, proposed innovations, such as PCS, might not only disrupt current practices, they are often viewed as inappropriate, illegitimate, and even "unthinkable."

Nonetheless, practical needs drive organizations to seek innovations (Greve 2003). When their current practices prove to be inadequate for the work and resources at hand, pioneering organizations search for and adopt (or invent) new practices (Leblebici *et al.* 1991). Further, there is often a group of later adopters of innovations who, though they initially resist change in practices, face external social pressure to use practices that other organizations in their field are increasingly using (Abrahamson 1991).

In other words, once some organizations adopt new practices, other organizations slowly but surely come to view these innovations as necessary. Indeed, social pressure to adopt new practices often increases with time, and such pressure may result in innovations even in organizations that do not need them for technical reasons (Fligstein 1991). These social pressures drive the imitation phase of the diffusion of innovations. In addition, pioneers may derive real economic benefits from the new practices they have adopted, benefits that become visible externally and that influence others to adopt as well.

In sum, these arguments suggest that nations' use of PCS/DRG systems was driven, on the one hand, by local concerns about managing resources and health care providers and, on the other hand, by social pressures that were both internal and external to health care systems. We examine these issues in more depth below.

Rogers' model

In addition to analysing PCS diffusion from an institutional perspective, we also draw on the work of Rogers (2003). Based on extensive reviews and analyses of the innovation literature, Rogers developed a simple, yet powerful, framework, which argues that both the innovation stage and imitation stage of the S-curve pattern are driven by characteristics of the innovation itself (e.g. can the innovation be modified to fit local circumstances?), characteristics of the potential adopter or adopting system (e.g. how strong is the technical infrastructure related to the innovation?), and interaction between the two.

Building on our discussion above about important technical and social aspects of PCS as an innovation, we organize the discussion below around two sets of key factors: (1) characteristics of the adopting system (i.e. the national context for PCS adoption and use); (2) interaction between adopting systems and the innovation that is driven by individuals who acted as carriers of ideas and champions for PCS, networks of PCS users, and other key constituents.

National context: The role of economic, political, social and technical forces

Context may matter a great deal in the extent to which innovations, ranging from new consumer goods (e.g. Tellis and Stremersch 2003), to management practices (e.g. Guler, Guillen and MacPherson 2002), and market-oriented political reforms (Henisz, Zelner and Guillen 2005), are adopted and implemented. We argue that key economic, political, and social factors matter specifically in the case of PCS.

Economic and performance pressures

At base, PCS are concerned with accounting for resource allocation and consumption in the health sector. In nations that are not so concerned with the performance of their health systems, including its costs, or the value that such systems are delivering relative to costs, one would expect less emphasis on accounting for resource allocation, cost control, or planning for expenditures, and, hence, less interest in using PCS.

Of course, one could argue that most nations in the world have been highly concerned with controlling costs in the health sector and, as a result, have some motivation to at least consider the use of PCS to achieve fiscal control. Thus, a key question is the extent to which decision makers perceive PCS as useful for cost containment: the more this is the case, the more likely it is that a nation will attempt to implement PCS.

Nonetheless, though most nations are concerned with the performance of their health care systems, we argue that fiscal concerns vary from one nation to another, both in their intensity and timing. England provides an example of this argument, as until quite recently, England spent less on health care than almost any other developed Western nation. In this context, it was difficult to make the case that PCS was an important managerial tool to help control costs, at least on a relative basis. As a result, it is only now that England's PCS will be used in combination with prospective payment as a means to control the use of resources.

Similarly, we expect less pressure to adopt PCS in countries that are experiencing economic stability, growth, or periods of economic well-being. Further, in nations that do adopt PCS in such economic periods, we expect the use of such systems to be relatively limited and driven by social, as opposed to economic, pressures. Sweden and Denmark fit this argument, and though they experimented relatively early with PCS, their implementation has lagged behind other nations.

In contrast, we expect nations that are experiencing a general economic downturn or an increase in health care expenditure, particularly increases that affect general business performance, to be more likely to adopt PCS, and to do so more quickly and extensively. The early development and use of PCS in the US is a good example. The implementation of the DRG system was driven by rising health care costs, which affected employers who pay for employees' health insurance. Employers had to pass on these rising costs to consumers in the form of the prices they charged for goods and services (e.g. the US auto industry) and, in the early 1980s, the US experienced a financial recession that fuelled the motivation for DRGs.

It is important to note, however, that, in practice, PCS that involve a prospective payment scheme (such as in the US) may improve hospitals' efficiency, but PCS, even combined with prospective payments, do not seem to contain costs, unless other changes are made to limit the volume of services provided (e.g. as in Italy, Hungary, and Denmark). In other words, under PCS with prospective payment, hospitals have a direct incentive to increase the volume of services they provide, and unless the productivity gains due to PCS balance volume increases, total national expenditure increases.

Technical context

Kimberly (1993) noted, and we agree, that PCS require considerable investment in information systems, computing capacity and technical expertise. More generally, a relatively complex managerial innovation, such as PCS, is more likely to be embraced to the extent that there are other managerial systems in place to support it. Perhaps the most important of such systems are computerized – electronic information systems. It appears that the relatively smooth implementation of PCS in Hungary, Japan, and Singapore occurred in part due to the strength of related technical systems, some of which had been in development for many years before PCS was considered. In Hungary, for example, the Ministry of Health had been gathering and evaluating data from samples of inpatient care cases since 1974.

Political agendas

An important aspect of political context concerns national political agendas, as expressed by ruling governments and political parties. The role of political agendas, especially agendas for health care, is obvious, but nonetheless it is important to consider them (Kingdon 1984). When improving the performance of the health system has been a political priority, the adoption and implementation of PCS have moved more quickly and smoothly. Examples include Portugal, whose PCS was implemented fairly easily between 1987 and 1990, and Singapore, which implemented its system between 1997 and 1998.

The structure of national political and health care systems

We focus here on the structure of national political and health care systems, more specifically, on the structure of decision making that governs these systems. To what extent are decisions that affect the "rules of the game," and the allocation of resources, centralized vs. decentralized, and how many different actors are involved in such decisions (Meyer, Scott and Strang 1987)?

In decentralized and fragmented political systems, many actors have the potential to influence critical decisions, making the resource allocation process contentious and hence both slower and potentially less uniform across political sub-units. In centralized and more unitary systems, the resource allocation process can unfold more quickly; once a decision is made to move ahead in a particular domain, resources can be allocated relatively quickly and uniformly across the entire system. The same arguments are true for the structure of decision making in a nation's health care system. More fragmented health care systems have both a greater number of, and more varied, actors whose interests need to be taken into account (e.g. public and private payers and service providers).

It is important to note that centralization in political systems does not always imply centralization and lack of fragmentation in health care systems. Though it has a relatively centralized political system, France, for example, has a relatively fragmented health care system. The system includes a mix of both public and private health care providers, and sickness funds that are independent from the national state (i.e. a Bismarck system). In contrast, England, which like France has a centralized political system, also has a centralized, relatively unitary health care system (i.e. a Beveridge system). The English health care system is characterized by relatively hierarchical decision making, with services that are paid for primarily by national tax revenues and provided mainly by a large public bureaucracy, the National Health Service.

In general, we argue that nations with more fragmented political and health care systems will have more difficulty in adopting PCS, simply because such systems have more actors and these actors are more heterogeneous. Further, not only will fragmentation slow the process of PCS diffusion, but it should also be related to more variation in the uses for PCS because different actors are more likely to see different uses for PCS.

In Italy, Switzerland, Denmark, Germany, and Sweden, nations with a federalist form of government and relatively decentralized and fragmented decision making, the structure of government decision making slowed the adoption of PCS (Ring, Bigley, Khanna and D'Aunno 2005). Germany, for example, has strong political decentralization, and though it has a universal health insurance system, it also has many sickness (insurance) funds. There is also a mix of public and private service providers, with weak integration between hospital care and primary care. This combination of characteristics creates a relatively fragmented system for both politics and health care and, as Kimberly and de Pouvourville (1993) argued, the PCS concept failed to diffuse in Germany because there were too many people to convince to promote its diffusion. It was 2005 before the German federal government was able to impose a policy for PCS and health care cost control at a national level.

Similarly, though Switzerland is a smaller country, it mirrors Germany's structure in politics and health care, and although there was early experimentation with PCS, it diffused only in a few areas (Geneva and Lausanne) where hospital managers wanted to use it for utilization review. In contrast, we observe that in Singapore, Portugal, and Japan, countries that have more unitary and centralized systems, once a decision was made to adopt PCS, the result was a national roll-out in a relatively short period of time.

It is important to note, however, that decentralization in national governance may mean strong centralization at regional levels (provinces in Canada are a good example). Thus, there could be rapid diffusion of PCS *within* local centralized governments that support the concept of PCS. In fact, national political agendas for health care are often so overcrowded with reforms (e.g. concerning public health and primary care) that it is quite difficult to maintain an emphasis on one reform versus another. This problem is particularly evident in national governments that are centralized, whereas at the regional level, governments may have more capacity to set agendas that focus on PCS.

Finally, the size of a nation and its health care system may be another structural characteristic that explains differences in the speed of PCS diffusion. To the extent that other contextual factors (i.e. performance pressures; political agendas; centralized decision making) are supportive, PCS diffusion may be more likely to occur more rapidly in smaller countries (e.g. Portugal, Singapore, and Hungary).

Context and innovation interact: The roles of social actors

Though national context and characteristics of the initial innovation (the US-DRG system) influenced PCS adoption and use, individuals and social networks have also played, and continue to play, a central role. As we look across the experience of the fifteen countries included here, we see three sets of actors as being particularly influential: (1) individuals who were carriers of, and champions for, the innovation; (2) networks of users, including those who developed a PCS research industry; and (3) major stakeholders at the local level in health care systems, especially physicians and regional and local hospital managers.

The roles of carriers and champions

We distinguish here between individuals who play two types of roles: those who carry to their nations the ideas, concepts and principles of patient classification analysis (often researchers linked to universities or public agencies) versus individuals who are champions for change and promote the use of PCS. Carriers of ideas are similar to the so-called "boundary spanners" or "cosmopolitans" identified in prior research on the diffusion of innovation (Kimberly 1981): these individuals are likely to travel across national boundaries and are connected via social networks and communication channels (e.g. professional journals) to varied sources of information.

Champions, on the other hand, are individuals who, for a variety of reasons, are deeply committed to an innovation and who are willing to invest significant amounts of their time and resources to implement it. Their principal challenge is resistance to change, a universal phenomenon found in all social systems. Some individuals such as George Palmer in Australia, Jean de Kervasdoué in France, and Jean Blanpain in Belgium played the roles of both carrier and champion.

Both carriers and champions are important. Carriers focus more on communicating about, and studying various aspects of, PCS; champions are needed because they focus more on action than ideas. To illustrate, consider the case of Switzerland. Here we see that there was an active group of carriers who conducted studies of patient classification systems in the mid to late 1980s. But the absence of real champions for change in the political system has undoubtedly contributed to Switzerland's relatively slow adoption of PCS.

The importance of individuals, or small groups of individuals, playing both these roles should be obvious from the preceding chapters but, at the same time, they should not be overlooked. Some of these carriers and champions were linked directly to Fetter, Thompson, and the Yale group. For example, George Palmer, whom we consider both a carrier and champion, played a pivotal role in DRG development in Australia, and from 1970 to 1987 he periodically travelled to the US and worked with the Yale group. Similarly, Jean de Kervasdoué came into contact with the Yale group in the late 1970s and subsequently used his position as Directeur des

Hopitaux in the Ministry of Health in France to motivate experimentation with a system based on DRGs.

Another observation is that champions who were not closely linked to decision makers within health care systems were not as effective as champions who were somehow part of those systems. In other words, implementation of PCS was facilitated by champions who occupied positions of authority in their health care systems that gave them the power to allocate critical resources. Though decision-making authority is never absolute, individuals who are both champions and decision makers face fewer obstacles to implementing PCS than others. The case of Singapore illustrates this point: the Ministry of Health was both a carrier and a champion, and held decision-making power, and PCS was implemented relatively quickly. In sum, carriers and champions heavily define the path by which an innovation enters a social system. Variation in who plays these roles, and how well they play them, affects PCS adoption and implementation.

Within institutional theory, an important new literature has emerged on carriers and champions for change (e.g. Scott *et al.* 2000). This literature describes and analyzes individuals who lead change in systems that are highly institutionalized, such as national health systems (Battilana 2006). Battilana and her colleagues reviewed forty recent papers that examined the role of what they term "institutional entrepreneurs" (ie. individuals who attempt to change organizations and practices that are so widely accepted that they are taken for granted (see also Fligstein 1997).

One conclusion from this review, and from Battilana's (2006) study of leadership and change in England's NHS, is that institutional entrepreneurs are not necessarily "insiders" who hold formal positions of authority. Rather, challenges to the status quo often come from those individuals and organizations that are outsiders; they are relatively less powerful and occupy positions at the periphery of organizational networks (Leblebici *et al.* 1991).

How well does this conclusion fit our arguments and the data for PCS carriers and champions? Evidence from the chapters here suggests a good fit insofar as, in many cases, the individuals who brought the ideas, concepts and principles of PCS to their nations (carriers) often were not insiders in government or national health systems, but rather researchers and academics. As outsiders, they had the advantage of being able to see the strengths of PCS. At the same time, however, as outsiders they did not necessarily have the authority or power to be effective champions with the ability to implement changes such as PCS. This may help to explain why many nations have experimented with PCS, but not implemented them as fully as possible.

Networks of users

Recent research indicates that networks, such as those we discuss here, have promoted the worldwide diffusion of a wide range of innovations, including economic policies (Henisz, Zelner and Guillen 2005), organizational practices (Guler, Guillen and MacPherson 2002), and educational systems (Schofer and Meyer 2005). We first discuss the development of PCS user networks and then examine their effects on PCS diffusion.

In his analysis of the migration of DRGs to Western Europe, Kimberly (1993) identified a series of programs, conferences, and events that developed networks of PCS users. These initiatives ranged from an annual one-week educational program begun at Yale in 1978 to promote the use of DRGs, to the formation of an association of Patient Classification Systems in Europe in 1985. In addition, Kimberly (1993) noted that a modest, though significant, DRG-focused research industry has developed whose purpose is to evaluate various aspects of DRG use and implementation. As a result, research on DRGs has produced a set of individuals with particular skills and interests in the analysis of PCS.

The networks that grew from these various initiatives and research programs now span national boundaries and involve multiple stakeholders. In fact, the Association of Patient Classification Systems recently held its 22nd annual conference, with 270 individuals attending from thirty-four countries.

These networks appear to have had several beneficial effects on the adoption of PCS. One is that they facilitate information-sharing about technical issues and problems that PCS pose. Perhaps more important than the technical information within the networks, is the sense of community that they generate. In other words, these networks create both social structures (such as the PCS Association) and a shared world view. From this cohesion comes the legitimacy and support that are needed to promote PCS in the face of obstacles to their adoption and implementation. Finally, as these networks have increased in size and prominence, they also have created a sense of momentum, suggesting that PCS are the way of the future and a necessary management tool for modern health care systems.

Major stakeholders

In addition to the role of individuals who influence or make policy decisions within health care systems, three other groups of actors must be considered: physicians, hospital managers, and to some, though a lesser extent, regional health system managers, who are particularly important in nations that have decentralized public health care systems (such as Italy, Sweden, and Denmark). Of these actors, physicians are typically the most powerful and they hold particular power when it comes to implementing PCS. Though they may not be able to resist policy makers' plans to adopt a PCS, physicians can make it very difficult to implement one smoothly.

In Belgium, for example, physicians expressed strong opposition to PCS on the basis of concerns about losing their autonomy and practising medicine with a focus on money rather than quality of care. Motivated by these concerns, physicians were apparently able to slow down the implementation of the system until recently. This is despite the fact that Fetter spent a sabbatical year in Belgium in the late 1970s and the Ministry of Health supported relatively extensive research on PCS. In general, the evidence supports the view that the more involved physicians are in the development of a PCS from its inception, the more likely they are to accept its use. Japan and Hungary provide good examples of this.

Further, it may be the case that involving physicians adequately means that a PCS must be developed or at least modified to fit, or at least appear to fit, local circumstances. A clear trade-off is that when local physicians are involved in developing or modifying a system, it takes longer to develop or modify. But there also is likely to be a significant decrease in the time that it takes for the system to be used.

Of course, it is inaccurate to consider that PCS pose only threats to physicians' interests and that they will universally see them as such. The Hungarian experience seems to indicate that physicians, like other stakeholders in Hungary, viewed a patient classification system as a better way to allocate scarce resources and, as a result, they supported, and actively participated in PCS development and implementation.

Though physicians typically hold more power than hospital and regional health system managers, these latter two groups matter as well. Their support for PCS seems to be mixed. On the one hand, PCS increases managers' uncertainty in the short run. This is especially true to the extent that hospital payment has been linked to a PCS (as in the US). In these cases, managers have been uncertain about how PCS would affect hospital financial performance and, importantly, their relationships with physicians. To what extent would the implementation of a PCS drive a wedge between hospital managers and physicians?

Further, PCS clearly puts more responsibility on managers to be accountable for hospital performance. In the US, for example, hospital managers did not initially embrace DRGs and their introduction compelled managers to significantly improve their skills in cost accounting, and financial analysis and planning (Gapenski 1999). Duckett's chapter on Australia also emphasizes the changes in managers' skills that were necessary with the introduction of DRGs.

On the other hand, PCS data give local and regional managers a tool to improve planning and monitor resource use. Perhaps more importantly, PCS data also give managers a foundation for efforts to change physician behavior. Physicians often respond well to data-driven arguments about the need for changes to improve their performance. PCS data provide managers with information that they had previously lacked. Thus, despite managers' short-term concerns about the introduction of PCS, managers' interests often align well with their use and in many nations, though managers were not cited as early advocates of PCS, they have rarely been cited as vocal opponents.

When PCS is introduced in nations that have decentralized health care systems, it is important to consider regional managers. Their interests appear to be similar to those of local hospital managers. Italy provides perhaps the best example because it is divided into twenty-one regions and each one is responsible for administering its own PCS. As Tedeschi notes above, regional managers in Italy must balance a global health care budget and DRGs enable them to plan for, and monitor, resource use. It should be clear, however, that in Italy, as elsewhere, the ability to plan and monitor resource use does not necessarily enable managers at any level to control costs. Other examples of nations where regional, county or municipal managers should be considered include Denmark and Sweden. Their experience seems comparable to that of Italy.

Finally, though we have discussed the interests of major stakeholders separately, it should be clear that it is more likely that a PCS will be adopted and implemented (both in a timely manner and more fully) to the extent that these actors share similar values and views about PCS. Hungary probably provides the best example of such alignment; to a lesser extent, this promoted DRG diffusion in Portugal (though in this case, DRGs were not accompanied by a payment plan). It is well-known, however, that stakeholders in health care systems often hold different, rather than similar, interests and this is yet another reason why we do not observe the typical S-curve of innovation adoption for DRGs/PCS.

What does the future hold?

Given the uneven migration of DRGs/PCS around the globe, it is somewhat risky to speculate about future developments. Nonetheless, two trends seem likely. First, we expect to see the continued migration of PCS to nations around the world. As noted above, representatives from thirty-four nations recently attended the 22nd annual meeting of the Association of Patient Classification Systems and this number has increased year on year. At the same time, evidence from the chapters here suggests that this migration will not proceed smoothly or in a simple S-curve fashion either within, or across, nations.

Second, we expect to see continued evolution in DRGs/PCS themselves and, more generally, in the use of classification techniques to analyze and manage health care services. In particular, there have already been efforts to extend the use of classification systems to patients and services that are non-hospital based in several nations (e.g. Canada). These efforts are likely to increase as policy makers and managers seek ways to improve use of scarce resources.

The Netherlands is considering perhaps the most innovative use of classi-fication systems in health care. Rather than classifying medical conditions and treatment, this approach classifies care episodes. For example, an episode of care for an elderly diabetic individual might consist of transportation to and from a primary care clinic for a routine physical exam. That is followed by a nutrition consultation with a dietary specialist. In other words, this approach classifies a bundle of related services, rather than using discrete medical con-ditions and treatments as the units of analysis. Focusing on such care episodes provides a more comprehensive and accurate picture of resource use and, as a result, this approach holds the potential to be very useful.

There are clearly challenges to such extensions of DRGs and they raise key questions: are there limits to the use of classification systems? How well do these systems deliver on the promises that advocates make for them? Of course, to the extent that patients, services or care episodes vary considerably, it is difficult to develop reliable classifications. In the case of psychiatric care, for example, there is a great deal of variation in patient characteristics, symptoms, etiology of problems, and treatment. Nonetheless, Canada and Sweden are examples of nations that are now using classification systems for psychiatric care and many other nations are working with similar extensions for ambulatory (outpatient) care in general.

Efforts to extend the use of classification approaches to focus on care episodes underscore one of this chapter's most important points: PCS is better thought of as an idea or a set of principles rather than a technology in the traditional sense of the term. Similarly, PCS is a malleable tool that has been modified to fit local circumstances. These characteristics of PCS make its migration difficult to analyze and predict. But, perhaps rather than viewing DRGs narrowly as the innovation of interest, we should focus attention more broadly on empirically-derived classifications of a wide range of units of analysis, including events, activities, processes, patients, medical conditions, and treatments.

Implications for policy makers, managers and researchers

Drawing on prior analyses of the diffusion of innovations in general (Rogers 2003) and DRGs in particular (Kimberly and de Pouvourville 1993), this chapter proposed a three-part model to assess PCS adoption and implementation. We argued that key characteristics of national context, DRGs as an innovation, and social interaction combine to account for patterns of PCS migration and use around the world.

Several themes emerge from the analysis above. First, policy makers and managers need to think carefully about the purpose of using PCS/DRGs. National policy makers and regional and county managers, as well as local hospital managers, are using these systems for a wide variety of purposes. The more ambitious objectives, such as using a system to pay for acute inpatient hospital care or even outpatient, ambulatory care, are difficult and often take several years to achieve. Perhaps the most important distinction is between using PCS to plan for and monitor resource use, versus using PCS to pay for services. Given the difficulties of introducing PCS in a health care system of any size, it appears that policy makers should give strong consideration to using PCS as a planning tool initially, even if their ultimate objective is to design a payment plan around their classification system.

Second, in only a minority of cases have nations adopted a system developed externally without making at least minor changes to it. Using systems developed in other nations is difficult due in part to the power of local-level actors, especially physicians, who are likely to resist changes that originate externally and are externally imposed. The major consideration here is the extent to which a system needs to be developed locally and what role various stakeholders will play in development efforts. As noted above, one strength of PCS is its malleability, and it may be wiser to draw on this strength rather than focus on the efficiency of importing a system in its entirety.

Third, as in other cases of social and organizational change, implementation of this innovation takes more time and resources than anticipated; politics are common. Many incremental changes are needed to fine-tune systems over time and promote their use. In many nations (though not all) there has been a game of "cat and mouse" played among government agencies, policy makers, and health care providers. The latter want to use PCS/DRG to promote accountability and efficient use of resources, while the former are concerned about the fairness of payment systems and protecting their autonomy to use resources as they see fit for local patients and communities. These conflicts seem inevitable, and should be taken into account by implementation plans.

Fourth, this leads to a related observation: understanding the structure of decision making and the pattern of relationships among actors in a health care system will be critical for selecting approaches to implementation. In nations with fragmented health sectors, the involvement of local actors will be more than in nations that are less complex, and where decision making is more unified or centralized. In such cases, top-down decision making and implementation of PCS/DRGs are more likely to be successful.

Fifth, the availability of good data and effective information systems is critical to the effective use of PCS/DRGs. Effectively innovating in this management area depends at least in part on having relatively sophisticated information systems in a nation's health care sector. In other words, policy makers and managers should take into account the technical conditions that promote success in PCS adoption and use. This includes the technical ability of local hospital and regional managers whose skills in accounting and financial planning and analysis will be taxed by the implementation of PCS, especially if it involves a payment plan.

Sixth, following the above points, successful innovation in this area seems to require small-scale experiments and trial-and-error. There is a need for health care systems to become learning systems. It is important for researchers and policy makers to collaborate on studies that can inform policy and management decisions. Indeed, it would be very difficult to adopt a classification system without strong contributions from researchers conducting empirical studies to support PCS development and implementation. Studies of implementation, as opposed to work that focuses on the development of classification systems per se, are especially needed to support PCS use.

Finally, in many cases we observe that an individual (or small group of individuals) emerged as leaders to promote the adoption of PCS/DRGs. Despite the importance of analysing the social context and structure of nations and health care systems, there is still an important place for understanding the role of institutional entrepreneurs, champions, and social networks in the process of innovation. These are individuals who see the need for changes in current systems and who are motivated to make them. It is important to understand who these individuals are, and how they leverage resources to promote the adoption of PCS/DRGs. Identifying champions for change and linking them to established networks of PCS users is a critical first step. The more that carriers of ideas are isolated from champions for change, the longer it will take to adopt PCS in a country or region, and the less smoothly implementation will proceed.

REFERENCES

Abrahamson, E. (1991). Managerial Fad and Fashions: The Diffusion and Rejection of Innovations. *Academy of Management Review*, 16(3), 586–612.

Barley, S. R. (1986). Technology as an Occasion for Structuring: Evidence from Observations of CT Scanners and the Social Order of Radiology Departments. *Administration Science Quarterly*, 31, 78–108.

Battilana, J. (2006). Initiating Divergent Organizational Change: The Enabling Role of Actors' Social Position. Cambridge, MA: Harvard Business School Working Paper.

Callon, M. (1987). Society in the Making: The Study of Technology as a Tool for Sociological Analysis. In W. E. Bijker, T. P. Hughes and T. J. Pinch (eds.) *The Social Construction of Technological Systems*, 83–103. Cambridge, MA: MIT Press.

Fetter, R. B. (ed.) (1991). *DRGS: Their Design and Development*. Ann Arbor, MI: Health Administration Press.

Fetter, R. B., *et al.* (1980). Case Mix Definition by Diagnostic Related Groups. *Medical Care*, 18(2), 1–53.

Fligstein, N. (1991). *The Transformation of Corporate Control*. Cambridge, MA: Harvard University Press.

(1997). Social Skill and Institutional Theory. *American Behavioral Scientist*, 40, 397–405.

Gapenski, L. C. (1999). *Healthcare Finance: An Introduction to Accounting and Financial Management*. Chicago, IL: Health Administration Press.

Greve, H. R. (2003). *Organizational Learning from Performance Feedback*. Cambridge: Cambridge University Press.

Guler, I., Guillen, M. F. and MacPherson, J. M. (2002). Global Competition, Institutions and the Diffusion of Organizational Practices: The International Spread of ISO 9000 Quality Certificates. *Administrative Science Quarterly*, 47, 207–33.

Henisz, W. J., Zelner, B. A. and Guillen, M. F. (2005). The Worldwide Diffusion of Market-oriented Infrastructure Reform, 1977–1999. *American Sociological Review*, 70, 871–97.

Kimberly, J. R. (1981). Managerial Innovation. In P. C. Nystrom and W. H. Starbuck (eds.) *Handbook of Organizational Design*. New York: Oxford University Press.

(1993). DRGs in Western Europe: Lessons and Comparisons in Managerial Innovation. In J. R. Kimberly, G. de Pouvourville and Associates. *The Migration of Managerial Innovation*. San Francisco: Jossey-Bass.

Kimberly, J. R. and de Pouvourville, G. (1993). Managerial Innovation, Migration, and DRGs. In J. R. Kimberly, G. de Pouvourville and Associates. *The Migration of Managerial Innovation*. San Francisco: Jossey-Bass.

Kingdon, J. W. (1984). *Agendas, Alternatives, and Public Policies*. Boston, MA: Little Brown.

Latour, B. (1987). *Science in Action: How to Follow Scientists and Engineers through Society*. Cambridge, MA: Harvard University Press.

Leblebici, H., Salancik, G. R., Copay, A. and King, T. (1991). Institutional Change and the Transformation of Interorganizational Fields: An Organizational History of the U.S. Radio Broadcasting Industry. *Administrative Science Quarterly*, 36, 333–63.

Meyer, J. W., Scott, W. R. and Strang, D. (1987). Centralization, Fragmentation and School District Complexity. *Administrative Science Quarterly*, 32, 186–201.

Ring, P. S., Bigley, G., D'Aunno, T. and Khanna, T. (2005). Perspectives on How Governments Matter. *Academy of Management Review*, 30(2), 308–21.

Rogers, E. M. (2003). *Diffusion of Innovations*, 5th edn. New York: Free Press.

Schofer, E. and Meyer, J. W. (2005). The Worldwide Expansion of Higher Education in the Twentieth Century. *American Sociological Review*, 70, 898–920.

Scott, W. R. (2001). *Institutions and Organizations*, 2nd edn. Thousand Oaks, CA: Sage.

Scott, W. R., Ruef, M., Mendel, P. and Caronna, C. (2000). *Institutional Change and Healthcare Organizations*. Chicago, IL: University of Chicago Press.

Tellis, G. J. and Stremersch, S. (2003). The International Takeoff of New Products: The Role of Economics, Culture and Country Innovativeness. *Marketing Science*, 22(2), 188–208.

Index

AN-DRGs (Australian National DRGs) 234–6, 277
APRDRGs (All Patient Refined DRGs) (United States) 25–6
AR-DRG (Australia), use in Germany 160–1, 162, 165
Australia
  Australian Health Care Agreements 231–2
  health care system 231–2
  universal health insurance system 231–2
Australian casemix system
  bureaucracy of policy monitoring and management 246–7
  casemix development program 233–4
  casemix funding of hospitals 236–8
  clarity and consistency of policy objectives 247
  classification development process and criteria 234–6
  comparison of NSW and Victoria funding systems 238–42
  data monitoring and auditing 248
  development of Australian National DRGs (AN-DRGs) 234–6
  factors in retention of casemix policy 239, 242–4
  history of casemix development 232–4
  hospital management impacts 248–9
  impact of policy change rhetoric 245
  impacts of introduction in Victoria 238–42, 251–2
  influence of Yale DRG development 232
  lessons from the experience in Victoria 242–50
  moral hazard and gaming behaviour 248
  New South Wales funding policy 238
  political appeal of casemix policy 242–4
  regulatory strategies in casemix funding 237–8
  requirements for long-term organizational change 247
  role of George Palmer in development 232–3
  transition to the new budget system 244
  use of casemix incentives to promote other policies 250
  Victorian casemix funding of hospitals 236–8, 238–42, 251–2
Austria, LKF system 160–1

Belgium
  APDRGs 146–8
  assessment of the application of DRGs 149–51
  data collection and checking 151–2
  history of casemix systems 144–5
  how DRGs are used 146–8
  impacts of shift towards prospective payment 149–51
  objectives of using DRGs 148–9
  potential adverse effects of reform 150–1
  progressive implementation of DRGs 144–5
  technical aspects of MBDS data collection 149
Bentes, Margarida 54–5, 58
Blanpain, Jean 363–4

Canadian approaches to casemix
  analysis of variations in coding practices 333–5
  Canadian Case Mix Groups (CMG) development 322–4, 324–6
  CMG age group adjustments 323
  CMG complexity overlay (Plx) 323
  CMG+ development 335–9
  CMG+ national pilot 339–40
  Comprehensive Ambulatory Classification System (CACS) 324
  Day Procedure Groups (DPG) methodology 323
  Discharge Abstract Database (DAD) 322, 323
  Expected Length of Stay (ELOS) indicator 322
  factors in successful application of casemix tools 343
  future developments 335–43
  history of casemix development 322–4, 325
  impact of changes in classification systems 332–3

Canadian approaches to casemix (cont.)
  introduction of CMG methodology 322
  ongoing development of methodologies 324
  redevelopment of acute care inpatient grouping
    (CMG+) 335–9
  refinement of DPG and CACS methodologies
    340–1
  refinement of RIW, ACW and ELOS
    methodologies 341–3
  Resource Intensity Weights (RIW) indicator
    322
  responsibility for casemix development and
    maintenance 324–6
  role of the Canadian Institute for Health
    Information (CIHI) 322–4, 324–6
Canadian casemix methodologies 326–32
  Ambulatory Cost Weights (ACW) 332
  Case Mix Groups with Complexity Overlay
    (CMG/Plx) 326–8
  Case Mix Indices (CMI) 332
  Comprehensive Ambulatory Classification
    System (CACS) 328
  Day Procedure Groups (DPG) 328
  expected length of stay (ELOS) indicator 330
  Functional Independence Measure – Function
    Related Groups (FIM–FRG) 329–30
  health resource indicators 330–2
  length of stay (LOS) indicators 330
  Major Clinical Category (MCC) 326–7
  Most Responsible Diagnosis (MRDx) concept
    326–7
  Resource Intensity Weights (RIW) 331–2
  Resource Utilization Groups – Home Care
    (RUG–III–HC) 329
  Resource Utilization Groups (RUG-III)
    328–9
  System for classification of inpatient psychiatry
    (SCIPP) 329
Canadian health care system 320–1
  Canada Health Act 320
  health care spending 320–1
  health insurance system 320
  population size and spread 320
casemix, global diffusion see PCS (patient
  classification systems) diffusion and
  specific countries

DAGS (Danish outpatient grouping system) 97,
  113–14
Danish casemix system
  activity-based financing outside the DkDRGs
    107
  activity-based financing using DkDRGs 104–6
  activity-based government pool 100, 101–3

current situation 100–7
development of the use of DRGs 112–13
DkDRG development from NordDRG 97
DkDRG rates calculation process 113–14
DkDRG system 84, 89–90
DRG as a means of payment 97
DRG system uses (2006) 106
impacts of activity-based financing 107–8
impacts of political-administrative structural
  reform 110–12
implementation of DkDRG and DAGS 97
improvement of activity-based financing
  models 108–10
influence of Jørgen Lotz 95
influence of Karin Kristensen 95, 96, 98
influence of Poul Erik Hansen 95–6, 98
information system (eSundhed) 103
introduction of casemix systems 94–6
NordDRG adaptation to DkDRG 97
NordDRG-based productivity analysis 96
NordDRG system 84, 89–90
patient choice of hospital 97–8, 100, 101,
  103, 108
productivity analysis based on casemix 96
waiting times 98, 100, 103, 108
Danish health care system 92–4
  private hospital sector 94
  spending on health care 93–4
DkDRG system 84, 89–90, 97, 113–14
DPC (Diagnosis Procedure Combination), Japan
  258–9, 260

Estonia, NordDRG system 84, 89–90

Fetter, Robert 9–13, 22, 122, 145
Finland, NordDRG system 84, 89–90
Finley, Joanne 13–14, 22–5
France
  access to health care 118–20
  funding of health care 118–20
  health care system 116–21
  health care system performance 116–17
  organization of health care 120–1
  population health indicators 116–17
  population size 116
  spending on health care 117–18
French casemix system
  casemix-based financing 131–4, 138–41
  current development 129–31
  debates over casemix-based financing
    138–41
  debates over the GHM classification 136–8
  drivers for development 124–6
  extensions of casemix 130–1

GHM (Groupe Homogène de Malades) system 116, 121, 125–6, 128–9, 136–8, 160–1
impacts of the introduction 135–6
implementation of the GHM system 128–9
influence of Jean de Kervasdoué 126–7, 363–4
introduction of casemix 121–9
key players in implementation 126–8
lessons from the French experience 141–2
PMSI (Programme de Médicalisation des Systèmes d'Information) 116, 121–31
potential uses 134–5
requirements for implementation to succeed 136
support from Yale University group 122
timing of the implementation 121–4
uses for casemix 131–5
German DRG system
decision to implement a DRG system 160–1
development of the German DRG system (G-DRGs) 163–4, 165–6
DRG introduction process 162–4
effects of DRGs on hospital partners 170–2
effects of DRGs on patients 173
effects of DRGs on sickness funds 172
expectations of the DRG system 161–2
future of DRGs in Germany 173–4
German Institute of Medicine Informatics (DIMDI) 162–3
hospital system impacts of DRGs 168–70
impacts of DRGs 166–73
impacts of political change 160–1
Institute for Calculating DRG cost weights (InEK) 162–3
internal hospital effects of DRGs 166–8
investigation of possible DRG systems 160–1
reform of the hospital reimbursement system 158–60
resistance to DRGs 161–2
selection of Australian AR-DRG system 160–1, 162, 165
situation before DRG development 158–60
test of AP-DRG system 160–1
German health care system 153–8
competition 157
coordination of demand and supply 156–8
demand for health care 153
financing of health care 154–5
hospital reform 157–8
hospital services provision 155
sickness funds 154–5
social health insurance system 153

GHM (Groupe Homogène de Malades) system (France) 116, 121, 125–6, 128–9, 136–8, 160–1
global diffusion of casemix *see* PCS (patient classification systems) diffusion

Hansen, Poul Erik 95–6, 98
HBCS *see* Hungarian DRG system (HBCS)
HRGs (Healthcare Resource Groups) (UK) 36, 37–9, 42–7
Hungarian DRG system (HBCS) current situation 295–308
access to health care data 308
activity volume control 304–5
budget planning for inpatient care 307
casemix skills training 307
chronic care 300
cost-weight uniformity 301
coverage procedure for new providers and services 304
definition of hospital case unit and category 302–3
disease treatment protocols 306–7
extension of casemix systems 298–300
financing of brief emergency cases 300
harmonization of outpatient and inpatient fees 305–6
health provider performance limits 304–5
local information system requirements 307–8
quality assurance elements 306
quality indicators 306
refinement of reimbursement parameters 301–2
refinements in definition of groups 296–8
rehabilitation 300
reimbursement for one-day surgery or clinic 298–300
reimbursement of 'serial' outpatients treatments 300
rules for very expensive devices and interventions 303–4
service provider operating licence 306
submission of data for settlement 307–8
treatment management system 305
uniform reimbursement parameters 301
Hungarian DRG system (HBCS) future development 315–17
contribution to viability of the health care system 317
cost-effective support for new technologies 316–17
equipment utilization improvement 316
expansion into new health areas 315–16

Hungarian DRG system (HBCS) impacts 308–15
  better utilization of care 311
  control of health care costs 311
  DRG creep 311
  effects on the health market 315
  growth in hospital sector output 310
  problems and weaknesses 312–14
  quality of patient care 312, 314–15
  quantification of hospital care results 310–14
  redistribution of tasks between hospitals 311
  reduction in hospital length of stay 310
  reduction in number of beds 310
  role in development of hospital management
    314
  role in realization of health care policy goals
    308–10
Hungarian DRG system (HBCS) introduction
  adaptation of DRG for use in Hungary 288–9
  allocation of risks of reimbursement 294–5
  development of an independent system 292–3
  development role of the Ministry of Health
    289–90
  drivers for introduction 286–7
  factors in successful development of
    casemix 290
  features of the first DRG-based reimbursement
    system 294–5
  history of the introduction of casemix systems
    286–95
  hospital base rate calculation 294
  international comparisons of data 293
  objectives of introduction 287–8
  preconditions for introduction 288
  questions debated during development 290–2
  range of applications for the casemix system
    293–4
  similarities to HCFA DRG version 295
Hungarian health care system 284–5
  acute inpatient care 285
  financing of health care services 284
  general practitioners 285
  outpatient care 285
  private health care providers 285

Iceland, NordDRG system 84, 89–90
Italian casemix system
  characteristics 202–7
  coding procedures in hospitals 212
  criticisms 194–5
  current situation 207–12
  decentralization of health systems 195–6
  DRG system 202–7
  DRG tariffs adopted by regions 196–202
  drivers of implementation 193–4

drivers of introduction 192–218
financial flows leading to funding
    207–8
future of casemix systems in Italy 219–25
goals 194
hospital budgeting 208–10
impacts on hospital financial systems
    196–202
impacts of political changes on health systems
    195–6
impacts of the introduction of DRGs
    212–19, 220
implementation 193–4
introduction 192–4
maintenance of the casemix system 211–12
national tariffs and regional adjustments
    202–7
path dependence in health policy 193–218
regional adaptations of the casemix system
    193–218
regional control of health systems 195–6
RODs (Italian name for DRGs) 193
shift to a DRG-based hospital financial system
    193–4
use of DRGs in hospital planning 210–11
weaknesses 219–25
Italian National Healthcare System (SSN)
    189–91
  AOs (Hospital Trusts) 189–90, 190–1
  APPs (accredited private hospitals) 189–90,
    190–1
  ASLs (Local Health Authorities) 189–90, 191
  evolution under the casemix system
    196–202
  funding 191
  impacts of regionalization reforms 191
  population characteristics 189
  public spending on health 189
  structure 189–90

Japanese approach to casemix
  classification development 258–9
  code finder program 261
  DPC (Diagnosis Procedure Combination)
    258–9
  DPC and innovation in hospital management
    269–70
  DPC as a tool for health reform 270–1
  DPC-based cost analysis project 263–4
  DPC project team 258
  DPC refinement process 263
  efficiency of use of health resources
    264, 265
  evaluation of the DPC system 264–6

extension of DPC to other medical services 268–9
future developments of the DPC project 266–71
health insurance system reform 270–1
history of introduction of casemix systems 255–8
hospital information system 260–3
impacts of an ageing population 270–1
incremental approach to per case payment 268
international comparison of tariffs 267–8
need for standardized medical profiling 255–7
need to create a Japanese system 257–8
patient choice and information 264–5
quality assurance program 265–6
receipt data download system 260–1
reimbursement system based on DPC 261–3
structure of the DPC code 260
universal health insurance system 254–5, 255–7

Kervasdoué, Jean de 126–7, 363–4
Kristensen, Karin 95, 96, 98

length of stay (LOS) as measure of output (US) 10–11, 12
LKF system, Austria 160–1
Lotz, Jørgen 95

Major Diagnostic Categories (MDC) (US) 11

NordDRG system 77, 82–5, 89–90
Norway, NordDRG system 84, 89–90

Owen, Jack 14, 16, 22

Palmer, George 232–3, 363–4
PCS (patient classification systems) adoption patterns, and management innovation 346–7
PCS (patient classification systems) as innovation
   social aspects 347–53
   technical features which promote diffusion 353–5
PCS (patient classification systems) diffusion
   analysis of variations in adoption 356–67
   carriers and champions 363–4
   drivers for adoption of new practices 356
   economic and performance pressures 359–60
   factors influencing variation in adoption 356–67
   future developments 368–9
   implications for policy makers, managers and researchers 369–71
   influence of major stakeholders 365–7

national context 358–62
networks of users 365
political agendas 360
Rogers' model of diffusion of innovations 358
role of social actors 362–7
S-curve model of diffusion of innovations 356
structure of national political and health care systems 360–2
technical forces 360
variation in duration and difficulty of PCS adoption 348, 356
variation in origins of the system 348, 353–4
variation in purposes and use for patients 348, 355
variation in timing of PCS adoption 348, 356
Pettengill, Julian 6–7, 15–16, 22–5
Portugal
   health care system 51–3
   Institute for Financial Management and IT (IGIF) 51–2, 61–3
   Ministry of Health 51–2, 53–5
   private sector 51
   Regional Health Authorities 51–2
   role of central government 51–2
   spending on health care 53
Portuguese casemix system
   ambulatory surgery DRGs 60–1
   concerns about coding of diagnoses 67
   concerns about DRGs and hospital funding 68
   current situation 55–63
   data collection 61–3
   DRG creep and splitting stays 67
   factors in the continued use of DRGs 68–9
   future of the DRG program 70
   HCFA DRGs 61
   history of introduction 53–5
   hospital coding audits 62
   hospital feedback reports 58–60
   hospital funding system 57–8
   impact of introduction of DRGs 63–7
   implementation costs 70
   implementation of a DRG-based system 53–5
   national and local databases 61–3
   national base rate 57–8
   objectives of a DRG-based system 54–5
   performance and quality indicators 58–60
   potential benefits of a patient classification system 70
   potential uses for DRG-produced information 69–70
   relative weights of DRGs 56
   role of João Urbano 54–5
   role of Margarida Bentes 54–5, 58

RODs (Raggruppament Omogenei di Diagnosi, Italy) 193

Schweiker, Richard 14, 16–17, 22–5
Singapore
  health care financing 273
  health care system 272
  population characteristics 272
  spending on health care 272
Singapore casemix system
  areas for further study and action 282
  choice of system 277
  data coding accuracy 277–8
  data quality and integrity 277–8
  enhancing system efficiencies 281
  factors in successful implementation 282–3
  funding formula 274
  implementation 273–80
  improving cost consciousness 280–1
  initial adoption of AN-DRG system 277
  managing the transition 275–6
  objectives 273–4
  pilot run 278–9
  progress thus far 280–1
  quality of care indicators 279–80
  technical considerations 277–9
Stockholm model of DRG introduction 78–81
Sweden, health care system 73–6
Swedish DRG system
  Centre for Patient Classification Systems (CPK)
    77, 84–5
  coding systems 90
  cost weights 90
  current situation 82–5
  developing a national grouper 88
  future of DRGs in Sweden 88–9
  health data registers 82
  impact of DRG-based PPS 85–6
  importance of good data 87–8
  importance of information systems 87–8
  incentive structure 87, 88
  introduction of DRG-based PPS 77–8
  introduction of the DRG system 77
  lessons learned 86–9
  national coordination on DRG issues 77
  NordDRG system 77, 82–5, 89–90
  productivity and cost containment 87
  quality of care issues 82
  realistic expectations of DRGs and PPS 86–7
  reasons for introduction of DRGs 73–4
  Scania approach to DRG introduction 81
  Stockholm model of DRG introduction
    78–81
  Swedish version of NordDRG 77, 82–5, 89–90

Västra Götaland approach to DRG
    introduction 81
Swiss casemix system
  AP-DRG version adapted for Switzerland
    179–80, 180–2
  'APDRG Switzerland' group 178, 179–80,
    180–1, 182, 186
  current situation 180–2
  data abstraction and coding 182
  drivers for introduction 179
  extensions of casemix 181
  history of introduction 177–80
  impacts of AP-DRG introduction 182–3
  implementation 179–80, 186–7
  key players in introduction 178
  lessons from AP-DRG implementation 186–7
  limitations on casemix in Switzerland 187–8
  monitoring of quality of coding 183–4
  PCS Switzerland 178
  quality of care indicators 184–5
  readmission rates 184–5
  role of the Swiss Federal Statistical Office 182
  split stays 184–5
  SwissDRG project 185–6, 186–7, 187–8
  technical issues 182
  University of Lausanne IUMSP casemix study
    (1984) 177–8
  uses of casemix 180–1
Swiss health care system 176–7
  private health insurance 176–7
  sickness funds 176–7
SwissDRG project 185–6, 186–7, 187–8

Thompson, John 9–13, 22

United Kingdom casemix system
  casemix classifications (HRGs) 36, 37–9, 42–7
  concerns of health commissioners 48
  concerns over 'upcoding' by hospitals 48
  current situation 39–42
  financial pressures on hospitals 47–8
  HBGs (Health Benefit Groups) 38–9
  history of the introduction of casemix 36–9
  HRGs (Healthcare Resource Groups)
    development 36, 37–9
  HRGs revision process 42–7
  impacts of implementation 47–8
  narrowing of services by hospitals 48
  National Casemix Office (NCMO) 36
  NHS Information Authority (NHSIA)
    36–7, 43
  NHS Plan 34, 39–42
  Payment by Results system 40, 41–2
  slow rate of implementation 47–8

Wanless Report into English NHS funding
39–40
United Kingdom health care system 34–6
English health service 34–6
four national divisions 34
National Health Service (NHS) 34–6
Northern Ireland health service 34
Primary Care Trusts 35–6
reform of the English health service 34–6
Scottish health service 34, 47
Strategic Health Authorities 36
Welsh health service 34, 47, 48
United States DRGs (Diagnosis-Related
Groups) system
adoption by American states 16–17
adoption by the federal government 16–17
APR (All Patient Refined) DRGs 25–6
calculation of payments to hospitals 7
competing patient classification systems 4
controversies over adoption 19–21
decision tree structure 5–6, 11–12
defining and measuring a hospital's products
9–13
DRG classification process 5–6
DRG creep concept 19–20
DRG segmentation and partitioning 11–12
DRG special interest groups 25
DRGs as dominant design 4
exceptions and anomalies 25–6
experience of New Jersey 13–14, 20–1
factors which led to adoption 21–5
future of DRGs 25–6
hospital casemix index 6–7
impact on health policy and management
mindset 12–13
impacts on health care costs and quality 17–19
impacts on hospital management behaviour
20–1
implications for hospital management 12–13
influence of interpersonal networks 22
influence of Jack Owen 14, 16, 22
influence of Joanne Finley 13–14, 22–5

influence of Richard Schweiker 14, 16–17,
22–5
influence on health care management and
financing 4–5
lack of adjustment for severity 12
length of stay (LOS) as measure of output
10–11, 12
Major Diagnostic Categories (MDC) 11
number of DRGs 6
pilot study by Pettengill and Vertrees 6–7,
15–16, 22–5
political response to the health costs crisis
14–17
pressure for a prospective payment system with
casemix index 14–17
principles of the DRG system 5–7
proposed severity adjustments 25–6
recalibration of DRG weights 7
relative weight (RW) of each DRG 6–7
response to hospital costs crisis 14–17
review and amendment of DRGs 6
role of the Center for Medicare and Medicaid
Services (CMS) 6–7
timing and conditions for acceptability 21–5
use by the United States government 26
use of averages 12
work of Fetter and Thompson 9–13, 22
Yale University research and development
9–13, 16, 22
United States health policy environment 7–9
influence of dominant coalitions 9
political power and influence 8–9
role of the technical medical care system 8
sociocultural influences 8
Urbano, João 54–5

Vertrees, James 6–7, 15–16, 22–5

Yale University DRG research group 122
consultancy service for potential users 354
DRG research and development 9–13, 16, 22
influence in Australia 232

Printed in the United States
By Bookmasters